D0959943

DISCARDED

MAKING SENSE OF PAKISTAN

25⁰⁰

FARZANA SHAIKH

Making Sense of Pakistan

DS
379
S445
2009

Columbia University Press
New York

EL CAMINO COLLEGE LIBRARY

Columbia University Press
Publishers Since 1893
New York   Chichester, West Sussex

Copyright © 2009 Farzana Shaikh
All rights reserved

Library of Congress Cataloging-in-Publication Data

Shaikh, Farzana.
Making sense of Pakistan / Farzana Shaikh.
    p. cm.
Includes bibliographical references.
ISBN 978-0-231-14962-4 (alk. paper)
  1. National characteristics, Pakistani. 2. Pakistan—Civilization. 3. Pakistan—Social
conditions. 4. Pakistan—Foreign relations. 5. Islam and state—Pakistan. I. Title.

DS379.S445 2009
954.9105—dc22

                    2009007314

∞

Columbia University Press books are printed on permanent and durable acid-free paper.
This book is printed on paper with recycled content.
Printed in India

c 10 9 8 7 6 5 4 3 2 1

References to Internet Web sites (URLs) were accurate at the time of writing. Neither
the author nor Columbia University Press is responsible for URLs that may have expired
or changed since the manuscript was prepared.

CONTENTS

ACKNOWLEDGEMENTS

In the preface to my first book published twenty years ago I reflected on the challenges posed to South Asian Muslims confronted with the contradictions of their faith and with the uncertainties that plagued the role of Islam in shaping the demand for Pakistan. This book returns to the theme by carrying the story forward and demonstrating the consequences for Pakistan of those unresolved contradictions. As before I feared I had set myself an impossible task, but as before I soon found myself buoyed up by the support of colleagues, friends and family without whom this project could not have been realized.

This is especially true of those in Pakistan. Many gave generously of their time; others helped open doors for me that may have remained shut: to all of them I extend my heartfelt thanks. Some, however, deserve special mention. In Islamabad and Rawalpindi Dushka Saiyid and Syed Mushahid Hussain provided me with invaluable contacts and sources. I am also deeply indebted to General (retd.) Mahmud Ali Durrani, General (retd.) Asad Durrani, General (retd.) Malik Iftikhar and General (retd.) Muhammad Rafi Khan, who agreed to spend long hours with me discussing changes in military thinking over several generations. I want to thank the Royal Norwegian Embassy in Islamabad and its ambassador to Pakistan in 2003, Janis Kanavin, for making available to me his embassy's premises for a series of dialogues on Islam and Islamic education with Hafiz Muhammad Anwarul Haq Haqqani of the Dar ul Uloom-e-Haqqani in Akora Khattak, and with Hafiz Fazl-ur Rahim and Muhammad Yousaf Khan of the Jamia Ashrafia in Lahore. Among others in Islamabad who extended their warm hospitality and who shared with me their views on Pakistan were Tasneem Beg, Parwaiz Iqbal Cheema, Rifaat Hussain, Roedad Khan, Shaheen Rafi, Tariq Rahman, Ahmed Salim, Ikram Sehgal and Mohammad Waseem.

ACKNOWLEDGEMENTS

In Lahore my greatest debt is to the late Qamar F.R. Khan, a true model of generosity and matchless courage. In Lahore, I also wish to express particular thanks to Dr Mubarak Ali, the late Farrukh Aziz, Air Marshal (retd.) Zafar Choudhry, Brig (retd.) Rao Abid Hamid, Mubashar Hasan, Tahira Mazhar Ali Khan, Kamil Mumtaz, Abbas Rashid, Ahmed Rashid, I.A. Rehman, Rashid Rehman and Fareeda Shaheed, who all patiently fielded my questions on the many causes of Pakistan's misfortunes. In Karachi, the city of my birth and of much of my education, I benefited from discussions with Arif Hasan, Adrian Husain and Sohail Lari. Amjad Awan, Nina Aslam, Mariam Ali Khan and Nigar Khan helped ease my many practical difficulties. In London, Maleeha Lodhi, Pakistan's accomplished former high commissioner to the UK, kindly offered to share her insights. My big sisters, Farida, Muna and Anwara, bore the stress of my endeavors with unfailing humor while making sure that every resource was put at my disposal.

The support of colleagues at institutions in the UK, the United States, Europe and India has been invaluable in helping me stay the course. I wish particularly to thank the Royal Institute of International Affairs (Chatham House) in London for electing me as an Associate Fellow of its Asia Programme and for giving me the opportunity regularly to share my ideas on Pakistan with its distinguished membership. I also want to acknowledge my debt to the Institute for Advanced Study in Princeton for inviting me as a Visitor to the School of Social Science in 2006–07, and especially to Professor Joan Scott, whose enthusiasm for my work on Pakistan was a real stimulus. At the Institute I learnt greatly from the wisdom of Lakhdar Brahimi and from the critical insights of Steve Feierman, Kristen Ghodsee, Rosalind Morris, Susanna Hecht, David Scott and rest of the 'Third World Now' seminar group. I want to thank Professor Simonetta Casci and Professor Georg Kreis of the universities of Pavia and Basle, respectively, for giving me the opportunity to rehearse some of the ideas that have since found their way into this book. In India the professional integrity, unflinching support and friendship of Mushirul Hasan of Jamia Millia Islamia, who made possible my contacts with Indian colleagues, has been a source of inspiration and immense encouragement. I also owe an equal measure of debt to Professor T.N. Madan, whose keen interest in my work on South Asian Islam over the years has been a privilege.

The author also wishes to acknowledge the editor of the Third World Quarterly and the publishers, Taylor and Francis, for material used on pp. 107–115 and pp. 151–157, which previously appeared in her article 'From Islamization to Shariatisation: cultural transnationalism in Pakistan', *Third World Quarterly*, Vol. 29, no. 3 (2008) and which was reprinted in Radhika Desai (ed.), *Developmental and Cultural Nationalisms* (London: Routledge, 2008).

Few authors could dream of a more supportive editor than Michael Dwyer of Hurst publishers, who patiently put up with a string of missed deadlines, but whose thoughtful comments and meticulous editing of the final manuscript serve as testimony to his innate graciousness. The acute observations of an anonymous reader were invaluable in helping me both to broaden the book's narrative and tighten its argument.

My greatest debt, however, lies closer to home. Patrick and Emile—my dual anchors—ensured that this book saw the light of day even if in the process I fared less well as wife and mother. From the start their involvement with this project was sustained and intense. Patrick read the manuscript more than once bringing to it his gifts as an outstanding scholar, logician and master of the written word. To Emile and his new found passion for intellectual inquiry I owe the good fortune of having avoided the tedium that could so easily have stood in the way of getting the job done. To these two mighty sources of support, I dedicate this book.

For Patrick and Emile

Pakistan in 2009

INTRODUCTION

More than six decades after being carved out of British India, Pakistan remains an enigma. Born in 1947 as the first self-professed Muslim state, it rejected theocracy; vulnerable to the appeal of political Islam, it aspired to Western constitutionalism; prone to military dictatorship, it hankered after democracy; unsure of what it stood for, Pakistan has been left clutching at an identity beset by an ambiguous relation to Islam.

This book—a work of interpretation rather than of historical research—addresses the political, economic and strategic implications of Pakistan's uncertain national identity. Such uncertainty has had profound and far-reaching consequences: it has deepened the country's divisions and discouraged plural definitions of the Pakistani. It has blighted good governance and tempted political elites to use the language of Islam as a substitute for democratic legitimacy. It has distorted economic and social development and fuelled a moral discourse that has sought to gauge progress against supposed Islamic standards. It has intensified the struggle between rival conceptions of Pakistan and set the country's claim to be a Muslim homeland against its obligation to act as a guarantor of Islam. More ominously still, it has driven this nuclear-armed state to look beyond its frontiers in search of validation, thus encouraging policies that pose a threat to its survival and to the security of the international community.

That Pakistan should face a particularly acute challenge in forging a coherent national identity will scarcely surprise those who have long pointed to its artificiality as a nation-state. Indeed, at independence, the country was largely bereft of the prerequisites of viable nationhood. The exceptional physical configuration of the new state, in which its eastern and western territories were separated (until 1971 and the secession of Bangladesh) by more than a thousand miles of

1

Indian territory, was an immediate handicap. So was its lack of a common language. Its choice of Urdu—spoken by a small minority—to serve as a national language was fiercely resisted by local regional groups with strong linguistic traditions. They expressed powerful regional identities that separated the numerically preponderant Bengalis of the country's eastern province from their counterparts in the west, where Punjabis dominated over Sindhis, Pashtuns and Balochis. Pakistan's national integration was further handicapped by the lack of a common legacy grounded in a strong nationalist narrative informed by a mass anti-colonial struggle.

Yet, these severe limitations were judged to be of secondary importance when set against the fact of a shared religion—Islam—held up by Pakistan's founder, Muhammad Ali Jinnah (1876–1948), as the real test of the Muslim 'nation' that would inherit Pakistan. At its simplest, Jinnah's claim rested on the assumption that, insofar as the Muslims of British India were members of a separate religious community, they were also the bearers of a distinct and potentially sovereign political identity. This assertion, although in many ways quite extraordinary, appealed to Jinnah's many followers for whom the force of Islam was judged to extend beyond the sphere of religion to touch vital matters of temporal existence, including the conditions of modern nationhood. It is this vexed relationship between Islam and nationalism that has proved to be deeply problematic and is arguably the single greatest source of ideological uncertainty in Pakistan.

I

This ideological uncertainty has deep historical roots. The building blocks that shaped the idea of Pakistan—community, nation and power—though largely informed by Islam, were all strongly contested. The different standpoints, articulated in the course of intense intellectual and political debates among South Asian Muslims in the late nineteenth and early twentieth centuries, reflected a marked lack of consensus regarding the meaning of Islam. This resulted in competing conceptions of the religious community, the nation and indeed the proper ends for the exercise of Muslim power in South Asia. The legacy of these conflicting notions has decisively influenced Pakistan, above all in the resolution of its 'consensus problem'.

The parallels between the South Asian Muslim search for consensus and Pakistan's attempts to come to terms with pluralism are striking. For what emerges is that, with few exceptions, an awareness of doctrinal and ideological diversity among thinkers engaged in defining a Muslim community in India did not usually add up to a positive pattern of acceptance, acknowledgment or appreciation of diversity. This ambiguity, I suggest, stemmed from an attachment to the idea of the Muslim religious community as defined by a singular 'communal' purpose, whose multiple meanings were treated as an enduring problem to be solved.

This conundrum of 'consensus' has marked Pakistan. Despite broad (if uneasy) acceptance that Pakistan meant (and continues to mean) different things to different people, its multiple meanings have invariably frustrated the cohesion of a national community that is anchored in, and is still widely judged to be representative of, an undifferentiated religious community. Indeed, the burden of its presumed status as the bearer of a religiously informed 'communal consensus' has compounded the uncertainties attached to Pakistan's national identity.

These uncertainties were accentuated by the contradictory expectations embodied in Pakistan. One called attention to the affirmation of a universal Islamic community, whose geography in the minds of many South Asian Muslims remained open to question. The other emphasised a Muslim 'nation' whose so-called 'communal' political and economic interests were circumscribed by territorial boundaries. The problematic relationship between Islam and territorial nationalism, which preoccupied Muslim intellectuals and ideologues as different as Muhammad Iqbal (1877–1938) and Husain Ahmed Madani (1879–1958) compounded the challenge of reconciling these expectations. It is no wonder that, as heir to these contrasting expectations, Pakistan started life ridden with contradictions.

These contradictions were swiftly exposed. Though touted as a 'homeland', Pakistan (unlike Israel) refused to adopt a 'right-of-return' policy, appearing to make a mockery of its claim to serve as the refuge for a Muslim 'nation'. Nor was it ever clear whether the 'nation' that stood to inherit Pakistan applied to an all-India Muslim diaspora or only to the settled Muslim majorities in north-western and eastern British India, poised to exercise political sovereignty over these regions.

Pakistan soon became the object of contestation between Muslim migrants from India and local Muslim populations settled in the territories that comprised the new state. With access to power and economic resources at stake, migrants and natives set about projecting ideas of the 'nation' that conformed to their distinct visions of Pakistan and of 'the Pakistani'. In time these differences hastened the disintegration of the country in 1971, without securing a consensus either on 'Islam' or on the terms of 'Pakistani-ness'.

Other historical ambiguities also left their mark. Earlier generations of South Asian Muslims had wrestled with two versions of 'Islamic universalism'. One, which espoused the 'universal', entailed a 'one-and-only-one-way' to Islam—a view favoured, for example, by the prominent Indian Muslim theologian, Shah Waliullah (1703–1762). The other, in which the 'universal' stood as testimony of Islam's universal appreciation of pluralism, was a stance adopted by the equally eminent Indian Muslim theologian, Abul Kalam Azad (1888–1958).

The first, positioning the 'universal' against 'difference', was common and found a strong voice in Pakistan among Muslim revivalist thinkers, notably Abul Ala Mawdudi (1903–1979), who in 1941 founded the Jamaat-i-Islami (or Islamic Party). The second, placing both universalism (that is, recognition of our common humanity) and difference in the same conceptual space, was rarer, and has been the source of much uncertainty. It lies at the heart of struggles around the multiple identities (ethnic, sectarian, religious) marking out Pakistanis and which are deemed to 'await' resolution through their incorporation into some version of the 'universal' Pakistani.

The historical quest for consensus about the meaning of Islam among South Asian Muslims also triggered important questions about the proper way to express the terms of Islam, and indeed the proper way to be a Muslim, in Pakistan. This has led to the promotion of exclusionary political discourses and practices that seek to impose ever narrower definitions of the Muslim and to establish the pre-eminence of a particular type of sectarian Islam as emblematic of the Pakistani.

They have led to the disenfranchisement of the country's Ahmedi minority, who have been adjudged not to be Muslim for subscribing to a different version of Islam. It has also resulted in attempts to justify discriminatory laws against Pakistan's Shia minority, who stand accused by sections of the country's Sunni majority of failing properly to express Islam. The promotion of exclusionary discourses has also been conducive to the dismantling of institutional protection for the country's small non-Muslim minorities, thus fuelling doubts about their claims to qualify as real Pakistanis.

INTRODUCTION

Uncertainty about national identity and the lack of consensus over Islam greatly affected the country's constitutional and political development; they also impinged on the construction of a coherent economic and social vision. Jinnah was famously ambivalent about his understanding of the relationship between Islam and politics. While he had done more than most to tighten the bond between religion and nationalism, thus laying the foundations of Pakistan, he was by all accounts a reluctant convert to his own idea. Moreover Jinnah, like the political and military leaders who succeeded him, was unable to resist the temptation of mobilising the language of Islam to generate power—power that lay for the most part beyond the reach of mass democratic politics, about which Jinnah was also ambivalent.

It is no wonder then that, after Jinnah's death in 1948, within months of Pakistan's independence, many of its political elites were uncertain about, or hostile to, his understanding of the role of Islam in defining the nation's constitutional foundations. It took lawmakers almost a decade to reach agreement in 1956 on the country's first constitution and its long and arduous ratification was bedevilled by controversy over the issue of an Islamic constitution for Pakistan—one that the final document failed to resolve.

What divided opinion was not whether an Islamic constitution was justified for a country that at the time was still home to a significant non-Muslim minority (almost 14 per cent of the total population, albeit concentrated mainly in East Bengal), but what the terms of such a constitution might imply. These terms, in turn, drew attention to the very question of the meaning of Islam—on which consensus among lawmakers was palpably lacking. While Jinnah's worldly political successors, plagued by uncertainty about the public role of religion, were content to acknowledge Islam as a fundamental component of the country's identity, religious parties pressed for Islam to be embodied in an Islamic state—although they too were notoriously vague about what that entailed.

The political repercussions of this doubt over Pakistan's constitutional identity were immense. Within three years of the constitution's promulgation and with the country still bereft of an elected national government, a military dictatorship had assumed charge that ushered in a cycle of military and civilian administrations. Although each pursued a distinct agenda, each did so by struggling to articulate a monopoly on the expression of Islam.

Again historical antecedents played a part. There was dissent from the beginning. Jinnah's claim to be the 'sole spokesman' for Muslims had vied with Maulana Mawdudi's authoritarian reading of a 'holy community of Islam'. In turn, General Ayub Khan (1958–68), in collaboration with various *pirs* (Muslim holy men), competed with the revivalist Jamaat-i-Islami to gain a monopoly over the discourse of 'modernist' Islam. In the late 1960s and early 1970s, the Awami League's espousal of 'Bengali Islam' stood (again mainly versus the Jamaat-i-Islami) in opposition to the authority of 'Pakistani Islam'. Zulfiqar Ali Bhutto (1972–77), championed 'folk Islam', again in collaboration with an assortment of mainly Sindhi *pirs*, to challenge the dominance of 'scripturalist Islam', advocated both by the Jamaat-i-Islami as well as by sections of the country's modernizing elite. Later, General Zia ul Haq (1977–88), who initially worked with but then against the Jamaat, favoured a 'legalist' interpretation of Islam with a strong punitive bias that aimed to stem both its popular as well as its modernist expressions. In time it strengthened the hold of an ulama-inspired, 'shariatized Islam' which, by the 1990s, openly challenged the legitimacy of the nation-state and further aggravated Pakistan's consensus problem.

The uncertainties that dogged the country's national identity led to wide swings in policy that exacerbated the divide between competing visions of the country's socio-economic change. With no clear appreciation of the role of Islam in public life, policies were pursued and judged not in terms of their success or failure to deliver broad social and economic benefits, but in terms of whether they weakened or strengthened the putative Islamic purpose of the state.

Here too there were historical precedents. Although Jinnah showed relatively little interest in economic matters compared to his counterparts in Congress, he nonetheless saw fit to prevail upon the Muslim League in the months leading up to Partition to define an economic programme for Pakistan that could be justified with reference to Islam. But with no consensus on the economic terms of Islam, it was not long before wildly contrasting economic systems ranging from the public ownership of property to private enterprise, from socialism to capitalism, were touted as compatible with Islam and therefore, also with the desired objectives of Pakistan.

The resulting incoherence was compounded by the emergence of a parallel discourse of corruption. It sought to judge the economic failures of the state, and especially its failure to curb the use of public office for private gain, not as the consequence of inequitable economic policies or poor governance, but as the moral failure of a state that claimed responsibility, and was held accountable, for upholding Islamic values in public life. Here too the absence of a consensus on Islam transformed the debate on corruption from a concern with the economic complexion of the state to a struggle over which version of Islam was most representative of the moral probity of Pakistan. Ranged in opposition to each other were those who associated corruption as being symptomatic of the endemic hold of regional and rural-based expressions of unreformed and custom-bound 'low' Islam, and those who associated it with the pretensions of a predominantly urban, legalist-scriptural 'high' Islam favoured by the country's dominant, modernizing elite and sections of the religious establishment.

This core ideological ambiguity generated a powerful puritanical counter-reaction, most evident in debates over the value of Islamic religious education. Beset by ambiguity over the precise relationship between the Muslim and the Pakistani, the state has had to acknowledge such education as vital not only for the training of the good Muslim, but also as the prerequisite to the moulding of the good Pakistani citizen. In so doing, it has allowed the managers of such education—the ulama and assorted Islamists—to emerge as influential purveyors of Islamic standards and as proponents of the argument that the latter ought to determine the state's putative Islamic identity and that of its citizens.

The influence of these religious authorities was considerably enhanced by their growing links with Pakistan's most powerful state institution—the military. Like the political leadership, the armed forces were compelled to confront the multiple meanings of Pakistan and the diverging interpretations of Islam that attached to the country's identity. Because of its repeated intervention in national politics, the military leadership has been forced to engage in these questions, which arise from the imperatives of managing two conflicting discourses of Islam in pursuit of political objectives.

The first, with which the military has more commonly been associated, was a Muslim 'communal' narrative that emphasised Pakistan's identity in opposition to India. The second reflected a discourse more closely modelled on Islamist lines, which projected Pakistan as the focus of a utopian Islamic vision underpinned by military expansion predicated on jihad (holy war). Since the late 1970s the military has sought to reconcile these opposing discourses and in the process has attempted both to determine the national interest and to define the very meaning of Pakistan. To do so, it has increasingly relied on Islamic religious parties whose co-operation it had come to value in the wake of a close and covert working relationship forged during the Soviet invasion of Afghanistan.

Yet the terms of this alliance were inherently unstable. While the military looked to Islam to strengthen the Muslim communal discourse and keep alive opposition to India by extending Pakistan's regional interests in Kashmir and Afghanistan, its jihadi protégés invoked Islam primarily to strengthen the putative Islamic character of the state. Furthermore, this tenuous balance was clearly expected ultimately to favour the military, owing to its overwhelming control of the state. But events after 11 September 2001 caused a dramatic shift in this equation, forcing the military to consider a re-orientation away from opposition to India towards a more aggressive posture vis-à-vis militant Islam. In the process, it also weakened the Muslim communal discourse of Islam upon which the military had depended to secure its political fortunes and which had served as a powerful counter-narrative against the Islamist tide seeking to impose a strictly confessional identity on Pakistan. Bereft of this counter-narrative, the military has been left floundering in its attempt to craft a fresh narrative resting on claims to speak on behalf of a more authentic Islamic constituency in Pakistan than that represented by its Islamist foes. Such a situation is likely further to frustrate the search for consensus over the meaning of 'Islam', the cancer that threatens Pakistan's body politic.

The fragility of its identity also explains why Pakistan has been driven to compensate for its ill-defined sense of nationhood by seeking validation abroad, and why of all its foreign engagements none has been as central as its opposition to India. This negative identity is rooted in the specific character of Pakistani Muslim nationalism that was moulded in opposition to the claims of India nationalism rather than in response to British colonial rule. Overcoming the limitations of this 'negative' identity is not only Pakistan's single greatest foreign policy challenge, but is also vital to the construction of Pakistani identity. Nowhere has this been more emphatically pursued internationally than in its struggle with India over Kashmir.

At least as important has been the affirmation of Pakistan's historical claim to parity with India—a claim that rested above all on the idea of power as a Muslim prerogative. Based on Jinnah's historical insistence that Muslims were a potentially sovereign nation entitled to parity with the Hindu nation, it has since defined the country's perennial international quest to be validated as the equal of India. Pakistan's alliances with the great powers, especially the United States and to a lesser extent China, though informed by considerations of security, have been concerned to establish its national and international parity with India, with damaging consequences. For Pakistan has sought also to emulate India by aspiring to the status of a regional power—a status it associates with India—and to realize it through control over subordinate powers, most notably Afghanistan, and through the possession of nuclear weapons.

II

That Pakistan today struggles still with a coherent national identity is widely acknowledged. Yet, the absence of such an identity is, more often than not, merely alluded to rather than squarely addressed, for the state's dysfunctionality is seen to stem primarily from other causes. They range far and wide and many provide compelling explanations of Pakistan's key problems: its failure to withstand military dictatorships; its uneven social and economic development; its severe ethnic divisions, and even the pursuit of questionable foreign policies. Yet these explanations are treated, for the most part, as *causes* of Pakistan's fragility as a nation-state rather than as *symptoms* of the underlying uncertainty about its identity—an uncertainty that stems from the lack of consensus over Islam.

One of the main reasons for this apparent oversight is the hold of the still powerful idea that Islam, as a religious ideology, had nothing to do with the quest for Pakistan. This view was largely inspired by the work of the eminent Pakistani sociologist, Hamza Alavi.[1] His neo-Marxist argument rested on the claim that the movement for Pakistan was driven not by religious motives, but by the economic and political interests of a salary-dependent class of Muslims, who he described as the salariat. It was this class, he maintained, that stood most to gain from Pakistan, and it was also this class that used religion (Islam) as an ideological ploy (as classes do) to justify the creation of Pakistan. After independence, this 'secular-minded' salariat, bound by reference to 'Muslim ethnicity' (rather than religious ideology) faced disintegration. Strong regional identities linked to the Bengalis, Sindhis, Pashtuns and Balochis resurfaced to mount a challenge. Their target, Alavi claimed, was the Punjabi salariat, whose 'hegemonic' powers they opposed, but whose determination not to share power ruined the prospects of a common national identity.[2]

Alavi's arguments have influenced a generation of scholars.[3] Buoyed by support from the Cambridge School of history with its emphasis on interests rather than ideas as engines of historical change, they have projected the movement for Pakistan as a struggle, above all, for political and economic gain rather than the promotion of Islam.[4] Their scholarship has been invaluable in deepening our understanding of the dynamics of Indian Muslim separatism and the creation of Pakistan. Yet, as I have argued elsewhere,[5] the excessive attention paid to material interests in the movement for Pakistan risked ignoring the very real force of powerful normative concerns informed by an Indo-Muslim religious discourse. These concerns were at least as important in shaping the demand for Pakistan as were the interests of the Muslim salariat.

While regional competition over access to salaried employment, especially in government, certainly played a part in thwarting the development of a shared national identity in Pakistan, this competition was deeply rooted in a struggle over rival versions of Islam. The role of ethnic and regional forces in challenging the 'hegemonic' national discourse of the Pakistani state[6] would, I suggest, be vastly enriched if their resistance could be set against the religious orientation of a dominant salariat who had long harboured a contempt for regional expressions of Islam that were seen to be at odds with their modernist versions of Islam. Exploring the differences grounded in these competing conceptions of 'reformed' and 'corrupted' Islam might not only illuminate the multiple meanings attached to Islam in Pakistan, but also explain how Islam as a key component of Pakistan's national identity came to be a divisive rather than a unitary force.

This is not to say that the challenge of forging a national identity for Pakistan should be attributed solely to the terms of Islam or to a discursive tradition rooted in Islam. On the contrary, as Talbot has persuasively demonstrated, many of Pakistan's difficulties stem from the historical inheritances of the colonial era.[7] As he argues, the authoritarian legacy of colonial rule had a profound effect, especially in the western regions of Pakistan. Here exceptionally low levels of political participation effectively pre-empted the development of participatory politics, which could have strengthened the basis of a national identity for Pakistan. This is a powerful argument and few would deny that the time it took Pakistan to shake off the constitutional strictures of the colonial state significantly damaged its prospects of resolving the sharp differences that impinged on the construction of the new state.

But Talbot also acknowledges that one of the legacies of colonial rule was the problematic relationship between Islam and Muslim nationalism in a state that, although created in the name of religion (Islam), was opposed by the men of religion—the ulama. Nevertheless, he is certain (as indeed was Alavi and those Alavi influenced) that Pakistan's problem lay not in the contested terms of Islam, but merely in the lack of 'fit' between the 'secular outlook of the League' and the 'temporary millenarian enthusiasm' of its followers.[8] This, as Metcalf has rightly observed, makes little sense when set against 'the self-conscious identification of Pakistanis with Islam [which] is notable even to other Muslims'.[9] Nor, she emphasises, can one differentiate in the case of Pakistan between 'some authentic statement of Islam' and 'the opportunistic use of Islam'.[10] There was (and is) much uncertainty as well as a lack of consensus regarding the meaning of Islam and this has plagued both the secular leaders of the Muslim League as well as the ulama and their millenarian Islamist allies.

There were of course important differences between the League's secular-minded politicians and their more religious counterparts in their approach to Islam. Drawing on the insights of Metcalf and Nasr,[11] I argue that two rival discourses of Islam—the communal and the Islamist—have struggled for ascendancy in defining Pakistan's national identity. The first, rooted in a Muslim separatist discourse of power that Alavi would have recognized as typical of the Muslim salariat, has been espoused by the country's ruling elite, which includes the military. The second, grounded in a more religious and at times radical reading of Islam, has been favoured by parties dedicated to the protection of Islamic values. It is these contested versions of Islam, rather than any disjunction between a 'secular' leadership and a 'religious' establishment that account for the difficulties in forging a coherent national identity.

There is also much interplay between these contested versions of Islam. In Pakistan's early days secular politicians relied on radical readings of religion to drive programmes of far-reaching economic and social change and to outline their vision of Pakistan as an Islamic society. More recently, sections of the conservative clergy have backed the military in pursuit of regional policies against India that aimed to strengthen a secular Muslim communal notion of power. But all struggled with the uncertainties inherent in the multiple meanings of Pakistan and the diverging interpretations of Islam that were held to attach to the country.

What it also shows is that these uncertainties, long seen as afflicting Pakistan's political leadership, were no less prevalent in the military. If that is the case, then the common perception that divisions and doubts among politicians in Pakistan left them especially vulnerable to an early assault by a more self-confident military[12] may need to be revisited. Most of Pakistan's politicians, especially in the early years, lacked a political base in the regions and were unsure of democracy, thus leaving them open to the appeal of authoritarian rule. However, their doubts over the fundamental question of Pakistan's national identity and of the place of Islam in defining that identity were no more acute than those of their military counterparts.

Siddiqa has offered a more nuanced understanding of the military as deeply embedded in the dynamics (and indeed the uncertainties) that plague Pakistan's civilian political leadership.[13] She argues that the army's position has been enhanced not so much by the weakness of the country's political elite, but the 'class' interest complicity between the two, which has served the military well. This focus on 'class' interests (for which Siddiqa is by her own account indebted to Alavi), however, obscures the complex relationship between Pakistan's religious identity and its most powerful state institution. It lay at the centre of the military's own engagement in the question of Pakistan's identity—an engagement prompted by the urgency of transforming the military from a colonial to a national institution. But this process was also beset by uncertainty that stemmed from conflicting perceptions of Pakistan's identity as a nation-state defined by territorial borders and as a Muslim state created in opposition to territorial nationalism. Uncertainty over these terms helps to explain why, notwithstanding its immense coercive powers and its repeated intervention in politics, the military has consistently failed to impose any single vision of Islam as the basis of Pakistan's national identity.[14]

Nevertheless, the military continues to play a key role in shaping questions of national interest. That it does so has been widely attributed to the support it has enjoyed from external powers, especially the

United States. These relations of dependence between the 'over-developed' Pakistan state dominated by the military and 'metropolitan' [read American] capital' have received the attention they deserve.[15] But these accounts signally fail to analyse or to deconstruct this relationship through the prism of Pakistan's fragile identity. While the contested terms of this identity are often alluded to,[16] their implications for Pakistan's external relations have rarely, as here, been systematically explored. They are judged either to be irrelevant to the country's strategic options or dismissed as mere extensions of state ideology, and therefore open to political manipulation. Neither of these claims, I suggest, can be sustained with regard to Pakistan. Nor can Pakistan's place in the international economic and political order be understood solely with reference to the imperatives of strengthening the state and/or the class interests of its dominant elites

Ultimately, however, what will determine Pakistan's stability as a nation-state is not so much greater certainty or a stronger sense of consensus. Rather, it will depend on the nature of the consensus itself. One possibility is that a consensus will emerge regarding the value of pluralism itself. Such a consensus—around, say, the nature of ethnic, religious or linguistic pluralism—would be conducive to greater national stability. Another possibility, however, is that Pakistan will pursue a strict consensus underpinned by an exclusive definition of the citizen and a one-and-only-one-approach to Islam. This kind of consensus would have damaging effects for Pakistan. It would not be conducive to internal economic stability, nor would it bode well for the geopolitics of regional stability. Without a doubt, the nature of consensus will determine Pakistan's future as a nation and the limits of its contribution to a more secure international community.

1

WHY PAKISTAN?

HISTORY AND IDEOLOGY

It is well-known that the term 'Pakistan', an acronym, was originally thought up in England by a group of Muslim intellectuals. P for the Punjabis, A for the Afghans, K for the Kashmiris, S for Sind and the 'tan', they say, for Balochistan. (No mention of the East West, you notice: Bangladesh never got its name in the title, and so eventually it took the hint and seceded from the secessionists....). So, it was a word born in exile which then went East, was borne across or translated, and imposed itself on history; a returning migrant, settling down on partitioned land, forming a palimpsest on the past. A palimpsest obscures what lies beneath. To build Pakistan it was necessary to cover up Indian history, to deny that Indian centuries lay just beneath the surface.[1]

Can history settle the fundamental matter of Pakistan's raison d'être? Many in Pakistan have no doubt that it can. Many others, and not just its detractors, claim it cannot. What is indisputable (and remarkable) is that the question should still be asked even as Pakistan settles into middle age, more than sixty years after its creation in 1947. But why should an inquiry into the historical meaning of Pakistan be at all relevant for an understanding of its present dilemmas or, indeed, its future course? To answer this question is to acknowledge the profound conviction among its people that Pakistan's purpose has been ill-served—indeed that something has gone wrong with the country's history. Yet few are willing to scrutinise that history for fear that it will shred the fragile national palimpsest and, with it, expose a past brutally at odds with the country's political mythology.

The architecture of this mythology has rested on two fraught notions: community and nation. Neither is unique to Pakistan, which, like Israel, enjoys the rare distinction of embodying a form of religious nationalism that involved the transformation of a religious community into a nation. Other suggestive points of comparison have also been noted: both countries shared a vision of themselves as a refuge for the persecuted; both attracted the hostility of the religious establishment; both sought to balance the expression of communal interests with demands to justify them on religious grounds; and both held to the vision of impregnable fortresses dedicated to the creation of just and humane societies.[2]

Yet what distinguished Pakistan were the grounds that defined the transition of the Muslims of British India from a religious community into a nation with political aspirations. At its simplest it involved the assumption that a distinct religious identity (Islam) had forged a mono-lithic community that predisposed Muslims to assume a separate iden-tity, which determined all other lines of social and political difference. The real significance of this identity lay in the ostensibly special status of Muslims that was seen to rest above all on their pre-eminent claim to power. It flowed from the experience of Muslim dominance in India, which reinforced the idea that an essential part of being Muslim entailed belonging to, or identifying with, the ruling power; but it also derived from an Islamically informed discourse that valued power as an instrument in the service of God's Law.[3] This collective conscious-ness was frustrated by the search for consensus over the definition of an Indian Muslim 'community', a difficulty that was compounded not only by divisions of region and class that eroded the binding force of a common religion, but by the multiple meanings attached to Islam itself. They reflected the extreme doctrinal and ideological complexity of the Islamic tradition. Yet, with just a few exceptions, an awareness of this diversity among South Asian Muslims, including Muslim intellectuals and ideologues, has generally not produced a positive pattern of acceptance, acknowledgement or appreciation for that diversity.

This was nowhere as pertinent as in the understanding of the notion of a Muslim community—an idea that has been more fundamental to Pakistan than the relatively recent construction of a Muslim nation upon which the country is assumed to rest. Indeed, no explanation of the relationship between religion and nationalism in Pakistan would be complete without addressing the idea of the Muslim community. It formed the very basis of the claim by the father of the nation, Jinnah, who declared Indian Muslims a nation precisely because they represented a community defined by Islam. Though the meanings attached to this community in South Asia have been infinitely varied, the epistemological value attached to the idea of a communal consensus in Islam has consistently challenged the broad acceptance of these multiple meanings. The legacy of a community whose internal differences were said to have frustrated the Muslim quest for consensus also profoundly influenced Pakistan's efforts to subscribe to the nation as a political (and therefore negotiable) concept. Just as the multiple meanings of the Muslim community in India were once judged to undermine its authority as a focus of individual allegiance, so too have the multiple meanings of Pakistan (and of Islam) presented an enduring problem—one that must be solved in order to transcend the social and political cleavages that undermine Pakistan's claim to a national identity. But while many had hoped that the substance of this identity would be strengthened by the ready-made assumptions of a putative Muslim community, Pakistan's history has merely underscored the deeply contested meanings of the latter.

Community

Indeed, no concept in South Asia has developed in as contested a manner as the notion of a Muslim community. Yet, as a concept it has been marked by ambiguity stemming from the vagaries of history and a discursive tradition that sought to reconcile opposing definitions of the community as both universal and exclusive in scope. Historically, the idea of a Muslim community in India evolved in the context of the suggestion that while British rule helped promote the idea of a common Indian nation, it also fragmented that nation by casting India as a land of disparate and seemingly irreconcilable religious communities. Some, like the Muslims, were seen to have the potential to develop separate political identities as nations. The movement for Indian self-government launched by the Indian National Congress, founded in 1885, and the recognition of a separate Indian Muslim political identity under reforms introduced in 1909 accentuated the tensions between an emerging Indian national consciousness and a burgeoning Muslim communalism.[4] In the years that followed, the peculiarly subcontinental phenomenon of Muslim 'communalism', which has been described as 'the community-wise exclusiveness of material interests and cultural concerns',[5] came to be associated almost exclusively with the separatist agenda favoured by the All India Muslim League (henceforth the Muslim League, founded in 1906).

From the outset, the Muslim League campaigned for the protection of Muslim interests and openly questioned the validity of Indian nationalism. Although recent scholarship has emphasised the shared genealogies of nationalism and communalism,[6] in practice they emerged as rival ideologies. Armed with opposing versions of Indian history and contrasting interpretations of the significance of lines of social difference, they juxtaposed an Indian nation against a Muslim community. Integral to this tension was the questionable privileging of an all-inclusive secular Indian nationalism over the exclusionary concerns of a Muslim communalism associated with narrow religious dogma.[7]

Yet, the notion of a Muslim community upon which Muslim communalism was seen to rest was far from universally understood or appreciated. This was true as much among the Muslims of the north-central provinces of British India, who would later emerge as the strongest advocates of Pakistan, as of Muslims from the north-western and eastern provinces, who were less enthusiastic.[8] Indeed there is now an uneasy acceptance even among Pakistanis that, far from representing a single identity, Pakistan meant (and continues to mean) different things to different people. These multiple meanings have been difficult to reconcile with the carefully nourished myth of a single communal purpose, anchored in the idea of an undifferentiated Muslim community.

Some historians of South Asia have warned against the tendency to make religion the sole marker of a Muslim community, which, they insist, is a legacy of colonial policy. In so doing, they claim, it risks 'essentializ[ing] the religiously informed identities of a highly differentiated subject population … called upon to conceive of itself as members of communities bound by doctrinal creeds.'[9] At the same time, they recognise that British social engineering alone cannot explain the emergence of a Muslim communitarian ideology and acknowledge that Indian subjectivity, including presumably that of Muslims, also had a role to play in shaping this communitarian discourse. But, they insist, this discourse varied over time and place: while communalism in one context drew upon religion as a signifier of cultural difference, in others it was erroneously conflated with religion as faith or worse, 'religion as political ideology'.[10] Others too have implicitly questioned the usefulness of relying on the term 'communalism' to suggest Indian Muslims as a monolithic community. They blame the 'Hindu nationalist imagination, with its desire for a clear definition of Indianness based on an exclusive sense of culture ... [as] decisive in imposing an artificial cohesion to the diverse local Muslim identities on the subcontinent'[11]—a claim that would certainly have been familiar to Jinnah, who accused Hindu opinion of 'foisting' and 'fathering' the idea of Pakistan.[12] Since then it has found an echo in the revisionist scholarship on Partition that emphasises the Congress' role in encouraging perceptions of a Muslim community, whose separation was judged to be vital to the future of a secular state in India.[13]

These arguments, though well taken, remain contested. While the distinctions between religion as cultural difference, as faith, and as political ideology are no doubt useful for analytical purposes and may well illuminate the process of community formation in South Asia in the nineteenth and twentieth centuries, it is far from clear whether they were at all meaningful as distinctions to Indian Muslims. Historically, the boundaries between Islam as a religious doctrine, as a force for the projection of Muslim culture and as a political tradition based on the notion of power as a Muslim prerogative, have been far more blurred in South Asia than is perhaps acknowledged. It is one thing therefore to insist on definitions of the Indian Muslim community that conceptually distinguish religion as faith, culture and politics—not least to avoid conflating these affirmations of difference in the South Asian context as communalism.[14] It is another to suggest that historically Indian Muslims were at odds with these overlapping registers or indeed averse to ideas of community that simultaneously embraced contrasting imperatives.

Similarly, while it may be instructive to set the emergence of a monolithic Muslim community against the background of an emerging nationalist discourse that placed a high premium on uniformity and to call attention to the Congress's interest in promoting the idea of a Muslim community united in opposition to its vision of independent India, both interpretations confuse convergence with causality. By arguing that the idea of the monolithic Muslim community chimed with the nationalist imagination and its interests (represented predominantly by Congress), it is mistakenly assumed that the notion of the community was itself a creation of these extraneous influences. In so doing, one runs the risk of underestimating the compelling appeal among Muslims of a spiritual community, whose fulfilment lay in its realization as a social and political community in the service of higher ends sanctioned by divine purpose. It is this quest for power that emerged as the common theme in otherwise diverging conceptions of the Indo-Muslim community and that would later legitimise the claims of a Muslim nation qualified for separate statehood.

Two broad meanings have attached to the idea of the Muslim community as it took shape in the context of nineteenth-century colonial India. The first drew attention to the universalist dimensions of the Muslim community by emphasising its inclusive nature, although it also narrowed its parameters by defining the community in strictly religious terms as faith-based. The second, more exclusive in character, restricted its definition to the sum total of Muslims in India but allowed for the meanings of the community to extend the strict tenets of the faith to encompass the realms of culture and custom. However, both were predicated on a clear understanding of the political imperatives that marked out the community and that were believed to enjoy divine sanction.

In the late eighteenth century the main representatives of what might be called a faith or *sharia*-based conception of the Muslim community in India, which arose in response to Mughal formulations of the cosmopolitan community, were, not surprisingly, religious leaders. Some, like Shah Waliullah of Delhi (1703–62), were towering intellectual figures, who exercised a decisive influence on later Indo-Muslim reform movements in the nineteenth century.[15] Others, like Sayyid Ahmed of Rae Bareilly (1786–31), were better known as men of action, whose legacy of *jihad* has continued to rumble on to the present day.[16] Notwithstanding these differences, they all shared a common concern with the moral regeneration of Indian Muslims and with the need to purify the faith and purge it of local (mainly Hindu) influences. By doing so, they hoped not only clearly to demarcate the boundaries of the Muslim community, but to do so by defining those boundaries as quintessentially faith-based. This apparent 'shrinkage in the substance of Islam'[17] to a faith-based community did not, in the minds of these reformers, signal a compromise with the community's universalist pretentions. On the contrary, their insistence on correct religious practice stemmed from the belief that only a return to the essence of the faith could restore the community's universal and historical importance.

Nevertheless there were tensions between this sharia-based understanding of the community and more cosmopolitan versions favoured by the Mughal courts, especially under the emperors Akbar and

Jehangir. Both rulers had been keen advocates of social harmony (*sulh-i-kul*), which later reformers such as Waliullah and his son, Shah Abdul Aziz (1746–1823), would vigorously oppose for compromising the governing principles of the *sharia*. But as Alam has persuasively demonstrated, the Mughals' attachment to inter-confessional harmony did not mean that they were unconcerned with the maintenance of the *sharia*. Rather, their version differed from the more juristic interpretations defended by later reformers. Informed by a system of ethics (*akhlaq*) and grounded in a tradition of political accommodation, this non-juridical reading of the sharia favoured 'the balance of the conflicting interests of groups and communities, with no interference in their personal beliefs'.[18] For Waliullah, by contrast, the *sharia* was less an agent of balance than a force to restore the community's internal coherence. To achieve this he sought above all to purify the faith by delineating more sharply the boundaries between Muslims and non-Muslims, but also by cementing divisions among Muslims. Their exposure to pre-Islamic local customs and their ignorance of the Quran and the Prophetic traditions, he believed, had widened these fissures.[19]

But Waliullah's search for communal coherence was not restricted to religious reform. Central to his understanding of the Muslim community as the embodiment of a universal order based on Islam was the revival of Muslim power in India. His passionate dedication to the moral regeneration of the community must be understood primarily as a response to the loss of Muslim power following the disintegration of the Mughal empire. However, the universal community that Waliullah sought to reform as the foundation of Muslim worldly power diverged sharply from the more cosmopolitan Mughal model that had legitimised Muslim dominance. For while he clearly equated the universal with the universal acknowledgement of 'one and only one Islamic way', the Mughal construction of the 'universal' amounted to a universal appreciation of pluralism. The first (more commonly) positioned universalism against difference; the second (unusually) placed both universalism and difference in the same conceptual space. The tension between these opposing versions of the Muslim community, based on different readings of the 'universal', remained unresolved. Yet, despite these differences both were united by a profound belief in the status of Muslims as a righteous community with a pre-eminent claim to power.[20] Although Waliullah and his peers may have been concerned to reserve power exclusively to Muslims, and the Mughals inclined to distribute it more widely in the interests of balancing different groups and communities, both saw the Muslim community at the apex of universal order, whose relationship to power was divinely endorsed.

The steady consolidation of British rule in the nineteenth century and the final disintegration of Muslim power after the mutiny of 1857 forced a redefinition of the community. With little social space and even less political room, many Muslims retreated in order to reinforce the scriptural foundations of their community. They included the pioneering *ulama* of Deoband, who set out to recast the community as the site of individual religious responsibility: a means of coping with a hostile and unfamiliar environment. They believed that the force of overwhelming British power required the community's withdrawal at least until such time as the process of reform was complete. Only then, they argued, would the community be able to re-claim its rightful political inheritance, albeit under the tutelage of a clerical leadership. This led to a greater emphasis on the need for religious reform, which in turn entailed sharpening the religious dimensions of the community.[21]

But conceiving of the community in these strictly religious terms was as pragmatic as it was problematic. Indeed, it has been argued that while the Deobandi *ulama* may well have steered clear of political engagement, their 'retreat from an active programme of re-establishing the Muslim state was more a tactic than the enunciation of a new principle'.[22] Some have also implicitly questioned whether the Deobandi *ulama*'s concern with 'the interiorization of reform' in the nineteenth century was entirely independent of public and political concerns, especially given their turn to political activism within a few decades.[23] This was to become particularly clear in the 1920s, when the *ulama* of Deoband had succeeded in forging a powerful and enduring anti-colonial alliance with the Congress Party. Ironically, this led some like the prominent Deobandi *alim*, Maulana Husain Ahmed Madani (d. 1957), to seek to deepen the religious kernel of the community and tighten its boundaries even while maintaining that Indian Muslims were part of a common Indian nation (*qaum*).[24] Some have explained this apparent contradiction by suggesting that few Deobandis envisaged the outcome of Indian independence as anything other than a mere blueprint 'for a federation of religious communities with little common social and political life'.[25] Be that as it may, what is worth underlining is that this position was fundamentally in keeping with the Deobandis' predominantly faith-based conception of the Muslim community as a union that was ultimately sustained by the force of its religious message. At the same time, this affirmation of the community's religious core did not imply any diminution of its universal status. Indeed, Madani was clear that unlike other communities such as a nation (*qaum*) or a faith-based organization (*millat*), the Muslim community was distinct in its reach as a trans-historical and trans-national union. For Madani the idea that Hindus and Muslims could not form a single nation was, as Zaman has perceptively observed, at least 'as insidious a notion as the idea that the Muslims of India were separate from the global Muslim community'.[26]

Maulana Abul Kalam Azad (1888–1958), the *bête-noire* of separatist Muslims, shared these sentiments. His conception of the Muslim community, strongly informed by the sharia, clearly emphasised its scriptural roots, but unlike his fellow theologians in Deoband, who were more concerned with the sharia's legal injunctions, Azad stressed its broader moral and ethical principles. With his profound conviction in Islam's universalist message, Azad remained steadfast in the view that the pursuit of national and political separatism of the kind that underlay the demand for Pakistan fundamentally violated the spiritual priorities of the Quran by 'placing a question mark around Islamic capacity to survive without frontiers and among other religions'.[27]

Of course some have since claimed that Azad cynically tailored his theological stance to suit his programme of political co-operation with Congress and its model of 'composite nationalism'.[28] Others have pointed to the hollowness of this suggestion by underlining Azad's life-long engagement (however 'disembodied' and 'dislocated') with religious ecumenism.[29] Yet others have claimed that Azad's pluralist model, far from being a secular or multi-religious enterprise, was no less than a form of 'jurisdictional apartheid'.[30] Their views have been reinforced by those seeking to unpack Azad's notion of the united community (*umma wahida*), who regard it as more suggestive of an alliance between Muslims and non-Muslims rather than of any understanding of unity between the two groups. They argue that, despite Azad's inclination in his later years to equate the idea of the united community (*umma wahida*) with a united Indian nation (*muttahida qaumiyyat*) in support of a partnership between Muslims and Hindus, he never lost sight of the essentially contingent nature of this relationship.[31]

This line of thinking is certainly persuasive when judged against Azad's impatience with the constraints of temporal politics, which he clearly judged to be peripheral to a community in the service of a higher end. Nowhere was this more explicitly stated than in 1912, when he urged Indian Muslims to support India's liberation alongside Hindus by suggesting they call on their reserves of 'Islamic self-assurance' to banish their minority complex. In a declaration that would be echoed decades later by Jinnah in his own quest to liberate Indian Muslim from their condition of 'minorityism', Azad denounced 'this pre-occupation with majority and minority [which] has become the root of our problem'. Mocking his fellow-Muslims for their cowardice in the face of Hindus, he reminded them that they were 'members of a [global] brotherhood of four hundred million believers in the unity of God', and who had therefore no reason to be 'afraid of two and twenty million idol worshippers of India'.[32] More explicitly than any of his contemporaries, Azad here was giving voice to a vision of the community as synonymous with the Muslim idea of a global brotherhood or *umma*. In so doing, he set the stage for a challenge to emerging discourses of the community that sought to equate it more squarely with the Muslims of India rather than a universal Muslim *umma*.

This much narrower discourse of community had been in evidence since at least the late 1880s. It coincided with the emergence of nationalist politics under the aegis of the Indian National Congress and had developed in response to the colonial restructuring of India's political economy. The first had prompted fears of impending electoral reforms that promised to empower the numerically preponderant Hindus at the cost of India's Muslim minority. The second threatened to undermine the influence of a hitherto dominant Muslim service class, or salariat, who after almost two centuries at the helm of administrative affairs under the Mughals now faced the prospect of being displaced by a more advanced Hindu salariat conversant in English and buoyed by the demands of a burgeoning Indian nationalism.[33] Both forced an urgent review of the place of Indian Muslims in any future political dispensation.

The most prominent Muslim engaged in working out the implications of these developments was the educational reformer and thinker, Sir Sayyid Ahmad Khan (1817–1898).[34] Widely credited for lending substance to the idea of a modern Muslim community that would combine the pursuit of religious and secular goals, he sought to break free from the rigours of scriptural discourse. Not only was his Muslim community restricted to its Indian frontiers, it also stood opposed to any suggestion of extra-territoriality such as to stoke the fires of pan-Islamism or to leave his fellow Indian Muslims vulnerable to charges of disloyalty to their colonial masters. Indeed, it was precisely Sir Sayyid's loyalty to the Raj that would also encourage a more secular understanding of the community. As Sir Sayyid's politics was to demonstrate, what underpinned the community was less the authenticity of its Quranic message than the Muslims' special status in India's political hierarchy. Restoring this special status, in part through access to modern education and in part by winning concessions that would formalise the community's undisputed claim to an equal share of power, constituted an integral part of Sir Sayyid's community politics.

However, it would be erroneous to assume that Sir Sayyid's understanding of the community encompassed or extended to *all* Muslims in India. On the contrary, the object of his attention was mainly restricted to the community of a largely Urdu-speaking Muslim salariat concentrated in and around northern and central regions of British India, including the United and Central Provinces, Bihar, Orissa, Bombay, Delhi and a handful of princely states. They were the chief beneficiaries of Sir Sayyid's programme of partial secularization and modernization and it was they, more than any other group of Muslims, who came to be identified as the Muslim community. Muslims from the north-western and eastern provinces, which later constituted Pakistan, were barely affected by Sir Sayyid's reforms except for those who had seized the opportunity of an education at the Mohammedan Anglo-Oriental College established by him in the northern town of Aligarh in 1875. Indeed, the Muslims of the north-west and north-east appeared to be relatively peripheral to Sir Sayyid's developing ideas of the Muslim community. The causes, it has been suggested, may have been economic. The Muslim landed classes in the north-west had little need of Sir Sayyid; they already enjoyed privileged relations with the Raj and had cemented powerful alliances with local religious leaders, who helped buttress their standing in rural areas. As for Muslims in the north-east, they were mainly of peasant stock and as such were seen to have little use for the modern education favoured by Sir Sayyid and which was geared to the needs of the salariat.[35]

This would appear to suggest that Sir Sayyid's conception of the community was not so much religious as ethnic—unmistakeably rooted in India and with a strong regional bias towards North Indian Muslims. Yet, there is little doubt that Sir Sayyid was responsive to, and aware of, more religiously informed notions of the community. In a remarkable observation in 1888 he declared that, 'as regards Bengal, there is, as far as I am aware, in lower Bengal, a much larger proportion of Mohammadans than Bengalis. And if you take the population of the whole of Bengal, nearly half are Mohammadans, and something over half are Bengalis.'[36] What is revealing here is an understanding (and separation of) the community of Muslims in Bengal as a religious community divorced from its ethnic and regional Bengali roots. This apparent denial of the validity of a Muslim's regional ties and indeed the rejection of regional expressions of Islam would, in time, come to be closely associated with the religious stance of Pakistan's governing elite, whose modernist orientation is widely seen to be a legacy of Sir Sayyid.[37] However, it is difficult to establish to what extent Sir Sayyid's extra-territorial understanding of the Muslim community stemmed from an awareness of Islam as a universal faith and to what extent from a Mughal cosmopolitanism that valued foreign ancestry as a hallmark of the Muslim ruling classes, whose ties of kinship tightened solidarity in the face of non-Muslim competition.[38] Sir Sayyid's speeches are littered with references to the foreign ancestry of his community and like the many Muslim notables he spoke for, he was conspicuously shy in defining himself territorially as Indian, preferring to evoke his place among Mughals and Syeds with foreign roots.[39]

These different ways of imagining the Muslim community as both universalist and extra-territorial on the one hand and culturally determined and locally grounded on the other, resurfaced in the thinking of the poet and politician, Muhammad Iqbal (1877–1938). Along with Sir Sayyid and Muhammad Ali Jinnah, he forms part of the triumvirate presiding over the pantheon of Pakistan's national heroes, and might even lay claim to be the 'patron saint of the Pakistani elite'.[40] Much of Iqbal's standing rests on what has been described as the 'liberating thrust' of his vision which, in celebrating individual freedom, is seen to depart from 'the existential community chained to the worldview of the religious guardians of Islam'.[41] Certainly Iqbal left few in doubt that the *practical focus* of his concerns lay with the community of Muslims in India rather than with Muslims as a worldwide community of believers or *umma*.

Beset by anxiety over their constitutional status as a minority in a future all-India federation dominated by Congress, he concluded that the only practical solution lay in Muslim self-government managed through a territorial arrangement that involved the consolidation of 'a Northwest Muslim Indian State'.[42] In this Iqbal, like Sir Sayyid, favoured a regional, if not ethnic, understanding of the community as coterminous with the Muslims of northwest India rather than with *all* Indian Muslims. His political vision of an autonomous Muslim state 'within the British empire or without the British empire' showed that the community he had in mind was, first and foremost, the immediate community of Muslims in the north-western provinces of India, comprising Punjab, the North-West Frontier Province, Sind and Balochistan.[43] While this exclusion of the Muslims of Bengal and of Muslims from elsewhere in India sat uneasily with the vision of a universal community, it demonstrated Iqbal's remarkable grasp of the power of geography in shaping the limits of a viable political community.

Iqbal's own unease with this restricted view of the community was expressed in his unusual claim that the demand for a Muslim state in the northwest could not be taken as evidence of a primordial Muslim attachment to territory such as to qualify them for nationhood in the European sense of the term. Muslims, he declared, were a 'nation', not because of their contingent presence in a particular location but because of their essential, that is to say, their enduring and non-negotiable, membership in a common religious community that also served as the model for a universal society. What had necessitated the recasting of this community along 'national' lines bounded by territory, he argued, was not the espousal of 'European political thinking,' but the realization that 'the survival of Islam in India depended upon its centralization in a specified area'.[44] At the same time, Iqbal was keen to distance himself from any model tied too closely to *sharia*-inspired versions of the 'community' that relied on *ulama* and Islamist conceptions of Muslim society.

Equally important was Iqbal's hostility to Persian-inspired popular Sufi mysticism (*tasawwuf*), which he blamed for encouraging versions of a universal Muslim community that came to be closely associated with sections of the Deobandi *ulama* and the thinking of Maulana Abul Kalam Azad.[45] While Iqbal shared their view of the universal concerns governing the Muslim community, he diverged sharply in his understanding of what this entailed by way of political implications. Unlike Azad, for example, for whom the universal was synonymous with the idea of unity (*wahdat*) and with a community that accommodated difference while grounded in commonly defined rules of righteous action, Iqbal argued that the idea of *wahdat*, tainted by its association with pantheistic Sufism, was neither desirable nor intrinsic to Islam. The essence of Islam and its community, he declared, lay in monotheism, which in its opposition to polytheism (*shirk*) had 'nothing to do with ... *wahdat* and *kathrat* (plurality)'.[46]

Indeed, its practical application as spelt out by Iqbal in 1921 appeared to demonstrate that there would, in fact, be little room for plurality and difference in the universal space of his community. 'If you want to make it [universalism] an effective ideal and work it out in actual social life, you must start ... with a society exclusive in the sense of having a well-defined creed and a well-defined outline but ever enlarging its limits by example and persuasion. Such a society, according to my belief, is Islam.'[47] This understanding of the 'universal' Muslim community was to serve as a powerful template for later ideas seeking to reconcile the imperative of Muslim nationhood with the prescriptions of a community that claimed universal sanction.

For the moment however this rarefied and learned dialogue of ideas could not escape the imperatives of British rule or the parochial affiliations of tribe and class that sought to challenge any tidy construction of community. The requirements of indirect rule, which came to be associated with the method of British control over India, demanded above all a stable and hierarchically organized society. Indirect rule also required the management of social divisions through a complex pattern of authority involving rulers of princely states, the landed aristocracy and tribal leaders. These divisions were as much vertical as horizontal, reflecting not only the separation between rulers and ruled but distinctions between class, caste, races and tribes. A common argument running through the corpus of modern Indian historiography has been that the organization of society along these lines was deliberately 'constructed' to delay the onset of nationalism.[48] Most historians now recognize that they also served to reinforce strategic alliances between the British and local Indian power-holders in the northwest of India, especially in Punjab.[49] Both sides stood to gain from this co-operation: the British by strengthening their hold over rural areas, which allowed them to facilitate trade and extract revenues from taxation *and* local chiefs by strengthening feudal and tribal affiliations threatened by emerging discourses of the Muslim 'community' that were potentially hostile to parochial loyalties.[50] This was much less marked in eastern regions of British India (later to emerge as East Pakistan), where the subservient Muslim peasantry was scarcely in a position to act as a bulwark of colonial rule. This is not to say that the development of parochial or local ideas of the community at odds with *sharia*-centric versions of a universal community was any less robust in these areas. In East Bengal, a strong regional culture buoyed by a nascent Bengali Muslim bourgeoisie helped to promote a socio-territorial idea of a Bengali community that soon came into conflict with *sharia*-inspired notions of the supra-regional community that gained momentum during the 1920's—and which later informed the idea of Pakistan.[51]

The application of colonial law also helped to consolidate parochial loyalties and seal attachments to the local community, especially in parts of the north-western regions. Here, unlike elsewhere in India where colonial law worked in tandem with Islamic law to create new legal interpretations and institutions (mainly in the domain of personal law), customary law was the order of the day. Its enforcement was often left to tribal councils (*jirgas*) and, as in parts of the Punjab, mediated through feudal structures permeated by kinship and clan ties.[52] The aim was to help British administrators forge alliances between the colonial state and rural intermediaries. They included large landowners and tribal heads, who acted as key agents of social control in rural areas. By allowing local chiefs to formalise their power, sanctioned by means of customary law, British officials helped to strengthen alternative notions of the community based on local political configurations. However, even these local communities were not entirely divorced from the framework of Islamic prescriptions. Many were legitimated by the institutions of rural Islam ranging from the *pirs* (spiritual mentors) of Sind[53] to the *sajjidda nashins* (guardians of Sufi shrines) in Punjab.[54] Nevertheless, on the whole they tended to be instinctively hostile to the *ulama* and other purveyors of *sharia*-inspired notions of the community, whose vision of the socio-political order ran counter to conceptions of authority favoured by tribal and customary law.

Nation

The transition from these many-layered and often conflicting ideas of the Muslim community to the rhetoric of an Indian Muslim nation was far from straightforward. It certainly precluded any linear development from community to nation. At the same time, there were links, however nebulous, that helped sustain the idea of a pre-existing Muslim community in India as the foundation of a future Muslim nation in Pakistan.

In his seminal Radhakrishnan lectures, Bayly has argued that more attention should have been paid to indigenous traditions that fuelled and gave meaning to the development of nationalism in India. Although he is careful to warn against falling prey to teleology of the sort that would suggest that modern nationalism was somehow preordained by the past, he argues that any explanation of its development must be 'epistemologically and socially rooted in these inheritances'.[55] Thus, even while conceding that Western models of the nation came to dominate political discourse after the 1880s, Bayly emphasises that the crucial question is one of how this 'derivative concept' of nation and nationalism came 'to be rooted in the institutions of the Indian environment *and understood in terms of its own ethical and political ideas*'.[56]

The observation is especially pertinent when exploring the sense imparted by Indian Muslims to the idea of a Muslim nation, and its relationship to the community, especially after the Indian Mutiny of 1857. What emerges is a fluid, ever-changing, picture that both shaped and was shaped by a framework drawing on traditional ideas of the community as the repository of righteous government as well as on indigenous sources of local authority rooted in what Bayly describes as 'regional patriotism'. The result is a more complex representation of the transition from Muslim community to Pakistani nation than is allowed for by those who argue that Muslim separatism should be seen primarily as the manipulation of communal cultural symbols that were consciously selected to further the political interests of a dominant elite.[57] The risk here is that by focusing too closely on the material underpinnings of nationalist discourse and the putative motives of nationalist utterances, the narrative loses sight of 'the emotional, ideological and institutional context within which nationalist ideas gained currency, value and weight'.[58] Among the ideas jostling for a place in this firmament of nationalist discourse after 1857 were the concepts of *qaum, watan, mulk* and *millat* used by Muslims to confound and obscure the meaning of the nation.

The creation of the Indian National Congress in 1885 marked a turning point in the emergence of an alternative Muslim discourse on the nation. What propelled it was a different interpretation of India's past shaped as much by a collective memory of Muslim rule in India as by Muslim unease over how best to reconcile the claims of Islam as a locus of power with those of the nation as the centre of political loyalty. Sayyid Ahmed Khan was instrumental in setting the tone of this alternative discourse. Apparently riddled with contradiction, it nevertheless made sense to those among India's Muslims who had grown fearful of the nationalist vision projected by Congress. Their concerns were articulated by Sayyid Ahmed, who argued that Hindus and Muslims were not one nation (*qaum*) but two,[59] even if their blood had mixed at times.[60] They shared little except a common territorial homeland (*watan*)—Hindustan. This was but one of many variations on the theme of the Muslim nation that Sayyid Ahmed deployed to tease his audience and confound later generations of historians. At least as common were his frequent references, especially before 1885, to Hindus and Muslims as members of one *qaum*.[61] What is undeniable is that for Sayyid Ahmed *qaum* rarely, if ever, implied the global brotherhood of Islam.[62] Indeed, his hostility to the universalist pretensions of the Turkish Caliphate, which might have sustained this view, was almost as strident as his antipathy to Congress—both, he believed, aimed to rip apart the fabric of loyalist politics vital to Muslim fortunes under the British *Raj*.

Notwithstanding these inconsistencies, there were some elements that remained constant in Sayyid Ahmed's understanding of the nation. They included notions of class and ancestry, which suggest that his Muslim 'nation' was an exclusive enterprise managed and directed by men (for it was also an essentially patriarchal organization) of high, preferably foreign, birth. It also suggested that, to the extent that foreign descent was a key component of the nation there was no *a priori* understanding of the 'nation' as rooted in native soil. This reading of the *qaum* was quintessentially a product of Sayyid Ahmed's cosmopolitan Mughal heritage, which tended to shun the crude divisions of faith such as were the preserve of contemporary religious reform movements. It comes as no surprise that, when in 1861 three non-Muslims—the princely rulers of Patiala and Benaras and the prime minister of the princely state of Gwalior, Sir Dinkar Rao—were included in the Viceroy's Legislative Council, Sayyid Ahmed 'rejoiced' that they had been called upon to 'discharge their duties manfully and right well'.[63] Well-born Hindus were, then, as much a part of the Sayyid Ahmed's Hindustani 'nation' as well-born Muslims. Or were they?

By the time Sayyid Ahmed had come to terms with the full import of the 1857 uprising, his thinking on the 'nation' appeared to be undergoing a shift. By 1888 there were clear signs that he was set to recast Hindus and Muslims as bearers of distinct identities—'two eyes' of a 'beautiful bride' (Hindustan)—even while suggesting that he still equated the term *qaum* among Muslims not with a country or race but with religion.[64] This idea of the *qaum* as an expression of a separate Muslim religious identity would appear to confirm Bayly's suggestion that it was merely an aspect of 'old patriotism' consistent with the idea of Hindustan as an 'ancient royal realm' rather than suggestive of a proto-nationalist community synonymous with what later nationalists would imagine as a territorial homeland (*watan*) or country (*mulk*).[65]

Yet, it would be naive to assume that Sayyid Ahmed's notion of the *qaum* was devoid of a political dimension. For to do so would be to gravely underestimate the force of his conviction that Muslims as a *qaum*, understood both as a religious fellowship and a sub-culture defined by a common ruling-class ancestry, had a special relationship to the political order. Sayyid Ahmed understood better than most that the transformation of the colonial state and the re-organization of the Indian legal and administrative systems in the 1880s entailed fundamental shifts, which were set to challenge the political dominance of well-born Muslims. They now faced the introduction of a range of unfamiliar criteria for admission to the higher echelons of state service. This included a mastery of English, rather than Persian (the former language of administration), which mainly privileged western-educated Indians, drawn from the Presidency towns of Calcutta, Madras and Bombay. Lumped by Sayyid Ahmed under the rubric of 'the Bengalis', they came to represent for him the single most potent challenge to his *qaum*. It would be fair to say that this scramble for government jobs, which made manifest the decline of Muslim privilege, proved to be almost as traumatic for Sayyid Ahmed's later politics as questions about the dubious quality of Muslim loyalty were for his early politics. It triggered an urgent reassessment of his *qaum*: now more closely to be informed by the political concerns of Muslims from well-born (*sharif*) families with a service class background, who hailed from the provinces of north and central India and, to a lesser extent, parts of eastern India, including Bihar.

It was this focus on well-born Muslims with their long and distinguished tradition of close links to the centres of power that led Sayyid Ahmed increasingly to equate power with bureaucratic access and to demand that such access be secured for Muslims on a basis of equality with Hindus in any colonial devolution of power to Indians. But this also led to a subtle shift in Sayyid Ahmed's thinking towards a more ethnic definition of the Muslim *qaum* as representative of the regionally-specific and upwardly-mobile Muslim salariat with a distinct 'culture' based on Islam. This 'ethnicisation of religious identity'[66] was of course greatly facilitated by the parallel process of Islamic revivalism in north India in the late nineteenth century, which accentuated cultural and religious differences and significantly widened the political fault lines between Muslims and other communities. Together they set the stage for a new, but by no means unproblematic discourse of the Muslim nation.

Among those who revealed its inherent tensions was Iqbal, whose ambivalence towards nationalism was symptomatic of a deeper struggle to reconcile the claims of an extra-territorial community informed by a universal religion with the demands of a Muslim ethnicity seeking expression within a geographically circumscribed nation. Like many of his generation, Iqbal's early political consciousness was fuelled by an instinctive attachment to the homeland of India, which has been used to substantiate the claim that Iqbal started out as an Indian nationalist before dedicating the rest of his life to Muslim separatism. However, Iqbal's political trajectory was more complex and more internally conflicted than has generally been recognized.[67]

Whilst the idea of the nation as an aspect of belonging clearly did exercise its charms on Iqbal, he proved to be far more resilient to nationalism as a focus of primary, if not exclusive, allegiance. This emerged most forcefully in his opposition to the nationalist credo favoured by the Congress, which he condemned as an attempt to import the evils of Western materialism and to undermine the spiritual basis of Indian society by recasting the nation as an object of worship. Iqbal's objections to the Congress' creed were not, however, dictated solely by his antipathy to an alien doctrine. At least as important was his sense of apprehension about what majority Hindu rule might signify for Muslim power and, by extension, for Islam as a 'cultural force'. For it had become obvious to Iqbal that the two were, in fact, inseparable. In the years following his return from Europe in 1908, the over-riding refrain of his political discourse was not so much the issue of guaranteeing the economic, social or political rights of Indian Muslims but of securing a safe haven for Islam in India. Iqbal probably did more than anyone to sow the seed of the claim that the demand for a separate Muslim state was primarily a demand for a Muslim enclave where Islam would no longer be 'in danger'.

Iqbal's instinctive hostility to the idea of the nation also led him to resist, intellectually at least, any link between a Muslim nation and a separate Muslim state—a link that would have compromised his engagement with Islam as a 'universal community' which could brook no divisions of the sort implied by national differences. Therefore, when in 1930 he laid out his scheme for a territorially demarcated and centralized Muslim state in the north-west of India, he justified its formation not on the grounds that Muslims were a nation, but that 'the life of Islam' depended on it.[68] It is now understood that what Iqbal was proposing was not an independent Muslim state as such, but an autonomous entity with the option of choosing either to remain 'within or without' the Indian federation. Nevertheless even if he had pressed for total independence, it is far from certain that Iqbal would have done so by recasting the Muslims of India as a nation.

Although he harboured strong reservations about separate Muslim territorial statehood, regarding it as a blow to communal solidarity, Iqbal always stated that territorial borders to secure Islam were essentially temporary devices destined over time to wither away by ever enlarging the frontiers of the Islamic community 'by example and persuasion'.[69] As such, the territorial nationalism espoused by Congress would surely have appeared to him to be especially pernicious in as much as its support for a permanent geographical space for an Indian nation rested on the dubious premise of a distinction between Indians and non-Indians. By contrast, his reluctant admission of territorial nationalism suggested that he believed such boundaries could only be justified when sustained by the force of a far more fundamental dichotomy between Muslims and non-Muslims that, in the context of India, necessarily required 'the creation of a Muslim India within India'.[70]

The power of this vision of a safe haven for Islam in India stemmed also from the deep-rooted mystique that Muslims like Iqbal attached to the idea of a protected enclave, where the practice of their faith could continue unhindered. While debate still rages about whether or not Iqbal ever envisaged an Islamic state of the sort demanded by some of his protégés, including Maulana Abul Ala Maududi of the revivalist Jamaat-i-Islami, he made no secret of his support for a Muslim homeland. The basis and justification for this (possibly independent) homeland lay not in the controversial proposition that Muslims were a nation, and therefore entitled to a separate state, but in the far more compelling myth that Islam itself was in danger. Once this was acknowledged—and Iqbal did more than most to press the case—there were two options: migration or resistance. Iqbal understood that the second made little sense in the context of India, which by the 1920s and 1930s appeared to be moving inexorably towards a democratic transition and an eventual transfer of power to a Hindu majority. There remained the option of migration, but this was to prove just as problematic given the demographic make-up of colonial India, where Muslims lived cheek-by-jowl with non-Muslims across the subcontinent. Iqbal's ingenious scheme of 'amalgamating' the lands lying to the north-west of India, which were already defined by their Muslim majorities, offered a practical way out to secure his ultimate objective—the protection of Islam as 'a cultural force'. Though he did not go so far as to make a case for the large-scale migration of Indian Muslims to a putative protected haven, the vision he invoked in his speech as president of the Muslim League in 1930 was clearly suggestive of the mythical place to which early Muslim pioneers, led by their Prophet, retreated to escape subjugation and slavery by the enemies of their faith.

That Iqbal was less concerned with forging a Muslim nation than ensuring a place where Islam could survive in India was perhaps most emphatically underlined by his failure to factor into his scheme the Muslims of the Gangetic plain, especially those concentrated in the eastern half of Bengal. Like Sayyid Ahmed Khan, for whom the *qaum* was essentially a regional configuration confined to the Muslims of north and central India, Iqbal's vision of the 'Indo-Muslim' community was most immediately shaped by the local world of north-west India, dominated at the time by the major political configurations of the Punjab. His intense if haphazard involvement in this localised (mainly Punjabi) sphere of influence would also explain why the imperatives of all-India politics, which ultimately forced Jinnah to resort to the rhetoric of nationhood in order to carve out a separate political space for Muslims in India, remained marginal to Iqbal's worldview.

This is not to say that Iqbal was wholly oblivious to the presence of Muslims beyond the north-western regions with which he was most familiar. By the mid 1930s the preponderance of Bengali Muslims in the east was beginning to influence his thinking about the future shape of Islam in India. In his letters to Jinnah in 1937 he demonstrated his awareness of the Muslims of east Bengal, demanding 'Why should not the Muslims of North-West India and Bengal be considered nations entitled to self-determination?'[71] Yet, Iqbal's interest in Bengali Muslims as a constituent element of a putative Muslim nation was ultimately peripheral to his main objective, which aimed primarily to secure 'the enforcement and development of the Shariat of Islam' through the consolidation of 'a free Muslim state or states'.[72] His overriding concern was not so much to confront the challenge of transforming Muslims from a minority to a nation, but in deciding how best to adapt a community with universal pretensions into a regionally circumscribed entity with a limited remit. Indeed, when faced with the untenable logic of extending national self-determination to Muslims in provinces where they were in a minority, he concluded that 'personally I think that the Muslims of North-West India and Bengal ought at present to ignore Muslim minority provinces' and concentrate instead on a 'line of action' for the Muslims of north-west India (followed, if need be, by a 'separate federation' for the Muslims of Bengal). In so doing, Iqbal echoed both a discourse that equated the Muslim *qaum* with the Muslims of the north-western provinces and contemporary schemes that assumed more than one Muslim federation to resolve the issue of Muslim self-determination in India.

Iqbal was not alone in promoting the idea of a separate Muslim state as a safe haven for Islam. Maulana Mawdudi (1903–1979), the founder of the sub-continent's premier revivalist movement, the Jamaat-i-Islami, also shared this view. During a decade-long association with Iqbal in the late 1920s and 1920s, Mawdudi came to be closely involved in an institutional programme of Islamic revival aimed at facilitating the creation of a Muslim national homeland.[73] Although these relations were soon crippled by Mawdudi's political ambitions and by his increasingly antagonistic stance towards the Muslim League, which he denounced as an ignorant 'party of pagans' (*jamaat i jahiliya*),[74] they left a lasting imprint on Mawdudi's thinking. His competing version of the Muslim nation was clearly modelled on the idea of a homeland for Muslims that would also serve as a haven for Islam. Like Iqbal, he too was closely focussed on the Muslims of the north-western provinces, whose interests he tended to equate with the Muslim 'nation' of India. Finally, like Iqbal he remained deeply

35

ambivalent about nationalism, preferring to frame it in the language of power as a necessary condition for the survival of Islam.

Mawdudi's version of the 'two-nation theory', formulated in response to the model of secular nationalism favoured by the Congress party, contained all the hallmarks of the crude binary opposition between a supposed Hindu nation and its Muslim counterpart. According to Nasr, it also represented Mawdudi's 'binary view of the world as sacred and profane'.[75] His two-nation theory, outlined in 1938, described Muslims as 'a distinct people whose social life is based on a particular ethical and cultural norm' and envisaged a state within a state that echoed Iqbal's vision of a 'Muslim India within India'.[76] Indeed, like most such schemes then in circulation, Mawdudi's blueprint, which provided for two 'culturally autonomous' entities, presupposed neither the physical partition of the sub-continent nor lip-service to Muslim 'national' self-determination. Rather, like Iqbal, his concern was to secure a safe haven—a *Dar ul Islam*, which he explained 'means only a Muslim cultural home and not a Muslim state, but if God wills it, the two may become one'.[77]

Though Mawdudi soon moved in favour of secession and the creation of a separate Islamic state, which he emphatically sought to distinguish from Jinnah's model of a less theologically inspired Pakistan, it is far from clear that he did so on the basis of a commitment to any ethos of nationalism—about which he remained deeply ambivalent. It is worth noting that he was perhaps more prepared than most of his peers to confront the full implications of a Muslim homeland by recognizing that it would have to guarantee the right of any Muslim to migrate to a consolidated space designated as such. In plans for a loosely confederal structure proposed at the same time, Mawdudi endorsed what effectively amounted to 'a right of return' for Indian Muslims living outside thirteen designated Muslim 'territories' (the fourteenth and largest being reserved for Hindus) by furnishing a timetable over twenty-five years to complete an exchange of population.[78] This scheme, though lacking any semblance of practicality, was nonetheless consistent with Mawdudi's overall objective, which was less to engage in the logic of Muslim nationhood than to establish an Islamic state in a designated Muslim territory. Ultimately, for Mawdudi as for Iqbal (both ideologues *par excellence*) the merits of an independent Muslim state had little or nothing to do with affirming the authenticity of a Muslim nation. What made an independent Muslim state imperative was the need to restore to Muslims the privilege of power both believed was a divinely sanctioned prerogative.

For Muhammad Ali Jinnah, ever the pragmatic politician, these *a priori* positions were far more difficult to sustain. Initially he had been reluctant to lend his support to Iqbal's territorial scheme outlined in 1930, fearing it would divide Indian Muslims and fuel civil war. As Ziring observes, 'he [Jinnah] could not envision a viable Muslim state as described by the renowned poet [Iqbal]'. Balochistan was still a wild, arid, border region and Sind had not yet been split off from the Bombay presidency. The North West Frontier Province was a rugged mountain area along the Afghan border, its inhabitants largely tribal, and, with the exception of a limited settled area around Peshawar, it was subject to no known central authority. Only the Punjab represented the contemporary world of South Asia and there Muslims had to find communion with the Sikhs in addition to resident Hindus.[79] Jinnah also recognized the problem of hundreds of thousands of Muslims from the Muslim minority provinces, for whom Iqbal had made little or no provision in his version of the Muslim majority state. Nor indeed is there any evidence that Jinnah at this, or any other, stage was inclined to back the mass migration of Indian Muslims to a putative Muslim 'homeland'; on the contrary, he was persuaded that the presence of substantial numbers of Muslim and non-Muslims minorities in each of the successor states of India and Pakistan would act as an effective deterrent against attack by the other, serving as hostages to good behaviour. Even so, his position on Pakistan as a 'homeland' was no less fraught with contradictions. For while he was keen to encourage qualified Muslim doctors, teachers, lawyers and others to migrate to Pakistan from Muslim minority provinces in India, he is said to have been averse to the idea of the exchange of population on religious grounds. These ambiguities surrounding Jinnah's idea of Pakistan as a homeland contributed significantly to its anguished history. Gyanendra Pandey, the Indian historian, has underscored this point noting that '[t]here was always going to be some doubt about the ethnic and territorial basis of this religiously defined nation. For there was never any suggestion that the ninety million Muslims of undivided India—spread out all over that territory, with Muslim-majority regions existing in north-western and north-eastern India and in pockets (towns and districts) elsewhere—could all be accommodated, or even wish to migrate to the areas that became Pakistan'.[80] Nevertheless, the idea of a 'homeland' exercised, as it still does, a powerful hold on the Pakistani imagination. For many of Jinnah's supporters, and indeed for subsequent generations in Pakistan, it bears all the hallmarks of a modern restatement of the Prophetic migration, complete with the sacrifices and sufferings endured by a beleaguered community forced to abandon hearth and home.

Werbner has drawn attention to the influence of these elements as founding myths of Pakistan and as essential to an understanding of its 'civil religion'. She shows how the struggle for Pakistan's national independence is most vividly accounted in terms of the 'the central Judaeo-Quranic myth' of migration and liberation. She takes as examples celebrations marking Jinnah's birthday that serve as the 'enactment on the *political* plane of an established world vision constituted in its axiomatic principles on the *religious* plane. Just as on the religious plane the Islamic nation, the *umma*, is constituted, above all, in the person of the Prophet ... so too the Pakistan nation is constituted in its visionary perfection in the person of the Quaid-i-Azam'.[81] What is paradoxical is that the idea of Pakistan as a Muslim 'homeland' (in contrast to an Islamic state) has also exercised its hold on the country's liberal intelligentsia, which has generally been hostile to theological myth-making. For them, the idea of a Muslim homeland has always represented a softer and more pluralistic conception of Pakistan than that suggested by a theologically-inspired version of an Islamic state.

Jinnah however was unmoved, at least until the 1930s, by any of these concerns. His aim until then had been quite simply to achieve a constitutional arrangement at the centre of a broadly federal India that he hoped would guarantee his place (along with Gandhi and Nehru) as an architect of India's freedom and, in the process secure his role as an 'ambassador of Hindu-Muslim unity'. Unlike Gandhi and Nehru, Jinnah faced the awkward problem of being without a political constituency. This was brought into sharp relief in the 1920s, when the devolution of power to the provinces under the new colonial dispensation (the Government of India Act 1919) meant that Muslims like Jinnah, from provinces where Muslims were in a minority, were ruthlessly shunted aside in favour of regional and party bosses. For a man like Jinnah, who had made no secret of his disdain for mass politics, returning to resume life as an English gentleman with a lucrative legal practice was an option he found hard to resist. By the time he was persuaded by the then almost moribund Muslim League to return to

India in 1935, he had done some hard thinking. It was not long before the fundamental shift in Jinnah's discourse emerged to suggest that the terms of reference for what had until then passed for Muslim separatist politics had changed dramatically. Where once had been talk of a Muslim minority with constitutional safeguards, the clamour now was about a Muslim nation and a non-negotiable right to parity with the majority Hindu nation.

The remarkable twist by which Jinnah persuaded a minority to arrogate to itself the attributes of a nation bound by little more than a common religious identity is still widely regarded as a *tour de force*. His skills in bringing together the disparate interests of Muslims in the Muslim majority areas of the north-west and east, more interested in regional autonomy, with those of Muslims from the minority provinces of northern and central India, more interested in securing equal partnership with Hindus at the centre of an all-India federation, has continued to win admiration. That he, a secular-minded Muslim with a taste for ham sandwiches, did so by employing the language of Islam to further his political ends, is remarkable. Far from proving an embarrassment, it is seen either as evidence of a master tactician at work or as the moves of an honourable politician reluctantly forced to resort to desperate measures to salvage the interests of his community.

Jinnah's most notable success lay in attaching to Muslims the label of a modern nation. As such it stood in marked contrast to the use of the old-style *qaum* favoured by Sir Sayyid, more suggestive of an 'old' Indian regional patriotism. Indeed, these parochial loyalties—whether of region, tribe or kin—were regarded by Jinnah as deeply threatening to his political project, which aimed above all to secure the recognition of the League as the exclusive representative of Muslim interests in India. The exceptional nature of these ambitions largely determined the exceptional nature of Jinnah's project, for while the demand for a separate Muslim state remained open to negotiation, the prerogative of the League and its leader exclusively to represent the Muslim nation was not. Those who challenged it were ruthlessly suppressed. They included Muslims who had thrown in their lot with Congress (so-called 'nationalist Muslims') and strongly resisted Jinnah's idea of equating the civilizational unity of Muslims with Indian Muslim nationhood. But they also included Muslim regional leaders, especially in the Punjab and Bengal, who sought to chart a difficult course between Muslim separatism and the demands of their local constituencies, which included significant non-Muslim minorities. Jinnah's determination to crush these awkward compromises set a precedent which some believe sowed the seeds of Pakistan's 'post-independence political culture of intolerance'.[82] In time it would also stifle a culture of dissent and strengthen the politics of 'hegemonic discourse' in Pakistan.[83]

Power

Yet what Jinnah clearly realized, unlike his predecessors, is that while the notion of communal solidarity remained a desirable ideal for many Muslims, its moral purchase rested on its relation to political power—conceived not as intrinsically corrupting, but as an instrument in the service of higher, divinely ordained, ends. And while the idea of Muslims as a political minority might well have secured constitutional safeguards to protect their rights, they could not convey the significance of the special status of Muslims or enhance their claim to political parity with a non-Muslim majority. By defining Muslims as a nation Jinnah was able both to encompass their entitlement to political power and to establish their parity with a putative Indian nation, thereby at a stroke affirming their potentially sovereign status.

At the same time, Jinnah's attempt to recast Indian Muslims as a nation solely on the basis of religious affinity was clearly fraught with contradictions. Not least were the deep ethnic and linguistic divisions that separated Muslims across the sub-continent. Few doubted (rightly as it turns out) that they could be subsumed under, or be replaced by, an overarching Islamic identity that would form the basis of a nation. More important still were the very different expectations of Muslim nationhood harboured by Jinnah's growing band of followers. For his supporters in the so-called Muslim minority provinces of central India, the idea of a Muslim nation promised to restore their special status as Muslims, which they feared had been compromised by the exigencies of proto-democratic politics. For others in the north-eastern provinces of Bengal and Assam, the rhetoric of Muslim nationhood clearly offered the region's rural Muslim majority the prospect of economic emancipation from a dominant class of Hindu landowners. Yet others in north-western India were drawn to Iqbal's idea of a viable safe haven for Islam in India: for them Muslim nationhood served as a compelling ideal and an 'outlet for expressing their religious concern in the political arena'.[84]

How then, despite these different expectations, was the problematic transition from community to nation managed, thus providing Pakistan with its *raison d'être*? The notion of a Muslim community, bound by a putative Islamic solidarity could not be supported either by the deep-seated ethnic and linguistic differences that divided Muslims or by the boundaries that separated local Muslim tribal and feudal elites, especially in the north-west. Nor indeed was there agreement among Jinnah's followers on the scope of this community. While visionary Muslims like Iqbal chose to highlight his community's supra-territorial or universalistic aspects (in opposition to the territorial nationalism of the kind espoused by Congress), his more pragmatic-minded counterparts set its limits more narrowly within the broad though as yet notional boundaries of Hindustan. Meanings attached to the 'nation' and the 'homeland' were also fractured. For the embattled Muslim gentry of north India, influenced by indigenous versions of 'old patriotism', the nation was clearly tied to a sense of place with specific modes and methods of communication, whether of language, literature or religious structures. But their status in a province where they were in a minority triggered a disjunction between the nation and the land that could only be resolved by recasting the idea of Pakistan as a homeland—as a point of destination rather than as a centre of consolidation.

This, in turn, has lent a certain force to the description of Pakistan as a 'migrant state',[85] conceived by and for those who were to leave their native homes to re-settle in a new land they wished to govern as a nation-state. The bond between the nation and the land was altogether more secure for Jinnah's supporters in the north-western provinces and the eastern regions of Bengal and Assam. Although divided, especially in the north-west, by linguistic, ethnic and tribal affiliations, the idea of the nation emerged there as more tangible and less elusive. Instrumental to its consolidation was the attachment to the land. However, strong pre-existing ethnic identities rooted in these territories meant that Jinnah's hastily cobbled 'two-nation' theory was vigorously (if unevenly) challenged by Muslims in these so-called Muslim majority areas. Perhaps not surprisingly, it was in Bengal that the idea of a Muslim nation proved to be most problematic. Firmly grounded in a specific territory, blessed with a common language that cut across a relatively homogenous Muslim population, its ambiguous relationship with a Bengali regional identity (or putative nation) with a large

41

non-Muslim component effectively challenged Jinnah's alternative, ethnic conception of a Muslim nation.[86]

But the latter, which equated religion with culture—and which Jinnah had sought to employ against the Congress's self-avowedly political definition of the Indian nation—met with an especially uneasy reception in Bengal. There, the distinction between religion and culture had been sustained by a powerful regional identity, which now threatened to set the imperatives of a more robust Bengali nation on a collision course with Jinnah's fragile conception of a Muslim nation. That dilemma was given its most coherent expression in 1944 by Abul Mansur (himself a Bengali Muslim) and president of the Bengal Muslim League, who declared that, '[r]eligion and culture are not the same thing. Religion transgresses the geographical boundary but *tamaddun* (culture) cannot go beyond the geographical boundary [...]. For this reason, the people of *Purba* [Eastern] Pakistan are a different nation from the people of the other provinces of India and from the "religious brothers" of Pakistan.'[87]

The increasingly ambiguous relationship between nation and territory, between religion and culture, and, most fundamentally, between (cultural) community and state, which emerged in the 1940s, led Jinnah to reshape Muslim politics by using the language of Islamic universalism. By doing so, he hoped to forge an instrument that not only chimed with Muslim sentiment, but would also serve as a powerful tool to mobilize Muslim opinion in favour of his campaign for the consolidation of a distinct Muslim political entity. At the heart of this universalist vision lay the notion of the Muslims as a righteous community that aspired to reunite morality with power under a 'true' leader, who by embodying the virtues of honesty, persistence and unwavering steadfastness, qualified for divine selection and as the 'natural' choice of the community.[88]

While the paradigmatic example of this vision has been most fully expressed in the community of Muslims assembled by the Prophet Muhammad, it has left a lasting impression on Muslims for whom historical change has been closely associated with exemplary leaders able to redeem and renew society. Though some have argued that Jinnah's own personality 'was antithetical to mystical notions of charisma',[89] his style of leadership evoked a complex blend of temporal and righteous power that in the minds of many of his followers would have sanctioned the notion that 'democracy under ["true"] leadership is paradoxically absolute since it allows no room for disagreement'.[90] Jinnah's claim to be the sole spokesman for Indian Muslims and his insistence on the League as their exclusive representative, though judged at times to be arbitrary if not ruthless, were nevertheless widely accepted by his followers as necessary to the process of Muslim collective redemption. In the context of the 1940s, it became synonymous with the struggle to liberate Muslims from the servitude of 'minority-ism' to make possible their equality of status (parity) with non-Muslims and justify their bid for national self-determination.

Yet, the theme of liberation in the historical narrative of Pakistan is troubled with ambiguity. The narratives of anti-colonialism that were central to anti-colonial struggles in Asia and Africa inevitably remained muted, for this was a nation forged not in reaction to a foreign colonial master, but in opposition to competing colonial subjects, who though mainly Hindus, were also non-Muslim. By incorporating the struggle for freedom and the myth of Pakistan into the broader mythology of Islam, Jinnah successfully evoked a compelling civil religion that represented 'the struggle of true believers against idolators (Hindus) and people of the Book (Jews and Christians) who deny the message of the Prophet and persecute his followers'.[91] This civil religion would become vital to the political life in Pakistan, whose historical trajectory has been singularly devoid of the strong ideological moorings characteristic of long drawn-out mass struggles for independence against foreign colonial rule.

Jinnah himself contributed to this process by appealing to the language and rhetoric of Islamic universalism as a means of defeating the tribal, racial and linguistic affiliations that threatened to ruin his Muslim nationalist project. Unfortunately for Jinnah, much of the discourse of Islamic universalism upon which he had been forced to rely to realize his political project had been shaped by the *ulama* and their version of a *sharia*-based Islam.[92] Furthermore, by using the language of universal Islam to lend substance to his concept of a Muslim nation Jinnah also pre-empted any understanding of the political community (or 'nation') as either 'limited' or 'sovereign'.[93] Its implications would surface in years to come in debates over the merits of divine versus popular sovereignty as the basis of Pakistan's constitution and in questions about the 'transnational' dimensions of the country's identity.

For at the heart of Islam's universalist posture lies the idea of the *umma*, which unlike the nation, *is* imagined as both unlimited and coterminous with mankind. The contradictions of using the language of Islamic universalism to drive a nationalist project left their mark on the new state, which though inspired by visions of a putative ever-enlarging universal community was yet forced to recognize its finite boundaries. Nor did the discourse of Islamic universalism facilitate the idea of the Pakistani nation as a 'sovereign' political community. For while the modern nation was imagined, as Anderson reminds us, as an Enlightenment project that sought to challenge the divinely ordained bases of political legitimacy, Islamic universalism presupposes a community that seeks to authenticate divine sovereignty. At the heart of this tension lay the question of allegiance, which Jinnah used to masterly effect by employing the language of Islamic universalism to secure the Muslims' loyalty to a higher power against the claims both of parochial and tribal affiliations and of a putative Indian nation as elaborated by the Congress. The consequences of such formulations have significantly moulded Pakistan's identity as a sovereign nation-state.

Yet, if the universalist logic of Islam was at odds with Pakistan as a national project, it was essential to the much larger purpose that underlay the movement for Pakistan. This, as Iqbal had intimated, had little or nothing to do with Muslim nationhood—an idea, he emphasised, which made no sense to Muslims. It is perhaps no accident that the idea of a Muslim nation should have entered so late into the political lexicon of the League. While political developments after 1937, especially the steady erosion of trust between the Congress and vast numbers of Muslims, helped quicken the shift from Muslims as a minority to Muslims as a nation, the change from one status to the other was less fundamental to the emergence of Pakistan than is generally assumed. For what linked both ideas, and was eventually to legitimise and lend meaning to Pakistan among its supporters, was the notion that power and its management were a divinely sanctioned Muslim prerogative.

The historical roots of this assumption are now generally, and quite rightly, held to flow directly from the experience of Muslim rule in India, which though loosely and sometimes unevenly established had, by about 1300, stamped itself across much of the subcontinent. By the time the Mughal empire came to dominate vast swathes of India in the 1550s, the force of Muslim overlordship had been so firmly projected onto the collective memory that it sustained the myth of power as a Muslim birthright. Although more marked among the Muslim nobility and well-born service classes (the *ashraf*), this assumption reached wider and deeper in society than is generally acknowledged. In Bengal, for example, among the Muslim peasantry these perceptions of power were not uncommon. The Bengali scholar Rafiuddin Ahmed has observed that while 'British rule did not hurt the Muslim peasantry of Bengal any more than it did the Hindu [it] left amongst Muslims a sense of deprivation that was uncommon among the Hindus. After all, they thought, the British had wrested power from "them", as if to suggest they had descended from ancestors who had ruled India long before the coming of the British.'[94] There can be no doubt however that it was among the Muslims of north India, with their proximity to the centres of power until the arrival of the British in the eighteenth century, that the collective memory of Muslim rule was most effectively forged as a political instrument. Even as Muslims in India were forced by the 'inescapable political accountancy of the Raj'[95] to don the garb of a mere minority, many were determined not to allow its logic to compromise their special status or their historical claim to power.

This idea of the special status of Indian Muslims was to prove a vital link in bridging the gap between their condition as a minority and as a nation. It fuelled both the League's early insistence upon securing recognition for the political importance of Muslims as well Jinnah's later demand for Muslim parity with Hindus in the all-India centre that dominated the political landscape in the decade leading up to Partition. While the transition from Muslim minority to Muslim nation was necessary to render more intelligible to others the nature of Muslim opposition to Congress, its real significance to Jinnah's Muslim followers rested squarely on the assumption that Muslims were 'special', and specially qualified to ensure the just dispensation of power. But as Pakistan's subsequent history was to demonstrate, the country's search for consensus was to repeatedly frustrate this Muslim quest for power.

2

WHO IS A PAKISTANI?

CULTURE AND IDENTITY

Nowhere has the lack of consensus over the meaning of Pakistan and its ambiguous relation to Islam surfaced more sharply than in doubts over the definition of 'the Pakistani'—a definition that is still deeply contested. Soon after independence conflicting discourses of Pakistan as both a point of destination for Indian Muslims and a consolidated centre of Muslim power accentuated tensions between Muslim migrants and indigenous groups, each armed with rival versions of 'the Pakistani'. On the one side were the moral claims of Muslim refugees from India, who sought to establish their pre-eminence as 'real' Pakistanis by comparing their migration to the archetypal Muslim exodus (*hijrat*) led by the Prophet Muhammad to establish the first Islamic community in seventh century Arabia. On the other, there prevailed the political logic of so-called 'sons of the soil', who appealed to their demonstrable (if sometimes imagined) roots in the regions of Pakistan.

This conflict to establish the alpha-citizen of the new country was symptomatic of the lack of resolution between two opposing ideas of political belonging that had informed the idea of Pakistan: the first, resting on an ideational construction of a natural Muslim community, the second on the notion of a locally negotiated national community. In the late 1960s this struggle developed in tandem with a related discourse on 'the Pakistani' as 'Muslim', whose wide-ranging implications were reflected in the civil war that led to the break-up of the country in 1971. They centred on attempts by the Bengali majority to strengthen an ethnic definition of the Pakistani in opposition to others that favoured an identity more closely tied to Islam. Although these efforts were brutally suppressed, they radically challenged the two-nation theory that emphasised allegiance to 'Islam' over regional loyalties as the *sine qua non* of being Pakistani.

Pakistan's altered contours after 1971 precipitated fresh uncertainties over Pakistani identity, which now assumed more complex forms. At issue were perceived attempts to Punjabise it, which triggered a reaction among the country's smaller regional groups (especially those of Sind and Balochistan), where there emerged a strong shift in favour of more plural expressions of Pakistani identity. The country's turn towards the Islamic lands lying to the west of Pakistan also encouraged fresh interest in equating 'the Pakistani' with 'the Muslim'. The hardening of the state's Islamic identity in the 1980s intensified these concerns, but also sharpened sectarian differences that fostered the preference for a certain type of Sunni sectarian Islam as a defining feature of the 'universal' Pakistani. Together these currents have significantly weakened the drive to achieve a pluralism friendly definition of Pakistani identity. The persistent lack of consensus over Islam and its role in relation to the state further undermined this effort. Its consequences have contributed towards the dismantling of institutional protection for the country's non-Muslim minorities and fuelled doubts about their claims to qualify as 'real Pakistanis'.

Migrants and natives

The uncertainty over who qualifies as Pakistani owes much to the nation's emergence in 1947 as something of a migrant state, one that is often compared to Israel. Yet there were differences. Unlike Israel, which at independence housed a few hundred thousand Jews, who readily made place for the thousands who fled Europe at the end of World War II, the new state of Pakistan already included in 1947 well-settled communities of more than 70 million Muslims. With independence these communities faced not only the uncertainties of defining themselves as Pakistanis in a land to which they had hitherto belonged simply as Punjabis, Sindhis, Balochis or Pashtuns, but also the challenge of positioning themselves in relation to more than 7 million Muslim refugees from India who arrived claiming an equal right to be Pakistani. At issue was a conflict that resonates to the present day. It centres on who can claim to be the true heirs of the new state and who thereby best qualifies as a 'real' Pakistani.

At independence the two sides of this titanic battle involved so-called Muslim migrants (or *mohajirs*) from India and others long settled in the lands that made up the new Pakistan, who saw themselves as native sons of the soil. Much has been written about the refugee crisis that faced Pakistan in 1947 as well as the long-term economic and political consequences of such massive migration.[1] Attention has focussed on the limitations of the new state, which bereft of any recognizable infra-structure, was quickly overwhelmed by a refugee crisis that (astonishingly) few had anticipated—notwithstanding the feverish rhetoric of a homeland and refuge for Muslims fleeing Hindu tyranny. Worse, the violence triggered by such mass migration was such that the Muslim League (never known for its administrative skills) soon ceded the task of governance to the evidently more competent members of the civil bureaucracy and the army. The critical role assumed by these institutions at the inception of the state would set the tone for their future dominance in national life.

Most of the refugees who arrived in Jinnah's Muslim homeland headed towards the north-western rather than the eastern territories of the regions designated as Pakistan: Punjab and Sind bore the brunt of the influx. Many chose to settle in the towns of Sind, especially Karachi, the country's commercial and administrative hub. Better educated and more urbanized than the local population, and distinguished by their use of Urdu rather than Sindhi as their language of preference, their integration was to prove far more fraught than that of their Punjabi-speaking counterparts, who had migrated to West Punjab.[2] Elsewhere, in East Bengal, the pressure was no less intense though the number of migrants here, mainly from neighbouring Bihar, was far smaller than in the west. But their integration too would emerge as a problem in years to come when their preference for Urdu rather than Bengali heightened resentment among the local Bengali-speaking population, who marked them out as ciphers of the country's Urdu-speaking dominant elite based in West Pakistan.[3]

Most historians now acknowledge that one of the most significant consequences of the refugee crisis was how it fundamentally altered the balance of power, especially in the country's western provinces. Here, better-educated migrant communities quickly dominated the institutions of the new state, which were for the most part concentrated in the west. This included influence over the ruling Muslim League already under the control of a predominantly migrant leadership, headed by Jinnah and his chief lieutenant (and later the country's first prime minister), Liaquat Ali Khan. It also ensured that Urdu—the language most commonly associated with non-Punjabi migrant communities—came to be recognized as the national language of Pakistan, although only a small minority spoke or understood it at the time.

But the ascendancy of these mainly Urdu-speaking migrant communities in the early years was also reinforced by powerful myths, whose strong Islamic resonance ensured that their claims to 'be Pakistani' assumed a significance that set them apart from indigenous communities settled in the five Muslim majority provinces that constituted Pakistan in 1947. The most important of these myths referred to the Islamic exodus (*hijrat*), which by association nourished the claim that Muslim refugees fleeing India for Pakistan were engaged in an act of heroic sacrifice comparable to that performed by the founders of the first Islamic community in seventh-century Arabia.[4] Popular perceptions of Pakistan as variously a Muslim homeland, a safe haven and a refuge from persecution reinforced these myths. Just as those who accompanied the Prophet on that migration had come to be accepted as the first real Muslims, so too, it was believed, had those who had journeyed with Jinnah to the land of the pure earned the right to be recognized as the first real Pakistanis.

Although officialdom in the form of the 1951 Census studiously avoided the use of the term *mohajir* to describe Muslim migrants from India, choosing instead to rely on the word 'refugee'—that is, one forced to flee his home 'as a result of partition or for fear of disturbances connected therewith'—the status of Muslim refugees in the early years was strongly coloured by their association with myths centred on the Islamic exodus and the inauguration of a new era. Judged by Muslims as the defining moment of the universal Islamic experience, these myths came in time to serve as a powerful symbolic resource for Muslim refugees from India. The latter sought to compensate for their lack of local roots by committing to a project whose definitions of a 'natural' (Muslim) community would soon be challenged by regional expressions of a negotiated 'national' community.

Historically this tension had been implicit in the lukewarm response of the main Muslim-majority provinces to the idea of Pakistan as a 'universalist' Muslim enterprise—at least until such time as it was defined as a national option that re-cast Pakistan as a territorial arrangement with the potential for independence. But this uncertain engagement with the idea of Pakistan by those who would later claim to be its sons of its soil, paradoxically, also facilitated most Urdu-speaking Muslim migrants to stake their claim as alpha-citizens of the new state.

The pre-eminence of these Urdu-speaking migrant communities, sustained by the language of Islamic universalism, soon clashed with the imperatives of a national project, which assumed birth to be a hall-mark of citizenship. Yet it is significant that, in marked contrast to Israel, Pakistan eschewed a 'right-of-return' policy that would have given any Muslim the right to settle in this self-proclaimed Muslim homeland. Although the new state had little choice but to allow the mass migration of Indian Muslims in the immediate aftermath of Parti-tion, the introduction of permits, passports and visas for Muslims seeking entry in the 1950s left few in any doubt that, whatever the claims of the new state, 'being Muslim' did not automatically translate into 'being Pakistani'.[5]

Among the first to challenge early attempts to cast Urdu-speaking Muslim migrants from India as the archetypal Pakistanis were local Punjabis from the new Pakistani province of Punjab. Although Pun-jab's Muslim leaders before independence had been less than enthusi-astic about Jinnah's idea of Pakistan as a platform for Muslim representation at the centre of an undivided India, Jinnah's success in dividing their ranks and winning the support of powerful landlords and local religious leaders (pirs) proved to be decisive in securing the province he acknowledged as the cornerstone of Pakistan.[6] The Punjab was also of course the main recruiting ground for the British army—a military legacy that continued after the creation of Pakistan with sig-nificant implications for its national life. Higher than average levels of urbanization, particularly in the east of the province had also ensured that large numbers of Punjabis enjoyed access to superior education, allowing many to occupy key posts in the civilian bureaucracy. Con-trol in the west over some of the richest agricultural land in the sub-continent reinforced these patterns of dominance.

Significantly, Punjabis were also able to lay claim to their own mythology of migration, which was at least as compelling as that asso-ciated with Urdu-speaking migrant communities. Of the estimated 7–9 million Muslims who are believed to have migrated to Pakistan in 1947, the majority (almost 5 million) came from East Punjab. Their migration was attended by acts of horrific violence, the scale of which dwarfed most others in the wake of Partition. Many suffered dreadfully as they fled scenes of mass communal killing, lending to their experience the heightened poignancy associated with the notion of religious flight. As those who had made sacrifices *and* suffered with their lives, Punjabi-speaking *mohajirs* were clearly on par with their Urdu-speaking counterparts to lay the strongest moral claim to qualify as real Pakistanis.

The refugees from East Punjab appeared however to care little for the term *mohajir* or the moral standing it bestowed on those who bore the label. Part of the explanation, as Talbot has suggested, lay in their easy absorption into West Punjab, where they were not required to make the linguistic or social adjustments forced upon their Urdu-speaking counterparts from the United Provinces who had resettled in Sind. It was just a matter of time before their separate refugee identity was subsumed under a broader Punjabi ethnic identity.[7] By contrast, Urdu-speaking migrants enjoyed none of these advantages. The vast majority (more than 60 per cent), who settled in Sind, found its culture far removed from the idealised mores of a tiny elite, whose courtly style still held many in thrall, while others sought refuge in the creation of Urdu-speaking enclaves where they nourished a melancholic attachment to a world left behind.

Verkaaik has argued how the *mohajir*-driven idea of Pakistan as a homeland was influenced by Indo-Muslim debates in the late nineteenth century, which emphasised Islam as foreign to India. These debates reinforced the assumption that Muslims were a 'diasporic nation, a nation without a homeland'[8]—a status that many later expected to be resolved with the creation of Pakistan. This link between migration and the idea of Pakistan underwent a profound change after independence. Whereas the use of the term *mohajir* had been intended in the early years to convey the solidarity between Muslim migrants and local Muslim populations, it gradually came to accentuate their differences. By the late 1980s these had widened as *mohajirs*, marginalised by the resurgence of regionally based ethnic politics, especially in Sind, appealed to the 'uniqueness of the migrant experience'[9] to shape an ethnic identity of their own. Migration now came to be associated with a 'new mentality that combined cosmopolitanism, modernity and a sense of patriotism'.[10] Lacking this experience, locals were also judged, by extension, to lack the attributes that flowed from it—attributes that the country's dominant modernist elite had long favoured as the hallmarks of the quintessential Pakistani.

The struggle to decide who qualified as the real Pakistani unfolded against the backdrop of another battle that was waged early in the life of the new state, involving the Bengalis of East Pakistan. Accounting for a clear majority of the country's population, they demanded the right to redefine the meaning of 'Pakistani' by insisting on its equation with the national majority, which they defined not in religious, but in ethnic terms. At the centre of this debate, which came to a head in the 1950s, was the status of the Bengali language. The Bengalis insisted that it should be recognized as the national language of Pakistan. They argued that as Urdu, the language of choice of the governing elite, was spoken at the time by less than four per cent of the population, it could not claim to be that of 'the Pakistani'. This controversy has been widely seen as symptomatic of an intensifying power struggle between a Bengali middle class determined to secure a share of power in central decision-making commensurate with their demographic weight and dominant Urdu-speaking *mohajir* groups, who feared that the recognition of Bengali as a national language would erode their opportunities in education and government employment.[11] This is unquestionably true, but it also set in motion a process that questioned the existing assumption that 'the Pakistani' was synonymous with the Urdu-speaker.[12]

Many of these assumptions had been shaped by debates concerning Indo-Muslim separatism. In the late nineteenth century, Urdu, with its lexicon of Persian and Arabic words, had been adopted by Muslim separatists as a key cultural symbol and a marker of Muslim identity (along with Islam), to lend substance to the claim that Muslims were a 'nation'.[13] The creation of Pakistan exposed the difficulties of adopting a national language, whose significance was lost on the local population who had their own regional languages. More importantly, Urdu's association with the migrant population also served to underline that it was a language alien to 'the Pakistani'.[14]

This perception of Urdu found a powerful echo in East Bengal, where its use as a marker of Pakistani identity was most vigorously challenged. For a time, the migrant perspective equating Urdu with Pakistani identity had attempted to hold its ground by denouncing calls for the state recognition of Bengali as 'anti-national'. Jinnah, himself a migrant (with a shaky grasp of Urdu), set the tone. In March 1948 he told a public meeting in Dhaka: 'the state language of Pakistan is going to be Urdu ... anyone who tries to mislead you is really an enemy of Pakistan'.[15] His statement met with widespread anger, which finally bubbled over in fierce riots in the provincial Bengali capital, Dhaka, in 1952. The Bengalis eventually secured the recognition of Bengali as an official state language alongside Urdu in the 1956 constitution, but their gains were mixed. Their rejection of Urdu came to be perceived in West Pakistan as tantamount to a rejection of the language that many had long associated with the language of the 'Islam', which was judged to be constitutive of the 'Pakistani'.

There were more insidious myths at play that were rooted in the enduring tension between versions of 'authentic Islam' associated with migrant culture and the 'corrupted Islam' of the local population. Nowhere was this tension more marked and nowhere was it to have more devastating consequences than in East Pakistan. Here Urdu-speaking Muslim immigrants (mainly from West Bengal and Bihar) nurtured the belief that 'their' Islam was superior to that of the indigenous Bengali Muslim population, whose 'syncretistic' practices, suffused with local Hindu and Buddhist rituals, were regarded as an affront to the identity of 'the Pakistani'.[16] The historical roots of this divide lay in the Mughal period, when Muslim officials posted to the region had expressed disdain towards recently converted local Muslim still attached to rituals commonly associated with Hinduism.[17] Like their Mughal counterparts, immigrants who arrived in East Bengal were often culturally and racially distinct—many spoke Urdu and were in appearance more North Indian than Bengali. But like their Urdu-speaking counterparts in the western regions of Pakistan, they also aspired to shape the identity of the Pakistani in line with their own image of the universal Muslim.

The influence of this migrant discourse was sustained by doubts over the quality of the Bengali's Muslim-ness, which was judged to fall short of the necessary credentials required to qualify as a Pakistani. The brutal army campaign in East Pakistan in 1971 stood as a grotesque testimony to the notion that the Bengalis' uncertain attachment to their faith rendered them less-than-perfect Muslims and thereby also undermined their aptitude to be less-than-perfect Pakistanis. In short, Bengalis were deemed to be guilty of betraying both Islam and Pakistan. But as Cohen observes, the only way West Pakistanis could ultimately justify the bloody crackdown against the Bengalis was 'to conclude that the Bengalis were not "truly" Pakistanis, that is, they were not truly Islamic or Muslims—theirs was a moral and religious failure, not a political one'.[18]

53

The secession of Pakistan's eastern wing, which emerged as Bangladesh in December 1971, dealt a severe blow to Jinnah's already fragile construction. It fuelled the explosive question: was Jinnah's two-nation theory dead and if not, who now represented the Pakistani? It is undeniable that the creation of Bangladesh marked the end of the less than plausible two-nation theory, thus exposing the tenuous basis of Pakistan. Yet it has been argued that the country that emerged after 1971 was more homogeneous in that it was 'no longer a geographical, cultural, religious, or economic absurdity'.[19] Many now expected the uncertainties of the country's *raison d'être* and the struggle over conflicting identities finally to be resolved.

One attempt to overcome this problem of 'uncertainty' after 1971 was to re-cast the two-nation theory by arguing that, despite the large number of Muslims in India, the vast majority (almost 70 per cent) of Muslims in the subcontinent still chose to live independently of 'Hindu domination'.[20] The creation of Bangladesh, it was claimed, did not so much negate as validate the premise that Muslims and Hindus were indeed two nations, qualified for separate statehood. Ironically, the Muslim League's 1940 Lahore Resolution, which had called for two independent Muslim states in the north-west and north-east of India, was now enthusiastically resurrected. However, it also prised open a veritable Pandora's Box by encouraging Pakistan's remaining constituent units after 1971 to re-interpret the spirit of the original resolution. The question now turned to whether the right to autonomy implicitly granted to the Bengalis under the Lahore Resolution could be extended to Pakistan's other regional groups with recognisably distinct cultures.

Pakistan's altered contours after 1971 accentuated these concerns. While the loss of East Pakistan had helped smooth some sharp differences, the new fault lines of nationhood had become more complex and more persistent. Ethnic nationalism continued to gain momentum, especially among Sindhis and Balochis, and to a lesser extent among the Pashtuns. Together they pressed for a more territorial definition of 'the Pakistani' in opposition to state-promoted versions still rooted in an extra-territorial discourse of Muslim nationalism that was seen to favour Urdu-speaking *mohajirs*. Paradoxically, there was little support for ethnic nationalism in the Punjab. Although Punjabis qualified in every sense as true sons of the soil, their broad control over the state, and especially the army, had transformed them into agents of a larger

Pakistani identity that stood in opposition to other regional claims. In time this perception of Punjabi dominance would foster claims that the 'Punjabisation' of Pakistan had opened the way to the creation of 'Punjabistan' and had blurred the distinction between the Pakistani and the natives of its largest province.[21]

These tendencies were accentuated by Zulfiqar Ali Bhutto's landslide electoral victory in 1970. It fuelled a regional Sindhi nationalism and heightened antagonism between Bhutto's fellow-Sindhis and Urdu-speaking migrants. But it also triggered the emergence of a new *mohajir* ethnic identity that signalled fresh reflections on 'the Pakistani'. According to Verkaaik, until 1971 every Pakistani could lay claim to a double identity, each with a strong extra-territorial dimension: as a Muslim (s)he belonged to the *umma* or the universal Islamic community, as a Pakistani (s)he belonged to the *millat* or local religious community. However, neither of these identities was wholly disconnected from territorial realities, for while 'the *umma* explained Pakistan's eastern border with India, the *millat* did so for the western borders with other Muslim countries'.[22]

Bhutto lent substance to these territorial dimensions by adding a third identity to 'the Pakistani': that which was attached to an ethnic-territorial 'nationality' (or *qaum*), each corresponding to one of the country's four regions (Sind, Balochistan, Punjab and the North West Frontier Province). This development was significant for two reasons: first because it sought to reconcile regional identities with a Pakistani national identity so that the two were no longer seen to be mutually exclusive; second because it effectively discarded the two-nation theory of Muslim versus Hindu in favour of a reconstructed three-dimensional model that emphasised simultaneous attachment to *umma*, *millat* and *qaum*.[23]

This shift from religious to ethnic nationalism was hugely problematic for migrant communities like Urdu-speaking *mohajirs* settled mainly in urban Sind, who now emerged as 'flawed' Pakistanis 'with neither history nor a sense of territorial attachment, urban, on the move, and unreliable.[24] Faced with the threat of being relegated to the status of outsiders they now opted to re-define themselves as Pakistanis by fashioning an identity based on ethnicity rather than religion. This involved the creative appropriation of Sindhi regional traditions that were used to project the idea of *mohajirs* as Pakistan's 'fifth nationality' with a 'territory' of its own carved out of Sind's main city—Karachi—designated 'Karachi *suba*' (province of Karachi).[25]

By the late 1980s, however, this territorially and regionally-based understanding of 'the Pakistani' had given way to a vigorous state-sponsored program of Islamization that sought to call attention to the supra-territorial dimension of Pakistani identity. It had been facilitated by a parallel process that involved Pakistan's geopolitical turn towards the Middle East following the secession of Bangladesh, which devalued attachment to the regions of South Asia and heightened consciousness of a 'transnational' Islamic brotherhood. The 'new' Pakistani that emerged after 1971 was therefore more, rather than less, conflicted—he was called upon proudly to declare allegiance to an ethnic-territorial nationality while under pressure also to affirm his identity as a de-nationalized Muslim.

Since the 1990s struggles to define 'the Pakistani' have returned to familiar lines of division between sons of the soil and outsiders. Many of these have been concentrated in Balochistan, where a violent nationalist insurgency has been aggravated by the settlement since the 1980s of Pashtun refugees from Afghanistan, who seek acceptance as Balochis and 'Pakistanis'.[26] Their claims have been stiffly resisted by Baloch nationalists seeking to restrict control over the province's assets, especially natural gas, to real Baloch, or sons of the soil. The decision by former President Pervez Musharraf, who seized power following a military coup in 1999, to launch an ambitious development program centred on the expansion of a deep sea port in Gwadur triggered fresh Baloch resistance. This time Baloch opposition was aimed not at ethnic Pashtun migrants from Afghanistan seeking to settle in the province, but at ethnic Punjabis, who were accused of planning to colonise Balochistan.[27] In so doing, Baloch nationalists invited hostility for restricting the right of 'the Pakistani' to freedom of movement. While these claims and counter-claims are by no means new to the politics of regionalism in Pakistan, what is unusual is that the language of the native was now employed not against migrants from beyond the borders of the state, but against those perceived to be outsiders *within* the state.

These shifts reflected the legacy of earlier attempts to inject Pakistani identity with a clearer ethnic-territorial dimension. They failed, however, to compensate for the fact that Pakistan's founding ideology lay in ruins after 1971. Instead, the tension between regional and Islamic expressions of Pakistani identity has remained unresolved. For a time after 1971 some Pakistani historians, led by the eminent archaeologist A.H. Dani, sought to ease these tensions by projecting Pakistan not as a separate Muslim homeland, but as the centre of a territorially defined nationality that acquired its distinctive features from an Indus Valley civilization rather than from Islam.[28]

These ideas have recently been developed further by one of Pakistan's leading public intellectuals, Aitzaz Ahsan, who wants to strengthen a more secular conception of 'the Pakistani'. At the heart of his vision is the idea of Pakistan as the successor of the primordial 'Indus state', while 'the Pakistani' emerges as the heir of a so-called 'Indus man' or woman.[29] Though Ahsan recognizes the distinct features of Indus society that mark it out from the culture of the Gangetic plains, he is less emphatic than Dani about the role of Islam in de-linking this society from its Indian habitat. Indeed, what is particularly noteworthy is that Ahsan's 'Pakistani' must embrace his 'Indian-ness' in order to claim his identity: 'by denying the Indian', Ahsan declares, the Pakistani 'den[ies] the Indus'.[30] But Ahsan is also aware of the ambiguities that flow from Pakistan's character as a 'migrant state'. Since the 1970s, he observes, 'locals' and 'migrants' have undergone 'personality switches'. While the 'local', who once evoked his roots in the region with pride has assumed 'an extra-territorial personality' that looks to, and is captivated by, an alien 'Arab element', the peripatetic *mohajir* 'continues to recall, and relive, life in [an imaginary] Indian birthplace'. Together they have re-fashioned a 'denationalized' Pakistani for whom 'the very rationale of Pakistan must be a total divergence of the attributes of the Pakistani from the Indian'.[31]

The idea of this denationalized Pakistani received strong encouragement during the 1980s, when Islamist forces gathered strength. They fostered fresh interest in defining the Pakistani as synonymous with the Muslim. But in a state still beset by the lack of consensus over Islam, differences resurfaced (reminiscent of the struggle in East Pakistan) over the proper way to be a Muslim in order to qualify as a real Pakistani. These differences have unleashed a violent sectarian struggle over attempts by militant protagonists of Pakistan's Sunni Muslim majority to establish a particular (Sunni sectarian) type of Islam as a necessary prerequisite of the universal or sovereign Pakistani.[32] They have also lent momentum to calls to widen the scope of constitutional definitions of the Muslim that would disenfranchise Muslim minorities, notably the Shias, who fail to conform to sectarian constructions of the Pakistani.

Sectarian myths

The arcane politics of sectarianism stands out as one of the many curiosities of modern-day Pakistan. Predicated on notions of legitimate authority more appropriate to seventh-century tribal Arabia than to a modern nation state with secular pretensions, it has surfaced repeatedly to dominate political discourse and precipitate violence that has threatened to tear apart the fragile national fabric. Current perceptions of sectarian conflict in Pakistan, which concentrate on differences between a Sunni majority and a Shia minority, have tended to blur the intricate patterns of its sectarian mosaic. They have also ignored a long tradition of sectarian politics in Pakistan that predates the current Sunni-Shia conflict, which has also sought to influence the debate on the rights of minorities and the question of citizenship.

Sectarian conflict between Sunnis and Shias in Pakistan was accentuated in the wake of General Zia ul Haq's far-reaching programme of Islamization introduced in the late 1970s. His measures met with stiff resistance from the country's Shias, who condemned them as a thinly disguised attempt to privilege Sunni interpretations of Islamic law. Regional developments at the time, notably the Shia revolution in Iran and the consolidation of Saudi-backed Sunni mujahedin groups involved in the anti-Soviet war in Afghanistan, also politicized the sectarian landscape in Pakistan. In time they contributed to broadening the base of sectarian discourse in Pakistan from an aspect of religious schism to a formidable force of religio-political activism.[33]

Yet it is also worth noting that sectarian divisions were rarely, if ever, relevant to the conduct of state leaders in its early years.[34] Indeed, Shias were prominent in the movement for Pakistan. The Aga Khan, co-founder of the All India Muslim League, the Raja of Mahmudabad of Lucknow, one of the largest landowners in northern India, and the well-known financier, M.A. Ispahani, were all Shias, who generously bank-rolled the All India Muslim League and campaigned tirelessly for a separate Muslim state. But it is Muhammad Ali Jinnah, who really stands out among these Shia luminaries and whose Ismaili Shia roots serve as a bitter reminder to those seeking today to establish Pakistan as a Sunni state.

An estimated 95 per cent of Pakistan's population is Muslim. Of these about 75 per cent are Sunnis, while an estimated 15–20 per cent are said to be Shias. Most Shias in Pakistan (as elsewhere in the Muslim world) are Twelvers (*ithna ashari* or *imami*) Shias, followed by a much smaller number of Seveners, also known as Ismailis. It is worth bearing in mind that despite their minority status, Shias in Pakistan, numbering an estimated 30 million people, account for the second largest Shia population in the world after Iran. At the same time, these broad, binary categories of 'Shia' and 'Sunni' mask the reality of a more complex sectarian landscape. In Pakistan, Sunnis, like Shias, are internally differentiated and sharply divided along doctrinal lines. Both encompass a host of sub-sects, cults, and rival religious traditions. Though most Sunnis in Pakistan subscribe to the moderate Hanafi school of law, they are daily challenged by a small but growing number of Sunnis, who favour the more orthodox practices of the Hanbali doctrine (*mazhab*) inspired by Arabian Islam. Sunnis in Pakistan are also influenced by rival doctrinal movements: Barelvis with their preference for devotional practices centring on the worship of hereditary saints outnumber the more strident, orthodox Deobandis.[35] Shias are no less prone to divisions.[36] The Twelvers or *ithna ashari* Shias, who represent the main body of Shi'ism, dominate in Pakistan. However, they have traditionally looked to Iran for spiritual leadership in contrast to the Seveners, better known as *Ismailis*, who predominate in northern Pakistan and parts of urban Sind and who owe allegiance to the Aga Khan.[37]

It is ironic that this rich sectarian landscape rarely figures in the discourse of religious politics in Pakistan. What has generally passed for a 'Shia-Sunni' divide, and what drives the country's politics of sectarian identity, is in fact more narrowly confined than is commonly supposed. It is limited mainly to followers of the Deobandi tradition, who in Pakistan have sought in recent years to appropriate the term Sunni for themselves.[38] Their main target is also more restricted with much of their wrath directed at ithna ashari Twelver Shias, who are singled out for their veneration of Shia imams and their elaborate ritual practices.

The sectarian overtones of this question first surfaced in the early 1950s, when radical Sunnis mounted a campaign against Ahmedis in Pakistan, who insist they are Muslim, but whose status as such has been questioned by orthodox Muslims.[39] The aim of the anti-Ahmedi protests, which erupted in 1953, was to force the government to declare Ahmedis a non-Muslim minority. Although the campaign failed to realize its aim until 1974, when Ahmedis were constitutionally designated

'non-Muslims' and stripped of their rights as full citizens, it set a precedent that significantly enhanced the power of Sunni groups pressing
for a sectarian construction of 'the Pakistani'.[40] Since then radical Sunnis have repeatedly pressured the state to consider ever narrower definitions of 'the Muslim' that would exclude the country's Shia minority
and reserve the constitutional rights of 'the Pakistani' to the country's
Sunni Muslims.[41]

These dynamics were fuelled by the chronic ambiguity and confusion over the meaning of Pakistan as a homeland for Muslims that
raised questions about the status of its non-Muslim minorities and
their claims to qualify as Pakistani.[42] Both fuelled a debate on citizenship that is still unresolved and that has left the field open to those
who would test the state's Muslim credentials by challenging its commitment to the equality of all its citizens. This dispute around the question of Pakistan's identity also explains why it has buckled under the
demands of notions of citizenship anchored in the management of difference. While much has been made of Jinnah's famous declaration of
11 August 1947 in which he announced his support for the 'fundamental principle that we are all citizens and equal citizens of one State',[43] it
failed to dilute the force of the divisive rhetoric he had helped nurture
in the decade leading up to the creation of Pakistan.

The fact that the exclusionist discourse favoured by sectarian groups
seeking to influence the citizenship debate should have become manifest so quickly after independence was testimony to this uncomfortable
reality. It suggested that, notwithstanding Jinnah's determination to
ensure 'that 'religion ... has nothing to do with the State,'[44] 'Islam' (in
this case) could not, after all, be selectively applied or manipulated
without incurring the risk of undesirable outcomes. By leaving open
until the very moment of independence the question of whether Pakistan would serve primarily as a homeland for Muslims without excluding others or whether its sole purpose was to exist for Muslims over all
others, Jinnah contributed to the ambiguity of the new state. Nor did
he seek to resolve these ambiguities after independence. On 25 January
1948 just months before his final exit from politics, and in failing
health, he publicly retracted his earlier commitment to democratic
citizenship by declaring that Pakistan's constitution would be based on
Islamic law (sharia) 'to make Pakistan a truly great Islamic State'.[45]

The new state's professed loyalty to Islam, however ambiguous,
heightened the risks it posed to democratic citizenship—risks that were

to be compounded by sectarian politics. In March 1949, the country's first Prime Minister, Liaquat Ali Khan, while moving the Objectives Resolution to determine the principles of Pakistan's future constituent assembly, declared that the state 'will create such conditions as are conducive to the building up of a truly Islamic society'.[46] This was put to the test within months. In May 1949, the Majlis-i-Ahrar (a Muslim communal off-shoot of the Indian National Congress) that was in the forefront of the movement against the Ahmedis, challenged the state to fulfil its obligations and frame a constitutional definition of 'the Muslim'. Although much of the debate at the time was clouded by esoteric idioms of prophetology, centering on the disputed messianic status of Mirza Ghulam Ahmed, who founded the Ahmedi movement in Punjab in 1889,[47] it prised open vital questions that have since underlined the state's fragile commitment to modern secular citizenship. By raising, and keeping alive, the question of who a Muslim 'really' is and what constitutional status a 'real' Muslim can legitimately claim, sectarian discourse brutally exposed the high cost of sacralizing political debate. In time it would also lend a decisive rhetorical edge to those seeking to translate this debate into a struggle to make the definition of 'the Pakistani' conditional upon that of 'the Muslim'.

Consensus on the meaning of the 'Muslim' remained elusive. As the judicial commission appointed by the government in 1953 to investigate the causes of the anti-Ahmedi movement gloomily observed, an agreement on the definition of a non-Muslim did not automatically translate into one on the definition of a Muslim. Its conclusion followed an invitation to a group of protesting *ulama* to define for the commission who they would consider Muslim. Their sharply diverging opinions led the commission to declare that, '[k]eeping in view the several definitions given by the *ulema* (sic), need we make any comment except that no two learned divines are agreed on this fundamental. If we attempt our own definition [of the Muslim] as each Divine has done and that definition differs from that given by all others, we unanimously go out of the fold of Islam. And if we adopt the definition given by any one of the *ulema* (sic), we remain Muslims according to that *alim* [Muslim religious scholar] but *kafirs* (apostates) according to the definition of everyone else.'[48] The Commission also debated the status of Pakistan's Shia community and charges of apostasy levelled against them by the *ulama,* warning that, 'what is happening now seems almost a writing on the wall, and God help us if we do not stop these ... people from cutting each other's throat'.[49]

Many hoped that the 1953 commission of inquiry into the anti-Ahmedi riots would curb the force of sectarianism and force it to retreat in the face of General Ayub Khan's relatively secular dispensation following his military take-over in 1958. But the state was soon embroiled in a fresh controversy that revived the political salience of sectarian identities. It was prompted by Ayub's contentious decision to engage with Sunni religious parties, which had called for the enforcement of the constitution and restricted Shia activities on the grounds that they violated the rights of the Sunni majority.[50] Whilst these demands were eventually rejected by Ayub, they nevertheless underscored the latent power of sectarian discourse.

The need for a fresh affirmation of Pakistan's Islamic credentials in the wake of the secession of East Pakistan (now Bangladesh) in 1971 lent new momentum to the sectarian debate. The provisions of the 1973 constitution promulgated by Zulfiqar Ali Bhutto reflected this concern. It strengthened the Islamic complexion of the state by requiring both the president and the prime minister to be Muslim. The constitution for the first time also made it incumbent for holders of both offices publicly to confess their faith as 'believers' by acknowledging the finality of Muhammad's Prophethood, thereby implicitly offering a definition of 'the Muslim'. As such it differed from Pakistan's first constitution (1956), which had required the president to be a Muslim but did not specify what this entailed. Within months of the enforcement of the 1973 constitution (which remains in force), anti-Ahmedi groups had swung into action. In early 1974 an eight-party alliance of religious parties launched a hundred-day campaign against the Ahmedis. An increasingly beleaguered Bhutto was forced to convene a special session of the National Assembly, which deliberated on 'the status in Islam of persons who do not believe in the finality of the prophethood of Muhammad'.[51] Conducted behind closed doors, it led to a constitutional amendment (the Second Amendment of 7 September 1974) that formally relegated Ahmedis to the status of a non-Muslim minority, thereby stripping them at a stroke of the citizenship rights they had enjoyed until then as Muslims.

These extraordinary developments marked a watershed in the debate on citizenship and minority rights in Pakistan. They established a precedent that enabled a political institution (the National Assembly), elected through a secular process (elections), formally to arrogate to itself the authority to pronounce on matters of faith pertaining to individual citizens. They also underlined the profound dilemma facing Pakistan—that is, upholding modern standards of citizenship in the context of a sacralized political discourse that could not (publicly at least) accommodate the separation between religion and the state. A telling reflection of this lay in the contradiction between the National Assembly's decision to criminalize the preaching of any doctrine that questioned the finality of Muhammad's Prophethood and Bhutto's (in the circumstances) fatuous declaration that Pakistan's 'secular constitution' would ensure that 'every Pakistani had the right to profess his religion, proudly, with confidence and without fear'.[52]

Subsequent measures adopted against the Ahmedis in 1984 as part of General Zia's Islamization programme further exposed the gap between the secular pretensions of the state and the growing reality of a discriminatory definition of Pakistani citizenship based on an exclusionary definition of Islam. It is worth noting that, even while the 1974 constitutional amendment had barred Ahmedis from holding any position reserved for Muslims, it did not abrogate Article 20 of the constitution, which guaranteed the right of religious minorities to propagate their faith. Nor had it suspended Article 33, which made the state responsible for safeguarding the legitimate rights and representation of minorities in parliament. By contrast, Zia's Ordinance 20 of 1984 not only institutionalised discrimination against the Ahmedis by further eroding their civil rights (for example, denying them the right to have their evidence in court treated on par with evidence submitted by a constitutionally recognized Muslim), but also transformed Ahmedi daily religious life into a criminal offence (for example, by threatening Ahmedis with criminal prosecution for calling themselves Muslims or referring to their places of worship as mosques).[53] Within a few decades of its formation, Pakistan had established new parameters for citizenship, dependent almost wholly on the definition of an individual's creed and religious profile. By doing so, it had also fundamentally revised the discussion on the status of non-Muslim minorities, who are now in danger of being increasingly regarded as *compatriots* sharing a common territory rather than as *citizens* with a claim to legal and political equality.

The resurgence of militant sectarian conflict in Pakistan since the late 1980s[54] has intensified the debate on the status of minorities and has added a new and more problematic dimension to it. It centres on the place of minority Shias, whose Muslim-ness and membership as equal citizens of the national community had not until recently been questioned (except perhaps within the confines of theological debates). This anti-Shia discourse is seen to be a direct consequence of Zia's Islamization policies, which sought to strengthen the state's monopoly over religion by enforcing a narrow, Sunni interpretation of Islamic law.[55] Shia protests against the programme gained momentum in 1980 under the auspices of the predominantly Twelver Shia movement, the *Tehrik-i-Nifaz-i Fiqh-i Ja'fariyya* (TNFJ or Movement for the Implementation of Ja'fari [Shia] law), which successfully secured guarantees that exempted Shias from subscribing to the new laws—for example, the payment of the Islamic alms tax (*zakat*),[56]—and which served thereby, paradoxically, to sharpen the Sunni profile of the state.

It was not long before Islamization moved inexorably towards 'Sunnification'.[57] This had profound consequences: it undermined the broad universalist claims that had until then been the hallmark of all Islamization projects in Pakistan and, by equating Sunnism with Islam, removed at a stroke the place of Shi'ism as a separate but equal voice. With Sunni law dominant and increasingly conflated with Islam, Sunni Islamists were now poised to claim that those who did not subscribe to Sunni law—that is, the Shias—were outside the pale of Islam and therefore deserved to be recast as religious minorities. Much of this debate has been shaped by the agenda of the militant Sunni organization, the *Sipah-i-Sahaba-i-Pakistan* (SSP or Pakistani Force of the Companions [of the Prophet Muhammad]), which is strongly informed by Deobandi ideology and dedicated since its creation in 1985 to making Sunni Islam the official religion of Pakistan.[58]

External factors, especially the regional rivalry between Iran and Saudi Arabia, also fuelled the deadly conflict between Sunnis and Shias that has engulfed Pakistan.[59] The Iranian revolution of 1979 left weak states like Pakistan especially vulnerable to the fall-out from the competition between these two rivals and significantly amplified the hitherto muted refrain of sectarian politics. The Afghan civil war, which raged for much of the 1980s, also acted as a catalyst, consolidating the power and position of Sunni mujahedin groups who, with the backing of Saudi Arabia and to a lesser extent Iraq, helped contain the regional ambitions of Iran and curbed the self-confidence of emboldened Shia activists.

The political landscape of Pakistan had by then undergone significant changes that encouraged the role of increasingly combative sectarian actors. As already noted, General Zia's Islamization programme, which was billed as an attempt to enforce the universalist prescriptions of Islam, was engaged in nothing less than laying the foundations for an essentially Sunni interpretation of Islamic law. Therefore, the external aspect was at best an enabling factor that sustained rather than generated the sectarian phenomenon. At worst, it was symptomatic of a political culture where the 'foreign hand' and 'intelligence agencies' have been routinely singled out for blame every time there is a crisis. Neither ought to be given much credence, absolving as they do both state and society in Pakistan of responsibility for an ever more violent sectarian conflict.

Indeed, what demands attention is the role of the state in constructing sectarian identities. While it is often assumed that the state at inception was 'neutral and had no sectarian agenda',[60] it has in fact since the late 1970s been actively complicit in the hardening of separate religious identities. In this it was motivated by the need primarily to neutralize regional identities, which were perceived to be a greater threat to its political hegemony than any challenge from sectarian discord. The support for religious parties in Balochistan in recent years, for example, has been widely used as a strategy to weaken the claim of Baloch nationalists. Equally, the appeal to an Islamic over a Pashtun identity has been systematically deployed to dilute the force of Pashtun nationalism in the border regions of the North West Frontier Province. Thus, the state's engagement with sectarianism is neither a recent phenomenon nor one that breaks with any established tradition of state neutrality. It is in part a legacy of the movement for Pakistan, which had sought to employ the language of Islamic universalism to lend substance to the national project. The fragility of the latter, which was soon reflected in the tensions between an autocratic centre and rebellious regional forces, meant that the state quickly developed an interest in Islamic social engineering as the means to ensure its own survival. This had serious consequences for the trajectory of sectarian identities which, because of the state's over-riding concern with the question of its religious identity, have enjoyed a degree of benign tolerance not accorded to the mobilization of other forms of identity—in particular, ethnicity, which has routinely been condemned as threatening to the integrity of the state.

The Islamic concerns displayed by sectarian politics have helped legitimate its power-brokers, but it has also sharply reduced the state's ability to infringe upon the religious space or to control it. This is most clearly demonstrated in the state's failure to curb the spread of sectarian forces in central and south Punjab, where the dynamics of local politics have accelerated religious divisions. In the districts around the urban centre of Jhang, anti-Shia rhetoric since the mid 1980s has been fuelled by tensions between a dominant class of Shia landlords and an emerging Sunni middle-class with political aspirations. Here, Sunni radicalism has served not only to mobilize popular Sunni support against the Shia elite, but has also offered an identity to new classes that lacked a place in traditional society. These represent the urban middle-classes, issued from Sunni Muslim families who had migrated from Indian East Punjab to adjacent regions in West Punjab allocated to Pakistan at the time of Partition. A large number of these migrant families were exposed to sectarian traditions favoured by the staunchly anti-Shia discourse of the Deobandi (and to a lesser extent the Ahl-i-Hadis) and Salafi movements. Both have a history of religious and political activism, and both have on occasion been associated with the Islamic populism of Punjab-based parties such as the Majlis-i-Ahrar, which spearheaded the campaign against the Ahmedi minority before and after Partition.[61]

Elsewhere, sectarian causes have also been well served by the dynamics of local politics. In the Federally Administered Tribal Agencies (FATA) of Kurram and Orakzai as well as in the so-called Northern Areas around the urban centre of Gilgit, local pressures arising from the influx of large numbers of Afghan refugees and a deliberate state policy to resettle Sunnis in the region have disturbed the fragile Shia-Sunni demographic balance. Since the 1980s these developments have accentuated sectarian tension and generated conflict. One of the worst affected areas in recent years has been Parachinar, the main administrative centre in Kurram. Its Pashtun population is mainly Shia, belonging to the Turi and Bangash tribes—a minority among Pashtuns, who are overwhelmingly Sunnis. However, the influx of large numbers of Sunni Afghan refugees in the 1980s and the resettlement of Sunnis from other parts of Pakistan disturbed this delicate equilibrium and has led Parachinar to be repeatedly convulsed by sectarian violence. Although the tension is rooted in competition over access to scarce resources, especially land, it has been sustained by a wider exclusionary idiom based on an imagined supra-local sectarian identity.

But it is in Pakistan's Northern Areas that the sectarian politics of exclusion has been most visible in recent years. Here, Ismaili Shias make up more than 60 per cent of the region's total population of about 1.5 million, and it is also here that in the late 1980s some of the worst sectarian violence flared, resulting in hundreds being killed around the region's urban hub, Gilgit. As in Kurram, this violence had local causes that included Shia hostility to the settlement of many Sunni businessmen from the Punjab and the NWFP attracted by the opportunities offered by the opening of the Karakoram Highway in 1986. Their resentment was sharpened by the latitude Zia gave to Sunni Islamist parties, which were blamed for widespread sectarian violence in 1988. In recent years sectarian politics has come increasingly to express local frustration over the lack of a constitutional identity for the Northern Areas. They occupy an anomalous position wherein they are administered by Pakistan but are denied the status of a province on grounds that they form part of the disputed territory of Kashmir.[62] A further grievance stems from the introduction in 1999 of textbooks by the federal education ministry, which local Shias claimed reflect a Sunni bias. It has led to strikes and protests only quelled in 2005 after the government agreed not to teach the contentious material in local schools—though the textbooks themselves still remain to be revised.

Is this yet another example of the ideological foundations of Pakistan leaving it ill-prepared to face the demands of modern citizenship, subject as it was to the conflicting claims of a religiously divided society? At its inception the state had to face the dilemma of choosing between rival interpretations of the dominant religion—Islam—and deciding which would receive state support. It also had to determine the criteria for citizenship and how its people comprised the national community. One aim was to recognize religious pluralism and accept non-Muslims (Christians, Hindus, Parsis and most recently Ahmedis) as citizens; another was to cast Pakistan as an unequivocally territorial state where religious affiliation should be immaterial to full and equal membership of the political community. Another sought to transform the country into an Islamic state with a clear Sunni dimension that could rival Shia Iran. Recently there have even emerged voices dedicated to recasting Pakistan's identity as a transnational state, carrying the message of Islam to other areas by peaceful means and, if necessary, by force. These are not hard and fast, let alone easily distinguishable, identities—indeed there is much interplay between Pakistan as 'cultural haven', 'homeland', 'Islamic state' or 'Islamic vanguard'. But, as Cohen notes, this complexity means that politics in Pakistan will always struggle with a heavy burden that cannot be removed without the resolution of its 'ideological puzzle': that is, 'reconciling the different permutations of state and religion in a country ridden with widespread ethnic and linguistic conflict and a dysfunctional oligarchic political order'.[63]

The mirage of citizenship

These uncertainties have also had decisive impact on the status of Pakistan's non-Muslim minorities. The question of whether or not they qualify to be Pakistani is to a very large degree rooted in the contradictions of Pakistan's founding ideology—the two nation theory. This presupposed two nations—not Indians and Pakistanis, but Hindus and Muslims. And while all nations, as Pandey has observed, are carved out of a 'core' or 'natural' citizen,[64] in Pakistan the exclusion of marginal religious groups, namely non-Muslims, has been more readily facilitated by the emphasis on a religious rather than a territorial understanding of the boundaries of the nation.

Many now recognize that for the vast majority of its citizens Pakistan's creation in 1947 represented the founding of a homeland for the Muslims of India—not all, but those who chose to go, those forced to flee persecution and those lucky enough to be in the right place at the right time. What precisely this newly created homeland signified for its non-Muslim members, who at the moment of Pakistan's creation constituted almost a fifth of its total population, was not however fully articulated. Some have explained this oversight by claiming that no one, including Jinnah, had anticipated the creation of a separate nation state. Others claim that Jinnah had always intended Pakistan to be an inclusive political community, as is shown by his rush to declare at independence that all who found themselves within the territory of the new state would be Pakistanis, entitled to equal citizenship. 'Every one of you,' he declared in August 1947, 'no matter to what community he belongs, no matter what relations he had with you in the past, no matter what his colour, caste or creed, is first, second, and last a citizen of this State with equal rights, privileges and obligations.'[65] It remains unclear whether in making his appeal Jinnah was offering a blueprint for the future state of Pakistan or simply responding to the crisis triggered by the mass communal violence that engulfed parts of Pakistan in the weeks leading up to Partition. According to some historians, Jinnah at the time had been keen to retain a non-Muslim minority in Pakistan to serve as 'hostages', in order to ensure fair treatment for Indian Muslims who chose to remain in India.[66]

Whatever Jinnah's motives in pressing for common citizenship, his successors found it an increasingly difficult challenge to guarantee the constitutional equality of all of Pakistan's citizens. Indeed, Pakistan appears to have moved far away from Jinnah's inclusivist model by sanctioning the political exclusion of its non-Muslim minorities and legalizing the disenfranchisement of Muslims whose status was in question. Explanations for these changes vary widely: they range from the supposed gulf between inclusive notions of citizenship and the imperatives of majoritarian nationalism (of which Pakistan's religious nationalism is one example), to confusion over the role of Islam in public life (which has been especially acute in Pakistan). Nevertheless, most of these interpretations implicitly recognize the narrowing of the political community in Pakistan that has resulted in separating membership in the community from any automatic claim to equal rights for all citizens.

What it suggests is that the imperatives of equal citizenship have been repeatedly challenged by the normative force of ideas that have favoured the mutual exclusion of Muslims and non-Muslims. Of course, Pakistan's dilemma is not unique. As Pandey has persuasively argued with reference to India, the construction of 'the real Indian' has depended upon a presupposed 'natural' or 'core' mainstream that is invisibly and unconsciously equated with the Hindu. The idea of the axiomatic 'Indian', he maintains, has depended upon the simultaneous creation of the hyphenated national, whose uncertain status as the 'Indian Muslim' or the 'Indian Christian' has reinforced the interchangeability of 'Indian' and 'Hindu'. More importantly still, the equation of the 'Indian nation' with a 'Hindu majority' has gone mostly unchallenged and since has shifted the focus of attention onto the 'designated' or 'proper' place of the minorities. That status is determined above all by a constant demand for a proof of loyalty to the state—a demand, he suggests, that is made only of those who are judged not to be its 'real' or 'natural' citizens.[67]

Although the axiomatic 'Pakistani' is rarely juxtaposed against a 'Pakistani Christian' or 'Pakistani Hindu', the equation of 'Pakistani' and 'Muslim' is, if anything, even more rigidly bound than in India. As in India this equation has tended not so much to raise questions about its problematic relation to more inclusive definitions of the Pakistani nation, but to concentrate attention instead on the status of non-Muslim minorities, who are under ever greater obligation to prove their loyalty and thus to qualify as Pakistanis.

The legacy of Partition made these obligations particularly acute for the Hindu minority in Pakistan, who much like their Muslim counterparts in India, were forced to endure the suspicion of harbouring divided loyalties. These loyalties were most sternly tested during the crisis leading up to the secession of Bangladesh in 1971. At that time, the Hindu population of East Bengal, which accounted for almost 12% of the country's total, was widely accused by Pakistani government forces of acting as a 'fifth column' in the service of India's military, which was accused of supporting Bengali nationalists and hastening the break-up of Pakistan. The Christian minority in Pakistan has also come under scrutiny to demonstrate its loyalty both because Christians stand as ciphers of anger against colonial rule and because of frustration over current Western policy that is judged to be anti-Islamic. As such, they have paid a particularly heavy price.[68]

What makes Pakistan a case apart from most other forms of majoritarian nationalism is the central yet ambiguous role accorded to Islam in the definition of both the nation and the state. It has served as a channel for exclusion that has led to the erosion of the rights of non-Muslims and furthered their disenfranchisement as citizens. In practice, any move that seeks to grant full legal and political equality of Muslims and non-Muslims must first wrestle with the perceived breach of the provisions of Islam that are judged to justify the boundaries of a nation, which unambiguously distinguishes between Muslims and non-Muslims. It is true that many Muslim states have successfully reconciled restrictive political norms derived from classical Islamic doctrine with modern egalitarian demands. But in Pakistan, the haphazard convergence of religion and nationalism that shaped the creation of the country and the uses to which it was put during extended periods of authoritarian rule has made the state more prone to institutional discrimination against non-Muslims. This has significantly enhanced the dangers for the latter. They run the risk of being relegated to their proper place as minorities on the fringe of the nation—entitled to share the same homeland (*watan*) or country (*mulk*) with a Muslim majority but without the legal and political rights owed to them as equal citizens.

The contradictions inherent in Pakistan's nationalist struggle were not the only factors to account for the steady political marginalization of its non-Muslim minorities. The structure and demographic composition of the new state were no less important in shaping attitudes towards the political rights of religious minorities. Although fractured by sharp ethnic and linguistic divisions, Pakistan at independence was more religiously homogeneous than India. Its population, estimated at around 80 million at the time, was overwhelmingly Muslim and tightly concentrated in 76 districts clustered in the north-west and north east of India.[69] This homogeneity was particularly marked in the country's western provinces, where the mass exodus of non-Muslims, estimated at between 5–6 million, mainly Hindus and Sikhs from urban areas in the Punjab and Sind, simplified a hitherto more complex demographic landscape. At the same time, the entry of more than six million Muslim refugees from India sharpened its Muslim contours. By contrast, migration in and out of East Bengal was much less significant. According to the 1951 census it only received some 700,000 Muslim refugees from India,[70] while only a fraction (about 1.5 million) of its non-Muslim, mainly Hindu, population, decided to emigrate, leaving it with a more religiously complex demographic pattern than in the west wing of the country.

Not surprisingly these differences induced very different perceptions about the legal and political status of non-Muslim minorities in the two wings of the country. One of the earliest indications surfaced within months of independence in December 1947, when the veteran Bengali Muslim League leader, H.S. Suhrawardy, tried unsuccessfully to open the membership of his party, the Muslim League, to non-Muslims. He argued that this would enable Bengal's sizeable Hindu minority (almost a quarter of the population of East Pakistan) to enter mainstream politics and would also reinforce the League's commitment to Jinnah's (albeit new-found) inclusivist ethos as the basis of the new state. However, neither of these proposals appealed to Suhrawardy's fellow-Leaguers. Their position was summed up, ironically, by one of Jinnah's closest associates from the North West Frontier Province, Sardar Abdur Rab Nishtar, who declared that such a move would 'finish the League' adding, 'I say if the League exists, Islam exists, Musalmans exist'.[71] As a result, non-Muslims chose subsequently to turn to the United Front—a Bengali regional coalition that inflicted a stunning defeat on the League in the 1954 provincial elections.

By then signs of alienation were already in evidence. In debates in 1949 over the framing of the country's first constitution, non-Muslim members of the Constituent Assembly, almost all Hindus from East Bengal, had raised serious objections to what came to be known as the 'Objectives Resolution' designed to serve as its Preamble. Of particular concern was its commitment to an Islamic rather than a secular constitution, which they feared would discriminate against the rights of Pakistan's non-Muslim citizens. In a series of wide-ranging amendments, they urged lawmakers explicitly to recognize the equality of Muslims and non-Muslims by substituting the state's obligation to ensure that 'Muslims shall be enabled to order their lives ... in accordance with the teachings and requirements of Islam' with an obligation instead to ensure that 'Muslims and non-Muslims shall be *equally* enabled to order their lives in accordance with their respective religions'.[72]

Remarkably, no Muslim member spoke up in favour of the amendments proposed by non-Muslim members. Indeed, they were roundly dismissed as unjustified and intended to make a mockery of what the Prime Minister Liaquat Ali Khan called the 'real Islamic society' to which Pakistan aspired. Nevertheless, Khan could scarcely have failed to ignore the warning from some non-Muslim members of the Constituent Assembly, who counselled him against pressing ahead with the Resolution on grounds that it would incur 'the curse' of 'posterity'.[73] This was not enough to deter Khan, who instead of seeking a consensus, put the Resolution to the vote. With the exception of one Muslim member, the left-wing politician Muhammad Iftikharrudin, who denounced the Resolution as a travesty of 'a proper Islamic constitution [and] real democracy', all Muslim members voted in favour of the original Resolution, while every one of their non-Muslim counterparts voted against.

These lingering doubts about the legal and political equality of Pakistan's non-Muslim citizens were scarcely resolved with the approval in March 1956 of the country's first Constitution. It barred non-Muslims from becoming President even while allowing for the possibility of a non-Muslim Speaker of the National Assembly, who would temporarily have had to assume this post in the absence of the President. No such ban however was imposed on the post of prime minister, which remained open to non-Muslims. Indeed, this parliamentary model, which vested real power in the National Assembly, was used to counter accusations by those critics of the Constitution who claimed it relegated non-Muslims to the status of second-class citizens. But the doubts persisted, fuelled by the Constitution's ambiguity over the electoral system. Unable to settle the question of whether to abolish separate electorates, which many still regarded as a pillar of the state's 'two-nation' ideology,[74] it was left to be decided by the National Assembly in consultation with the provincial assemblies. But in a startling demonstration of the uncertainty over the place of Islam, lawmakers in October 1956 approved a Bill that endorsed two separate electoral systems for the country's two wings. Under its provisions, non-Muslim voters in East Pakistan were given the same rights as their Muslim counterparts by voting jointly for all parliamentary candidates. In West Pakistan, non-Muslims were denied the right to elect Muslim candidates and restricted to separate electorates.

Although the Bill was subsequently amended in 1957 to give Muslim and non-Muslim voters in both wings equal rights to choose candidates under a system of joint electorates, the issue remained politically contentious. While most Bengali regional parties, including the Awami League and the Hindu Congress called for joint electorates to be declared irreversible, the Muslim League, which controlled power at the centre, dithered over its implementation. In the event, the issue was still unresolved by the time the Constitution itself was abrogated following the 1958 military coup. The debate served as a telling expression of Pakistan's continuing failure to reconcile notions of citizenship resting on two mutually exclusive models of statehood—the first grounded in territory (the nation-state), the second in a putative supraterritorial community (*umma*). As Jalal points out, '[Pakistan] could not be 'national' and 'Islamic'. It could not be 'national' because in the Islamic conception of the state non-Muslims do not have equal rights of citizenship; and it could not be 'Islamic' if the boundaries of the nation-state, as opposed to religious affiliations, were to distinguish citizens from non-citizens'[75]

These glaring inconsistencies are even better understood when set against the simmering tensions within a dominant political elite forced to balance the claims of a Western style democracy in which nationality and citizenship rights are held to be coeval, with a religiously informed nationalism in which Islam is judged to be the basis of political legitimacy. For a while, the change of regime that followed the 1958 military coup led by Ayub Khan appeared to ease some of these tensions. Not only did the military regime sideline the political classes' uncertain compromises over the issue of Pakistan as an Islamic state, and by extension the uncertain place of non-Muslims within it, but it also sought to project an image that underlined its secularizing mission. The new Constitution, promulgated in 1962, dispensed with the 'Islamic' prefix and firmly rejected a recommendation by the constitutional commission to restore separate electorates for non-Muslims.

Nevertheless, restrictions on non-Muslims holding the post of president remained intact, demonstrating that the regime's secular credentials were, in part, symbolic and possibly even open to negotiation. This was confirmed when, under pressure from the religious lobby, the 1962 Constitution was amended to recognize Pakistan as an 'Islamic Republic'. And though the 1962 Constitution broke with its predecessor by clearly endorsing a system of joint electorates, this time for the whole country, these provisions were rendered meaningless (as were all other provisions relating to the franchise) in a system which ruled out direct, universal franchise. Furthermore, Ayub's insistence upon retaining the One-Unit formula (which had amalgamated all four western provinces into a single entity to neutralize East Pakistan's political majority and impose parity with 'West Pakistan'), also meant that the representation of the interests of non-Muslims, who made up almost a quarter of East Pakistan's population, was effectively limited.

Despite these constraints, and the absence of any real shift in favour of greater legal and political equality for non-Muslim citizens, Ayub's modernizing social agenda has generally been credited with encouraging a climate of greater tolerance, which paved the way for the more complete integration of Pakistan's non-Muslim citizens. Many have pointed to Ayub's contempt for the Muslim religious establishment as the reason why, especially in the early years of his government, he ignored religious and sectarian divisions that were potentially damaging to his nation-building project. At the same time, the bitterness and rancour that followed Ayub's divisive economic policies meant that any gains made in bridging religious divisions were soon overwhelmed by the regional disparities that widened the gulf between East and West Pakistan. One of its most disturbing consequences was the revival of an exclusionary discourse against East Pakistan's non-Muslim, mainly Hindu, population. At the time, it took many by surprise.

For while Ayub's attempts to strengthen a secularized Islam were expected to have little effect on redressing equity grievances between

Pakistan's different regions, many had hoped that it would at least ease the latent tension between the country's Muslim and non-Muslim citizens. Instead, what it unleashed in the form of the 1971 civil war in East Pakistan was a violent reaction against Ayub's secular experiment. One of its consequences was to reject a secular and plural definition of 'the Pakistani' in favour of restoring its equation with 'the Muslim'. Nowhere was this more chillingly demonstrated than in the preoccupation with the question of the 'good Muslim' during the military campaign against Bengalis in East Pakistan. As a means of selecting who best qualified as a 'good' Pakistani, it made swift work of non-Muslims who, by definition, were least to meet the standards expected of 'the Pakistani'.

These trends became more pronounced after the formal secession of East Pakistan, which instantly transformed the rump state into a largely homogenous entity in religious terms. From having once had to confront the challenge of working out credible arrangements to guarantee equal citizenship for non-Muslims comprising almost 14 per cent of its total population, the new state could now afford merely to acknowledge its responsibility to protect the 3 per cent that remained. This was reflected in the 1973 Constitution drafted by the country's first elected assembly, which represented an overwhelming Muslim majority. It may explain why the Islamic provisions of the Constitution, which for the first time established Islam as the 'state religion of Pakistan', elicited much less discussion and why the bar placed on non-Muslims from holding both the post of President and Prime Minister generated only mild controversy.

With additional offices of state now constitutionally closed to non-Muslims, the charge of second-class citizenship and indeed the disenfranchisement of non-Muslims, could no longer be evaded. For all its democratic underpinnings, therefore, the 1973 Constitution (which remains in force) represented the first clear signs in Pakistan of a drift towards institutional inequality, allowing discrimination against the country's non-Muslim minorities. And it is Zulfiqar Ali Bhutto, who yielded to the pressure of declaring the Ahmedis a non-Muslim minority, and thereby sanctioned their disenfranchisement, who is held chiefly responsible for bringing into play the toxic demarcation between Muslims and non-Muslims.

While personally Z. A. Bhutto, the main architect of the Constitution, may well have favoured a more secular dispensation for Pakistan including a more egalitarian status for non-Muslims, he like many of his peers was unable to resist the lure of a 'real' Pakistan held out by the removal of the country's awkward eastern province. As Ziring has observed, the insistent presence of East Bengal's large non-Muslim population, with its disturbing Hindu undertones, had always suggested that 'Pakistan could never realize its potential as a Muslim country while connected to East Bengal'.[76] Some Pakistanis also acknowledged the opportunities presented by the separation of East Bengal. Reflecting on the emergence of Pakistan as a 'more viable entity' after 1971, the prominent Pakistani scholar, Burki, has argued that the separation of East Pakistan was a development rich with possibilities for Pakistan. The latter, he claims, were damaged by the perennial struggle over the meaning of Pakistan between the Bengalis and their compatriots in West Pakistan. It was this tension, he suggests, that was primarily responsible for confounding the issue of Pakistan's Muslim identity. 'As long as Pakistan remained divided into two wings', he argues, 'the question of Islam's role in the affairs of the state remained unanswered. The people of East Bengal were content to let Islam guide individual behaviour rather than become the religion of the state. The most the Bengalis were prepared to do in this respect was to pass the Objectives Resolution in 1951[sic] ... Only after ... Pakistan broke up in 1971 did the leaders' resolve to keep religion out of politics begin to weaken.'[77] Though he does not say so, the implication of Burki's remarks leaves no doubt that this apparent weakening of resolve paved the way for a recognisably Muslim nation with the power to forge a clear Muslim identity.

Whether or not, and how far, this identity depended upon the political marginalisation of non-Muslims is an issue that Burki chooses to side-step. Nevertheless, the sweeping changes associated with General Zia's Islamist brand of politics in the 1980s left little doubt that Zia himself associated the strengthening of Pakistan's Muslim identity with the steady erosion of the rights of its dwindling non-Muslims. His most decisive moves in this direction were contained in a series of judicial reforms (known as the Law of Evidence), announced in 1984. They barred non-Muslims from giving evidence against Muslims in newly established Islamic courts (so-called *sharia* courts), and obliged them to accept that their evidence in such courts would be worth half that submitted by a Muslim, thus making it easier for Muslims to pursue legal proceedings against non-Muslims.

These divisions were reinforced in 1985 with the restoration of separate electorates, which constitutionally stripped non-Muslims of the right to vote in territorially demarcated constituencies designated for the election of candidates to the national and provincial assemblies. Henceforth non-Muslims, divided into four groups (Christians, Hindus, Ahmadis and Sikhs, Buddhists and Parsis grouped together) were denied the right to vote for the same candidates or share the same constituencies as Muslims. Instead they were restricted to voting for candidates from their own religious group. While the selective manner in which these rules were applied suggested that their purpose (like most other measures introduced by Zia under the rubric of Islamization) was mainly rhetorical, there was no doubt that they did much to undermine secular politics, which since the separation of East Pakistan had come to be most closely associated with the PPP.

Indeed, the issue of separate electorates had resurfaced in 1977 precisely in the context of a campaign by pro-Islamic parties to abolish joint electorates, which they claimed favoured the PPP, whose liberal policies were judged to favour voters from religious minority groups, encouraging them to side with the party. Barring non-Muslims from the election of general seats, they believed, would be to their advantage and to the detriment of the PPP. Encouraged by Zia's own disdain for Bhutto's secular politics, they supported his move to push through an amendment in 1979 that restored separate electorates. The new system was implemented in elections to local bodies in 1983 and again in 1985 during party-less national and provincial elections. In a referendum held in 1984 to endorse his presidency Zia eschewed separate electorates. It was projected not as a test of the president's performance in office but as an endorsement of 'the process ... to bring the laws of Pakistan in conformity with the injunctions of Islam'—a question so carefully worded as to virtually exclude non-Muslims from pronouncing on it while making it difficult for Muslims to oppose it without seeming to be against Islam.[78]

The erosion of the political rights of non-Muslims and the equation in public discourse between Pakistani and Muslim occurred against the backdrop of other measures that institutionalized discrimination against non-Muslims and shifted perceptions about their position as constituent elements of the Pakistani nation. In a series of changes to penal code laws relating to religious offences, announced in 1985, Zia singled out disrespect to Islam and the Prophet as offences carrying a life sentence or death penalty. The amendments aroused wide concern among non-Muslims, who feared that they would be especially vulnerable to prosecution. At issue were not only their rights as citizens entitled to equal protection under the law, but also uncertainty over the state's religious neutrality. The latter had been an important consideration in the framing of the 1860 British Indian Penal Code from which many of the so-called blasphemy laws had been derived and which had served as a benchmark when incorporated into the statute books at independence.

Religious neutrality had also been undermined by Zia's decision to alter the status of the 1949 Objectives Resolution from a Preamble, which outlined the fundamental principles of the state, to a justiciable part of the Constitution enforceable in law. In so doing he removed the constitutional ambiguity at the heart of the Resolution that had allowed Pakistan's early law-makers to reassure the country's religious minorities about their legal and political rights. By contrast, there emerged under Zia a more categorical assertion of the state's primary obligation to its Muslim citizens that, for the first time, through the application of blasphemy laws, could potentially be tested in a court of law. These laws were an extension of Zia's ill-advised programme of Islamization, reflecting impatience with the undetermined question of Pakistan's Islamic identity—impatience Zia sought to resolve by hardening the boundaries of the nation through a system of legal exclusions aimed at non-Muslims.

The success of Zia's endeavours owed much to a cultural discourse that had been closely, if unevenly, associated with the foundations of the state, which held that being Muslim was a condition of being Pakistani. Under Zia the practical implications of these assumptions found more room to develop. One area in which they were more systematically pursued was in public education school textbooks. A recent and much cited study on the influence of the latter in shaping national identity in Pakistan found that a major consequence of the injection of 'Muslim majoritarianism' under the guise of Zia's Islamization programme into the national curriculum in the 1980s, was the idea that 'Pakistan is for Muslims alone'.[79] It shows how 'the process of equating Muslim and Pakistani identities starts in very early school education' and how distortions in the teaching of history have led to a perception of Pakistan's non-Muslims as lacking the requisites to qualify for full citizenship.[80] This has created an environment in which non-Muslims have been steadily relegated to second-class citizens, whose political loyalties have repeatedly been questioned and whose not inconsiderable contributions to Pakistani society systematically ignored.[81]

The 'democratic interregnum' of the 1990s changed little. The PPP, led by Benazir Bhutto, failed to roll back discriminatory legislation against non-Muslims, while Nawaz Sharif moved further to extend Zia's Islamization programme by formalising the application of *sharia* law. If implemented, it could well have served as the final repudiation of Jinnah's foundational statement endorsing the legal equality of all Pakistan's citizens. Nor did General Musharraf's vision of 'enlightened moderation' succeed in stemming the erosion of the rights of Pakistan's non-Muslim citizens. All blasphemy laws remain intact while an attempt by Musharraf to implement the laws in a less arbitrary manner than at present was jettisoned in the face of protest from pro-Islamic parties. Musharraf was also forced to back down on a proposal in 2005 to delete the so-called 'religion column'. First introduced in 1974 (and subsequently extended by Zia) to single out Ahmedis as non-Muslims, it still requires all Pakistani passport holders to specify their religious affiliation. Widely condemned by liberal politicians as intended to single out non-Muslim citizens by forcing them to declare their religious beliefs and thereby leave them more vulnerable to discriminatory legislation, it stands as an indictment of a state that has presided over the steady erosion of the constitutional and legal rights of non-Muslims, leaving them largely bereft of institutional protection.[82]

However, Musharraf's military regime did order the abolition of separate electorates in 2002, which finally restored to non-Muslims the right to vote for both general seats as well seats reserved for minorities. Initially welcomed as a necessary step to force Muslim candidates to canvass for support among non-Muslim constituents and possibly even encourage parties to nominate non-Muslim candidates, it has since been condemned by non-Muslim organizations as failing in practice genuinely to enfranchise their communities. In a system still dominated by the clan-based politics of patronage, they argue, it is Muslim politicians rather than non-Muslim voters who decide who is to represent non-Muslims in the seats reserved for religious minorities in national and provincial assemblies. Marginalised and ignored by political campaigns in the run-up to the 2008 general elections, they point to the fact that of the twelve non-Muslim candidates contesting general seats to the National Assembly and six contesting general seats for the provincial assemblies, most failed to receive endorsement from the main parties and thus none was successful.[83]

It is generally assumed that the erosion of Jinnah's pluralist and secular vision of Pakistan has been due either to a state centralization contemptuous of ethnic diversity or to state-driven Islamization intent on disciplining, if not marginalizing, religious difference. While it is undeniable that these processes have defined the criteria of 'belonging', the exclusionary political discourses and practices with which they are associated are a consequence of a more profound uncertainty about Pakistan's national identity and a lack of consensus regarding Islam's relation to the state. Much of this uncertainty was historically embedded in doubts about the value of pluralism, which so characteristically defined the movement for Pakistan. Pursuing a strict consensus informed by the language of a 'given' universal Islamic community, it lacked the imagination and confidence either to conceive of the nation as a 'political project' or to envisage the act of belonging as a 'political argument'.[84]

3

THE BURDEN OF ISLAM

THE SACRALIZATION OF POLITICS

It would seem self-evident that, as a Muslim homeland built in the name of Islam, Pakistan would be better equipped than most states to define the role of Islam in national politics. Yet the debate on the place of Islam in national life has raged on, muddied by the claims and counter-claims of its many protagonists. That it should continue to do so is in very large measure a reflection, if not a symptom, of the ideological confusion at the heart of a state still trapped in myths of its own making. All states rely on myths, which they nurture to lend meaning to the imagined political community. What is peculiar to Pakistan is that the myths so carefully cultivated to sustain the national edifice turned out after independence to be embarrassments that needed to be shrouded from view or embellished in ways that made them more palatable.

So it was that the carefully cultivated myth of Pakistan as a 'nation' of Muslims ill at ease with Indian secularism came to weigh heavily upon the country's first generation of leaders. Prompted by their own (often ill-defined) secular leanings, they chose to reconcile their quest for a modern constitutional framework based on religion by claiming that Islam was *not* a mere religion (as was Hinduism) but the blueprint for a comprehensive social and political order capable of adapting to the modernity of nationalism. In doing so, they drew heavily on an established modernist tradition of Indo-Muslim thinking that aimed to free Islam from the pre-modern associations commonly attached to religion.

At the head of this campaign was Muhammad Iqbal, who though significantly more radical in his thinking than his predecessors Sayyid Ahmed Khan and Amir Ali (1849–1928), like them proclaimed modernity to be Islam's birthright.[1] But this claim was also implicit in Jinnah's understanding of Islam as modern. As Metcalf has perceptively observed, while Jinnah's cosmopolitanism inclined him (like Nehru) to regard religion as archaic, what singled him out from his secular-minded peers in Congress was the claim that 'Islam was *not* a religion'—a view he then used formally to buttress the claim in March 1940 that 'the Muslims were a nation, not a religion'.[2] 'The problem of India' he declared, 'is not of an inter-communal character but manifestly of an international one and it must be treated as such.'[3] Nor, he later added, were Islam and Hinduism 'religions in the strict sense of the word'—they were two 'nations'.[4]

Jinnah, no romantic soon realized that, while the principles of Islam might represent a panacea for the resolution of the Muslim national question, they were unlikely to help address the real shortcomings of Muslim society. These shortcomings were brutally exposed at Partition, when Muslims (like others) demonstrated that the primeval impulses of their religion remained dangerously in place.[5] By August 1947 Jinnah was forced to recognize that, whatever the national claims on behalf of Islam, he could not tame the Islamic tiger. In his famous inaugural speech to the first meeting of the Constituent Assembly, he appeared to acknowledge the damaging effects flowing from the use of religious rhetoric to justify his demand for Pakistan. 'You will find,' he observed, 'that in the course of time Hindus would cease to be Hindus and Muslims would cease to be Muslims, not in the religious sense, because that is the personal faith of each individual but in the political sense as citizens of the state.'[6]

Many have since interpreted this extraordinary re-statement of Jinnah's vision as evidence of his unequivocal preference for a secular state—although he did not, significantly, go as far as to use the word secular. But Jinnah's speech also fuelled fears among others, who wondered whether he had reneged on his commitment to the new country's founding ideology—the two nation-theory. While neither claim has ever been decisively established, what it suggested was that Jinnah, having mobilised Islam's vote-winning potential, now sought to curb its destructive power by confining religion to the private sphere. It would set the tone for future battles over conflicting conceptions of Pakistan.

Holy battles

These tensions first surfaced in the constitution-making process, which extended for almost a decade, and culminated in the country's first constitution in 1956. This period was dominated by debates, the most sustained of which centred on the role of Islam in the new state. In and of itself, this was perhaps not unusual for a country with an overwhelming Muslim majority. But instead of the confidence that was expected to flow from this distinct Muslim identity, the process was dogged by uncertainties. Binder, one of the most perceptive observers of Pakistan's constitutional endeavours in these early years, concluded that 'nowhere has the element of democratic nationalism been so weak, the desire for an Islamic constitution so generally admitted, and the cleavage between the Western-educated and the ulama so wide'.[7] Divisions that have since been cast as ones between 'traditionalists' and 'modernists'—if not between 'fundamentalists' and 'secularists'— were by no means hard and fast distinctions. On the contrary, they often masked a more diffuse Islamic romanticism that cut across the political spectrum, making the task of fleshing out Pakistan's identity as a modern Muslim state even more difficult.

Jinnah's own prevarication did little to clear the confusion. In a speech to the Sind Bar Association in Karachi on 25 January 1948, he even seemed ready to abandon his earlier stance, which had called for religion to be kept out of politics, and denouncing as 'mischief' attempts to ignore 'Shari'at Law' as the basis of Pakistan's constitution.[8] While few would deny that these inconsistencies were to be expected from Jinnah, who by that time was consumed by fatal ill-health, they set an unfortunate precedent for his successors. Many have since used the ambiguity cultivated by Jinnah to negotiate their own positions and, in doing so, have continued the legacy of a movement that under Jinnah himself came to represent all things to all men.

The Objectives Resolution passed in March 1949, which has served as a preamble for all three of Pakistan's constitutions (1956, 1962 and 1973), was symptomatic of this ambiguity.[9] Though regarded as the country's 'constitutional *Grundnorm*',[10] its endorsement was marred by a discord that demonstrated the fragility of the consensus underpinning the new state. This became plain during clashes on the floor of the Constituent Assembly, where the gulf separating Pakistan's secularising elite and its men of religion marked the onset of a battle that rumbles on today. At issue was how best to provide a constitutional niche for Islam that recognized its importance in the creation of the state while containing its influence in dictating policy and framing laws.

The country's dominant, governing elite in these early years was drawn mainly from the urban professional classes of north-central India. Though they represented a formidable presence in Pakistan, their lack of local roots meant that few could do without some form of Islamic legitimation. But such legitimacy came at a price, which involved compromising the secular objectives with which these classes were closely associated. The religious lobby (consisting of both the traditional *ulama* and religious parties), although seemingly vigorous in style and rhetoric, was also constrained. Many of its members had been vocal critics of Jinnah's scheme for a separate Muslim state, which few believed was intended to be an Islamic state. The religious lobby was soon seduced when Jinnah, having failed to obtain constitutional concessions from Congress, promised an Islamic government to mobilize the hitherto tepid support of the Muslim-majority provinces of Punjab and Bengal. Nevertheless, many still harboured reservations about Pakistan—reservations compounded both by fears of Jinnah's instinctively secular preferences as well as by concerns that support for a territorial state was tantamount to rejecting the primacy of the universal Muslim community defended by classical Islam.

These reservations were not confined to the traditional men of religion, the *ulama*. Indeed it has been argued that 'the idea of making Pakistan an Islamic state began with the politicians and not the ulama'.[11] Among them were Islamist politicians, who were closely allied to the Jamaat-i-Islami, which acted as the main catalyst to ensure that Islamic concerns would be taken into account by law makers entrusted with drafting the 1956 Constitution.[12] These efforts, which were also instrumental in persuading the *ulama* to join the fray in support of an Islamic constitution, were finally rewarded with the adoption of the 1949 Objectives Resolution. Projected at the time by the Jamaat as a decisive victory for its campaign in support of an Islamic constitution, it has since come also to be regarded by many historians as the first in a series of major concessions secured by the Jamaat from the country's secular leadership. Just how far law-makers themselves accepted these claims remains unclear, but what is not in doubt is that the promulgation of the Resolution pointed conclusively to the growing political muscle of the religious lobby. The alliance between the

Jamaat and the religious establishment represented by the *ulama*, although uneasy, was successful in leaving its stamp on the Resolution.

Its influence showed especially with regard to two issues. The first was the affirmation of divine over popular sovereignty, thus setting limits on the scope of parliament and interpreting its responsibilities as a 'sacred trust'. The second concerned the obligation of the state to 'enable' Muslims to 'order their lives ... in accord with the teaching and requirements of Islam as set out in the Holy Quran and Sunna'.[13] Nevertheless the governing elite, led by the country's first Prime Minister Liaquat Ali Khan, vigorously denied that the Objectives Resolution, by recognizing divine sovereignty, proposed to erode the power or authority of 'the chosen representatives of the people' or that there was 'any danger of the establishment of a theocracy'.[14] Nor, he claimed, was the affirmation of divine sovereignty incompatible with the emergence of Pakistan as a 'sovereign independent state' as indicated in the second paragraph of the Resolution.

Addressing fears that the Resolution's so-called 'enabling clause', which committed the state to assist Muslims 'to order their lives in the individual and collective spheres in accordance with the teachings and requirements of Islam',[15] privileged Muslims over others, Liaquat invoked Islam's spirit of tolerance, insisting that it served as a model for the state's fair treatment of minorities. Not to show tolerance, he claimed, would be to 'transgress[ing] the dictates of our religion'.[16] But Liaquat also reiterated that 'the state was not to play the part of a neutral observer, wherein Muslims may be merely free to profess and practise their religion, because such an attitude would be a very negation of the ideals which prompted the demand for Pakistan'. Instead, he said, 'the state will create such conditions as are conducive to the building up of a truly Islamic society, which means that the state will have to play a positive part in this effort.'[17]

Liaquat was strongly supported by the leadership of the Muslim League, whose members in the Constituent Assembly backed the Resolution as consistent both with Islam and with what they believed to be Jinnah's vision of the state of Pakistan. But, even then, there was obviously little consensus on the kind of Islam that would underpin the constitutional foundations of the state, and much uncertainty about Jinnah's understanding of the state's relation to Islam. Some, like Mian Iftikharuddin, the left-leaning member from Punjab, voted against the Resolution on the grounds that it did not represent what he called 'a proper Islamic constitution' since it ignored the 'progressive', 'revolutionary' and 'democratic' dimensions of Islam.[18] Others however, including Jinnah's close political associate, Abdur Rab Nishtar, spoke in favour of the Resolution precisely for what he claimed was its accurate representation of Islam, which rejected any 'divorce between religion and politics'.

Citing Jinnah's often repeated claim that 'Islam was a complete code of life', Nishtar also declared that the Resolution was wholly consistent with Jinnah's notion that 'religion governs not only our relations with God, but also our activities in other spheres of life'.[19] More significantly, while he acknowledged that Jinnah had indeed pledged to protect the country's minorities, Nishtar doubted whether Jinnah ever questioned that his first obligation was to 'the Muslim majority' for whom the state had been created and for whom Nishtar claimed the Resolution had been primarily framed.[20] Interestingly, some among the *ulama* also justified their support for the Resolution by claiming that its goal to establish a state based on Islam chimed with Jinnah's 'ideas'. The prominent Deobandi *alim* and member of the Constituent Assembly, Maulana Shabbir Ahmed Usmani, was among them.[21]

Although the divisions between the Western-educated elite and the religious lobby were real, the tenor of these early constitutional debates suggests that the desire for some kind of constitution based on Islam was more widespread than is perhaps acknowledged. It is true that many secular politicians succumbed readily to the temptation of appealing to Islam in order to paper over the cracks that surfaced after independence. But most also found it hard to discard the memory of the closing years of the empire, which had been dominated by visions of an Islamically informed constitutional order, which they equated with a state governed by Islam, even if what they meant was obscured by the lack of consensus over Islam. What is also clear is that for the vast majority of this first generation of leaders, the Islamic basis of the Pakistani state was to be reflected not so much in legal injunctions embodied in the constitution of the state, but in the affirmation of Islamic ethical and social concerns—a legacy of nineteenth-century Indo-Muslim apologists who, by asserting that every social virtue was contained in Islam, often ended up romanticizing the principles of an Islamic polity.

The ambiguities of the Objectives Resolution and the so-called 'repugnancy clause' of the 1956 constitution, which committed the state to reject any law opposed to the Quran or Sunnah, testified to the influence of this legacy of Islamic romanticism. But it also reflected the weakness of Pakistan's secular politicians, who were fearful of the power of the religious lobby upon which they had to rely not only to ensure the final success of the movement for Pakistan but also to lend them a patina of legitimacy in circumstances where few could call upon the support of local constituencies. Bereft of their bases of power and faced with growing challenges from regional separatists in Bengal, Sind, the North West Frontier Province and Balochistan, they had little choice but to fall back on Islam as both a source of legitimacy and the basis of national unity. With the exception of a handful of Hindu members of parliament who opposed an Islamic constitution, few Muslim politicians, including the more secular-minded among *mohajir* politicians, were able to conceal their belief in the intrinsic superiority of an Islamic constitutional order.

The real dividing line between these separate camps lay then not in their differences over the desirability of an Islamically informed constitutional order but in their understanding of what that order entailed—a division reminiscent of the tension between the idea of a pre-existing Muslim nation and a Muslim nation in-the-making. The religious lobby, consisting of the *ulama* and religious parties dominated by the Jamaat-i-Islami, confidently declared that the nature of an Islamic state was knowable, if not yet known. On the other hand, the self-proclaimed secular Muslim intelligentsia was given to improvisation while still waiting for Pakistan's true Islamic spirit to unfold through the working of a yet-to-be-defined political system.

Not surprisingly, non-Muslims who uniformly opposed the Resolution were at odds with their Muslim counterparts. They claimed that the Resolution represented a deviation from Jinnah's vision and insisted that Jinnah himself 'most unequivocally said that Pakistan will be a secular state'.[22] Some even argued that 'were this Resolution to come before this House within the lifetime of the great creator of Pakistan, the Quaid-i-Azam, it would not have come in its present shape'.[23] Be that as it may, opposition to the Resolution was confined almost entirely to members belonging to Hindu and other religious minorities, who feared that its stress on an Islamic dispensation threatened to compromise the secular state and, with it, the right of non-Muslim citizens to claim equality with their Muslim counterparts. Their concerns raised questions that would return to haunt Pakistan in later years, for while the debate over divine against popular sovereignty appeared to fade away with each new constitution (1962, 1973), its implications resonate to the present day. Then as now these questions centred on the issue of whether, having acknowledged God's sovereignty, the state was also duty-bound to enforce His law (the *sharia*) as supreme.

Then, as now, many were persuaded that the question would have a vital bearing both on the rights of the country's religious minorities and on the future of Pakistan as a secular state committed to the equality of all its citizens. Hindu members of the Constituent Assembly, who represented almost a quarter of the population of East Bengal, voiced some of the strongest objections to the Objectives Resolution in 1949. They feared (not without reason) that the sovereignty clause, which sought to privilege Islamic law (*sharia*), would not only encroach upon the equal rights of religious minorities but also erode the authority of parliament to guarantee those rights. These fears would be confirmed in years to come but the signs were already apparent. Under the 1956 constitution the ceremonial post of Head of State (or president) was reserved for Muslims—a provision retained under the 1962 constitution. But by the time the 1973 Constitution came to be promulgated, non-Muslims were denied access to the posts both of president and prime minister.

This shift was particularly striking in the light of Liaquat's categorical statement, following the approval of the Objectives Resolution in March 1949, in which he condemned *ulama* groups as enemies of Islam for suggesting that non-Muslims in Pakistan would henceforth be denied the right to head 'the administration'. 'This,' he declared, 'was absolutely wrong,' insisting that the Objectives Resolution had accepted that 'a non-Muslim can be head of the administration', leaving many to understand that he intended 'the administration' to mean 'the government'. But in a fashion characteristic of the leadership, Liaquat immediately muddied the waters by invoking the idea of the 'Islamic state' that he believed would be 'established in accordance with this Resolution'.[24] This fuelled doubts about the secular commitments of Pakistan's first generation of leaders and re-opened the door to Islamic parties determined to regain the initiative at a time when the lack of consensus over the role of Islam in defining the state was palpable.

General Ayub Khan's military coup of 1958, which put an abrupt end to this process, temporarily salvaged the cause of Pakistan's secular intelligentsia. By steering Pakistan away from an overtly ideological (that is, Islamic) stance to more developmental concerns, he succeeded in shifting the debate along lines that favoured the country's secular elites. According to Nasr, national politics now came to focus not so much on 'why Pakistan was created' but 'where Pakistan was heading'.[25] This is not to say that Ayub's pro-secular regime had no vision of the role it intended to reserve for Islam in public life. But it was a vastly simplified formula that reflected Ayub's style of paternalistic politics and was clearly designed to fit what he fondly referred to as the 'genius' of the Pakistani nation.

It involved, first, harnessing Islam as a force for political unity; and second, projecting it as an engine of socio-economic development. In so doing, Ayub fell squarely within the Muslim modernist tradition to which he had been exposed as a young student at Aligarh College. There he had forged his conviction that Islam was not a mere religion but a 'movement' that was both 'dynamic and progressive'[26], thus echoing Jinnah's own description of Islam as *not* a religion but a comprehensive social order with the power to determine the contours of a modern Muslim nation. In this way, Ayub also sought, much as Jinnah before him, to appropriate the right claimed by both the *ulama* and religious parties, notably the Jamaat-i-Islami, to interpret Islam.

Ayub's use of Islam as a force for political unity differed in one important respect from his predecessors. By regulating religious discourse in the service of a strong state he assumed that, over time, the benefits of the latter would trickle down and create a strong nation capable of standing without the aid of Islamic crutches. The case for this so-called 'trickle-down' theory was supported in large part by the philosophy of Ayub's economic policy, which assumed that strong economic growth, however asymmetric, would eventually lay the foundations for wider economic welfare. Although none of these assumptions was vindicated, they served as powerful engines to modernise the regime.

Ayub's admiration for the Kemalist experiment in Turkey also played a part. Like the Turkish leader, Kemal Atatürk, Ayub hoped that wide-ranging social and economic reforms would help sever his country's links with its immediate past and, by extension, its ideological mooring in Islam. But as Ziring has persuasively argued, any comparison between the two was doomed to failure: while Turkey was successfully salvaged from the ruins of the Ottoman Empire to emerge as a sovereign state, Pakistan remained the prisoner of a 'colonial dispensation that had little relevance to the contemporary nation-state'. More importantly, he observes, while the circumstances of World War I had assured Turkey an 'instant national identity', Pakistan surfaced in the wake of a shambolic transfer of power by the British Raj 'as a truncated structure, housing a diverse, disparate and divided people'.[27]

Ayub eventually understood this but not before trying in vain to reformulate Islam in ways that would by-pass the religious establishment. The method he adopted was bureaucratic in approach and involved managing Islamic discourse through the official sponsorship of a flock of advisory councils and research institutes. Not surprisingly, it failed to win the backing of the country's religious parties, which were determined to challenge Ayub's attempt to curb its powers to interpret Islam. Having secured from the secular leadership the right to define the constitutional identity of Pakistan as Islamic, they now sought to consolidate those gains by strengthening its monopoly over the public expression of Islam. Nevertheless, Ayub did succeed, partially at least in the early years of his administration, in rolling back the space afforded to Islam as a guide to public policy. With hindsight it is clear that what he was engaged in was not so much evicting Islam from the public sphere as restoring to it a modernist rendering of Islam, which he believed more faithfully reflected the original vision of Pakistan. 'Our mind,' he declared, 'is the mind of Islam, which is capable of expressing ... the language of science, the language of economics and the language of current affairs.'[28]

There was little ambiguity about Ayub's own role in this venture. He sought nothing less than to steer Pakistan under his tutelage towards the right kind of Islam and away from the obscurantist Islam of the *ulama*. It has prompted some to suggest that, in so doing, he effectively 'Pakistanised' Islam and opened the way for Jinnah's secular two-nation theory to be replaced by a Pakistani 'ideology of Islam'— which would serve as 'a national ideology, a principle of unity between the two wings of Pakistan and a flexible code of life befitting the modern age'.[29] His most significant achievement in this regard was the promulgation in July 1961 of the Muslim Family Laws Ordinance, which aimed to establish greater consistency between the legally permissible and the morally acceptable in matters affecting Muslim marriage, divorce, the age of consent and inheritance.[30] But it also reflected a fresh and concerted move by the country's secular leadership to assert a monopoly on existing forms of religious expression—an attempt that set the stage for a bitter struggle between Ayub and pro-Islamic parties, which rallied behind the Jamaat-i-Islami to condemn the measure. The Jamaat's efforts to bury the Ordinance failed to make headway as Ayub moved swiftly to resist the challenge by seeking judicial protection for its provisions. It ensured that the Ordinance remained in force until it finally secured protection under the 1973 constitution. Nevertheless, its limited enforcement has lent credence to the view that the Ordinance 'functioned more as a symbolic point of attack by fundamentalists than as an instrument of large-scale social change' and that its modest gains have been largely overshadowed by the Islamic distortions of a criminal justice system for women that occurred in the 1980s.[31]

Ayub's campaign to ease the burden of Islam and encourage a more secular discourse had extracted a heavy price from his critics among the *ulama* and their Islamist allies. In 1963 they forced him to reinstate Pakistan as an Islamic Republic after months of protest against his 1962 Constitution, which had referred simply to the 'Republic of Pakistan'. Embattled and on the defensive, he now turned to the mainly rural-based purveyors of mystical or 'folk' Islam (*pirs*) in the hope of mobilizing their support against the predominantly urban-based clerical opposition. Just how far he succeeded in persuading the masters of rural Islam to legitimise his modernizing agenda remains unclear. Indeed, opinion is divided between those who claim that Ayub extended his modernizing programme into the rural hinterland by offering new interpretations of Sufi Islam more consistent with ideas of development,[32] and those who insist that his alliance with rural religious leaders actually retarded the process of modernization in the countryside by strengthening the hold of traditional forces.[33] What is not in doubt is that in so doing Ayub continued a long tradition involving secular leaders, who had relied on rural-based spiritual leaders (*pirs*) and guardians of local shrines (*sajjida nashin*) to curb the hostility of urban-based *ulama* doubting their Islamic credentials. They included Jinnah, whose canny alliance with local *pirs* in the Punjab in the 1940s had effectively neutralized opposition from the *ulama* suspicious of his secular discourse.[34] By working to forge alliances with Muslim spiritual leaders in the countryside, Ayub like Jinnah and those who followed him, grew less certain of the relationship between Islam and the state. This uncertainty was aggravated by their tendency to use the language of Islam to generate various forms of power—power that was neither accountable nor within reach of ordinary democratic processes, such as elections.

The embarrassment of an educated political elite fraternising with semi-literate purveyors of Islamic practice, commonly equated with backwardness and superstition, meant that these contacts had officially to be disavowed. Indeed, Ayub had pitched his regime's legitimacy on waging a successful campaign against forms of religion that he had repeatedly claimed were antithetical to the modern Muslim mentality. In so doing, he reflected the concerns of Pakistan's first generation of political leaders, who prided themselves as the heirs of the spirit of Aligarh, which had placed a high premium on rationality and frowned on the spread of popular or folk Islam. But this attachment to formal learning and disdain for popular Islam was also shared by sections of the Deobandi *ulama* and their Islamist allies, who used it to hone a national discourse dedicated to ridding Pakistan of the corrupt and impure customs associated with folk Islam. Their opposition to Ayub's modernist agenda tended to blur these similarities, much as in the years immediately following independence when the debate over Pakistan's Islamic identity had appeared to separate 'modernists' from 'traditionalists' even though both held tenaciously (albeit for very different reasons) to the idea of reserving a role for Islam in the definition of the country's national identity.

These apparent divisions resurfaced under Ayub, accentuated by the scope and pace of his secular reforms. His attempt to appropriate the *ulama*'s rights to interpret the role of Islam in the public sphere also antagonised them and their Islamist allies. In their opposition to the regime they could count on the support of regional parties, especially in Sind and Bengal, which had grown to resent the concentration of power at the centre and the widening disparities between Punjab and Pakistan's poorer provinces. Ayub's authoritarian style of government and his brutal suppression of ethnic conflict deepened this political alienation forcing him, in time, to appeal to Islamic solidarity in an attempt to overcome divisions and shore up the legitimacy of his regime.

The Combined Opposition Party (COP), which emerged to contest the 1965 presidential elections and staged a two-pronged attack against authoritarianism and secularism, failed to mount a realistic challenge. Led by a motley coalition of religious zealots, leftists and ethno-nationalists, it nominated the frail and politically inexperienced Fatima Ali Jinnah as its presidential candidate against Ayub. Though revered as the sister of Pakistan's founder, her symbolic appeal was not enough to oust the incumbent. As a woman, Fatima Jinnah also stirred feelings of profound ambivalence among the Deobandi *ulama* and the pro-Islamic parties, which were characteristically hostile to women in public life and which until then had typically refused to endorse a Muslim woman as head of state. That they did so was a measure of pragmatism since they ran the risk of being castigated as the peddlers of double standards. Worse, they stood to be out-manoeuvred by Ayub, who set aside his regard for the rights of women by declaring that a woman was not, after all, fit to rule! In this he called on the support of the Barelvi *ulama* and their network of local *pirs* and assorted *sajjida nashins* to vie with the Jamaat as representatives of true Islam— disturbing evidence of the manipulation of religious expression as a means to holding onto power.

With hindsight Ayub was more effective than most in riding the crest of Islamist opposition. When his regime finally collapsed its downfall was more readily attributable to Pakistan's defeat in the war against India in 1965 and to the strength of regional movements in Bengal and Sind than to any pressure from organized Islamist forces. Indeed the surge of populist politics spearheaded by the PPP and the Awami League threatened for a while completely to engulf Islamic parties, whose dismal showing in the 1970 elections reflected their political weakness. However, the political crisis in East Pakistan, which followed the general elections, gave Islamist forces the opportunity to regain the initiative. Their target was the Awami League's brand of secularism, which parties like the Jamaat-i-Islami vigorously opposed. Its student organization, the Islami Jamiat-i-Tulaba (IJT), played a key role in this, mobilizing its forces and driving a campaign against 'the enemies of Islam'. This was underscored by its involvement in counter-insurgency operations during the 1971 civil war in East Pakistan and its role in the organization of the para-military *al-Badr* and *al-Shams* brigades, which functioned as Islamist shock-troops. These alignments laid the foundations for a far-reaching alliance at the very heart of the state between Islamists and army, which would allow both sides to benefit in the decades to come. The army, soon to be embroiled in military adventures in Afghanistan and Kashmir, would receive religious sanction while religious parties, long denied access to state power, would gain in prominence.

This dramatic realignment between Islamist forces and their erstwhile secular-minded foes in the army was largely underpinned by the ethos imparted to troops drawn from West Pakistan. They were instructed in the belief that by fighting the local Bengali population, they were fending off India and, by extension, a Hindu challenge to the Islamic way of life. For Islamists the alliance proved to be an unexpected boon. Co-operation with a key state institution not only averted the threat of political marginalization posed by the election results but also helped see off critics who had questioned the nationalist credentials of Islamic parties, which had expressed reservations about the idea of Pakistan before independence. It was the popular turn to Islam following the secession of East Pakistan that allowed the re-entry of Islamist parties into national politics and ensured that they lived to fight another day.

But the dynamics of the new political landscape had also become more complex and the outcome of any struggle for supremacy less certain. At one level Islamic parties stood to benefit from a climate in which answers to the national predicament were being sought in Islam. This was merely a short distance from the claim that secularism itself was to blame for the crisis. The 'secular' ways of national leaders, and in particular those associated with the military regime of General Yahya Khan, who had taken over after Ayub's resignation in 1969, would soon come to serve as evidence. In a characteristic assessment of the time, the authors of the Hamoodur Rahman Commission report charged to investigate the events of 1971 civil war noted that, 'the belief appears to be universally entertained by all sections of our people that one of the major causes of our disgrace was the moral degeneration which had set in among senior army commanders' that included among others 'lust for wine and women'.[35] The most serious allegations centred on General Yahya, whose addiction to 'heavy drinking' and questionable friendship 'with a number of ladies of indifferent repute'[36] was held up as indisputable evidence that 'secularism' had corroded the moral fabric of the leadership and hastened the disintegration of the nation.

This shift was also reflected in the weakening of the country's founding ideology—the two-nation theory—which now came to be seen as too closely tied to the secular vision associated with Jinnah and the country's first generation of politicians. It led to the understanding that, having lost its eastern wing, the 'new' Pakistan could afford to shed the legacy of a historical past rooted in South Asia. Instead, it turned west towards the Muslim Middle East, where it hoped more firmly to anchor its Islamic identity, which many believed had eluded the state so long as it faced resistance from the Bengalis who were content to relegate religion to the private sphere. As such, there was an overwhelming sense that Pakistan could yet emerge from this crisis strengthened by a final reconciliation between Islam and nationalism. The long and uneasy co-operation between the country's two wings, it was felt, had stood far too long in the way of Pakistan realising its full potential as a Muslim country.

To a large extent Z.A. Bhutto, who assumed power as Pakistan's first democratically elected prime minister, encapsulated the mood of this new Pakistan. He steered the country more clearly perhaps than any other leader before him in the direction of closer relations with the Muslim heartland that lay to the west of its borders. He did so consciously observing that 'the severance of our eastern wing ... has significantly altered our geographic focus ... At the moment, as we stand, it is within the ambit of South and Western Asia. It is here that our primary concern must henceforth lie.'[37] Internally too Bhutto signalled changes that confirmed the new-found importance of Islam in the conduct of public affairs. His ruling PPP openly proclaimed the power of 'Islamic socialism' to drive its populist programme and, perhaps taking a page out of Ayub's book, moved quickly to forge alliances with various local *pirs*—although unlike Ayub he showed little inclination to challenge the Islamists by seeking to exercise a monopoly over public expressions of Islam.

On the contrary, Bhutto took credit for promulgating the country's most explicitly Islamic constitution yet. The 1973 constitution, which remains in force, reiterated Pakistan's identity as an Islamic Republic and for the first time recognized Islam as the 'State religion of Pakistan'. The teaching of Islam was made compulsory and a Council of Islamic Ideology was established to advise the national and provincial governments on legislation in keeping with the Quran and Sunna. In a further unusual and equally unprecedented move, the Constitution required the state also to 'endeavour to preserve and strengthen fraternal relations among the Muslim countries based on Islamic unity'.

With the stage thus set to respond to long-standing demands by Islamists and their allies among the *ulama*, it was expected that the era of holy battles involving secularists and religious parties would steadily lose momentum as a broader consensus emerged about the role of Islam in politics and government. But these expectations proved to be ill-founded as Bhutto tried in vain to render his regime's secular image more palatable to an Islamist opposition newly empowered by a cultural climate keen to reaffirm Pakistan's Islamic roots and a Constitution prepared to endorse it. The determination of the Islamists and their allies among the *ulama* to take on Bhutto emerged almost as soon as his government took power. An immediate issue on which religious parties rallied was against the recognition of Bangladesh, which they strongly opposed, claiming it compromised the principle of Islamic solidarity that had lent substance to Pakistan's founding ideology—the two-nation theory. They were supported by groups representing Urdu-speaking migrants (*mohajirs*), who had been strong proponents of the two-nation theory. Their stance on this occasion was informed however less by visions of a Muslim nation than by the cause of thousands of Urdu-speaking Biharis left stranded in Bangladesh, whose repatriation they expected would add clout to their campaign to resist Bhutto's pro-Sindhi policies. The Islamist opposition also drew on the support of public opinion in Punjab, the heartland of the army, which was still smarting from Pakistan's humiliating military defeat at the hands of combined Bengali nationalist and Indian forces.

Nevertheless, Bhutto's room for manoeuvre vis-à-vis the Islamist opposition was constrained by his need to win support for his new Constitution, which had come under scrutiny from Islamic parties pressing for Pakistan to be designated an Islamic republic. So evenly balanced was this contest that, despite Bhutto's strong electoral mandate, when he did finally announce Pakistan's official recognition of Bangladesh in 1974, he felt obliged to do so with the full backing of the international Muslim community gathered under the auspices of the Islamic Summit Conference in Lahore. The strategy was the clearest demonstration yet of Bhutto's part in consolidating a time-honoured tradition among Pakistan's political leaders to call on Islam to meet the Islamist challenge. And as with his many illustrious predecessors, starting with Jinnah, Bhutto too soon realized that the gains flowing from such appeals were ephemeral. More importantly still, and to his immense cost, he would also come to understand that Islam could neither be selectively applied nor easily manipulated and that by venturing to do so, he invited an Islamist backlash.

It was not long before Bhutto was caught off-guard by Islamic parties bent on forcing him to establish his Islamic credentials. The robustness of the latter had long been doubted by Bhutto's foes among the *ulama* and the Islamist opposition, who condemned his apparently wilful disregard of Islamic practices. His well-known taste for fine wine, and women, combined with a political style that reinforced his image as a Western-educated progressive all ensured that his secular demeanour remained a live political issue. Bhutto fuelled the controversy by publicly endorsing Pakistan as a 'citadel of Islam in Asia'.[38] Mindful of allegations that he was a wayward Muslim, and anxious to ward off claims that his party had relied on the financial backing of Pakistan's Ahmedi community, in 1974 he stripped Ahmedis of their Muslim status, hoping thereby to rehabilitate his image with his Islamist critics.

Like Ayub, Bhutto also relied on the guardians of folk Islam as an alternative spiritual power base, given the ideological legitimacy denied him by the keepers of high Islam—the *ulama* and their Islamist allies. Bhutto's patronage of the cult of the popular Sindhi saint, Lal Shahbaz Qalandar, which was frowned upon by the orthodox *ulama*, signalled his determination to draw on rival traditions of rural Islam. Not only was he persuaded of the importance of the appeal of rural Islam among the poor, but he was also certain that strengthening this nexus was vital to maintain his control over the countryside.[39] Ultimately these efforts failed: the appeal to popular Islam neither empowered Bhutto's regime nor protected him from the wrath of his Islamist foes.

Indeed, the Islamist opposition to Bhutto moved concertedly to outmanoeuvre him by sharpening their discourse and calling for the introduction of a Prophetic Order or *Nizam-i-Mustapha*. It was supported by local holy men in rural Punjab and parts of rural Sindh, who were closely allied to the Barelvi *ulama*, organized as the Jamiat-ul Ulama-i-Pakistan (JUP). They favoured a more lenient approach to promoting the cult of the Prophet and to intercession at the shrines of rural saints, both of which were routinely condemned by the more orthodox Deobandi clergy as well as by the urban supporters of the Jamaat-i-Islami. However, these differences were suspended as the campaign against Bhutto gained momentum and coalesced around a slogan that, by calling simply for the 'rule of the Prophet', appeared to be free from the confusion that had beset the pro-Islamic lobby's attempts to define an Islamic state.

By asserting that the Prophet was the perfect governor and the Quran a perfect book of law, the need to define the Islamic state and to produce an appropriate constitution, which had so confounded the early generation of secular and religious leaders, seemed much less urgent. Instead, the issue of Pakistan's putative Islamic identity now appeared to be premised more simply on a series of what were assumed to be, for Muslims at least, self-evident truths. Confronted with this challenge, Bhutto tried one last time to outwit his opponents, not by appealing to folk Islam, but by seeking to generate the power that flowed from the democratic process tied to the ballot-box. In March 1977 he ordered general elections and was widely accused by the Islamist opposition (freshly re-cast as the Pakistan National Alliance—PNA) of rigging them in his favour. Desperate to salvage his future, Bhutto now moved to co-opt the opposition by emerging as the champion of Islamization. In a series of dramatic and widely publicized announcements, he ordered a ban on alcohol, an end to gambling and the closure of nightclubs. All had been projected by the *ulama* and their Islamist allies as essential conditions of their vision of *Nizam-i-Mustapha*. The move marked the triumph of Islamic activists in Pakistan. Though thwarted by a military coup from making a bid for state power, their gains would henceforth be abundantly reflected in a new dispensation that, for the first time, not only took account of Islam in the very texture of state and society, but significantly eased the passage of Islamist forces from the margins to the centre of national political discourse.

In the name of Islam

This development was pushed forward by Pakistan's military ruler, General Zia ul Haq, who ousted Bhutto in July 1977. After hailing the 'spirit of Islam' that had forced Bhutto to relinquish power, he declared: '[i]t proves that Pakistan, which was created in the name of Islam, will continue to survive only if it sticks to Islam. That is why I consider the introduction of an Islamic system as an essential prerequisite for the country.'[40] While there is no doubt that, like many of Pakistan's political leaders since independence, including Jinnah, Zia's need for regime legitimacy fuelled his desire to tap the repertory of Islam, he was exceptional in declaring from the outset that he intended to ride the Islamist wave rather than stamp on it.

But like his predecessors, he too soon found that merely acknowledging the Islamist tiger was not enough; it was necessary to keep pace with it. And indeed it was the slow pace of Zia's Islamization programme and his reluctance consistently to endorse the Islamist conception of the state, rather any personal compromise with secular values, that eventually diluted the enthusiasm of his early supporters in the Jamaat-i-Islami, thus prompting him to turn to (and eventually bolster) the *ulama* parties. Conveniently for Zia, the *ulama*'s concerns lay not so much in plans to introduce an Islamic state, about which they remained famously ambiguous, but in the reform of society along lines deemed more in keeping with Islam.

Zia's reforms, to the extent that they came increasingly to depend upon the Islam of the *ulama*, reflected this subtle but fundamental shift away from the narrowly political concerns of the Jamaat's demand for an Islamic state towards changes aimed at transforming society as a whole. As such, Zia's vision of the Prophetic Order (or *Nizam-i-Mustapha*) called for the implementation of Islamic laws that would, in the first instance, regulate social and economic transactions—leaving for later the Islamization of the state itself. The working assumption was that an Islamic state had to be preceded by an 'Islamized' citizenry. While this assumption proved to be politically expedient for Zia, who was concerned above all to legitimize his military regime, it also carried force in a climate of national uncertainty that had prompted a fresh turn to Islam in order to address the crisis of identity caused by the loss of East Pakistan. Although Bhutto's economic and social policies had been widely expected to ease the sense of national malaise, his government's failure to live up to expectation was equated with the failure of secular regimes, which stood condemned for their tenuous attachment to Islam. Paradoxically, Bhutto's transparently insincere attempts to play the Islamic card, far from fuelling a revulsion against the political uses of Islam, intensified the drive to anchor the state more firmly in the principles of Islam.

It was in this climate of enduring uncertainty that Zia set about addressing the ambiguities that surrounded Pakistan's putative Islamic identity. His first port of call was the famous Objectives Resolution, which having served until then as a preamble to successive constitutions, was in 1985 made 'justiciable'—that is to say, made subject to enforcement by the courts.[41] The significance of the move lay in the formal application of the so-called 'enabling clause' included in the Resolution, which obliged the state to create conditions such as to 'enable' Muslims to order their public and private lives 'in accordance with the teaching and requirement of Islam as set out in the Holy

Quran and the Sunna'. It is worth noting that, despite the fanfare sur-rounding Zia's decision to make the Resolution a substantive part of the Constitution, his reforms did not wait for constitutional validation. Much of his Islamization programme was implemented between 1979 and 1984, sanctioned not by the Constitution but by Zia's own Provi-sional Constitutional Order of 1981, which had effectively subordi-nated the Constitution by guaranteeing the military regime immunity from judicial prosecution.

This has lent some credence to the view that Zia's Islamization pro-gramme was designed primarily to buttress his legitimacy rather than to reflect any real shift in favour of an Islamic constitutional identity. Indeed the question of legitimacy was particularly sensitive for Zia, coming as it did soon after the blanket denunciation of Bhutto's gov-ernment as illegitimate both for its fraudulent return to power and its failure to respect Islamic laws. However, Zia's own claim to legitimacy was equally fragile on both secular and religious grounds in that he was neither an elected leader nor recognized as an expert on the inter-pretation of Islamic law (*mujtahid*). But the general understood early on that as long as he could rely on the support of the religious parties, he could claim that together they would ensure that Pakistan fulfilled its destiny as an Islamic state. The question of legitimacy weighed no less heavily on religious parties. Their poor performance in the polls meant that, despite their Islamic credentials, their claim to power lay in agreeing to co-operate as junior partners with a military regime more concerned to restore the authority of the state than to further the agenda of Islamization.[42]

While there is much to substantiate this instrumentalist reading of Zia's Islamization programme, it was also rooted in expectations gen-erated by the struggle over the role of Islam in Pakistan. Zia was unex-ceptional among Pakistan's military rulers in seeking to legitimize his unconstitutional take-over nor the first to be concerned with building a strong state. But the fact that developmental goals such as had pro-vided the basis for Ayub's regime and defined Bhutto's reformist agenda were rejected in favour of a return to a 're-foundation' of the state, suggests that the idea of a national consensus that had lasted until the 1970s had broken down.

Some have gone further, arguing that not only had this 'liberal-modernist' consensus been rendered obsolete by changes in the social and political landscape since 1971, but that its viability had always been in doubt and may even have concealed 'the people's yearning for a simpler past' shaped by a diffuse attachment to Islam that many still associated with Pakistan.[43] The delicate equilibrium between the material interests of the few and the religious concerns of the many that had fuelled the demand for Pakistan, and had held the state together since independence, had effectively crumbled by the 1970s. This opened the way for a new regime to offer the possibility of restoring that balance, even while keeping its own political imperatives in sight. By espousing the Islamist cause, Zia promised nothing less than to elevate the reformation of Pakistan to a 'moral plane' not seen since the heady days leading up to the creation of the country in 1947.[44]

Between 1979 and 1983 Zia introduced a range of measures aimed at laying the foundations for a comprehensive Islamic system.[45] They included legal reforms, economic policy, educational planning and the enforcement of a harsh, religiously sanctioned, penal code. A new set of so-called *shariat* laws backed by *shariat* courts was rigorously applied with draconian punishments to curb adultery, false witness, theft and the consumption of alcohol. Far-reaching policies aimed at Islamizing the economy were announced, though these were less systematically applied. They involved interest-free banking and the introduction of a controversial Islamic tax (*zakat*) system that met with protest from the country's Shia minority, who resisted the extension of its Sunni Hanafi provisions.

But it was through education that Zia hoped most effectively to consolidate Islamization. Under his regime Quranic schools (or *madrassas*), established with the help of *zakat* funds and support from private sponsors with privileged access to coffers in Saudi Arabia, worked in tandem with state schools to help forge a new national consensus. At the heart of this exercise lay the promotion of the new notion of an 'ideology of Pakistan', which received official sanction in a 1981 directive instructing the authors of school and college textbooks to 'guide students towards the ultimate goal of Pakistan—the creation of a completely Islamised state'.[46] This now became the key reference point for debate and the benchmark against which to test the authenticity of Pakistan as an ideological 'Islamic state'.

Secular-minded critics of this new consensus have long regarded the notion of the 'ideology of Pakistan' as the brain-child of the religious right, especially the Jamaat-i-Islami. Its main purpose, they argue, was to inject this ideology with 'Islam' and to equate it with Pakistan's

EL CAMINO COLLEGE LIBRARY

founding ideology, the 'two-nation' theory, in an attempt to obscure the secular content favoured by Jinnah.[47] But they also recognize that the ease with which the two came to be used interchangeably after Zia seized power was facilitated by the persistent lack of a clear consensus on the identity of the state and by the failure to recognise the 'definite conflict' between the League's secular leadership and the party's more religious rank and file.[48] Most importantly, they acknowledge that Jinnah's increasingly equivocal stance on the place of Islam in public life, which led to his many compromises with the *ulama* in the run-up to Partition, enabled Zia and his religious allies to exploit Jinnah's failure to project a strong secular vision and to impose their own idea of Pakistan as an Islamic state.[49]

Others deconstructed the significance of the ideology of Pakistan by suggesting that vital differences separated Zia's vision of Pakistan as an ideological state based on Islam from Jinnah's more liberal understanding of a Muslim state diffusely informed by Islam.[50] They argue that while the former was set to enforce Islam, often of a doctrinaire variety, the second aimed (in the spirit of the Objectives Resolution) merely to create an 'enabling environment' for Muslims to organise their lives without judicial or legal sanctions. Over time these differences were steadily eroded owing largely to Zia's co-option of religious parties, which pressed for an ever more rigid understanding of Islam as 'a set of regulative, punitive and extractive commands'.[51] This particular understanding of Islam also helped secure Zia's main objective—to ensure that Islamization remained a state-sponsored and state-controlled exercise. By claiming that the Islamic state would act as a divine instrument with 'uncontested sovereignty', Zia hoped to widen the reach of the state.[52] In time these efforts met with resistance not from a re-invigorated 'liberal-modernist' consensus, but from emboldened *ulama* bent on a campaign of 'shariatization', which threatened the very existence of the state, as is discussed below.

Until then the real value of Pakistan as an ideological state was to inject Zia's military regime with some legitimacy. Zia himself skilfully managed to co-opt pro-Islamic parties, notably the Jamaat-i-Islami, whose standing among a burgeoning class of small merchants, shopkeepers and new professionals was an invaluable asset to a regime seeking to widen its support, especially in the early years. But Zia also understood that the backing of these new, and as yet insecure, middle classes demanded re-packaging his policies not as revolutionary, but as part of a process of Islamization that had already commenced at independence and had then been deliberately thwarted by the country's secular leadership.

It came as no surprise that Zia moved speedily to revive the debate about the so-called 'repugnancy clause' enshrined in the Constitution, which obliged the state to disallow laws judged to be inconsistent with 'Islam' but did not provide firm mechanism for doing so. In 1979 he ordered the creation of four Shariat benches in the High Courts of Punjab, Sind, the North West Frontier Province and Balochistan to establish a mechanism to rule on the 'repugnancy' of laws suspected of being un-Islamic. In the 1950s and 1960s agreement over the mechanism had been repeatedly frustrated by the struggle between those who favoured the creation of a special body of religious experts to decide on the matter and those who insisted that the final decision should be left to parliament. Constitutional debates over the question of repugnancy had also been mired over whether laws were required merely to be consistent with Islam (and if so which Islam) or specifically with the injunctions of the Quran and Sunna. Zia had little to fear from these debates. With parliament dissolved and a Constitution that still formally subscribed to the principle of divine sovereignty, he was confident enough to press ahead with his agenda.

Some argue that Zia's agenda bore all the hallmarks of a cosmetic exercise. For instance, limits were imposed on the Shariat benches of the four provincial high courts, since their rulings to bring laws in line with Islam were made subject to appeal to the Shariat Appellate Bench of the Supreme Court. The powers of the Federal Shariat Court, established in 1980, were also circumscribed by a bar on reviewing Ayub's Muslim Family Laws Ordinance, which was still widely condemned by the *ulama* and their Islamist allies as a blatant violation of the *sharia*. And their influence, now embodied in the Council of Islamic Ideology, was also curbed by the Council's strictly advisory role, making it in effect subordinate to the Federal Shariat Court, which reserved the right to issue mandatory rulings.

These measures, seeking to incorporate Islamic laws into the framework of the modern state, soon ran into difficulties. But unlike in the 1950s and 1960s, the struggle did not so much involve liberals and traditionalists divided by their interpretations of Islam, but the country's Shia minority, which was determined to resist laws it claimed were tantamount to the imposition of a Sunni programme of Islamization.

Their anger had been fuelled in 1981 by the failure to include any Shia as a full-time judge in the Federal Shariat Court of *ulama*. This led to mass protests by Shias, who also refused to accept the mandatory collection by the state of the alms tax (*zakat*). Their objections centred on claims that since no state was worthy of the respect enjoyed by the Prophet's order, Shias chose to give alms directly to the poor.

Although Zia was eventually forced to exempt Shias from laws relating to the payment of the alms tax, the bitter sectarian divisions unleashed by the controversy aroused suspicion that Islamization was a guise for the 'Sunnification' of Pakistan.[53] Zia also faced the wrath of his allies, especially the Sunni Deobandi *ulama* and an increasingly strident Sunni political constituency. They argued that as Sunnis were a majority in Pakistan, the state had the responsibility to enforce compliance with Sunni laws rather than agreeing to concessions for the Shia minority. This sectarian discourse, masquerading as the rights of the majority, soon triggered a wider campaign for the recognition of Pakistan as a Sunni state—a goal some believed was within reach with the application of Islamic laws that appeared to have settled the contested issue of Pakistan's identity as an Islamic state.

In fact, the issue of Pakistan as an Islamic state was far from resolved. This was nowhere as dramatically highlighted as in the prolonged campaign launched by women's groups, outraged by laws that sought to regulate the conduct of women and revise their status as equal citizens. In a series of decrees issued in 1979 the military regime had announced that it would replace existing (colonial) penal codes with what came to be known as the *Hudood* (punishment) Ordinances. These prescribed strict codes of punishment for criminal offences under Islamic law, including adultery. The Federal Shariat Court was also mandated to amend an 1872 law and replace it with an Islamic Law of Evidence (*Qanoon-i-Shahadat*), which regarded the value of a woman's testimony in court to be worth half that of a man.

Both measures aroused the fury of women's groups, most notably the newly founded Women's Action Forum (WAF), which campaigned against these and other measures, including discriminatory provisions relating to retribution and blood-money.[54] Though the agitation drew mainly on the support of urban middle-class women, it nevertheless represented the first co-ordinated opposition to Islamization. The WAF also drew strength from the emergence of a broad-based pro-democracy movement that brought together ethnic and Shia parties in alliance under the aegis of the Movement for the Restoration for Democracy (MRD).

Two issues were of particular concern to the WAF and its allies among other women's groups opposed to the reforms. First, there was the definition of sexual crimes under Islamic laws introduced by Zia's regime, which refused to distinguish between rape and adultery and equated sexual misdemeanours with crimes against the state punishable by death. Second, there was the introduction of a Law of Evidence, apparently sanctioned by Islam, which undermined the legal status of women and the equality guaranteed to them as citizens by the Constitution. Although some have argued that these measures were also cosmetic in that they were neither widely nor even deliberately aimed at women,[55] there can be little doubt that they amounted to an unprecedented attempt to institutionalise the subordination of women in Pakistan on the basis of the narrowest possible reading of Islam.

Indeed, for groups like the WAF, this was the nub of the problem. Their opposition to the reforms was framed not in the universal discourse of human rights but in the assertion that the laws bore no relation to real Islam. The emphasis on equal civil and political rights for women only seemed further to accentuate the dilemma underlined by Metcalf 'of trying to speak both an Islamic and a liberal language and yet to avoid what are commonly taken to be the ultimate implications of both'.[56] One of its many consequences was to force women's groups to oscillate between two equally hazardous alternatives: either to acknowledge the merits of Islamization (albeit with a reformist-liberal edge) to shake off the charge of impiety, or set even more stringent standards for real Islamic reform than those pursued by the regime and its orthodox allies.

These dilemmas were in part symptomatic of WAF's class origins, which rendered it both socially conservative and inclined to adopt a functional stance that has been described as the 'convenience of subservience'.[57] Determined by patterns of social hierarchy and powerful norms of social exchange, it encouraged educated, urban and upper-class women otherwise in favour of emancipation to resist 'challenging their prescribed roles in society ... which afford[ed] privileges not available to women lower down the rungs of the social hierarchy'.[58] Nowhere was this more in evidence than in the response to General Zia's Islamization programme, which outraged well-born *sharif* Pakistani women accustomed to enjoy the benefits accruing from access to elite education, class and social connections. It was this that drove an elite band of feminists to stage a rear-guard action, which sensitized more women across the social spectrum to new ways of engaging with politics.

Women were not the only force to challenge Zia's attempt to impose his version of revivalist Islam on Pakistan. Ethnic forces, which resurfaced with vigour under his regime, also took up the cudgels. Most of the tension was concentrated in Sind where Sindhi regionalists were still smarting from the humiliation of Bhutto's ouster and the pain of his execution. Many of Zia's Islamization policies were condemned as a ruse to perpetuate Punjabi domination with the backing of the army. Other ethnic groups, including the Baloch and the Pathans, also regarded his Islamization programme with suspicion. Zia won them over, albeit temporarily, by resorting to appeasement.[59] His alliance with *ulama* parties headed by the Jamiat-ul Ulama-i-Islam (JUI) was also instrumental in containing ethnic discontent in Balochistan where, as in the North West Frontier Province, it enjoyed influence. Indeed, the rhetoric of Islam then fuelling the war in Afghanistan was significant in curbing Pashtun sub-nationalism, which was to steadily give way to the language of militant Islam and then to support the covert, US-led, campaign to oust Soviet forces from Pakistan's neighbour.

But while some ethnic forces challenged Zia's rhetoric of Islamic solidarity by highlighting the importance of ethnic identity, others adapted by appropriating Islam to define their ethnic identity. This was nowhere more in evidence than in the political mobilization of Urdu-speaking migrants *mohajirs*, who by 'ethnicizing Islam' in the process of forging a collective muhajir identity, showed how profoundly Islamization had altered the complex relationship between ethnicity and religion in the 1980s. More importantly, it also demonstrated how the language of high Islam, once commonly associated with the state, could be reshaped in opposition to the state.[60] By the 1980s there were also indications that Zia's engagement with Islamism had wrought deep changes in the orientation of the country's religious establishment—changes that prompted a questioning of the very legitimacy of the state as the repository of Pakistan's national identity. Where Islamization had once loudly proclaimed the reach of the strong state, the state's very susceptibility to a new process of 'shariatization' revealed the formative weaknesses of both the Pakistani state and the country's national identity.

The lure of shariatization

Indeed, the process of shariatization[61] needs to be carefully distinguished from the better-known phenomenon of Islamization that has been most closely associated in Pakistan with the military regime of General Zia ul Haq. The differences between the two are often blurred by the common assumption that both share an uncompromising emphasis on the enforcement of Islamic law, at the expense of a commitment to the broader ethical foundations of Islam that held sway in the early discourse about the nation-state in Pakistan. Nevertheless, the social and political forces behind each of these processes were recognizably different.

Islamization in Pakistan was largely a state-driven process, which at times has enjoyed the support of the country's powerful Westernized elites. The latter relied on a statist interpretation of Islam to oppose the populist policies favoured by Zulfiqar Ali Bhutto and, in time, increasingly espoused a culture that was distinctly Islamic in tone.[62] By contrast, the recent phenomenon of shariatization corresponds more closely to what some scholars have described as the indigenization of the post-colonial state in Pakistan and the steady nativization of its society.[63] Both have marked the rise of so-called vernacular groups, which are neither Anglicized nor Western but recognizably modern on their own terms—that is 'entertaining instrumental rationality' in the feverish pursuit of material advancement without, for example, inviting cultural intrusion into the domain of social, especially sexual, relations.[64] Politically, their aim is to share centre-stage with Pakistan's still largely dominant Westernized elites and lay claim to a slice of the country's economic and intellectual resources, while attempting to reshape society to secure their new position.[65] Among their intellectual resources is the language of religious sectarianism. Although it has been used to redefine the meaning of the national community by seeking to exclude Muslim minority sects, like the Ahmedis and the Shias, and to secure constitutional recognition for Pakistan as a (majority) Sunni state, it is in fact congruent with their very modern aims.

To highlight these differences is not to suggest that Islamization in Pakistan is synonymous with what commonly passes as establishment Islam—as found in some parts of the Middle East, notably Egypt and Saudi Arabia, where the state has worked closely with the Islamic religious establishment, especially the *ulama*. Nor is it intended to imply that shariatization should be understood as another version of so-called popular Islam. Indeed, both assumptions would be wrong: state-sponsored Islamization of the kind favoured by General Zia was primarily an exercise aimed *against* the Islamic religious establishment. Its main proponents were lay activists associated with Pakistan's premier Islamist party, the Jamaat-i-Islami, who made no secret of their hostility to the traditional, mainly Sunni, clerical establishment. Until the mid-1980s, it was these lay activists, rather than the *ulama* that were the driving force behind Islamization.[66]

For its part, the assumption that the roots of shariatization can be traced to some tradition of popular Islam in Pakistan is also ill-founded. Popular Islam, as commonly understood in Pakistan, is associated with Sunni Barelvis, who still predominate over vast swathes of the Punjab and the hinterlands of Sind.[67] Better known for their veneration of saints and shrines, their ritual practices show a clear preference for the Sufi 'way' (*tariqah*) over the *sharia*. In fact, the main Barelvi party, the Jamiat-ul Ulama-i-Pakistan (JUP), was very much a junior partner in the former governing coalitions in Balochistan and the North West, where shariatization was strongest. These former ruling coalitions were dominated, by the more reformist-minded followers of the Jamiat-ul Ulema-i-Islam (JUI), whose leadership represents Pakistan's religious establishment and which, until recently, was better known for its politically conservative inclinations.

Since the 1980s however this religious establishment has undergone a process of radicalization that has enabled it successfully to appropriate the rhetoric of political Islam, typical of the Islamist lay intelligentsia represented by the Jamaat-i-Islami.[68] Zia's military regime initially sought to exploit the tension between Islamists and traditional clerics as a means of staying in power. But faced with the risk of revolt by a disinherited younger generation, the regime turned to the conservative *ulama*, who it believed held the key to social peace. This concern with social order was reflected in Zia's economic policies, which placed a premium on the private sector. Their purpose was to ensure the creation of a middle- and lower-middle class base for his regime that could effectively resist any threat from the Pakistan People's Party's lower class base of support, whose aspirations had remained largely unfulfilled during the party's tenure in power. The *ulama*'s successful co-optation of those Kepel refers to as the 'devout bourgeoisie',[69] who formed the backbone of Zia's support, was the key to its political effectiveness in the service of Zia's regime. In exchange the *ulama* demanded greater autonomy, especially over the administration of quranic schools and religious seminaries (*madrassas*), which by the early 1980s were serving as magnets for a younger generation. Frustrated by the failure of Bhutto's economic policies, which had promised to secure *roti, kapara awr makan* (food, clothing and shelter), they now turned eagerly to the ethics of *sharia*-based Islam as an alternative precisely when it also seemed poised to define public policy and determine its direction in their favour. Through this complex process Zia helped create what has been described as 'an *ulama* wing of Islamism, which would increasingly assert itself at the cost of lay thinkers and organizations'.[70]

The *sharia*-based Islam which now emerged in Pakistan was rooted in the Deobandi school founded near Delhi in 1867.[71] Its discourse was less concerned with the creation of an Islamic state—the object of Islamization—than with the establishment of the 'political hegemony of Islam'. Unlike lay Islamists, for whom the Islamic nature of the state has always been more important than the strict application of the *sharia*, the primary objective of these 'neo-fundamentalist' *ulama*[72] has been (in true Deobandi style) the reform of society through the implementation of the *sharia*. In the worldview of the Jamiat-ul Ulama-i-Islam, which has been nurtured by its extremist off-shoots led by the so-called '*petty ulama*',[73] the state is, at best, an instrument to be used to transform society along Islamic lines. Its limited role is sustained by an Islamic discourse that has habitually regarded the territorial state as an artificial construct, whose physical boundaries are judged to be transient and subversive of a presumed universal community of believers (*umma*).[74]

The implications of this discourse for the development of Pakistani nationalism contrast sharply with those of Islamization. The latter was grounded in the Pakistani nation-state, despite the global scope of Islam. The importance attached to the capture of the state also meant that the legitimacy of any programme of Islamization had to be sought, above all, from a domestic and national constituency. By contrast, shariatization aims both to question the validity of the state and to influence the debate on national identity by redefining Pakistani nationalism primarily in terms of its relation to an imagined extra-territorial 'community of believers'. More significantly, perhaps, the secondary importance attached to the control of the state has diminished the value of nurturing a domestic constituency. This has come at a time when the manipulation of extra-territorial Islamic networks and a strategy of political violence are increasingly available to ascendant political forces, given Pakistan's deep involvement with the Afghan war and its aftermath.

Indeed, the ideology of shariatization emerged against the background of the Soviet invasion of Afghanistan and the Afghan civil war, which allowed transnational Islamic religious-political networks to compete with national states as sources of patronage. But it was also grounded in history. Its roots go back to the nineteenth century, when teams of peripatetic Muslim holy men and preachers journeyed from India to the Arabian Peninsula and returned armed with more doctrinaire readings of Islam. They inspired the great *jihad* movements of the 1820s, which galvanized thousands of Indian Muslims to trek across India's north-western frontier to Kabul to expand the social space for an ideal Muslim society purged of pagan practices.[75] This doctrinaire version of Islam competed with and retarded modernizing trends among British India's Muslims. A century later, as Muslims in the Middle East prepared to come to terms with the nation-state, thousands of Indian Muslims were caught up in a drive to protect the Turkish Caliphate. Tens of thousands once again migrated from India to Afghanistan—in their terms, from the realm of the infidel (*dar ul harb*) to the realm of the Muslim (*dar ul Islam*).[76] A decade later, in the late 1920s one of the most important transnational (and ostensibly apolitical) grass-roots movements, the Tablighi Jamaat, began to take shape among Indian Muslims. An offshoot of the Deobandi movement, it today enjoys wide support inside Pakistan, where it is dedicated to re-affirming a Muslim religio-cultural self and to forging an 'identity constituted without reference to territory'.[77]

This transnational vision in Pakistan is also a legacy of the intellectual tension between Islam and nationalism, which found one of its sharpest expressions in the thinking of Muhammad Iqbal. Widely credited with laying the ideological foundations of a separate Muslim state in India, Iqbal was never, ironically, a supporter of nationalism, let alone of nationalism among Muslims: he objected to the claim of modern nationalism to supplant the universal community (*umma*) as the sole focus of the Muslim's political loyalty.[78] Maulana Mawdudi, the leader until his death in 1979 of the Jamaat-i-Islami, though committed in principle to an Islamic state, founded his party in 1941 as a movement opposed to nationalism, which he condemned as a Western conspiracy. Mawdudi also denounced Jinnah's campaign for Pakistan not just on the grounds that it was a secular project but also because it embodied a particularism that undermined the transnational Muslim community.[79]

While these tensions between nationalism and transnational religions are by no means exceptional to Pakistan, they were of particular importance to the country owing to its formative weaknesses as a state, the indeterminacy of its political boundaries and the early onset of authoritarianism, which made resorting to Islam as a legitimacy bank of last resort endemic to its tortuous political history. In 1947 Pakistan had emerged out of a bloody partition as a territorial absurdity with its two wings (West and East Pakistan, now Bangladesh) separated by more than 1,000 miles of Indian territory. Moreover, for more than half their length, Pakistan's current borders to the west (the so-called Durand Line separating it from Afghanistan) and the north (the so-called Line of Control bordering Indian-held Kashmir) do not correspond to internationally recognized boundaries. In the areas to the west, bordering Afghanistan, there exist in addition large territories designated as 'tribal areas' which are subject to tribal laws rather than to the writ of the national government.[80] For almost a quarter of a century this state, which many regarded as merely a congeries of provincial units, endured, based on a volatile mix of a national culture founded on an ideology which transcended national borders, weak development efforts, political authoritarianism and US patronage.

Eventually this mix would yield to the contradictions inherent in the national imagining of Pakistan. The secession of the country's eastern wing was a watershed, reviving painful memories of the refusal in 1947 of millions of Indian Muslims to migrate to, or partake in, the great 'Muslim hope' that was Pakistan. Nevertheless, many hoped that, with the traumas of Partition behind it and the secession of East Pakistan a reality, the new country would emerge in 1971 as a more intelligible nation-state. It did not: new challenges surfaced in which the extra-territoriality of Pakistan's putative Muslim identity, hitherto contained, burst open in a changed, more conducive, context. Rather than any normalization, the re-drawing of Pakistan's borders after the secession of its eastern wing in 1971 merely strengthened the denationalizing tendencies inherent in Pakistan's founding ideology, Islam. This was prompted in part by a geo-political reorientation towards the

Muslim Middle East. Of course this re-orientation need not, as it did, have entailed a loosening of Pakistan's South Asian identity. But the loss of East Bengal meant that the very idea of Pakistan had to be reconfigured from a South Asian refugee experience, which demanded bridge-building between disparate communities, to one 'more akin to Islamist doctrine and precept than that suggested by the constrained and tortured secularism of the earlier vision'.[81]

Although Islamization in Pakistan is usually attributed to General Zia, its pull, as we have seen, was already evident in his immediate predecessor, Zulfiqar Ali Bhutto. But while Bhutto set the stage, it was General Zia who deepened the nexus between Islamization and the state, first establishing a connection between the lay Jamaat-i-Islami and the *ulama*, and then launching a comprehensive program of Islamic reform that paved the way for a distinctly legalistic (as opposed to an ethical) approach to Pakistan's Muslim identity. This focus on Islamic legal injunctions and their implementation called for a new Islamic bureaucracy, which in turn required new alliances such as that between the military regime and sections of the traditional religious establishment, namely the *ulama*. They presided over a vast network of religious seminaries—the *madrassas*—which now became the main suppliers of the cadres who were to administer Zia's Islamic state.[82] Significantly, the state patronage of the *madrassas*, to the extent that they revived in a new, more state-oriented and centralized form, Islamic educational networks that had hitherto depended upon local structures of political authority and social control, has been regarded as a sign of the growing indigenization of the post-colonial state in Pakistan.[83]

Although most *ulama*, who emerged as power-brokers in the later years of the Zia era were politically cautious Deobandis, Zia's new dispensation tempted enough of them with an opportunity to occupy a legitimate space in the political arena and in modern sectors of state and society.[84] Their control over the *madrassas* and the placing of their graduates in government agencies and state institutions also gave them the required leverage to train a citizenry that many hoped would be more inclined to accept Islamic ideology as 'an appropriate anchor for the conduct of politics'.[85] It was this close involvement of the *madrassas* with the state that made possible their transformation from centres of traditional religious learning into politicized, modernized (and also militarized) institutions that, in time, would radically challenge the state's right to control policy-making, interpret Islam, and define the parameters of Pakistani nationalism.

The newly politicized clerical establishment could challenge the state in this fashion, setting off shariatization, largely because of its traditional autonomy, which stemmed in good part from the financing of *madrassas*, especially the larger ones, out of voluntary contributions (*zakat*).[86] And although the *madrassas* that now proliferated in Pakistan (officially estimated in 2002 to stand at around 10,000 with more than a million and a half students under training)[87] benefited from extensive state funding in the 1980s, the *ulama* resisted the control that might normally have been expected to accompany such patronage. Indeed, influential *ulama* groups have continued to resist state encroachment into the domain of religious education—whether through financial or curricular regulation[88]—even under the military-dominated regime of former President Parvez Musharraf and despite intense international pressure.[89]

The institutional capacity of the clerical establishment to resist and stand aloof from the state was also encouraged by the increasingly strained relations between Zia's military regime and the Islamist intelligentsia, which under the Jamaat-i-Islami had by the mid 1980s lost confidence in the credibility of Zia's Islamizing agenda and opted to side with the nascent pro-democracy movement. In 1987 the party's new leader, Qazi Husain Ahmed, declared that neither Islamization nor the Afghan war justified Zia's abrogation of democracy, and more extraordinarily still, maintained that Pakistan's political predicament could be solved only by ending martial law rather than promulgating the shariat bill (which took effect in June 1988).[90] This afforded space to *ulama* parties like the Jamiat-ul Ulama-i-Islam, now undergoing a process of change from religious conservatism to political radicalism with the help of militant groups nurtured by the war in Afghanistan, to shape a new kind of Islamic discourse less concerned with the identity of the nation-state than with the transformation of society along the lines of a doctrinaire reading of Islam.

The Afghan civil war erupted in 1979 and its call to *jihad*, while heavily dependent on covert material assistance from the United States and sections of the Pakistan's ruling military establishment, relied for its day-to-day implementation on transnational Islamic religious networks. While the facts and profound implications of these events for Pakistani politics have already been extensively documented,[91] what needs to be emphasized here is how this involvement fundamentally re-shaped Pakistan's Muslim identity by gradually eroding popular attachment to local symbolic sites of traditional Islam, to the land and its frontiers, and to local hierarchies of rural and tribal society. What emerged instead, under pressure from an increasingly radicalized and politicized clergy, was the steady decontextualization of religious practices based on a strict, literalist reading of Islamic law, which many have since loosely described as 'neo-Wahhabi Islam'. While the United States' pursuit of its Cold War objectives were critical to this development, it is significant that Pakistan proved also to be environmentally friendly to this culture.

Part of the explanation lies in the re-emergence of the question of its Islamic identity after the loss of East Pakistan. New doubts arose about the merits of Pakistan's local, 'Indian' roots, and by extension 'Indian Islam', whose vulnerability to non-Muslim influences had been the subject of debate among Muslim reformers in the nineteenth century. They included Iqbal, who had already identified 'Arabian Islam' as a corrective to more 'corrupted' forms of 'Indian [and Persian] Islam'.[92] As such thinking assumed a new and greater resonance in redefining Pakistan's Muslim identity, the influx of more than three million Afghan refugees in the 1980s also radically altered the country's political landscape. They included a first generation of mostly literate and urbanized Afghans who, while in exile in Pakistan, quickly fell under the sway of the Jamaat-i-Islami, which until at least the mid-1980s was chiefly responsible for funnelling US and Arab funds to the Afghan mujahedin.

But the Jamaat's steady alienation from General Zia's military regime led the regime to woo the *ulama* parties such as the Jamiat-ul Ulama-i-Islam, which, having already been politicized under Zia, now sharpened its political profile. These parties appealed to by now 'de-tribalized' young Afghan refugees whose desperate circumstances made them especially responsive to a more radical brand of Islam. The *ulama* parties and their network of *madrassas* took in (almost always as boarders) Afghan children, who interacted with young Pakistanis of different ethnic origins—Pashtuns (like themselves) but also Balochis, Sindhis and Punjabis. Instructed in Arabic and Urdu, they became instrumental in the creation of a putative 'universal Islamic personality' structured around Deobandi ideology.[93]

This compelling vision exercised a powerful pull on Pakistan—a state still in search of an identity. Of course the vision also served the needs of Pakistan's most significant state institution—the army—which would rely on transnational Islamic groups to implement its regional foreign policy formula, and in so doing, emerged as a key agent of shariatization. But the shifts contained in this vision were equally symptomatic of economic and social decline in Pakistan—a decline that stemmed from core uncertainties about the direction of change and about the role of Islam in determining the priorities of national development.

4

THE DILEMMAS OF DEVELOPMENT

THE UNCERTAINTIES OF CHANGE

The ideological ferment of the 1970s and 1980s, which led to growing Islamic consciousness in Pakistan, compounded the uncertainty over the country's national identity and the role of Islam in shaping it. The constitutional debates of the 1950s had failed to resolve the question of whether Pakistan was intended to be an Islamic state that privileged Muslims, or a Muslim nation-state that would guarantee the equality of all its citizens. Ayub's secular-oriented military regime in the 1960s sought to ease these tensions by drawing attention away from the historical purpose of the state to a concern with economic and social development. But his divisive policies weakened the effort to mould a more secular national identity. The prospects of the latter were severely weakened after 1971 with the loss of East Pakistan and the rise of Islamist forces ranged against the secular discourse of Bhutto's People's Party. Their position strengthened in the 1980s and 1990s with their entry into the political mainstream, which dramatically sharpened the profile of Pakistan's putative Islamic identity.

The economic and social implications of the struggle over Pakistan's national identity and its relation to Islam took time to surface. One reason was the overwhelming importance attached to framing an Islamic constitution, which dominated public debates in the 1950. By contrast, the clamour over the direction of economic and social policies and their supposed agreement with the state's Islamic foundations was relatively subdued, notwithstanding the (albeit modest) attention given to these issues prior to the independence of Pakistan.

It was not until the 1960s, with the onset of Ayub's ambitious development programme that the spotlight turned on the economic and social complexion of a state that professed to be founded on Islam. By the 1970s this interest had widened, stimulated by the popular appeal of Bhutto's egalitarian economic and social agenda re-packaged as Islamic socialism. But it was also driven by a more pointed moral engagement in the 1980s and 1990s with issues of corruption in public life and the desirability of extending certain forms of Muslim religious education to protect the Islamic character of the state. Indeed one of the consequences of the pressure to measure economic and social policies against yet to be agreed standards of Islam has been to privilege a moral discourse of corruption. Though widely held to be a by-product of inequitable economic policies and poor governance, corruption has come increasingly to be judged in the light of standards of morality expected of a state that still claims responsibility, and is held accountable, for upholding Islam in public life. But here again there is little consensus on which Islam is more representative of the moral probity of the Pakistani state. There is a discourse on corruption in which the culture of a high scriptural Islam commonly associated with the country's religious establishment has long found an echo in the legalist bias of the modernist Islam advocated by Pakistan's elite. Together they have emerged as critical voices against the so-called low, regional expressions of Islam espoused by hereditary landowning classes backed by local religious authorities (Sufi *pirs*), whose habits of patronage (*riwaj*) are believed to have encouraged the spread of corruption. The refrain of this high Islam with its contempt for regional forms of unreformed Islam has intensified public engagement with economic and social issues. In so doing, it has also created a climate working to the advantage of a religious establishment whose long-standing interest in the moral reform of state and society has found a ready platform in the increasingly politicized agenda of the ubiquitous Qoranic school, the *madrassa*.

As in matters political and constitutional, the debate on economic and social change has been notable for its marked absence of consensus regarding the meaning of Islam. While secular politicians loudly claimed that Pakistan would be a laboratory for Islamic principles of economic equality and social justice, their failure to live up to the expectations fostered by these claims left them vulnerable to their critics among the *ulama* and Islamist parties intent on testing the Islamic credentials of the state. The differences between the two sides have also brought into focus the perennial struggle between those content to accept an *ad hoc* role for Islam in the sphere of policy, subject by definition to change, and those determined to elevate Islam to the status of an immutable Law.

Free and unequal

It is generally assumed that issues of Muslim welfare and equity were marginal to the idea of Pakistan. While this is true when compared to the overwhelming concern with the defence of Muslim cultural identity, upon which all else was seen to depend, they were by no means minor concerns. Although the material interests of the Muslim salariat, who set the agenda for Pakistan, rarely extended beyond the demand for bureaucratic access,[1] the emergence of non-salariat groups, such as the large Bengali Muslim peasantry, in the movement for Pakistan ensured that issues of equity had to be addressed. More importantly, for these non-salariat classes questions of equity were, more often than not, framed in the language of Islamic social justice.[2]

This was encouraged as much by the persistent if nebulous connection between Islam and the idea of Pakistan as by the influence of modernist interpretations of Islam that dominated discussion about the nation and that regarded the Pakistan project as a quest for distributive justice grounded in Islamic principles. Some core themes gained credence among prominent Muslims who favoured the idea of a separate Muslim political order in India and in time would come to be closely associated with Pakistan. They included luminaries as diverse as Iqbal in Punjab and the radical Bengali Muslim peasant leader, Maulana Abdul Hamid Khan Bhashani (1885–1976). Both held to the view that the consolidation of a Muslim political sphere was essential to put in place economic arrangements consistent with Islam. Indeed, for Iqbal the vision of a consolidated centre of Muslim power in South Asia was inconceivable without acknowledging the egalitarian ethos underlying Islam, which he believed could not be guaranteed in conditions marred by the structural inequalities of Hindu society.

There was little consensus on what economic terms of 'Islam' were required to ensure a more equal society for the Muslims of India. While Iqbal and others emphatically declared that some forms of capitalist development were inconsistent with the spirit of Islam, neither he nor those who shared his vision, especially in East Bengal, felt able to bring their version of Islam in line with socialism. The fear of being seen to compromise the spiritual foundations of Islam, and the hostility of the Muslim League's conservative leadership to any far-reaching economic reforms, undermined the practical influence of a socialist reading of Islam. Jinnah's own ambivalence about the direction of economic policy also compounded the uncertainty over Pakistan's economic complexion and its relationship to Islam. While known to give serious thought to the urgency of economic reform as an Islamic imperative, and even on occasion to question the compatibility of capitalism with Islam, Jinnah's economic instincts were overwhelmingly conservative and favoured private property. Like the leadership succeeding him, he addressed popular expectations by displaying his commitment to the *objectives* of economic and social justice believed to conform to Islam rather than by implementing an economic blueprint consistent with recognizably Islamic measures, such as interest-free banking.

The issue here is not so much Jinnah's sincerity as a politician, but his uncertainty over the socio-economic implications of Islam for Pakistan. The latter haunted the economic debate in the 1960s when ideological battles over the merits of public and private enterprise in Pakistan were judged as much by their success in meeting standards of economic efficiency as by meeting those consistent with the ideals of distributive justice endorsed by Islam. Bhutto's appeal to 'Islamic socialism' in the 1970s and General Zia's attempts to fashion an 'Islamic economic society' along capitalist lines in the 1980s offered two very different understandings of Islam.

Pakistan's developmental trajectory is often seen as an example of a 'dual paradox': while achieving extraordinarily high rates of growth, there has been hardly any significant expansion in public services or reduction in poverty.[3] Why have welfare and equity consistently taken second place in Pakistan? The question is worth re-visiting given claims that the demand for an independent Muslim state was as much a struggle for Muslim power as for economic justice, which Islam demands and, which, it was believed, could not be guaranteed under Hindu-majority rule. Historically, much of the explanation lies in the weakness of the League's popular roots. Stymied from the outset by the dominance of a leadership deeply entrenched in the Muslim landed and commercial classes of north and central India,[4] these roots were barely nourished during the League's campaign for separate Muslim nationhood. The League's near pathological fear of mass politics, which characterised the movement for much of the 1920s, found expression in Jinnah's preference for 'constitutionalism'. It not only justified the League's disdain for Gandhi's civil disobedience movement, but also distanced it from popular campaigns for greater social and economic equality unleashed by Gandhi. Although by the late 1930s the League seemed ready to temper this innate conservatism by calling for 'the social, economic and educational uplift of the Muslim rural population', its opposition to the expropriation of private property, in marked contrast to Congress, was to be a lasting fissure between the two organizations. In time it set the tone for the very different priorities accorded by India and Pakistan to social and economic welfare.[5]

These differences also expressed the gulf that separated Jinnah from his peers in Congress, notably Jawaharlal Nehru. According to Wolpert, Jinnah's highly respected biographer: '[e]ven as Jawaharlal placed increasing faith in socialist solutions for India's problems of poverty, Jinnah retreated more than ever behind the bastions of private property. His growing passion for real estate ... [would] soon rival his interest in politics. Private property, most of it forever rooted on Indian soil, became, ironically enough, almost as fascinating a diversion for Jinnah's mind and energies during the last lonely decade of his life as Pakistan itself.'[6] The League's development as a mass-based party in the early 1940s appeared, paradoxically, to strengthen rather than dilute Jinnah's appreciation of the value of private property. His entry into the so-called Muslim majority areas of Punjab and Sind required accommodation with the Muslim landed gentry, who dominated local politics. With the League bereft of any popular roots in these regions—the result of years of neglect stemming from its preoccupation with the interests of a mainly urban north Indian Muslim elite—it had no choice but to forge alliances with local, mainly landed elites. However, the price for their support of the League's still unsubstantiated claim to be the sole representative of Muslim India was nothing less than the freedom to protect their economic interests against the egalitarian currents then sweeping Asia. They were backed by a powerful coalition of rural-based Muslim religious leaders—the *sajjida nashin*—who themselves controlled vast estates and were often closely connected by marriage to the leading landlord families.[7]

This is not to say that the League or Jinnah acted out of compulsion or were reluctant partners of forces hostile to economic and social reform: on the contrary. In East Bengal, the party's high command, with Jinnah's support, actively sought in the 1940s to contain the fiery, radical rhetoric of popular Bengali leaders such as A.K. Fazlul Haq and Abul Hashim. Instead it sided with mainly Urdu-speaking, conservative, landowners out of touch with the concerns of the rising Bengali vernacular elite represented by Haq and Hashim. Both aroused fears of a 'revolutionary' agenda that conjured visions of a communist take-over among their detractors. Neither was ever nominated to serve as a member of the League's powerful Working Committee.[8]

Jinnah himself made no secret of his disdain for their brand of Bengali populist politics. But he was also quick to dismiss the landed barons of Punjab and Sind as 'spineless'.[9] These mutually contradictory positions have been interpreted as evidence of Jinnah's lack of interest in developing a coherent economic programme—the claim being that issues of power and representation far outweighed any concern with Muslim economic and social development.[10] This is true, but it also risks simplifying Jinnah's uncertainty about the economic implications of a Muslim national identity predicated on a relationship to Islam—especially as it pertained to the ownership, production and distribution of wealth. But with the seemingly inexorable drive in favour of a 'Muslim' Pakistan, Jinnah could no longer evade the question of which economic system (capitalist, socialist or mixed) would best achieve the standards of distributive justice endorsed by Islam.

In 1944 he took up the challenge during an address to the League's newly established Planning Committee, which he had delegated to frame a programme for Muslim development based on state intervention.[11] That its purpose was to address expectations of centralised planning compatible with Islam was made explicit by none other than Jinnah. He advised members that, 'In whatever problems you tackle there is one point which I must request you to keep in mind, and it is this. It is not our purpose to make the rich richer and to accelerate the process of the accumulation of wealth in the hands of a few individuals. We should aim at levelling up the general standard of living amongst the masses ... Our ideal should not be capitalistic, but Islamic and the interests of the welfare of the people should be constantly kept in mind.'[12] Warnings that Jinnah and his peers were set to join the battle over the economic boundaries of the new Muslim state surfaced almost immediately. Within days, the mouthpiece of conservative Muslim opinion, the Lahore-based *Civil and Military Gazette*, had denounced Jinnah's preference for a non-capitalist economy as contrary to the 'spirit of Islam'.[13]

Just why Jinnah came to regard capitalism as antithetical to Islam and inappropriate to Muslim economic development is unclear. His personal preference for private ownership and his indifference to religious injunctions would appear to run counter to both. What is known, and could well contain clues to his apparent change of heart, was a brief but pointed correspondence with Iqbal in 1937.[14] In it Iqbal made a strong case for a brand of socialism compatible with the spiritual foundations of Islamic Law as the best way 'to solve the problem of Muslim poverty' and to ensure 'the right to subsistence'.[15] He also warned that unless the League addressed the problem, 'the Muslim masses will remain indifferent to it'.[16] With his finely honed visionary instincts, he offered Jinnah a way out. The solution, he claimed, lay in 'the enforcement of the Law of Islam and its further development in the light of modern ideas'; neither however was possible 'without a free Muslim state or states'.[17] Nevertheless, Iqbal was optimistic about the prospect of success for he was convinced that, unlike the threat posed by Nehru's socialism to the rigid hierarchies of Hinduism, 'the acceptance of social democracy, in some suitable form and consistent with the legal principles of Islam, is not a revolution but a return to the original purity of Islam'.[18]

Iqbal's urban, lower middle-class background had made him an early recruit to the cause of socialism with its promise of a more egalitarian (though not classless) society. With his radical Islamic piety, he was irresistibly drawn to the serious if nebulous idea of Islam as a social and economic system founded on the principles of brotherhood, equality and social solidarity. But how these principles were to be translated in the context of a modern industrial society and how they would be expressed in the socio-economic system of a free Muslim state, or indeed who would control the means of production where Muslims held sway, were questions that Iqbal, who died in 1938, did not have to confront. Yet his struggle to hold on to Islam's theistic base as the necessary foundation of any free Muslim state, while subscribing to the ethics of modern socialist doctrine, anticipated later debates in Pakistan. These would be concerned overwhelmingly with how far, if at all, the economic and social programme of a Muslim state had to reflect the moral concerns of Islam, and how they could best reconcile Jinnah's claim that Islam was *not* a mere religion of medieval practices, but a socio-economic order that could serve as the basis of a modern nation.[19]

The search for consensus was also undermined by the colossal problems that faced Pakistan in its early years. Although Iqbal and Jinnah may well have thought that containing the worst excesses of capitalism was more 'Islamically desirable', Pakistan's economy at independence offered few opportunities to put in place the socialist objectives that Iqbal believed could be justified by Islam and that Jinnah later appeared to endorse. The challenge of accommodating almost eight million refugees from India, the lack of an industrial base and a material inheritance from the Raj that was wanting, meant that Pakistan's early leaders, including Jinnah, soon turned to private enterprise as the main engine of the fledgling economy. Success depended on the engagement of private entrepreneurs, who were overwhelming drawn from the Muslim merchant classes, many with close links to Jinnah.[20] But their concern with high returns on investments would, over time, greatly weaken the impetus of social democracy and stifle debate about its relevance to a Muslim Pakistan.[21]

Yet, even in these early decades, when economic issues were far less embroiled in the question of Pakistan's relation to Islam, those pressing for more equitable economic policies did so in line with Islamic expectations that were assumed to be embodied in Pakistan. One such instance was the movement for land redistribution in the 1950s, which owed much to the leadership of outspoken leaders such as Mian Iftikharuddin from the Punjab and his Bengali counterparts, Abul Hashim (Secretary General of the Bengal Muslim League in the 1940s) and Maulana Bhashani (whose left-wing politics had earned him the sobriquet, 'red maulana'). Closely allied to radical factions in the League,[22] whose quest for Muslim power they equated with the pursuit of Islamic economic and social justice,[23] they were among the earliest precursors of the idea of 'Islamic Socialism' that gained ground in the late 1960s and 1970s. But the perennial lack of consensus over what kind of Islam defined Pakistan's national identity meant that their particular understanding of Islamic moral concerns about economic and social relations in Pakistan was vigorously contested. The strongest challenge came from the *ulama* and the Islamist groups allied to religious parties. Although they may have shared with their socialist foes a common desire to restore Muslim power, their objectives varied. The Muslim socialists who supported Pakistan seized on it as an opportunity to apply principles of economic and social justice they believed were consistent with Islam. For their part, the *ulama* and their Islamist allies were drawn primarily to the idea of Pakistan as a space for the fulfilment of obligations prescribed by Islam, which included obligations tied to the ownership of private property such as the payment of *zakat*.

These differences over the socio-economic implications of Islam for Pakistan sharpened in the 1960s and 1970s. At first, they were muted—overwhelmed by the more intense debate over the place of Islam in the constitutional definition of Pakistan. There were also powerful forces at work immediately after independence that tended to conceal the lack of consensus over economic and social policy. The civil bureaucracy, which had emerged as a powerful stabilizing force, looked to the nascent industrial bourgeoisie to help off-set the influence of indigenous landowning and tribal groups. Their belated and lukewarm response to the idea of Pakistan still aroused suspicion while their devotion to forms of popular Islam appeared to jar with the tradition of reformed Islam favoured by most bureaucrats and entrepreneurs. Dominated by a small minority representing urban Muslims from India, with few local roots, they tended also to be indifferent, if not instinctively hostile, to regional and ethnic expressions of Islam favoured by the local, largely rural, majority. Nevertheless, their control of the state and of its resources ensured that these influential urban elites soon developed a powerful socio-economic base, which successfully resisted competing versions of Islam.[24] This is not to say that local, especially landholding, interests held no sway over the direction of socio-economic change in these early years. On the contrary, they still commanded enough authority in the ruling Muslim League effectively to thwart all attempts to introduce tenancy and land reforms until forced to make modest concessions in the 1960s.

Ethnic and regional conflicts accentuated the lack of consensus over Islam, minimising the risk to ruling elites of any immediate threat from below of the kind that had forced asset redistribution in East Asia. But while the struggle over Islam may have eased the pressure for more equitable economic policies, it could do little to restrain the excessive consumerism that flowed from these policies and that came, in time, to be associated with state corruption. By the mid 1960s, there was a sustained debate that fuelled controversy over the state's responsibility to meet economic standards consistent with its Islamic objectives. Ayub Khan's economic policies, which were implemented from 1958–68 (and hailed by his supporters as the Decade of Development), failed to address equity issues.[25] Not only was there evidence of a steep rise in levels of absolute poverty, but there was, by all accounts, also a staggering concentration of wealth in a handful of mainly West Pakistan-based families.[26] The fact that Ayub's preferred economic strategy of 'functional inequality'[27] paid scant attention to the development of social welfare sectors, such as education and health, further alienated the masses and eroded government legitimacy. More dangerously still, these trends were symptomatic of wider regional disparities between East and West Pakistan that had fuelled resentment among Bengalis, who accused Ayub's regime of reducing the east to an internal colony.[28] It was also the perception and the popular feeling[29] that inequalities had increased under his regime that brought disaffection with Ayub. A major indicator 'was the considerable increase in the level of conspicuous consumption and wasteful expenditure on extravagant and lavish housing and other consumer durables by the richer classes in the country ... in the face of ... extreme poverty'.[30] At issue was Ayub's secularizing agenda, which was implicitly held responsible for promoting economic inequities and encouraging corruption in violation of 'Islam'. While opposition to his regime was certainly not restricted to differences over economic priorities, the apparent disjunction between Ayub's policies and Islam's commitment to distributive justice served as a particularly potent symbol in Pakistan, where the state was still inclined to put its Islamic commitments on display.

The unfettered growth of private enterprise, the absence of meaningful land reform and the massive concentration of wealth and power during Ayub's decade of development questioned how compatible these could be with an Islamic economic order in Pakistan. While the space to be accorded to Islam in formulating public policy remained unsettled, fundamental questions on the desirability of private property, the merits of public against private ownership and the state's responsibility to ensure a social welfare system still continued to be debated within an Islamic framework. What separated the two sides of this debate was not whether Islam should determine economic policy, but which Islam should serve as its engine.

This lack of consensus also accounted in part for the wild swings in economic policy that have characterised Pakistan's political trajectory.[31]

The creeping socialism[32] apparently endorsed by Jinnah on the eve of independence derived from a modernist reading of Islam that emphasised distributive justice as the cornerstone of the modern national community. The more robust modernist interpretation of Islam preferred by Ayub was shaped by radically different assumptions, which also tended to equate true Islam with personal piety. This modern understanding of religion, Metcalf observes, implied that when 'it [Islam] intruded on socio-economic issues, it did so in conformity with Western standards of practice and interpretation'[33]—derived from the legacy of 'classic modern Western economic theory in which economics was wholly divorced from moral considerations'.[34] Its most potent expression was the doctrine of 'the social utility of greed', adopted by Ayub, which justified inequality on the grounds that it led to economic growth.[35] By the mid 1970s, these modernist variations of an Islamic economic order were challenged by Bhutto's version of Islamic socialism before a return to private enterprise in the 1980s was justified by Zia as consistent with his programme of Islamic reform.[36]

During these decades there emerged sharp differences that frustrated the search for a consensus on Pakistan's most efficacious economic policies. This applied even to those apparently in agreement over the desirability of introducing a Muslim socialist order as a corrective to the unbridled capitalism of Ayub's regime. Opinion in the late 1960s and 1970s was divided between those who propounded Islamic socialism and those who appealed to 'Muhammadan equality' (*musawat-i-Muhammadi*): both were vulnerable to criticism. While the former were accused of surreptitiously fostering a materialistic worldview that was antithetical to Islam (and therefore inappropriate for Pakistan), the latter were said to have substituted a moral philosophy of Islam for sound economic doctrine. Both dismissed their critics by insisting that they were guided, above all, by the need to re-orientate national policy along lines that would privilege the economic and social concerns of Islam, which they claimed had been eroded during Ayub's regime.

They were also united in their opposition to private property, condemning it as 'un-Islamic' on the grounds that Islam judged labour to be the sole value in economic production.[37] Indeed, they sought to buttress this claim by suggesting that Islam's unequivocal ban on interest amounted to a rejection of any concession to capital—implying thereby that private enterprise was itself 'un-Islamic'. These views received wide currency in the mid 1960s in the monthly magazine *Nusrat*, which was the main ideological organ of the PPP. The objective, according to one authoritative assessment, was 'to develop Islamic Socialism as an intellectual movement that would enable Pakistan, fully in consonance with its religious foundations, to find a route to modernity between atheistic materialism on the left and the wholesale westernization and religious obscurantism on the right.'[38] Its essence would eventually find its way into Bhutto's own poorly crafted rhetoric of 'Islamic socialism' in the 1970s.

What is worth noting is that there was little in this discourse on the socialist foundations of an Islamic economic order to suggest that it could become the basis of a more coherent Pakistani national identity of the sort that had come to be commonly associated with Arab nationalism. A rare exception was Hanif Ramey, who made his name as a PPP stalwart and one of the party's chief ideologues in the 1970s. He called for a socialist re-interpretation of Pakistan's national identity that would unite 'the oppressed classes' and strengthen national solidarity. Nevertheless, as Jawed perceptively observes, it was social justice rather than national solidarity that moved most Islamic socialists in Pakistan.[39] This would be consistent also with Metcalf's view that, by the early 1970s there was less concern than in the 1950s and 1960s with Islam as a focus of national unity in Pakistan than with Islam as a 'programme of government action'.[40] This is not to say that there was unanimity about Pakistan's national identity or indeed consensus over the place of Islam in the expression of that identity, but that the link between Islam and Pakistan ensured that 'an Islamic language' remained the dominant language of national debate. While richly diverse in its use of symbols, it effectively pre-empted the development of any other rival language, whether couched in terms of secular nationalism, liberalism or socialism. Nor, as Metcalf emphasises, was this the language of 'Islamic tradition'—on the contrary, it represented 'a self-conscious and deliberate reformulation of Islam by people who were literate, often professional, and usually urban'.[41]

They included Zulfiqar Ali Bhutto, whose promise to restore the principles of distributive justice and equity to the forefront of Pakistan's development strategy was famously projected as Islamic socialism. It is true that Bhutto, unlike Ayub, 'did not seek to reinterpret Islam to serve the needs of development', but rather 'to serve populism'.[42] His concern with distributive justice as Islamically desirable was neither unusual when set against the wider discourse of radical

127

egalitarianism in Pakistan's early years, nor so easily dismissed as the opportunistic use of Islam when the separation of East Pakistan in 1971 demanded a fresh affirmation of the popular roots of Pakistani Islam. It found a voice in the thinking of 'Islamic Socialists' led by Ramay, Rasul Bakhsh Talpur and others who, encouraged by the appeal of Bhutto's heady mix of egalitarianism and popular Sufi Islam, redoubled their efforts to find Quranic support for radical land reforms and the nationalization of basic industries.[43] By doing so they hoped both to respond to their supporters, who feared that the PPP's brand of socialism would compromise the Islamic ends associated with Pakistan, as well as to see off criticism from religious parties, whose alternative interpretations of Islam favoured radically different economic policies.

These interpretations had also surfaced in the late 1960s in response to the inequities encouraged by Ayub's policies, and they were widely promoted by the *ulama* and lay Islamist parties, led by the Jamaat-i-Islami. Unlike the Islamic socialists, who were preoccupied with the issue of distributive justice in a Muslim state like Pakistan, the *ulama* and lay Islamists were concerned primarily with creating the right conditions to fulfil the obligations demanded by Islam. They argued strongly in favour of private property and free enterprise on the grounds that they were necessary to meet obligations demanded by Islam such as the payment of *zakat* and the pilgrimage to Mecca (*hajj*)—neither of which they claimed was possible if all wealth was owned by the state.[44] This is not to say that *ulama* groups had no regard for questions of economic justice; rather the redress for poverty and inequality was sought not in the design of economic instruments but in the more rigorous compliance with religious obligations centring on the various forms of institutionalized charity.[45] However, the *ulama*'s support for private property did not readily translate into an endorsement of capitalism. On the contrary, they saw the moral failings of capitalism (usury, speculation, hoarding and exploitation of the poor) as far outweighing any benefits flowing from the respect for private property.[46]

These broad concerns were systematized by the Jamaat-i-Islami and its leader, Maulana Mawdudi. Fiercely hostile to Ayub's version of modernist Islam, but no less antagonistic to socialist readings of Islam, he mounted a spirited defence of private property and free enterprise as being fundamental to the economic objectives of Islam.[47] Those were identified as the freedom of economic action, the creation of a charitable network, and the rejection of class conflict. The rules designed to achieve these objectives were the sanctity of private property, the freedom of enterprise and the circulation of wealth.[48] Such considerations converged with the *ulama*'s own concerns to resist state control, deepen religious obligations and strengthen Islamic solidarity. In 1970 the Jamaat launched its election manifesto, which set out its vision of an Islamic economic order for Pakistan. Regarded by some as 'a Western-type capitalist system with a social security scheme',[49] it failed to win popular support at a time when the stark disparities in wealth that followed Ayub's regime demanded a more rigorous treatment of socio-economic issues than the Jamaat offered.[50] Yet, it was not so much the Jamaat's treatment of socio-economic issues along emphatically Islamic lines that worked against it, but rather its assumption that the relation between Pakistan's national economic priorities and Islam was self-evident.

Bhutto's attempts while in power to forge a new consensus on Islam as a socio-economic movement with the potential to address inequalities set him on a course of confrontation with both Islamists and the *ulama*. By that time he had also lost the support of the left-wing factions in his own party, who had grown disillusioned with his authoritarian style of government and disregard for equity objectives embodied in the PPP's extensive nationalization programme.[51] His unwillingness to challenge the dominance of the landed classes and enact land reforms also alienated supporters, who had expected Bhutto to fulfil the promise to remove 'the remaining vestiges of feudalism'.[52] But, ultimately, it was the combined power of the small propertied classes represented by traders, merchants and shop-keepers hard hit by nationalization, and Islamist parties appealing to the sanctity of private property, that sealed Bhutto's political fate.[53]

These groups emerged as the main beneficiaries of General Zia's military regime which ousted Bhutto in 1977. Among its earliest measures was a review of Bhutto's socio-economic policies. The aim, to restore private enterprise as the main engine of growth though denationalization, was to be carefully calibrated. Instead of dismantling the whole edifice of Bhutto's economic programme, the emphasis shifted to opening up sectors previously closed to private enterprise.[54] Nevertheless, the move from state-led 'Islamic socialism' to state-led 'Islamic capitalism' was unmistakeable, preparing the way for growth that would eventually compare favourably with Ayub's 'Decade of Development'.

Exogenous factors, notably US financial and military aid in support of Pakistan's role as a front-line state against the Soviet invasion of Afghanistan, sustained the boom.[55] So too did overseas remittances by Pakistani workers in the Gulf, which helped fuel a parallel economy. It served as a magnet for private entrepreneurs, who preferred to bypass conventional banking channels in favour of alternative systems, such as *hawala* or *hundi*, which relied on the informal transfer of capital through private individuals.[56] This flourished in many rural areas and small towns, which also served as the main recruiting grounds for migrants to the Middle East and acted as the nodes of the informal economy. Private initiatives mushroomed, boosting sectors from tourism to transport, but also encouraging investments in so-called 'collective goods' informed by notions of Islamic charity, including the building of mosques and religious schools (*madrassas*).[57] The regime vigorously encouraged these charitable initiatives as the necessary tools to forge an Islam that would come to define Pakistan's new economic order.

This reading of Islam was predicated on an orthodox rather than a modernist reading which re-imagined Pakistan as a state unambiguously created to apply Islamic law. In matters of socio-economic policy, the aim was not to bring 'Islam' in line with conditions prescribed by modern ideologies but to adapt modern conditions in ways that would facilitate Islam. The belief in class conflict that had informed the PPP's social-democratic reading of Islam now gave way to rival interpretations stressing the idea of a co-operative society of Muslims under obligation to secure the economic objectives of Islam—as most closely associated with the Islam favoured by lay Islamist parties, such as the Jamaat-i-Islami and the traditional *ulama*. Indeed, they emerged as the strongest supporters of Zia's military regime. While they never threatened to supplant it as an alternative centre of power, their influence over socio-economic change, especially in the early years, was unmistakeable. Questions first raised in the 1960s about how best to make Pakistan more responsive to an Islamic social and economic system were explored with keen interest by the regime, which relied both on the expertise of traditional *ulama*, such as Maulana Taqi Usmani, and on the advice of prominent lay Islamists from the Jamaat-i-Islami, like Khurshid Ahmad, who served as a senior minister in Zia's first cabinet.

In 1980 Zia appointed a committee to review how the main objectives of an Islamic system of economic management could be applied to Pakistan.[58] Echoing themes already rehearsed among the *ulama* and the lay Islamist parties in the 1960s, the committee concluded in its report that the main purpose of an Islamic economic system was the achievement of justice and kindness (*al adl wal ahsan*). Its fulfilment in the context of Pakistan, it declared, depended upon universal education, land redistribution and a ceiling on inherited wealth. While the committee's recommendations were singled out by most critics as purely cosmetic, designed for public consumption, what was striking was its admission of uncertainty regarding the instruments necessary for an Islamic economic order. Neither the abolition of interest nor wealth and land taxes (*zakat* and *ushr*), identified by the *ulama* and most religious parties as indispensable to Islamic economics, were deemed to be so by the committee.[59]

Its members were also ambiguous about the role of the private sector in leading economic growth. While the committee had no doubt that 'an Islamic economy will require the state to play a tangible role' in the interests of guaranteeing the standards of social welfare expected of an Islamic system, it was unwilling to countenance a role for the state that would allow it to occupy the 'commanding heights' of the economy.[60] This underlying uncertainty was confirmed when the committee's members, possibly anticipating that there was nothing new or specifically Islamic about its proposals, agreed that 'these are the objectives of *any* economic system; but that does not disqualify them from being the objectives of the Islamic economic system as well, particularly as they follow directly from Islam's own distinctive economic philosophy'.[61]

By the mid 1980s, a consensus over Islam and, by extension an Islamic system, was as yet nowhere in sight. The military regime's Sixth Five year Plan (1983–88) placed fresh emphasis on a reduced role for the state as quintessentially 'Islamic'.[62] But the state enforcement of *zakat* and other Islamic taxes, traditionally regarded as voluntary acts of Muslim piety,[63] which had been implemented in defiance of the finance committee's recommendations, gave a dominant role to the state, one that was to be further extended by its close supervision of the abolition of interest. These wide variations in the understanding, and selective application of 'Islam' by the regime were largely responsible for the scepticism with which Zia's policies on Islamization came to be regarded. In time, they reinforced the impression that the terms employed to define 'Islam' were governed mainly by considerations aimed at boosting the regime's political legitimacy through the choice of measures that carried the greatest symbolic association with Islam.[64]

The end of the Zia era in 1988 signalled a fresh debate about the relation between 'Islam' and Pakistan's socio-economic order. This came increasingly to focus not so much on 'Islam' and the direction of change ('capitalist', 'socialist' or 'Islamic'), but on 'Islam' and the *consequences* of change. Where earlier uncertainty had concentrated on which reading of 'Islam' would define the course of Pakistan's socio-economic development, doubts now surfaced over which 'Islam' could best contain the damaging consequences of socio-economic change, notably corruption. To some extent the shift in emphasis reflected global currents, which showed a decisive shift in favour of economic liberalization and privatization. The return to power of the PPP under Benazir Bhutto in 1988 and again in 1993 was accompanied with none of the fanfare of 'Islamic socialism' associated with her father's party. Instead, forced by Pakistan's ballooning debt crisis to accept the conditions set by multilateral lending agencies, notably the IMF, it gave free rein to the private sector to kick-start the economy.

With political institutions all but destroyed by the previous regime, this set the stage for a wholesale assault on the state by eager entrepreneurs ready to pay to break through bureaucratic hurdles in order to establish new enterprises. These trends became even more acute under Nawaz Sharif, whose use of state resources to further economic liberalization precipitated even more dramatic changes. According to one respected commentator, 'the 1990s were the moment where the economic interests of middle and elite Pakistan became articulated into politics and into a desire to use politics for economic gain'.[65] It was also the moment when the question of corruption, long associated with the vestiges of a backward rural Islam, would come to be more closely linked to the rational and modernist Islam associated with the governing elite.

The culture of corruption

Of the many issues that have surfaced about Pakistan, especially since the early 1990s, few have so consumed the attention of observers as corruption. Perceptions of its scale and pervasiveness have been reinforced by the prevalence of international corruption league tables, which have consistently deemed Pakistan one of the most corrupt countries in the world.[66] Although successive governments have been willing (publicly at least) to launch ever more ruthless anti-corruptions campaigns, it appears still to be deeply entrenched. So grave is the problem now held to be that some have even argued that what Pakistan needs most urgently is good government—that is, instituting a system of accountability rather than democratic government based on holding elections.[67]

Despite this recent global attention, corruption in Pakistan has long been symptomatic of deeper concerns about a state whose distortions are judged to be the results of the moral failings of a leadership ignorant of Islam. Moreover the debate on corruption has been mired in rival interpretations of Islam, each accused of corrupting socio-economic change in Pakistan. While some regarded corruption as flowing from the distorted priorities of the new, modernist, Islam espoused by the country's governing elite, others saw it as proof of the resilience of the unreformed, popular Islam that held sway over vast swathes of Pakistan's rural society. Since the 1980s the emergence of a more self-conscious Islamic identity has lent momentum to yet other forms of more puritanical Islam which have intensified the debate and threatened more systematic campaigns in favour of reforming standards of public and private morality.[68]

The relationship between forms of Islam and the debate on corruption has a curious pedigree in that it has often represented a nostalgic yearning for Pakistan's first generation of leaders, whose respect for the high ideals of Islam are believed to account for their apparent reluctance to raid the public purse.[69] Stories abound of Jinnah's frugality (despite his immense wealth), while the high standards of financial probity and accountability set by his close associates (many of them devout Muslims), such as Liaquat Ali Khan and Khwaja Nazimuddin, serve as bench-marks by which to judge and routinely condemn subsequent generations of Pakistan's leaders. Not surprisingly, the common view has tended increasingly to endorse the view that 'the business of politics now attracts the scum of the community and a legion of scoundrels. In the name of democracy, unspeakable crimes are committed ... larceny, loot and plunder in broad day light, with no fear of accountability'.[70] Corruption in Pakistan is often regarded as the new evil that marked a break with the values of an older and more glorious period.

This may explain why attitudes towards corruption, at least during the earlier part of Ayub's regime in the 1960s were relatively tolerant. One influential economic assessment suggested that corruption under Ayub was instrumental to economic efficiency even if it did fuel 'anecdotal evidence that the recipients of import and industrial licenses either were close friends of the regime or had greased the palms of people in authority to grant them'.[71]

But tolerance for the high levels of corruption unleashed by Ayub's model of unbridled growth found no place in the hostile discourse of its critics, especially the traditional *ulama*, who singled out the regime's version of Islamic modernism for encouraging corruption. At issue was Ayub's attempt to codify elements of a modernist tradition he first imbibed as a student at Aligarh by subjecting the legal injunctions of Islam to critical and rational scrutiny. Outstanding examples ranged from the far-reaching 1961 Muslim Family Laws Ordinance, which formalized Islamic injunctions as legal rules relating to polygamy, divorce and inheritance [see chapter 3] to the regulation of the Islamic lunar calendar by reference by a central meteorology department. Measures such as these, the *ulama* feared, strengthened the forces of secularism and eroded the state's Islamic purpose 'to command right and forbid evil'.[72] It was precisely Ayub's 'modernist' zeal for innovation (*bida*) that had fatally divorced statecraft from moral considerations and opened the way for widespread corruption.

Ayub also faced a stiff challenge from Islamist parties like the Jamaat-i-Islami. While the *ulama* had condemned the regime's unhealthy desire for innovation as the source of corruption, the Jamaat attributed it to Ayub's authoritarian style of politics, which it claimed ran counter to Islam.[73] Yet, the Jamaat was more restrained in its critique of Ayub's modernization programme and its resulting disparities, fearing that to do so would trigger a populist reaction against private property—an institution the Jamaat vigorously defended.[74] No less important was the Jamaat's own engagement with modernism, which left it more ambivalent about Ayub's modernizing agenda than the traditionalist *ulama*. The Jamaat's vision of Islam squarely encompassed the modern and the new; neither was seen as threatening or necessarily corrupting. Indeed, the Jamaat's leader, Maulana Mawdudi, emphasised that modernity, albeit under the auspices and name of Islam, was vital to overcome the economic and political weakness affecting Muslims. It was not Ayub's modernity as such that was the source of corruption, but his failure to Islamize modernity that was judged by the Jamaat to be corrupting.[75] Ultimately, their struggle centred not so much on the respective merits of two rival versions of Islam—the traditional and the modern—but on rival claims to define the parameters of a modern Islam with the power to free Muslims from retrograde practices such as corruption. For the Jamaat, it was precisely Ayub's failure to bring Pakistan in line with reformed Islam and his subsequent compromises with the popular Islam of Sufi *pirs* to secure his political future that were held to be responsible for corruption.

Ayub vigorously resisted these claims, repeatedly stressing his commitment to the principles of Islam. But, as Metcalf observes, his Islam was 'modernist', concerned less with 'providing a blue-print or guide to policies and actions' (let alone delineating a regime of public morality) than serving as the 'ultimate interest' of his policies.[76] Ayub's attempt to separate Islam as a focus of national loyalty from Islam as a programme of action could not be sustained. By the late 1960s his style of Islam had failed to respond to urgent calls for more equitable wealth distribution and, worse, it appeared to foster an 'un-Islamic' outlook favouring the ostentatious display of wealth in the midst of squalor and poverty. Notwithstanding these weaknesses, Ayub's modernist understanding of Islam served as a powerful weapon in the service of a dominant discourse opposed to local cultures, whose preference for custom (*riwaj*) over the rule of law was deemed to be the root cause of corruption. In recent years it has found an echo in the suggestion that corruption in Pakistan is fundamentally an expression of the country's old indigenous regional traditions, which habitually favour custom over the rule of law and seek the sanction of a popular and unreformed Islam to perpetuate arbitrary practices. Representatives of this view argue that the revival of old cultures sustained by regionally entrenched landed elites (*jagirdars*) and tribal chiefs (*sardars*) have been responsible for damaging the quality of governance and bringing corruption into the country.[77]

The process gained momentum when the old feudal elites, threatened by the emergence of a new class of capitalist farmers under Ayub, mounted a rear-guard action to reassert their authority. Ill at ease with the modernist vision of Pakistan as a state sanctioned by the rule of law, local leaders reasserted the customary rules of reciprocity and the exchange of favours to undermine the institutions of the modern state.

By the mid-1960s, it is claimed, the state's legal foundations had been eroded, leaving it prey to a cultural environment that predated Pakistan and in which corruption, conceived as the granting and withholding of favours in exchange for political support, became the norm. The modernizing elite, who sided with Ayub in the hope of eclipsing this old culture of corruption, were unable to withstand the challenge. Lacking local constituencies, they were no match for local landed magnates and tribal chiefs who held sway over many of the north-western regions that became part of Pakistan in 1947.

While much of this critique levelled against this 'ancient culture of corruption' can be read as a means of justifying the modernizing imperative common to any nation-state, it acquired a particular significance in Pakistan, where the Islam of the governing elite has left a decisive imprint on thinking about the consequences of corruption for socio-economic change. Metcalf identifies two main features characteristic of the Pakistani elite's treatment of Islam. The first was its 'modernist orientation', which has favoured a degree of 'jurisprudential radicalism' (and impatience with existing forms of popular Islam), which is a legacy of nineteenth-century Indo-Muslim reform movements.[78] Partial to rational thinking, it lent itself readily to the demands for a modern Muslim state. The other, more implicit, was its disdain for 'regional forms of Islam' in Pakistan, which were seen to be instinctively hostile to legally established authority.

These elements, characteristic of modernist thinking, converged with the outlook of most revivalist organizations, notably the Jamaat-i-Islami, which was otherwise opposed to the Islam of the ruling classes.[79] What drew them together was a common understanding of corruption as a nexus between powerful landed and tribal authorities, who appealed to custom rather than law to stamp their authority *and* the network of Muslim holy men (*pirs*), who relied on customary religious practices rather than Islamic law to control the lives of rural worshippers. Together, these forces were believed to have weakened the impulse of an enlightened society, leaving it vulnerable to corruption. While there are unquestionably wide differences among Muslim reformists in Pakistan over the interpretation of Islamic law—ranging from the liberalism of Aligarh modernists, who have dominated state power since independence to the more rigid posture adopted by revivalist supporters of the Jamaat on the margins of power—all share a common concern to establish legal supremacy as a corrective to the corruption of the 'old' order.

Three main assumptions have flowed from this idea of corruption as a feature of the indigenous order in Pakistan—assumptions that have had a vital bearing on the perception of the country's economic and social development. The first is that corruption is inherently a feature of the indigenization of the post-colonial state, which so long as it was under the control of so-called modern elites had successfully withstood its damaging effects by appealing to an ethic of public service sanctioned by the rule of law. The second is that the indigenization of the Pakistani state heralded the return of old feudal and tribal classes, whose customary modes of predatory authority had been legitimized by the electoral democratization. The third is that elected politicians, who have been the chief beneficiaries of this process, to the extent that they depend electorally upon local and regional constituencies, have become carriers of this old culture—leaving them more vulnerable to corruption than their more modern counterparts in the civil bureaucracy and the military.

Pakistan's first democratic election and the return to power of the Pakistan People's Party in 1970 reinforced these perceptions. For some, the election of Zulfiqar Ali Bhutto, a scion of one of the oldest landed families of Sind, formalized the resurgence of the old order, deepening the hold of corrupt practices.[80] That Bhutto was not perceived to be 'as straightforward a modernist as Ayub Khan'[81] lent credence to this view. Bhutto's complex style of politics, combining an urbane Western education with a decidedly rural idiom that found common cause with rural elites, represented by landlords and *pirs*, reinforced this perception. As such, his decision to empower regional elites and promote regional, especially Sindhi, cultures appeared to signal a break with 'Iqbalian modernism'.[82] The 'corrupted' forms of Islam popular in the regions, including the worship of saints and shrines, had long been regarded by Iqbal's followers as inappropriate for a modern nation such as Pakistan. Revivalist supporters of the Jamaat also made no secret of their opposition to Bhutto, whose secularism appeared to them as morally reprehensible as his attachment to the 'unreformed' Islam of Sindhi shrine culture: both were seen to have corrupted the fabric of the modern state in Pakistan.

This unlikely convergence of modernist and scripturalist Islam would explain, in part, why opposition to Bhutto eventually crystallised under the banner of Islam—although, characteristically, what this really meant remained uncertain. The Jamaat's revivalist blue-print for

Pakistan clearly held little appeal for the modernists, who made up the ranks of the secular and leftist factions allied to the anti-Bhutto Pakistan National Alliance (PNA).[83] But their shared distaste for the old culture of feudal and tribal patronage and for the unreformed Islam they believed helped sanction it, lent substance to the claim that they were all acting to salvage the Islam they believed was the bulwark of Pakistan as a modern Muslim state. According to Mawdudi, this Islam had little place for 'these Brahmins and *pirs*, these nawabs and ru'asa [sing, *rais*, traditional leader] these *jagirdars* and feudal lords ... to rob ... [and] to satiate [their] selfish demands.'[84] Nor, according to their counterparts among the modernist elite, was this Islam compatible with 'the economics of *riwaj*' favoured by the 'old establishment', which they claimed had been provided opportunities by Bhutto 'on a grand and unprecedented scale', leaving the way open for a sharp rise in corruption.[85]

Whether or not Bhutto went further than any other leader in corrupting the institutional foundations of the modern state in Pakistan is open to question. Nevertheless, his status as a politician who nurtured his links with local cultures and their versions of folk Islam, reinforced popular perceptions that politicians were more predisposed to corruption than their modern counterparts in the civil bureaucracy and the army. The idea gained wider currency in the 1990s during the troubled prime ministerial tenures of Benazir Bhutto and Nawaz Sharif, which, according to some assessments, left Pakistan more unequal and corrupt than at any other time since the 1960s.[86] Like her father, Benazir was accused of corrupting the state by entrenching its feudal character and transforming public institutions into instruments for the arbitrary exercise of power.[87] The compromises with indigenous feudal and tribal cultures were less stark in the case of Bhutto's successor, Nawaz Sharif, who twice succeeded her in 1993 and 1997. His skill in the art of patronage politics appeared to be firmly grounded in rules devised by an emerging, predominantly urban, industrial-based, middle class, which had consolidated its gains under Zia.

Regarded by the state's purportedly modern elites (the bureaucracy and the military high command) as committed to development, Sharif raised expectations that he would revive the country's modern industrial sector along lines reminiscent of the Ayub era. While reports of the misappropriation of public funds and the accumulation of bad debts by business associates and family members soon surfaced, Sharif's commitment to economic modernization tended (as during the Ayub era) to encourage a more forgiving attitude to corruption, deemed a necessary evil to grease the wheels of an economy in disrepair. The fact that he hailed from an urban, industrial background that made no secret of its attachment to reformist currents within Islam, also fuelled expectations that Sharif would be less vulnerable to the corrupting influence of popular and folk Islam characteristic of local cultures. His and his closest political associates' involvement in the Tablighi Jamaat, an off-shoot of the reformist Deobandi movement, reinforced these expectations. Although indifferent to matters of Islamic law and juris-prudence, the Tablighi movement actively discourages 'deviant' cus-toms centring on the veneration of holy men (*pirs*) and the practice of syncretic rituals associated with popular Sufism.[88]

Since Sharif's ouster in 1999 following a military coup led by Gen-eral Musharraf, who was forced to resign in 2008 under pressure from a democratically elected government, the issue of corruption has come under fresh scrutiny. Critics have challenged the claim that it is prima-rily the class of elected politicians that is chiefly to blame for corrup-tion by pointing to the failings of the civil-military alliance that has run the country for much of its history. What is unique about corruption in Pakistan, they suggest, is not the resurgence of an old culture repre-sented by 'corrupt political leaders, inept political parties, and ruthless landlords' contemptuous of the rule of law, but the vice-like grip of a 'modern' civil-military alliance, whose members, as 'the real perpetra-tors of corruption have cleverly manoeuvred to shift the blame to scapegoats'.[89] This is believed to be especially true of Pakistan's mod-ern armed forces. Their supremacy in the form of successive military regimes transformed them from a state institution into a 'political class' with significant economic interests tied especially to the acquisi-tion of agricultural land.[90] These changes have led to the development of the military 'as one of the many land barons or feudal landlords' with a pattern of social behaviour that 'is like that of any big feudal landlord'—a trend that intensified under General Zia's government (and later vigorously encouraged by Musharraf).[91]

Until then, it is argued, the army was relatively well-placed to claim the moral high ground as agents of the modern state pitted against the corruption of the old order. But it soon lost the reputation it thought it enjoyed. Hamza Alavi was among the first to signal these changes. He identified two factors that had made the army more prone to the logic of an informal system at odds with the rules governing military professionalism. The first was the granting of land to army officers, which he believed sensitised them to the socio-cultural logic of reward and reciprocity, 'so that even those who did not come from substantial landowning families acquired landed interests and a corresponding class commitment'. The second involved the participation of the military in business (ostensibly to help equip its members to manage state corporations), which offered 'much greater scope for patronage and nepotism'.[92] Indeed entry into business through careers in the state service, both civil and military, has since the 1980s become a marked feature of military rule in Pakistan, leading to a steady decline in levels of transparency and accountability.[93] Other informal networks have also influenced the military and made it vulnerable to corrupt practices. Since the 1980s, allegations have surfaced of an established nexus between the then ruling military regime and shadowy drugs syndicates with close links to key members of Zia's military administration.[94] They suggest that the dominance of Yusufzai and Khattak Pathans, who are entrenched in military and industrial circles, may have forged connections between senior army officers and drug traffickers, though these charges have always remained open to question.[95]

Paradoxically, it was its informal alliance with Islamist parties that rendered the military more vulnerable to the moral discourse of corruption. Having freely employed the rhetoric of Islam under General Zia, the armed forces now found themselves under pressure also to abide by Islamic standards. The accent on the public adherence to Islamic norms since the 1980s had fuelled expectations of higher standards of public morality consistent with Islamic standards, but they came precisely at a time when the gap between personal piety and public morality appeared to be widening. One response to the growing strain was the hardening of an Islamic language that found expression in a puritanical tendency[96] that now seeks to dominate debates on Pakistan's putative Islamic purpose.

The puritan backlash

Nowhere has this puritanical tendency been more actively nurtured than in the defence of Muslim religious education, whose main institution—the *madrassa*—is regarded by its guardians as a bastion against corruption, and possibly even a microcosm of the Islamic state they believe was envisaged for Pakistan. In a striking confirmation of this vision, the distinguished *alim*, Maulana Rafi Usmani, president of the well-known *madrassa*, the Dar al Ulum in Karachi, told an assembly of new students in 1997 that they were poised to enter 'a secure fortress' ... [where] God has created a small world for us ... [which] the rest of the world does not know'. 'Its purpose,' he claimed, was 'to show everyone what an Islamic government is like. We can tell them to come and see our little model, our example of an Islamic society.'[97]

It is undeniable that the hermetically sealed world of the *madrassa* can no longer be isolated from the currents now sweeping across Pakistani society. While this has been a cause of serious misgiving among some sections of the traditional religious establishment, others within it have seized upon the opportunity to use the pedagogical objectives of the *madrassa* as a means of pressing for the reform of public standards along lines consistent with the Islamic purpose of the state. In that sense, the debate on the value of religious education, which is said to have contributed to the exponential growth of *madrassas* in Pakistan[98] has also stimulated public engagement with issues of moral probity as a means of testing the state's 'Islamicity'. Among those hastening to set the tone of this debate are the *ulama*, whose interest in the moral reform of state and society are rooted in their long involvement with traditional Islamic education. As purveyors of this education they have long claimed that they are also best placed to steer state and society away from anarchy and corruption.

Their claims are partly grounded in the historical status of the *madrassa* in South Asia, which has been closely associated with both the protection of a Muslim identity and the formation of the 'morally respectable' Muslim. This role was enhanced in colonial India when *madrassas* as diverse as Farangi Mahal in Lucknow and the Darul Uloom in Deoband came increasingly to be preoccupied with models of right conduct (*adab*) and its relation to the definition of Muslim identity and the defence of Islam.[99] The prominent place occupied by Islam in independent Pakistan restored the elements of this debate to centre-stage so that, as Zaman notes, 'the [Pakistani] ulama's vision of how an Islamic identity is best preserved is closely tied to the institution of the madrassa'.[100] So too are the moral foundations of that identity which, in keeping with the broad pedagogical aims of religious education, are dedicated both to providing basic education and ensuring 'socialization to certain norms of proper behaviour and knowledge'.[101]

Recent studies that investigate the appeal of Islamic religious education in Pakistan also confirm that the preference for such education
stems not so much from financial compulsion (for example, poverty),
but from a clear value attached to such learning in Pakistan, where the
training of the good Muslim is seen to be a prerequisite of the good
Pakistani citizen.[102] Moreover uncertainty about which Islam is best
suited to producing the good Muslim and, by extension, the good
Pakistani has widened the space for contestation while allowing the
madrassas and their managers—the *ulama* and Islamist groups—to
emerge as influential purveyors of Islamic standards.

They have been encouraged by the ample space afforded by successive governments concerned with Islamic religious education in Pakistan and its role in setting standards of public life that are judged to be
consistent with a state committed to Islam. The assumption that religious education is vital to the broader Islamic aims of the state has
been nowhere more in evidence than in repeated attempts to reform
the *madrassa* curriculum. Paradoxically, Ayub Khan, who made no
secret of his hostility to the *ulama* and Islamist parties, appeared to
share this assumption. In 1962 he appointed a committee charged with
overseeing the reform of the *madrassa* curriculum. In its report, it
emphasised that 'it was Islam which gave birth to Pakistan and more
than anything else it is Islam which will guarantee its future greatness.
The importance of religious education is therefore obvious in a country
like Pakistan'.[103] At the same time, the report declared that religious
education of the kind imparted by *madrassas* could not be restricted
merely to the study of the Qoran and other religious texts, but was also
responsible for creating 'an Islamic nation'. More significantly, in an
apparent break with the regime's style of Islam, which understood it
above all as an aspect of personal piety, the report called for religious
education that would reflect Islam as a total system and that would
'cover all aspects of human life'.[104] While it is more than plausible, as
Zaman suggests, that the committee may have intended to use this
recommendation to justify bringing the sphere of traditional religious
education more closely under state control,[105] it is unlikely that either
the *ulama* or Islamist parties saw the recommendations in quite the
same light. Indeed, the support of the Jamaat-i-Islami[106] suggests that
it may well have construed the committee's recommendations as
endorsing the Jamaat's position that the values imparted through a
modern religious education were vital to set the standards expected of
Pakistan as a modern Islamic state.

This was certainly the guiding assumption of the 1979 report on *madrassa* reform commissioned by Ayub's more devout successor, General Zia ul Haq. Strongly backed by Islamist parties, including the Jamaat-i-Islami, it left no doubt that the purpose of religious education in Pakistan was to enhance the state's Islamic identity. Mindful of the part played by *madrassas* in fostering Muslim identity in colonial India, the committee came out strongly in favour of the *madrassa* in Pakistan as the 'anchor which holds the entire society together'.[107] Despite the stated intentions of his regime to enhance the role of religious education, Zia failed to inspire the confidence of the religious establishment dominated by the *ulama*. They feared the imminent loss of their autonomy, but also condemned as 'irreligious' proposals to transform *ulama* organizations into official institutions.[108] By doing so, they signalled their determination jealously to guard their prerogative to pass judgement on the presumed Islamic character of the state.

Their position was buttressed by the failure of President Musharraf's sustained efforts to bring religious education in line with his vision of Pakistan's identity as a beacon of 'moderate Muslim enlightenment'. Regarded by the *ulama* and Islamist parties as a ruse to justify his pro-Western policies, it served nevertheless as an opportunity for Musharraf to reiterate the state's role in ensuring a prominent role for Islam in the public sphere. The government's White Paper on Education, which was published in 2006 (and revised the following year), stressed the importance of religious education in Pakistan by insisting that 'Islamic ideology must determine the policy of education ... and provide for options that will enable the Pakistani Muslim to develop himself or herself as a true Muslim'.[109] While the report made much of 'true Islam' as endowed with the power to 'meet modern challenges with modern responses',[110] it shared with its predecessors a readiness to flaunt the state's Islamic credentials by appearing to subscribe to the worldview of the *ulama* and other religious groups. 'The responsibility of the state', it declared, 'was to provide its citizens with [a] ... knowledge of individual and social values as ordained in the Quran.' As such, 'the importance of madrasas as a supplement to State's efforts cannot be over emphasised.'[111]

This is not to say that the state has necessarily, or always, deferred to members of the country's religious hierarchy as the guardians of Pakistan's Islamic identity or as keepers of its public morality. Indeed, the history of Pakistan is replete with instances of conflict between the state and its critics within the religious hierarchy. At the same time, the state's ambiguity about the place of Islam in public life and the need of authoritarian regimes to prop up their tenuous legitimacy by recourse to the rhetoric of Islam has ensured that the spokesmen of religion are given license not only to remain actively engaged in public life, but also to arbitrate on the state's Islamic character. It is worth noting that, since Pakistan's controversial engagement in the US-led 'war on terror' in 2001, some *madrassas* such as the Jamiat-ul Ulum al-Islamiya in Karachi and the Dar-ul Ulum Haqqaniya in Akora Khattak in the North West Frontier Province, have questioned the state's Islamic credentials by denouncing proposals to reform the *madrassas* as evidence of the state's failure to protect the latter as bastions of Islam and as guarantors of Pakistan's Islamic identity.

But the state's role in fostering ambiguity about the place of Islam in public life is not the only reason to account for the salience of religious education in Pakistan. At least as important has been public disenchantment with the failure of successive governments to provide basic public services, and especially of their failure to provide a more equitable education system.[112] The latter has transformed the issue of religious education from one concerned with debating the merits of Islamic instruction in a modern state to one that now serves as the basis of a powerful moral discourse against the failings of the state. It has been strengthened by the persistence of deep divisions along lines of class and language in Pakistan's educational system that some have compared to 'educational apartheid'.[113] They have accentuated social and economic inequalities and produced what some describe as 'denizens of alien worlds', who 'live in the same country but are completely alienated from each other.[114]

Since independence access to quality education, especially to elite schools, where the medium of instruction is English, has been the preserve of classes with power and privilege. Bhutto's 1972 educational reforms sought to redress this imbalance by nationalizing most private schools with the exception of a number of prestigious English-medium schools and those owned by missionaries or run as charitable trusts. But his reforms also widened existing divisions by creating a new hierarchy within schools where the medium of instruction was English. They were now internally divided between poorly state-administered, so-called English medium schools, subject to a national curriculum, and privately run elitist English-medium schools with their own curriculum that prepared children from wealthy families for education abroad.

The 1980s witnessed further disparities following the reversal of Bhutto's nationalization programme. Under General Zia private entrepreneurs were encouraged to enter the educational market, where demand for English as the language of power had intensified at the same time as had demands for instruction in Islam necessary to qualify for service in the new, Islamized state. It led to a significant expansion in the numbers of *madrassas*,[115] but also in the numbers of private schools offering both worldly[116] and religious education. With their modest fee structure they served as magnets for students from lower middle class families seeking to be both modern, by mastering English, (however imperfectly) and Islamic. Many of the private schools that offered a 'mixed' education have garnered the support of Islamist parties keen to extend their appeal among politically disempowered classes seeking to lay claim to positions of power through access to English in the context of a more religiously grounded education. Ironically Islamist groups were at the forefront of anti-English campaigns that peaked in the late 1970s, but were cut short by Zia—himself once their greatest champion—who reversed an order imposing Urdu as the medium of instruction in all schools. Since the 1980s, Islamist groups have emerged as strong supporters of instruction in English. Differing in style from both the rejection and resistance of English by the *ulama* and its acceptance and assimilation by the westernized elite, their strategy reflects a bid by new groups, which have seized on the empowering potential of English, to sharpen the Islamic profile of the state.[117]

It has led to the claim that the majority of privately-financed English medium institutions in Pakistan have been effectively transformed into middle-class 'Islamist institutions'.[118] Others appear to confirm this trend. They point to the proliferation of private schools offering a 'mixed' education that combines religiously grounded education with instruction in English, and warn that current efforts to 'de-Islamize' the state educational system run against the preference of ever larger numbers of Pakistanis for 'a worldly education in religious environments'.[119] Ominously, they also suggest that 'these religiously oriented private schools may not be the government's allies in the production of Pakistani citizens'.[120] If so, they could be poised to usher in a more pointed puritan challenge against the perceived moral failings of a state that will come to be ever more closely judged against models of

145

presumed Islamic authenticity, whose claims to deliver fairer services will be enhanced by their claim to do so unambiguously in the name of Islam.

It is precisely the state's ambiguity and lack of ideological certainty over the place of Islam in the public sphere that has left it vulnerable to the charge by *ulama* and Islamist groups that its incompetence in delivering basic services to its citizens constitutes a *moral* rather than a political failing symptomatic of a lack of commitment to Islam. The state has responded by making ever more lavish claims to speak on behalf of Islam. Their implications have been especially marked in the debate on the value of Islamic religious education, where by projecting it as vital to the definition of Pakistan's national identity, successive regimes have allowed the pedagogical aims of such education, originally dedicated to producing good Muslims, to set the standards of the good Pakistani citizen. At the same time, these standards have imperilled the state by serving precisely as the yardsticks by which an increasingly restless citizenry, angered by the degradation of public life in Pakistan, has chosen to test the state's professed Islamic character.

But it is the absence of a consensus regarding the role of Islam that has, above all, severely constrained the economic and social reach of the state. Although Pakistan's early generation of leaders boldly declared that Islam would govern their economic system, the lack of unanimity over Islam effectively precluded the development of a coherent economic model. Competing ideas of Islam also influenced the social and economic discourse on corruption by injecting into it a strong moral component that has tended increasingly to equate poor governance with the state's fragile commitment to a more 'authentic' Islamic dispensation. It is against this morass of uncertainty that the armed forces have tried to stamp their own vision of Pakistan's national identity.

5

BETWEEN CRESCENT AND SWORD

PROFESSIONALIZING JIHAD

Few discussions of Pakistan can escape the armed forces' overwhelming dominance of national life and its less than benign role as a key political actor. The military's monopoly over the right to speak on behalf of the nation and its jealous control over the levers of power have long been recognized as characteristic features of the Pakistani state, even if their causes are still widely debated.[1] The most common explanations of the military's involvement in civilian affairs have centred on the traumatic circumstances that accompanied the nation's creation, which left it at birth with a fledging administration forced to turn to its army to confront simultaneous challenges arising from communal riots, the resettlement of millions of refugees and, above all, a hostile regional environment marked by tension with Afghanistan and a primordial fear of India.[2] Chronic structural imbalances also played their part. The leaders of the new country, many of them migrants from India, lacked constituencies in the territories they now claimed to control. They were left with no choice but to cede ever greater powers to the military that, with the support of external powers such as the United States, led to the terminal decline of civilian political institutions.[3] More recently, the causes of the army's iron grip on politics have come to be more closely analyzed less in terms of its claim to be the best guardian of Pakistan's national interest or of the weakness of civilian politicians lacking legitimacy, but as rooted in the predatory control over a vast economic empire (or 'Milbus') that is harnessed in the service of the military's class interests.[4]

These explanations all carry considerable force. Yet, by ignoring the implications of Pakistan's unresolved national identity and the lack of consensus over the role of Islam, they fail to explain how the military emerged as a major force attempting not only to determine the national interest but to define the very meaning of Pakistan. There are many interpretations recognizing that an Islamic outlook has increasingly permeated the military rank and file and that on occasion it has even threatened the army's professional ethos, making it more vulnerable to the ideologies of radical Islam. Yet, there is little understanding of how an institution assumed to be unequivocally 'national' fell prey to the multiple meanings of Pakistan and the diverging interpretations of Islam that were held to attach to the country. Like the political leadership, unsure of its secular credentials in a state where the nebulous association between religion and nationalism had progressively sacralized political discourse, the military too soon lost sight of its proclaimed 'secular' purpose.

The relative lack of interest in pursuing the complex relationship between the state's religious identity and its military institutions is partly explained by the widely held assumption that the military, unlike its weaker political counterparts, was under no pressure to accommodate Islam or yield to the temptation of mobilizing its symbols in order to shore up its authority. The common view is that, notwithstanding the adoption of religious symbols, the army's 'Islamic identity was only in name' and served to dress a 'largely moderate and secular' ethos.[5]

This is true as far as it goes but this interpretation conceals the more complex reality of a key state institution that has long sought to overcome the ambiguities surrounding Pakistan's national and Islamic identities. This concern was sharpened by the army's repeated involvement in political affairs, which encouraged its interest in matters of ideological nationalization, and by its jealous control over the projection of Pakistan's regional interests. In particular, the military has grappled with how best to mould itself as an institution that was simultaneously capable of accepting Pakistan's identity as a nation-state defined by the limits of its territorial borders while contributing to its distinctive features as a Muslim entity founded on claims that had historically called into question the validity of territorial nationalism.

That religious identity has counted for less in explaining the military's political ascendancy in Pakistan stems also from the assumption that such interest as there was in Islam in the military tended to be moderate and liberal. There was a presumption that any other form of Islam, such as the more orthodox brand promoted by General Zia's military regime, was aberrant and unrepresentative of the military.[6] In practice these distinctions were blurred and the military's relation to Islam more incoherent than is commonly supposed. Not only was there no consensus within the military on the strategic implications of Pakistan's putative Islamic character (as early and subsequent controversies over the doctrine of *jihad* as a legitimate instrument of military strategy demonstrates), but agreement was also lacking on which Islam best served the corporate and political interests of the armed forces (as the radically different positions on Islam adopted by Generals Ayub, Zia and Musharraf clearly testify).

These doubts were largely symptomatic of unresolved tensions between two conflicting versions of Islam which the military sought, over time, to manage in pursuit of its own objectives. The first pertains to the more liberal and moderate representations of Islam with which it is still widely (if questionably) associated. It flows from a recognizably Indo-Muslim communal discourse of power that defines Pakistan (marked by its Muslim identity) primarily in opposition to India (marked by its Hindu identity). The second, reflecting a more radical reading of Islam that is commonly judged to be at odds with military thinking, has sought to project Pakistan's Muslim identity as an expression of social aspirations informed by a visibly religious interpretation of Islam.[7] The uneasy relation between the two was brought to the surface most sharply in the 1970s and 1980s following the separation of East Pakistan and the outbreak of the war in Afghanistan. These events prompted the military to make a bid to reconcile Pakistan's Muslim (communal) identity, dictating the pursuit of strategic interests against 'Hindu India', with the country's Islamic identity as the focus of a utopian Islamic vision guaranteed by a policy of regional military expansion predicated on *jihad*.

But this shift had dangerous consequences. Far from easing the tension between a communal discourse concerned with Pakistan's 'Muslim' identity and a religiously informed ideology determined to enhance the state's 'Islamic' features, the strains have widened. The military's alliance with its *jihadi* protégés has also proved to be unstable. The army looked to Islam to strengthen Muslim communal discourse and prolong the conflict with India with the aim of buttressing its authority

149

at home and lending momentum to its regional policies in Kashmir and Afghanistan. Islamist forces, however, invoked Islam not so much in opposition to India (though they are undeniably opposed to Indian secularism) but more clearly to seek to assert Pakistan's internal Islamic character.

Forging an Islamic army

On the face of it, Pakistan's army would appear to be the least likely agent of transnational Islamist ideologies, which are ostensibly at odds with the consolidation of the institution over which the military has held sway for more than half of the country's history. Not only is the army one of the primary state institutions in Pakistan, whose importance has loomed ever larger as it has undermined the political process, but the top brass has long been an integral part of the modern governing elite for whom religion has generally been deemed to be a private matter. At its inception, the army's professionalism was defined more by its secular British colonial heritage than by the notionally Islamic character of Pakistan. On the face of it, until the late 1970s at least, there was little discernible interest among the officer corps in the question of the army's precise relationship with Islam or in an Islamic state.

Yet, the military was far from insensitive to the rhetorical power of Islam as a mobilizing force. It is of course true that prior to independence the military was relatively untouched by debates around the Islamic character of the Pakistani state. Some have suggested that this owed much to the fact that because the articulation of Pakistani nationalism was largely 'a civilian and constitutional enterprise', the military could not invoke the mythology of an armed 'national' resistance. This, it is believed, slowed the process whereby the military shed its 'colonial identity' in favour of one with clear 'national' credentials. Nevertheless, questions about the military's new identity, and its relation to 'nationalist state ideology' surfaced soon after independence.[8] They were triggered by Pakistan's military failure in Kashmir in September 1948, which led to an attempt by a group of senior military officers to force a radical shift in military thinking and transform the army into a 'national' force. The 1951 'Rawalpindi conspiracy case', as it came to be known, has been described as 'genuine, small and serious'.[9] Though swiftly crushed, it pointed to the presence of a simmering debate in the army unleashed by Pakistan's military defeat in Kashmir.

It focussed attention on the army's less-than-'national' complexion, which was held responsible for wrecking military operations in Kashmir. Resentment was especially strong against British officers in senior positions (including General Douglas Gracey, then commander-in-chief), whose concern to protect British interests, it was alleged, had undermined Pakistan's national interest in gaining control of Kashmir.[10] Although those implicated in the conspiracy were also said to have communist leanings, the evidence is far from clear.[11] What is not in doubt is that the accused were pre-occupied by the issue of army's 'national' image and the means to transform it from a 'colonial' into a 'national' institution. In so doing, they are very likely also to have confronted the uncertain relationship between religion and nationalism that defined Pakistan's national identity.

This was reflected in military thinking at the time, which equated nationalising the army with the adoption of religious symbols and historical allusions based on Islam, which were neither necessarily moderate nor liberal. Thus by the late 1950s and early 1960s, parallels were drawn between the armies of the classical age of Islam and the armed forces of Pakistan.[12] Models of 'Muslim' soldier-hood were discussed in army journals and Quranic verses invoked to explain and illuminate the Muslim conduct of war.[13] These developments emerged in tandem with other changes that heightened awareness of the need to forge a national military identity that would represent both a departure from colonial models influenced by Britain and America as well as a clear break with its Indian counterpart with which it had once shared a colonial-secular heritage. But it was far from clear how this military identity could be conceptualized.

Over time, the lack of any clear intellectual resolution of these issues at the national level was overtaken by shifts in the class composition and patterns of military recruitment that eventually forced the military to become more responsive to the language of Islam—even if the meanings attached to Islam still varied widely within the institution. At the same time, the army's growing involvement in politics meant that it now urgently required the use of Islamic symbols able to provide military regimes with legitimacy[14] and the power to re-cast the country's national identity in line with the military's domestic authority and the pursuit of its regional objectives.

Alavi was among the first to examine the nexus between sections of the army and pro-Islamic groups in a landmark study of the post-colonial state. He highlighted how new patterns of recruitment in the 1960s—from poorer districts of Punjab and from the North West Frontier Province—reshaped alliances in Pakistan's premier military institution.[15] Recruits with strong social grievances soon outnumbered the sons of wealthy landed families who had once supplied the bulk of the army's conservative generals. These new recruits were more prone to the religious extremism associated with the Jamaat-i-Islami, whose influence in the armed forces by the late 1970s had become well-established.[16] This has been confirmed by more recent research showing that those who joined the officer corps after 1971 were drawn from more modest social backgrounds than their predecessors, and that these recruits from the urban lower-middle and lower classes were also more inclined to favour 'conservative religious values'.[17] The tarnished image of the army in the aftermath of Pakistan's military defeat in 1971 also eroded its appeal among more affluent groups, which gave way to recruits from humbler backgrounds lacking exposure to Western influences and trained mainly at local military academies.[18] Increasingly the army was regarded as a source of employment for rural families of modest means and the urban lower-middle classes, encouraging trends that would eventually transform the military into the site of lucrative rewards and profit-making ventures.[19]

These changes had a profound effect on the officer corps, which left it more vulnerable to Islamist influences. In his now classic study on the Pakistan army, Cohen identified three generations of military men—the 'British', the 'American' and the 'Pakistani'. They were shaped by their distinct class and social backgrounds and by exposure to distinct events and cultural influences, which produced more or less homogeneous cohorts of officers.[20] Each showed distinct features: the ethos of military professionalism of the first 'British' generation;[21] the more pronounced liberal attitudes of the next 'American' generation of army officers[22] both of which sat well with the social background of the officer classes; and the new post-1971 'Pakistani' generation of army officers of a diminished and less well-funded army (due to cutbacks in US aid) who were 'more representative of the wider society in class origin ... least subjected to foreign professional influences, and ... drawn from a generation with no direct contact with India"'.[23] Regional and ethnic distinctions in the army between the numerically preponderant Punjabis and others,[24] changes in standards of professionalism that sought to de-link their attachment to 'Western' norms, and the introduction of subjective criteria (personal and family connections or religious zeal) for promotion in the ranks,[25] were other factors that altered the character of the army and its role in national politics—thus inducing a re-articulation of Pakistani nationalism.

The 'Pakistani' officer class that took over during Zia's military regime had had little exposure to Western professional influences. It represented a generation that was more familiar with the Muslim Middle East (especially the Gulf States) through training and security related programmes and that had no direct contact with India.[26] Although recruitment was still overwhelmingly biased in favour of the Punjab, where geographical proximity to Kashmir and overlapping kinship ties between local Punjabis and Kashmiri Muslims kept alive the 'communal' dispute with India, other influences began to compete for attention.[27] They re-opened the question of Pakistan's identity, which had been thrown in doubt by the separation of East Pakistan, and revived the issue of Islam—an issue largely deferred (if not entirely suppressed) by the 'British' and 'American' generation of army officers in the 1950s and 1960s. A weakening in standards of military professionalism in the period 1965–71 and overt challenges to the authority of senior officers, whose secular ways were blamed for the debacle of 1971,[28] intensified the pressures in favour of a more Islamically informed military identity—which under Zia would come to equate military professionalism with Islamic piety and the display of religious beliefs as a pre-requisite for advancement within the ranks.[29]

It was at this time that there began to emerge signs of a recognisable symbiosis between the senior military leadership and parts of the religious establishment committed to a vision of 'transnational' Islam.[30] The driving force behind this convergence was the military's policy of 'proxy war' in Afghanistan and Kashmir, which aimed at redressing the regional strategic balance with India.[31] It relied on an irregular force of volunteers drawn from militant Islamic groups who were prepared to execute the military's policy across Pakistan's porous borders by invoking the language of Islamic universalism. It was facilitated by volunteers, who included Islamic combatants with global connections, and whose training had been entrusted to Pakistani military commanders. Their role, in turn, was facilitated by the constraints of the Cold War, which required all US assistance to anti-Soviet forces in Afghanistan to be covertly channelled through Pakistan's intelligence agencies.

Although the Pakistani military sought mainly to establish control over Afghanistan in an effort to secure for it strategic depth in the event of an attack by India, many were also drawn by the appeal of a transnational discourse of 'shariatization', which served to legitimize the regime's policies of extra-territorial adventure in Afghanistan. Furthermore, at a time when the break-up of Pakistan as a territorial entity had revived fundamental questions about the country's national identity, many responded readily to a discourse that offered a sense of purpose that appeared to transcend the goals associated with a 'nation' constrained by territorial borders.

The Pakistani army's engagement with pro-Islamic groups was not unprecedented. In 1947 the army had called on the religious zeal of Pathan tribesmen to stage armed incursions into Kashmir in an effort to liberate its Muslim population from Indian control. Later in 1971 it had worked closely with the armed wings of pro-Islamic parties, notably the Jamaat-i-Islami, to secure religious sanction for its brutal campaign against the 'enemies of Islam' among Bengalis in East Pakistan.[32] However, it was during the Afghan civil war that the involvement of militant Islamic groups with the senior military leadership, notably in the army, was most firmly cemented. Islamic parties and their more radical off-shoots responded enthusiastically, making available volunteers dedicated to the pursuit of transnational Islam and eager to act as conduits for covert assistance to the Afghan mujahedin.[33] It has also been suggested that Zia's Afghan policy was premised on the twin options of playing the ethnic and Islamist cards simultaneously. By favouring Pashtun-led Islamist parties in Afghanistan and Pakistan and by appealing to Islamic solidarity, Zia hoped to neutralize the 'Pashtunistan' issue—that is, the demand for an autonomous Pashtun state in Pakistan's North West Frontier Province. According to Olivier Roy, '[I]nstead of repressing their own "Pathans", the Pakistani military establishment (in which Pakhtuns [sic] were over-represented in terms of their demographic weight), chose to turn the Pakhtunistan [sic] issue the other way round, *by blurring the contested borders and taking root inside Afghanistan*' (italics added).[34]

Despite these historical links between the military and pro-Islamic militant groups, the rank and file of Pakistan's army came into contact with transnational Islam not through their ties with militant groups but through their exposure to non-militant movements, notably the Tablighi Jamaat, whose ostensibly non-political and proselytizing mission stressed faith renewal through personal reform. Originally a loosely structured organization, with a local base in the central Indian region of Mewat where it emerged in the late 1920s as a response to Hindu revivalist campaigns, it had spread rapidly across South Asia by the 1980s. Its transnational message, while rooted in the critique of the Indian Islam of the nineteenth century, was developed on the assumption that 'the more the Jama'at expands transnationally the more universally its ideology is recognized'[35]—an approach that was naturally boosted during the Afghan civil war.

Much of the Tablighi Jamaat's appeal among Zia's officer corps stemmed from Zia's own strong preference for its organization and ideology.[36] He was the first Pakistani head of state ever to attend a Tablighi annual congregation (*ijtima*) in 1979 at the organization's national centre in Raiwind, near Lahore.[37] Its initial attraction within the army may, ironically, have been rooted in its apolitical character since feigning distaste for politics has also been, for the army, the necessary ideological counterpart of its repeated and active political involvement. Yet the Tablighi Jamaat's apolitical stance is fraught with ambiguity, suggesting as it does that by 'making Muslims conscious of their separate identity and aware of their social obligations from a religious perspective [it] ultimately serves a political purpose'.[38] Moreover, its invocation of the faith (*dawa*) is inspired by the Deobandi reformist tradition, which emphasises external aspects of the *Sharia* over its inner meanings as favoured by most Sufi traditions. This is reflected in the preference of Tablighi members for more orthodox, Deobandi *ulama* parties, notably the Jamiat-ul Ulama-i-Islam (JUI).[39] Finally, as a proselytizing force, the Tablighi Jamaat harbours a strong activist component based on 'enjoining good and forbidding evil' (*amr b'il ma'ruf wa nahiy 'anil munkar*)—a core concept in Tablighi versions of *jihad* as action (not excluding violent action) in the service of God.[40]

This public disavowal of politics by the Tablighi Jamaat has permitted many officers and enlisted men to engage in its activities and to demonstrate their religious disposition without fear of raising suspicions about their engagement in Islamic activism. By the mid-1980s the presence of so-called *tablighis* in the army was common knowledge. Few officers made a secret of their attendance at Tablighi congregations or masked their involvement in Tabligh-led missionary work. Indeed one senior Tablighi activist, General Javed Nasir, rose to head the military's intelligence agency, the Inter-Services Intelligence

(ISI) in 1992–93.[41] Entrusted with the task of continuing the ISI's responsibility for the execution of Pakistan's Afghan policy, he discharged his functions through a combination of conventional intelligence techniques and the holding of *dhikr* (ritual remembrance of God) assemblies.[42] The military authorities not only looked benignly upon these developments, assuming the Tablighi Jamaat to pose no political threat, but the organization was also encouraged as a counter to the more strident discourse of Islamist parties like the Jamaat-i-Islami, whose insistent demand for an Islamic political state was seen as a challenge to the military high command.

The army's role in fostering the influence of 'transnational' influences was also rooted in Zia's regional policies, which sought to privilege Pakistan's putative 'ideological' boundaries over its territorial frontiers. This was closely tied to Zia's quest for political legitimacy, which he believed could be secured by re-casting the army from an institution dedicated to the defence of the state's borders to one concerned with guarding the 'ideological' frontiers of a wider Muslim community, whose limits would be set by the *sharia*. But in doing so, Zia also opened up for debate the validity of Pakistan as a nation-state by calling into question its role in hosting a separate 'national' army that appeared to stand in opposition to other Muslim armies and that thereby undermined faith in a Muslim commonwealth. It is perhaps not surprising therefore that, in the late 1970s and 1980s, some Pakistani military strategists approached the territorial state as something of '*an interim measure*' that would in time be succeeded by a more broadly based Islamic political entity.[43] In its place there emerged a preference for an alternative model that was held to be more consistent with the aims of an avowedly Islamic state like Pakistan. This model was increasingly defined by reference to Tablighi ideas of '*umma* consciousness'[44] that, by drawing attention to global Muslim unity, offered an implicit critique of the nation-state system.

This model also redefined the nature and conduct of state institutions under Zia. Directly challenging the assumption that what was authentic was necessarily national, he 'transnationalized' Pakistan's army along lines more in keeping with the presumed norms of extra-territorial Islam. Its authenticity would now be judged by how far it could extend its reach beyond the frontiers of the nation-state, whether in Afghanistan or Kashmir. Owen Bennett Jones, who has explored the relationship between the army and the transnational Islamic militant networks it deployed in these countries, concluded that it is far from 'a one-way street'. Common perceptions that the army merely aided and abetted Islamic militant groups overlook an altogether more 'insidious aspect': the motivation of Pakistani soldiers who fought alongside the Afghan mujahedin in Afghanistan and, later, with pro-Islamic militant groups in Islamists in Kashmir. These soldiers, he writes, were 'affected by their experience of working and fighting with Jihadis. Caught up by the romance of the Mujahideen's struggle, [they] have come to admire their civilian militant counterparts'.[45]

The influence of the Tabighi Jamaat on the military establishment must also be assessed in the light of Zia's attempts to diversify the religious basis of his regime. Having started out as an admirer of the Jamaat-i-Islami and of its blue-print for an Islamic society, Zia grew increasingly wary of its strident politics and resented its impatience with the pace of his regime's Islamization. Soon the Jamaat, which once enjoyed exclusive access to the armed forces, found that it was required to share influence with other groups Zia regarded as less politically suspect, notably the Tablighi Jamaat. It has also been argued that Zia himself had become disenchanted with the Jamaat-i-Islami's failure to put forward concrete proposals for an Islamic state or to propose an effective substitute for the secular state, whose ideology Zia believed had hastened the demise of earlier military regimes.[46] But Zia's transnational vision would have mattered less for the state and the nation had the army itself not undergone changes that made it more responsive to its appeal. To a younger generation of officers commissioned after 1971, who were less confident about the identity of their nation and about the contested boundaries of their state, Zia's image of the Pakistan army as an 'army of Islam' entrusted to protect 'the territorial and ideological frontiers of the state' presented one way of resolving this issue of identity. His recourse to the normative symbols of Islam was dictated in large part by his concern to legitimise his regime, but it also furthered the debate that had raged inside the army since the 1950s about its transformation from a 'colonial' to a 'national' institution.[47]

Zia reasoned that this could not be achieved without re-defining Pakistan as a state. Increasingly what emerged in the discourse of the ruling officer corps in the late 1970s and early 1980s was the notion that while the frontiers of the state of Pakistan were territorially demarcated, the boundaries of its nation were not. On the contrary, these were judged to be ideologically parallel to, and informed by, broad adherence to the *sharia*—resurrecting thereby the historical uncertainties over the precise relationship between the religious community and the nation that has clouded the idea of Pakistan since its inception. But it would also explain the powerful resonance of Zia's appeal to mould an army, whose role as the defender of the 'territorial and ideological frontiers of the state'[48] appeared finally to hold out the prospect of settling the question of Pakistan's identity.

Jihadis and juntas

The symbiosis between successive military regimes and so-called *jihadi* or militant Islamic groups in Pakistan has rested on two broad foundations: first, the need for a putative Islamic ideology to legitimize military takeovers and enhance the military's claims for an institutional role in national politics; second, rhetorical support for a pan-Islamic discourse to buttress regional policies dictated by military priorities.

Mobilising Islam in order to substitute for the absence of political legitimacy was a legacy of Pakistan's nationalist movement and has defined civil and military governments since the state's inception. The League's political roots lay outside the territories that formed Pakistan and many of its leaders were without constituencies in the new state. These 'unrepresentative' politicians were led to justify their control over the state by appealing to Islam. What this meant in practice was an overwhelming emphasis on a shared ideology—Islam—as the most important basis of political authority over and above any shared economic or political interest. Ethnic divisions and conflicts increased this temptation to rely on religion as a unifying factor. The military, which took power for the first time in 1958 under General Ayub Khan, inherited this legacy.

Although Ayub attempted at first to shift the basis of his regime's authority from an attachment to the putative Islamic purpose of the state to developmental goals that emphasized modernization and the consolidation of a strong state, the success of these endeavours proved short-lived.[49] His ambitious programme of economic and social reform failed to secure either the legitimacy of his regime or resolve the country's problem of national identity and the lack of consensus over Islam. Soon Ayub, like his political counterparts, found that Islam could mobilise forms of state authority that ordinary democratic processes, such as voting, left beyond his reach.[50] Although he had also hoped that his focus on development would help unify the country and reduce regional disparities, especially between East and West Pakistan, it had the opposite effect. Not only did they widen class and regional disparities, but, as Nasr persuasively argues, they also deepened divisions between 'a secular and Westernized ruling class and a mass of people living according to time-honoured Indo-Islamic traditions'.[51]

Loath to call on the procedures of democratic legitimacy, Ayub turned to Islam to boost the legitimacy of his regime and to contain the class and ethnic divisions that threatened it. It is notable that he also consciously avoided 'an absolutist interpretation of Islam' and showed little interest in sectarian interpretations that favoured Pakistan's majority Sunni Muslims or questioned who a Muslim 'really' was. Instead, he appeared to throw his weight behind a 'communal' (rather than an 'Islamic') understanding of Pakistan that projected it as a state created not so much to further the cause of Islam, but to free Muslims from Hindu domination and to defend Pakistan from India.[52] This 'communal' discourse, that is, the belief in one monolithic Muslim community that stood in opposition to 'Hindu India', was appropriated by Ayub, for whom it appeared perfectly to encapsulate the rivalry between Pakistan and India upon which the military depended for its dominant position in national politics. He was to play a vital role in promoting this communal discourse of Islam—a role he expected both to enhance the standing of the military and strengthen its reputation at home and abroad as the purveyor of 'moderate' (rather than 'Islamist') interpretations of Pakistan's Muslim identity.[53]

But Ayub also understood that an identity predicated on mere opposition to India could not, in the long run, sufficiently legitimate military rule or contain the challenge posed to the centralized military state by the expression of regional ethnicities that had gained ground since independence. With the idea of 'Muslim ethnicity', which had informed the conception of the Muslim 'nation', having outlived its purpose with the creation of the state,[54] he had now to craft a new identity for Pakistan. The aim was to allow the military to retain the communal emphasis on Pakistan's identity as a Muslim homeland created in defiance of a united India while making room for a more robust Islamic interpretation of this identity that was capable of supporting the military's geo-strategic objectives against its neighbour. By doing so, Ayub set in motion the first of many efforts by the military to reconcile two

159

diverging interpretations of 'Islam' that had attached to Pakistan's identity and to resolve their uncertain relation in favour of the military's own political interests.

The tone was set in September 1965 with the onset of Pakistan's second war with India over Kashmir. In his address to the nation, Ayub warned his people that 'Indian aggression in Kashmir was only a preparation for an attack on Pakistan'. 'Indian rulers,' he claimed, 'were never reconciled to the establishment of an independent Pakistan where the Muslims could build a homeland of their own', but their defeat was imminent because 'the 100 million people of Pakistan whose hearts beat with the sound of 'La ilaha illallah, Muhammad ur rasool ullah [there is no God but God and Muhammad is His messenger] will not rest till India's guns are silenced.'[55] Here, more clearly than ever before, Ayub signalled the army's intention to mould an identity for Pakistan that recalled both its status as a territorial Muslim homeland and a fortress of Islam, each bound to the other through the army, the institution charged with their common defence. In his autobiography, *Friends not Masters,* Ayub had ruminated on man's yearning for 'an ideology for which he should be able to lay down his life. Such an ideology with us' he had observed, 'is obviously that of Islam. It was on that basis that we fought for and got Pakistan'. But this had complex implications, he concluded, for while it was 'true that in [Islamic] society national territorialism has no place, yet those living in an area are responsible for its defence, security and development'[56]— tasks he confidently expected would be most readily associated with the military.

Tactics, as much as ideology, played a part in pushing this military vision of Pakistan's identity. The use of irregular mujahedin forces under the command of army officers during the 1965 campaign in Kashmir underscored this point. Encouraged by simmering Muslim unrest triggered by the disappearance of a holy relic attached to the Prophet Muhammad's hair from the Hazratbal shrine in Srinagar, Ayub turned to armed Islamist volunteers in order to instigate an armed revolt in Kashmir against Indian authority.[57] By stoking grievances around expectations of a shared belief in a collective Muslim identity under siege, Ayub paved the way for the convergence of an Islamist movement to safeguard Pakistan's identity and the communal discourse that had shaped Pakistan's Muslim identity in opposition to India. The need to forge such an alliance appears already to have been under some consideration. A report by Ayub's Bureau of National Research and Reconstruction, established in 1958, suggested that in the event of a crisis in its military alliance with the United States, Pakistan should call on its 'long traditions of irregular fighting' informed by 'its own ideology ... of self-defense (jihad) which Islam has ordained makes it incumbent upon everyone to contribute towards the national defense'.[58] Ayub clearly took the advice to heart when he ordered senior army commanders in 1965 to arm and train a force of Kashmiri irregulars, the Mujahid Companies, to defend Pakistani positions along the ceasefire line.[59]

So vital did these religiously motivated irregular forces prove to be in the pursuit of the military's regional objectives against India in these early years that it was unsurprising that the military rulers who succeeded Ayub considered relying on them to consolidate their power at home. The 1971 civil war in East Pakistan was the first testing ground of the domestic potential of a nexus between the military and Islamic militant groups hitherto used for foreign policy purposes. The strategy employed remained much the same, with the army relying on irregular paramilitary forces to conduct brutal attacks against the Bengali opposition before the onset of the formal military campaign. Underpinning this venture was a close working relationship between the Jamaat-i-Islami and the new military government headed by General Yahya Khan. He had taken over after mass demonstrations, in which the Jamaat had played a key role, had forced Ayub to resign. Elections held in 1970 had raised expectations that the Jamaat might emerge as a major power-broker. In the event, it failed to capture more than four seats in the National Assembly, prompting many in the party to look for an informal alliance with the military regime. For its part, the military government was keen to contain the build up of populist pressures in East and West Pakistan under the aegis, respectively, of the Pakistan People's Party and the Awami League. The Jamaat's willingness to mobilize, on behalf of the military government, its shock troops in order to curb political dissent, especially in East Pakistan, sealed this unholy alliance.

As the military campaign against the Awami League in East Pakistan got under way, the Jamaat mobilized thousands of armed volunteers (*razakars*) to be put at the service of Pakistani troops engaged in East Pakistan. Two brigades in particular, designated *al Badr* (sun) and *al Shams* (moon), gained notoriety for their readiness to employ counter-insurgency tactics against the Bengali guerrilla force (Mukti Bahini) in advance of army operations.[60] The brigades attracted well-educated recruits from *madrassas*, who were drawn by their brief to mount 'specialized operations' during the civil war. Said to be a euphemism for the activities of the army's death squads, they have been held responsible for the murder of scores of Bengali intellectuals on the outskirts of Dhaka just hours before the surrender by Pakistani troops in December 1971 to Indian forces fighting in support of Bangladeshi resistance.[61]

While these links between the military and counter-insurgency groups allied to pro-Islamic parties operations are yet to receive detailed attention,[62] they were consolidated by General Yahya's resolve to co-opt sections of the religious right that fared poorly in the 1970 elections. In September 1971 he inducted four members of the Jamaat-i-Islami into the cabinet to oversee the establishment of 'peace committees' in East Pakistan organized by local branches of the Jamaat-i-Islami and *ulama* groups affiliated to the Jamiat-ul Ulama-i-Pakistan and the Nizam-i-Islam party. This fresh symbiosis between military and pro-Islamic groups, which some believed had been weakened by Ayub's avowedly secular stance on questions of social reform, was welcomed by both sides. According to Nasr, the terms of the agreement ensured that 'the army would receive religious sanction in its increasingly brutal campaign, and the Jamaat would gain in political prominence'.[63] An additional consideration was the opportunity it provided to pro-Islamic parties to salvage their ideological credibility. Most of them had opposed the movement for Pakistan on grounds that it envisaged the creation of a secular state. Now, it was hoped, their engagement in a campaign to 'save' Pakistan from disintegration in 1971would finally see off politically damaging accusations that they were 'anti-Pakistan'.

The return to power of Zulfiqar Ali Bhutto as Pakistan's first democratically elected prime minister in 1972 marginalized the working relationship between the military and its religious allies, which until then had dominated state policy. Instead, populist forces allied to left-wing parties moved to occupy centre-stage. But Bhutto's failure to assert the authority of elected institutions against stiff opposition from a powerful military-bureaucratic alliance and his half-hearted commitment to economic reform undermined his hard won gains. A critical factor contributing to his downfall and to the concomitant resurgence of Islamic parties opposed to his policies was the defection of the lower middle classes, including traders, merchants and shopkeepers, especially in the Punjab. They had been badly affected by Bhutto's nationalization measures. Many belonged to families that had migrated from India and that still harboured feelings of insecurity about their new home, making them susceptible to the appeal of Islamic parties opposed to Bhutto's government.[64] More ominously still, military officers unhappy with Bhutto's PPP now turned to rekindle their interest in Islamism, gravitating towards Islamic parties and renewing ties established in the previous decades.[65]

Ultimately Bhutto was fatally weakened by his inability to break free from an ideological paradigm that had already been heavily influenced by the army. His spirited anti-India stance, which projected India as 'an enemy of Islam and Muslims and, therefore an inveterate foe of Pakistan'[66] suggested that, whatever his differences with the military (and there were many), he was unable to resist the force of a carefully crafted identity for Pakistan that sought to bring the military's geostrategic vision in line with the state's presumed organic Islamic character. Nowhere was this more in evidence than in his justification of the need for a nuclear deterrent against India in terms of Pakistan's weapon in the service of 'Islamic civilization'.[67] Like the military Bhutto also came to rely on Islamist groups to secure Pakistan's objectives against Afghanistan. In late 1973 he approved plans to recruit conservative, pro-Islamic groups to mount an insurgency in Afghanistan against the powerful Afghan premier, Mohammad Daoud, whom he accused of fanning the flames of Pashtun nationalism and of encouraging Pakistan's Pashtun population to press their claim for an independent Pashtunistan. A newly created 'Afghan cell', supervised by Bhutto's close confidante and head of Pakistan's frontier paramilitary forces, General Naseerullah Babar, oversaw this covert Islamist insurgency, confirming the military's jealous control of Pakistan's regional policies and its by now habitual use of Islamist groups to further these policies.[68]

Yet even while Bhutto shared the military's understanding of Pakistan's national security objectives he was wary of relying on Islamist groups to pursue his domestic policies. There is no evidence, for example, that he called on the use of Islamic irregular forces to sustain his military campaign against nationalists in Balochistan in 1973–77. On the contrary, Bhutto regarded Baloch nationalism as primarily a challenge to his personal authority and a threat to the centralized state. As such he did not hesitate to crush it by crude military force, avoiding any of the Islamically enflamed ideological justification that had been judged necessary to contain Bengali nationalism in East Pakistan. This was also a reflection of Bhutto's confidence in the sources of his own domestic legitimacy: he believed that he could afford to be less dependent on Islamist groups. This did not mean that he ruled out the appeal of Islam to secure his own domestic political survival (as his concession over the Ahmedi issue demonstrated) or to enhance his international standing (as his mastery of the 1974 Lahore Islamic summit amply suggested). Rather, he was less tempted to cultivate the kind of linkages that bound the military and Islamists because he still believed that his legitimacy derived from a democratic mandate beyond the reach of the military and their Islamist allies.

No leader did more rudely challenge Bhutto's optimism than General Zia ul Haq. Under his regime, the military came closest to affecting a convergence between the country's armed forces and Islamist groups in matters of state interests and national identity. The context of this alliance had already been set by Zia's close working relationship with the Jamaat-i-Islami, which had played a key role along with other Islamic parties in ousting Bhutto. But it was the role Zia reserved for radical Islamic groups in helping to shore up the domestic legitimacy of his regime and extending the reach of its power beyond Afghanistan and Kashmir that marked a new departure in the military's engagement with the forces of Islamism. Zia's admiration for Islamic parties, especially the Jamaat-i-Islami, and later the *ulama*-dominated Jamiat-ul Ulema-i-Islam (JUI), was well known. His personal piety and the demise of the two-nation theory precipitated by the loss of East Pakistan in 1971 reinforced in him the vision of Pakistan as 'an ideological state' predicated on Islam. The defence of this identity allowed the military regime to reap rich dividends at home among Islamist parties that had long sought to project Pakistan as an Islamic state and to respond to changes in the regional environment precipitated by the Afghan war, which now opened 'new strategic vistas for Pakistan'.[69]

Zia's success in articulating these diverse concerns lay in his deft handling of the internal and external demands made by Islamist groups on the military. Internally, it involved the engagement of private groups emerging from within Islamic parties and religious organizations to facilitate the state's domestic *jihad* by penetrating the private sphere with the aim of regulating individual morality. Externally, it centred on the mobilization of private armies linked to religio-political groups by re-casting the military conflict with India as a religious war. By so 'privatizing' the concept of *jihad*[70], Zia tailored it to match both his vision of the internal 'Islamic' character of the state and to serve as a formidable instrument in the projection of the military's regional ambitions.

Initially Zia's impulse had been directly to involve the state in the management of both processes rather than to sub-contract them out to groups beyond the formal control of the state. But soon after announcing ambitious plans for the moral transformation of society in the early 1980s, he realized that the practical implementation of Islamic strictures relating to eating, drinking, prayer and fasting were beyond the capacity of the state. The rethink may well have been prompted by advice from the regime's preferred think-tank, the Council of Islamic Ideology (CII), which in 1982 called on the regime to seek the co-operation of like-minded groups in society to back its moral reform program, saying it could not be achieved through mere public legal enactment.[71] Zia's hopes that the state would take the lead in formulating an 'Islamic' foreign policy also had to be moderated when he was forced to agree, in exchange for generous US assistance, to the terms set by the United States for the conduct of the covert war in Afghanistan. It led the government effectively to relinquish control over the day-to-day management of the war to privately armed groups, whose proclaimed dedication to *jihad* was to prove the only test of their loyalty to the regime.

Buoyed up by these incentives and eager to extend their own separately crafted agenda of sharpening Pakistan's identity as a guarantor of Islam, there now emerged a clutch of Islamic groups who offered their services to the regime. They included groups such as Hizb-ul Mujahedin (HM) and Harkat-ul Mujahedin (HAM), which were closely allied to the Jamaat-i-Islami and the Jamiat-ul Ulama-i-Islam (JUI) respectively. Others developed as armed wings of religious organizations. One such example was the Lashkar-i-Taiba (re-named Jamaat-ud Dawa in 2002).[72] Its parent organization, the *Dawat-ul Irshad* (Centre for Preaching and Guidance), encouraged by Zia, had emerged as one the most influential purveyors of a new educational philosophy that justified the use of force to re-educate society along Islamic lines and further Islam's proselytizing mission.[73] Granted prime land by Zia in 1986 in the small, dusty town of Muridke, some 20 kilometers north of Lahore, it claimed the responsibilities Zia had hoped to reserve for the Islamic state. But the Lashkar-i-Taiba insisted that, in the absence of such an Islamic state, it was justified in monitoring both standards of individual behaviour expected of Muslims, such as the payment of *zakat* and in mobilizing individual Muslims to wage *jihad* wherever other Muslims were oppressed beyond the frontiers of Pakistan.[74] While its case with regard to *zakat* was broadly in line with Islamic tradition—which recognized the payment of *zakat* as a Muslim's religious duty and therefore within the private domain of piety[75]—Lashkar-i-Taiba's stance on *jihad* as an individual exercise represented a major break with Islamic tradition insofar as it required the declaration of *jihad* to be backed by state sanction.[76]

Other more amorphous groupings also emerged at this time, defined less by their organizational rigour than by the presence of charismatic individuals. One of these was a loose assembly of radical Islamists grouped around Maulana Abdullah, an obscure hard-line cleric who had set up base at the Red Mosque in the heart of Pakistan's capital, Islamabad. He won Zia's favour after agreeing to recruit thousands of Muslim holy warriors (*jihadis*) to take on Soviet forces in Afghanistan. In exchange, he secured permission in 1986 to expand his mosque complex and build two Qoranic schools. They were to become the target of military action by President Musharraf in 2007, who acted in retaliation against a series of vigilante actions in Islamabad aimed at imposing *sharia* law. Until then the Red Mosque had basked in the glow of patronage by senior members of Zia's military and intelligence apparatus for whom it served as the first port of call for eager recruits prepared to bolster the military's strategy at home and abroad.[77]

At the heart of these varied alliances lay the military's objective to harness Islamist groups in the service of its interests against Afghanistan and India. While the first centred on neutralizing the irredentist threat poised by Pashtun nationalism, the second involved a strategy of 'bleeding' India by fuelling militant unrest in Kashmir in the hope of winning concessions from New Delhi. In time both converged and were subsumed by the larger goal of resisting India. The control of Afghanistan came increasingly to be dictated by military perceptions of its value as a vital point of retreat in the event of an Indian attack on Pakistan. Support for insurgent groups in Kashmir pressing for secession from India would bolster the campaign in favour of the province's integration into Pakistan.

These objectives were fraught with risk. Fierce factional fighting between rival mujahedin groups following the withdrawal of Soviet troops in 1989 demonstrated that Pakistan's control was more tenuous than it once thought and threatened to compromise what Zia described as Pakistan's hard earned 'right to have a friendly regime in Afghanistan'[78]—a right it sought later to exercise by nurturing the Taliban. In the meantime, the end of the civil war in Afghanistan had also left thousands of Islamist volunteers recruited as fighters without an occupation. They stood as both a threat and an opportunity to the military. While mindful of the dangers of unleashing the zeal of these holy warriors in pursuit of their Islamist ideals at home, the military was clearly unwilling to squander their potential to wage a campaign, masquerading as jihad, in support of regional gains against India. Having mastered the art of covert warfare, the military now sought to replicate the 'liberation' of Afghanistan by mounting greater Islamist resistance against Indian forces in Kashmir.

The prospect of this new adventure was received enthusiastically by the military's Islamist protégés, who were heartened by the familiar rhetoric of *jihad*. Nevertheless, there were differences within these militant groups that were to become more pointed and, in time, render more difficult the military's task of controlling them. Some like the Harkat-ul Jihad al-Islami (HUJI), founded by a band of students at the radical Binori *madrassa* in Karachi who joined the Afghan resistance in 1979, were driven by the appeal of a pan-Islamic state. It was part of an organizational network that extended beyond Pakistan to include parts of Central Asia, China and Bangladesh.[79] Others, like the Hizb-ul Mujahedin (HM), founded in 1989 as an armed subsidiary of the Jamaat-i-Islami, had more limited objectives centring on the integration of Kashmir into Pakistan.[80] What united them was the shared rhetoric of *jihad*, their preferred instrument of choice to achieve their objectives.

At this time too some Pakistani military officers were irresistibly drawn to *jihad* as the means not only to defy India's military superiority, but also to settle the issue of Pakistan's Islamic identity. Among those pressing for the more creative use of jihad were senior military commanders, including Generals Hameed Gul and Javed Nasir. Both had been closely involved in training Pakistani and foreign fighters in Afghanistan and both would subsequently head the Inter-Services Intelligence (ISI). Gul, described as 'loudly religious',[81] took over as head in 1987. Disillusioned with the Geneva Accords and disenchanted with the United States, he soon emerged in his own words as a 'Muslim visionary' with an eye to purging Pakistan of Western cultural influences and paving the way for an Islamic revolution.[82] Nasir, a born-again Muslim, was involved in the recruiting, training and arming of militants under the auspices of a so-called 'Kashmir cell' supervised by the Inter-Services Intelligence (ISI). Both enjoyed privileged relations with local and foreign jihadi groups and neither made a secret of his desire to translate religious convictions into political practice.

The rhetoric of *jihad* served as a perfect vehicle for these concerns. Gul and Nasir held strong pro-Islamist views and favoured the projection of Pakistan's identity as a pan-Islamic hub. Under Nasir's leadership, the ISI (much to the consternation of Pakistan's ally, China) supported Chinese Muslims in the Xinjiang province, Muslim rebel groups in the Philippines, radical Muslims in Central Asia and channelled arms to Bosnian Muslims.[83] By the mid 1990s the links between sections of the military high command and radical Islamists had clearly fuelled confidence in the prospect of a military-led Islamist takeover such as came to light following the arrest in September 1995 of thirty-five senior officers on charges of planning to stage a mutiny and impose a strict Sunni Islamic state with a pan-Islamic agenda drawn up by the Harkat-ul Jihad al-Islami (HUJI).[84] The aim was to re-cast Pakistan's identity from an 'introverted' Muslim state confined to South Asia to 'an extroverted Islamic state', whose interests extended past its frontiers to the Muslim world beyond.[85] Although out of all proportion to Pakistan's real power to undertake military conquest, this geopolitical conception was designed to help ease the uncertainties that had plagued the debate about Islam and national identity.

The backing of civilian governments in the 1990s in favour of the use of *jihadi* groups as strategic assets in Afghanistan and Kashmir testified to this. Benazir Bhutto and Nawaz Sharif, who held power in turn as prime ministers during this period, readily agreed with the priorities, as well as the means, set by the military in the pursuit of Pakistan's regional policy. From 1989 onwards, both endorsed the use of irregular forces in Kashmir and Afghanistan—even if each did so as much to out-manoeuvre the other as to reinforce the military's objectives. Both leaders recognized that the space afforded to Islamist groups under Zia left them with no choice but to join them in using the issue of Kashmir as a means of bolstering the Islamic credentials of their respective parties. During her first government (1988–90), Benazir Bhutto moved to regain the initiative on Kashmir by declaring 5 February a public holiday to 'pray for the success of *jihad* in Kashmir'. This was in response to Sharif's call for a national strike to mark Pakistan's solidarity with the people of Kashmir.

By the time Bhutto took power for the second time in 1993 the stage was set for a more marked investment in militancy. It was facilitated by her government's alliance with the JUI, intended to divide the Islamist vote then being assiduously courted by Sharif. Her move was to prove vital in strengthening the so-called 'military-mullah' nexus by enabling her resourceful Interior Minister, General Naseerullah Babar (who had been recruited by her father on a similar military mission to curry favour with Islamist groups in Afghanistan—see above), to develop a working relationship with the JUI, whose string of Deobandi *madrassas* nurtured the Taliban. They took power in Afghanistan under Bhutto's watch in September 1996. This has led some to conclude that 'between 1993 and 1997 the most radical element of Islamism was associated with the military and the secular PPP, not with the mainstream Islamism of Nawaz Sharif and the PML'.[86]

This is not to say that Bhutto's opponent, Nawaz Sharif, eschewed links with the jihadist network. Sharif's umbrella organization, the Islami Jumhoori Ittehad (IJI-Islamic Democratic Alliance) included the Jamaat-i-Islami, whose militant arm, the Hizb-ul Mujahedin (HM), had by the early 1990s become the most organized and effective group in Kashmir. It enjoyed Sharif's active support for its role in Islamizing and, indeed, 'Pakistanizing' the conflict in Kashmir, seeking as it did to impose versions of Islam more compatible with the Jamaat's Islamist vision than with the Sufi interpretations more common to the region.[87] Sharif, who maintained close relations with the military high command and the ISI, especially during his first tenure as prime minister, was also said to have considered proposals by the ISI to back covert activities by foreign jihadi groups in Kashmir using the proceeds of the drugs trade.[88] Although Sharif strongly denied his involvement in any plan to finance pro-Islamic militant groups in Kashmir on these terms, his first tenure coincided with a clear change in tactics that pointed to greater emphasis on the covert use of intermediary groups in order to widen the conflict. It was demonstrated in 1993 with the emergence of the Harkat-ul Ansar (HUA, also known as the Harkat-ul Mujahedin, HAM), which would soon displace more public outfits such as the

Hizb-ul Mujahedin (HM), to become the chief agent for the covert recruitment, training and arming of foreign fighters in Kashmir on behalf of Pakistani interests.[89] This marked a pronounced shift in favour of groups dedicated to recasting the conflict in Kashmir as a global war between Muslims and non-Muslims.

Changes in the ethnic composition of the leadership of some militant groups facilitated this process, leading to the fragmentation of the *jihadi* landscape. One such case was the Harkat-ul Ansar (HUA), whose Pashtun leadership tended to be less motivated by concern for Kashmir than the cause of *jihad*. Not surprisingly, it soon split with most of its Punjabi rank and file, whose commitment to Kashmir led to the creation in 2000 of Jaish-i-Muhammad under the leadership of Masood Azhar from Bahawalpur in southern Punjab. By the time Sharif took over as prime minister for a second time in 1997, so-called '*jihadi* culture' had become far less of a monolithic phenomenon. At the same time, it had also developed as an endemic feature of Pakistan's political landscape, with the military's intelligence agencies believed to be casting long shadows on its trajectory.[90]

In reality, these bonds between the military and radical Islamist groups concealed tensions that stemmed from their competing visions of Pakistan. These tensions would exact a devastating price during the late 1990s and in the aftermath of the country's controversial engagement in the US-led 'war on terror' in 2001. Having used the language of Islam in the service of a Muslim communal agenda that justified opposition to India, the military was forced to confront the challenge of meeting the lavish expectations it had fostered. The most immediate focus of that challenge lay in the resolve of Islamist groups to bring home the *jihad* and sharpen the state's Islamic profile by targeting those judged not to be 'real' Muslims in Pakistan. It has led to unprecedented sectarian violence between Sunnis and Shias, but also to the dangerous fragmentation of Islam encouraged by so-called 'Talibanization' sweeping parts of the country's north-western regions, which now threatens the state and its institutions, notably the army.

The wages of sin

Of the many metaphors used to describe Pakistan's political turmoil on the eve of the twenty-first century, none appears to have so fully captured its flavour as the term 'blowback'. A leftover from terminology first employed by American agents in the 1950s to refer to the unintended consequences of covert actions in the pursuit of Cold War objectives abroad, it has come to epitomize Pakistan's acute crisis, at once victim and perpetrator of seemingly random events. These events have been closely tied to the conflicts in Afghanistan and Kashmir, which brought the military establishment and militant Islamists closer. In time this convergence blurred the lines between military priorities driven by a Muslim communal discourse of identity predicated on Pakistan's rivalry with India and Islamist concerns that relied on the structure of this rivalry to reinforce Pakistan's Islamic character. Although the soldier and the mullah began as rival contenders in the struggle to define the meaning of Pakistan, their common search for sources of power beyond the reach of the democratic process led them both to depend on the language of 'Islam'. This convergence became more palpable after the separation of East Pakistan, which resurrected entrenched uncertainties about the country's Islamic identity. The conflicts in Afghanistan and Kashmir, which depended upon the regional invocation of Islamism, accentuated these uncertainties by enhancing the transnational dimension to Pakistan's national identity. It paved the way for a fresh fight-to-the-finish among irreconcilable political and religious competitors, who today pose the most potent challenge yet to the survival of the state.

The repercussions of Pakistan's destructive engagement in these regional conflicts were quick to materialise. Its deadliest manifestation was the escalation of sectarian violence between Sunnis and Shias, which has scarred the country's political landscape and shaken the foundations of state and society. Although the discourse of sectarianism, and indeed sectarian conflict, had assumed political overtones since the implementation in the 1980s of pro-Sunni policies by General Zia, it was not until the mid 1990s that sectarian violence came to be recognized as a direct consequence of Pakistan's engagement in Afghanistan. Pakistan's support for the Taliban was unquestionably a key factor in accentuating sectarian violence in Pakistan insofar as it helped establish an internationalist 'Sunni sphere of influence'. It drew inspiration from Saudi Islam and relied on international connections furnished by its close, if amorphous, links with Al Qaida.[91] After the Taliban assumed power in 1996 they deepened their links with radical Sunni groups in Pakistan, providing sanctuaries and serving as a conduit for arms. Before long the Taliban's fiercely anti-Shia rhetoric came to serve the ends of Sunni sectarian forces, such as the Sipah-i-Sahaba-i-Pakistan (SSP) and its militant off-shoot, the Lashkar-i-Jhangvi (LJ), which were dedicated to the creation of a Sunni state in Pakistan.[92]

Yet the onset of sectarian conflicts flowing from Pakistan's involvement in Afghanistan clearly predated the Taliban take over, having assumed a new dimension when the Soviet withdrawal from Afghanistan brought home the *jihad* to Pakistan. The country soon became the site of two fundamentalisms: the 'red' variety, coming from Iran and the 'green' kind promoted by the military and its Islamist allies.[93] One significant measure of the sectarian blowback was the 1995 military coup attempt, which, with the help of Sunni militants allied to the Harkat-ul Jihad al-Islami (HUJI), had aimed to declare Pakistani a Sunni Islamic state. Support was strong in Punjab, where the HUJI followers (who came later to be known as the 'Punjabi Taliban') were active in sharpening the discourse of Sunni sectarianism in Punjabi districts around Raiwind and Jhang. Elsewhere, sectarian conflict was precipitated by the decision in the late 1980s to re-settle Sunni tribesmen from Afghanistan in an effort to alter the demographic complexion in regions such as the Northern Areas and the tribal agency of Kurram, both with a history of Shia activism.

Yet Pakistan's response to sectarian violence in the years following the Afghan conflict was ridden with contradictions. While the state was forced to recognize the scale of sectarian conflict and the dangers it now posed to its authority at home, the use by the military of sectarian groups in the pursuit of Pakistan's objectives in Afghanistan and Kashmir resulted in a policy of domestic appeasement dictated by self-interest. This explains how a campaign to stem the tide of Sunni sectarian violence in 1994–1996 in the Punjab, supervised by Benazir Bhutto's Interior Minister, General Naseerullah Babar, was actively pursued even while Babar approved arms and training for Sunni militants deployed to support military-backed operations in Afghanistan and Kashmir.[94] Thus groups implicated in sectarian violence at home were found co-operating with military commanders abroad.

They included militant off-shoots of political parties that enjoyed the confidence of the military high command. For instance, the Sipah-i-Sahaba-i-Pakistan (SSP) and its military arm, the Lashkar-i-Jhangvi, although blamed for numerous sectarian attacks against minority Shias, maintained privileged relations with the military through their organizational links with Jaish-i-Muhammad—which was one of the main Pakistan-based *jihadi* groups operating in Kashmir that worked closely with the military to sharpen the Kashmiri (and Punjabi) profile of *jihadi* activism against Indian forces.[95] What held these groups together was Pakistan's 'Afghan war', which aimed both to undermine the prospect of a secular regime receptive to India as well as to nurture an Islamist government friendly to Pakistan. Helping to create and later support the Taliban served the two interests but, as Rashid has observed, it was Pakistan's rivalry with India over Kashmir that came increasingly to dictate its Afghan policy.[96] Of singular importance was the Taliban's agreement to provide access to training bases for Pakistan-backed militants preparing for attacks against Indian forces in Kashmir.

A major legacy of this militant culture, encouraged by Pakistan's involvement in Afghanistan and Kashmir, was the emergence of what is now commonly referred to as 'Kalashnikov culture'—namely easy and ready access to arms, which makes it simple for militant groups to become para-military organizations. What is also noteworthy is the spread of this militant culture to parts of the country not commonly associated with the so-called 'martial races'—a notion popularized by the British in India to justify higher levels of military recruitment into the colonial armed forces from northern Punjab and the frontier regions than, say, Sind or Balochistan. In Sind, for example, criminal violence soared when, in the wake of the Afghan conflict, arms and drug mafias controlled by ethnic Pashtuns were forced to move south from the regions bordering Afghanistan. These criminal networks, with their extended financial interests, came to permeate the world of Islamist politics in Sind, where they promoted 'Islamic' issues such as sectarianism. It soon resulted in what has been described as the 'Islamization of criminal activity and criminalization of segments of Islamism in Pakistan'.[97]

The pattern was replicated elsewhere in parts of southern Punjab around Bahawalpur, Multan and Rahimyar Khan. Not formerly known as recruiting grounds for the armed forces, these areas emerged in the early 1980s as choice bases for the recruitment of fighters loyal to jihadi and sectarian organizations, who since then have intensified their activities in these regions.[98] It was also in Bahawalpur that one of the more prominent jihadi groups, Jaish-i-Muhammad, emerged in 2000 under the leadership of Masood Azhar (himself a native of Bahawalpur) with the aim of widening the armed struggle in Kashmir.

It is open to debate whether the Pakistan armed forces were enthused by this growing militarization of society, for it suggested the determination of some powerful groups to break away from their military handlers. One such was Lashkar-i-Taiba (LT). While regarded by the military as a key asset in promoting its covert campaign in Kashmir, Lashkar's activities at home, and especially its role in fuelling sectarian conflict, soon caused consternation in the army. In 1998, a delegation representing Sharif's government that was said to have the backing of military commanders prevailed upon the Lashkar-i-Taiba to sever its links with Sunni sectarian organizations in exchange for a promise to be allowed to enter the political mainstream.[99] It prompted a country-wide crackdown against armed sectarian groups and against erstwhile allies of the Lashkar-i-Taiba, notably the militant Sunni organization, Lashkari-i-Jhangvi, aimed at ending sectarian violence in the country.

Yet, these efforts were to prove short-lived. Within a year sectarian violence had resumed in parts of the Punjab and the urban centres of Sind, leading to the assassination of scores of Shia and Sunni activists and prompting the army to step in to contain the violence. For most astute observers however it demonstrated the military's unwillingness to confront evidence that the sources of support for militant sectarianism in Pakistan lay in Afghanistan and Kashmir, where the army depended upon sectarian groups to execute its regional policies. Groups such as the Harkat-ul Mujahidin (HAM), involved in military-backed operations in both Afghanistan and Kashmir, were especially implicated in fuelling Sunni militancy in Pakistan.

The military's reluctance to sever its connections with these groups also rested on the assumption that, ultimately, it could effectively control their scope for action. During the 1990s the military's patronage of radical Islamists involved it in engendering a series of splits that aimed to weaken groups judged to be crafting independent agendas. Ethnic divisions facilitated these efforts. In early 1991 the pan-Islamic group, Harkat-ul Jihad al-Islami (HUJI), which had been co-operating with the military in organizing foreign fighters to join the Afghan resistance, was challenged by a break-away group of Pashtun fighters, leading to the creation of the Harkat-ul Ansar (HUA) (since renamed the Harkat-ul mujahidin, HAM). The Harakat-ul Mujahidin (HAM) was widely deployed in Kashmir and played a key role in the military's ill-judged attempt to seize the Kargil heights in 1999.[100] By 2000 it came also to be widely implicated in promoting a sectarian agenda in Pakistan, where it faced a split triggered by a faction with a large Punjabi following that emerged as Jaish-i-Muhammad.

Jaish-i-Muhammad was widely known to enjoy the backing of military sponsors, who were keen to consolidate the development of an identifiably 'Pakistani' group that would be more responsive to the military's specific objectives in Kashmir than 'foreign' *jihadi* groups with keener pan-Islamic agendas spawned by the conflict in Afghanistan. Sections of the military had also become aware of the need to check the growing power of the Lashkar-i-Taiba, which had insisted on claiming pride of place among the six hundred or so mujahedin combatants involved in the Kargil operation, and whose success in recruiting retired army and intelligence officials was believed to have significantly strengthened its organizational and operational capabilities.[101] With its growing influence and ambition to establish its supremacy among *jihadi* groups, it was not long before the military moved to contain the Lashkar-i-Taiba by sponsoring the creation of the Jaish-i-Muhammad. But any hopes that the military might have harboured in using the Jaish-i-Muhammad in the quest for its own regional objectives against India in Kashmir were thwarted by the group's dedication to pursuing an altogether independent sectarian agenda at home in co-operation with radical Sunni militants loyal to the Sipah-i-Sahaba-i-Pakistan and its armed wing, the Lashkar-i-Jhangvi. Some have gone so far as to suggest that the 'SSP [Sipah-i-Sahaba-i-Pakistan], the JM [Jaish-i-Mohammad] [sic] and the Lashkar-i-Jhangvi appeared to be three wings of the same party: the SSP [Sipah-i-Sahaba-i-Pakistan] was the political umbrella while the JM [Jaish-i-Mohammad] [sic] and the Lashkar-i-Jhangvi were the *jihadi* and domestic wings respectively'.[102]

But the ability of the military to control the complex agendas and activities of this vast array of militant groups was in fact far from secure. This was less a reflection of the military's coercive powers, which remained intact, than of its need to rely on the Islamist lobby to shore up the legitimacy of its fresh engagement in national politics. In October 1999, the army chief, General Musharraf, seized power vowing to restore national institutions and to repair Pakistan's image as a beacon of moderate Islam. But this agenda was almost immediately undermined by the military's close working relationship with Islamist groups upon which it still relied to pursue its regional objectives, especially in Kashmir. It was also compromised by the army's longstanding interest in containing political parties dedicated to reaffirming the primacy of a popular mandate as the only foundation for constitutional rule.

While international pressure forced the military, publicly at least, to loosen its connections with Islamist groups in Kashmir, its search for legitimacy at home enhanced its dependence on the Islamist lobby. Forced by international pressure to surrender its objectives in Kashmir, the military could no longer call upon its claim to act as a bulwark against India, which had served until then as the military's main *raison d'être*. Bereft of a robust narrative to sustain his hold on power, Musharraf was led increasingly to fall back on groups that actively favoured the discourse of Islamism. In time it would severely constrain his power to weaken the props that supported Pakistan's Islamic identity. These included thousands of Qoranic schools (*madrassas*), which successfully resisted official registration, as required under the Madrassas Registration Ordinance 2001.[103] Further evidence of the regime's impotence lay in its failure to repeal General Zia's notorious blasphemy laws aimed at non-Muslim minorities,[104] and to annul the equally abhorrent Hudood ordinances that, despite some minor amendments approved in 2006, continue to undermine the constitutional rights of Muslim women.

These developments have been seen to be suggestive of the military's enduring ambivalence towards Islamist groups and their agendas. Musharraf's personal involvement in the training and recruitment of the mujahedin in Afghanistan during Zia's tenure and his role in suppressing a Shia uprising in Gilgit in 1988 with the use of Sunni radical militants, it is argued, heightened his ambivalence and deepened his own appreciation of the advantages of fostering the military's links with Islamists.[105] It is also fair to assume that these links were considerably strengthened by Musharraf's decision to involve large numbers of irregular mujahedin forces in the military operation he commanded in Kargil in 1999 and by his co-operation at the time with key military commanders who were known to be deeply committed to the Islamist cause.[106] Since then, these links have become more complicated in response both to the development of a more muscular Islamist lobby in Pakistan and to the international constraints imposed on the military's ambitions in the wake of the September 2001 attacks. Such ambivalence was reflected in the contradictions of a military regime that was now obliged to rail publicly against 'Islamic extremism'—all the while seeking to preserve its 'institutional views', which were that the Islamists were its best allies in the struggle against India.[107]

Ultimately, this balancing act could not be sustained in an international climate that had fatally undermined the bedrock of the Muslim 'communal' narrative, with its emphasis on opposing India, upon which the military had long pitched its claims. While the military's involvement with the Islamists, especially since the 1980s, had given it the means to co-opt the Islamist narrative to serve its institutional interests, it could not (despite Zia's grand efforts) in the end claim to *speak* on behalf of this narrative. In the context of Pakistani politics, where the articulation of national identity was still uncertainly poised between opposition to India and reference to 'Islam', there were fresh opportunities for the amplification of the Islamist narrative as a drive to strengthen Pakistan's Islamic identity. But the course of this Islamist narrative has been uneven and it has come fiercely to be resisted by a military unwilling to relinquish its role as the final arbiter of the country's national identity.

The military leadership's intentions were posted soon after 11 September 2001 when it was forced to revise its Afghan policy and shortly afterwards to tone down its support for the insurgency in Kashmir. The first led it to withdraw support from the Taliban; the second forced it to rein in the operations of Islamic militant groups. While it was understood that these changes had been exacted in response to the demands from the United States, some within the military hierarchy were encouraged to use the occasion to contain the violent 'blowback' unleashed by the military's controversial support for Muslim extremist groups in Afghanistan and Kashmir. They appeared to enjoy the confidence of Musharraf, who in January 2002 announced a ban on all militant groups, including sectarian outfits, signalling thereby a break in relations between the army and its militant protégés in Afghanistan and Kashmir.

His decision came in the wake of a daring attack by militants on the Indian parliament in December 2001, which had brought Pakistan to the brink of a dangerous military confrontation with India. In his speech justifying the ban, Musharraf recalled Jinnah's vision of 'the ideology of Pakistan', which he claimed stood in contrast to the 'theocratic state' advocated by Islamist parties and their militant allies. Their attempts to establish a 'state within a state', he declared, would be defeated by his military regime, which had come to recognize that 'today Pakistan is not facing any threat from outside ... the real threats are posed from within'.[108] This public renunciation of groups once considered linchpins of the army's Kashmir policy was widely seen at the time as representing a welcome paradigm shift in the military's strategic thinking that hitherto had emphasised opposition to India. But in accepting this paradigm shift the military also lost the potential to feed off the Muslim communal narrative predicated on rivalry with India upon which its fortunes had so long depended.

Severely weakened by the loss of its ideological anchor, the military moved to salvage what it could of its bargain with Islamism. Within months of Musharraf's ban on Muslim extremist groups, they resurfaced with new names and their members resumed their activities. With his programme of 'enlightened moderation' coming under scrutiny from an increasingly sceptical liberal constituency, but unable to call on the 'communal' narrative informed by opposition to India, the military regime had no choice but to turn, again, to Islamist groups to help buttress its legitimacy. The new arrangement between the military and Islamist groups was demonstrated in two ways. The Islamist lobby supported Musharraf's tenure as president, while retaining the post of army chief (in violation of the constitution). In exchange, the military regime ensured the success of the Islamist lobby (now organized as the Muttahida Majlis-i-Amal, MMA) in the 2002 general elections, which allowed it to gain control of the governments of the North West Frontier Province and Balochistan, thereby decisively entering the political mainstream. What marked this arrangement out from others before it was that the military was no longer in control of a narrative, let alone the dominant one. By 2004, popular opposition to US policies in the region and the spread of a pro-Taliban tribal insurgency in the border areas next to Afghanistan had energized the Islamist lobby, putting it in a position finally to make good its challenge to oust rivals in an increasingly deadly struggle to define the identity of Pakistan.

The military's response was to try to craft a new narrative based on the fear of an imminent Islamist takeover. This rested on the assumption that the military, once the country's best defence against external aggression, was now the only force that stood in the way of a domestic Islamist peril. Although this claim came soon to be dismissed by some as a myth cultivated by the military to tighten its political grip,[109] the military's warning resonated abroad, where Western governments, fearful that violent Islamists could gain control of Pakistan's nuclear weapons, rushed to heed the alarm raised by Musharraf. Domestically the military's new narrative was doomed from the outset. Its weakness stemmed not so much from the fragility of its claims, which may have been real enough given the strength of Islamism in parts of the north-western regions, but from its failure to construct an alternative discourse that could compensate for the loss of the communal emphasis on Pakistan's Muslim, as against its Islamic, identity. With opposing India and stoking the Kashmir conflict no longer compatible with the demands of the new international order, the military might have turned to the county's indigenous cultural traditions to try and bolster its legitimacy. But with sharp ethnic divisions pre-empting any recourse to cultural unity as the basis of the nation, it has been forced to appeal to the 'values of Islam'. And since there is no consensus on the role of Islam, its efforts to resurrect a variant of the communal approach to Pakistan's Muslim identity by rooting it in ideas of 'enlightened moderation', soon proved to be futile.

Yet, Pakistan's search for validation has rarely been constrained by these internal considerations. Indeed, the uncertainty over its national identity and the lack of consensus over Islam that has dogged the state since inception have made it all the more imperative for Pakistan to compensate for its poorly developed identity by seeking corroboration from others. This has taken multiple forms, whether claiming parity with regional rivals such as India, forming alliances with great powers, notably the United States, or manipulating dependent states like Afghanistan.

6

DEMONS FROM ABROAD

ENEMIES AND ALLIES

It is commonplace to observe that a country's foreign policy is determined by its national interest. It is less common to suggest that in the case of a country like Pakistan, foreign policy has been dictated by issues of national identity. Indeed, what is revealing about Pakistan is the extent to which its foreign policy, though naturally shaped by national security interests, has served as a vital compensation for the country's lack of a clearly defined sense of nationhood.

Of all Pakistan foreign engagements, none has been as central to its identity as its relations with India. The peculiar circumstances of the country's creation very largely account for this. For Pakistan was born not in a struggle against British colonial rule, but in opposition to the Indian nationalist movement. Overcoming the legacy of this 'negative' identity has been the defining feature of Pakistan's policy towards India, and the greatest challenge of all has been embodied in their dispute over Kashmir. It is here, amid the rhetoric of rival claims over territory and state sovereignty, that Pakistan has fought to assert itself and to liberate its identity from the uncertainties that have attached to its status as merely 'not India'. But the achievement of this identity has depended also upon affirming Pakistan's historical claim to parity with India. Grounded in Jinnah's insistence upon the equality of the nations of Hindus and Muslims as the basis of any territorial division of British India, this search for identity has served as a powerful incentive in Pakistan's quest for military parity with India and its determined pursuit of the ultimate force equalizer—nuclear weapons.

It was perhaps inevitable that Pakistan's primordial conflict with India—almost seven times its size in population and more than four times its land mass—should have driven it to seek assistance abroad. Security against an attack from India was certainly a major consideration in its decision early on to enter into an alliance with the United States. Yet the basis upon which it contracted to do so also reveals Pakistan's need for validation and its desire to win recognition of its special status. The alliance with the US as a strategic 'partner' ensured that Pakistan's military defences against India would also project the country's global image. But Pakistan's drive to validate its identity by partnering the great powers in pursuit of *their* strategic objectives has brought few gains and none of the international recognition which would confirm its status as a power to rival India.

Nevertheless, the desire to play a role that is disproportionate to its actual power has been a fundamental aspect of Pakistan's self-perception. Rooted in the determination to free the country from its historical association with a Muslim minority discourse shaped in response to a Hindu majority, whose claims to nationhood it sought to emulate, it has left a lasting legacy on the conduct of the country's foreign policy. For the very attempt to emulate India has led Pakistan also to seek to match the foreign policy aims of its larger neighbour. Chief among these, and of overwhelming concern to Pakistan, was India's claim to be a regional power, which Pakistan has sought to imitate, particularly in its relations with Afghanistan. Although the consequences of these foreign policy ambitions have often been devastating to Pakistan and the strategic costs immense, no price is yet seen to be too high to validate Pakistan's claim to nationhood.

Standing up to India

No analysis of Pakistan's conflictual relations with India can avoid the question of historical antecedents. Of these, the violent and bloody events around the Partition have defined the bases of the unmitigated hostility between the two countries. They have fuelled a climate of suspicion that has led to three wars and that many now believe threatens a nuclear confrontation. At the heart of this deadly rivalry is Kashmir. While ostensibly a dispute over the control of territory, any proposed resolution has been complicated by issues that touch upon questions of national identity, the viability of national legitimation projects and conflicting interpretations of history.

Yet it is worth noting that even in the midst of the unremitting hostility which has triggered three wars (1948, 1965 and 1971) and two major military stand-offs (1999 and 2002), dialogue between the two sides has been kept alive. It has resulted in major agreements, ranging from an understanding to share river waters (the 1960 Indus Waters Treaty) to normalizing relations, albeit tenuously, over Kashmir (the 1972 Simla Agreement). Since 2002 there have been further efforts to break the deadlock over Kashmir.[1] These efforts have encouraged a so-called 'composite dialogue' that has boosted confidence-building-measures (CBMs), including bilateral trade, the relaxation of visa regimes, cultural exchanges and the settlement of lesser disputes involving troop withdrawals from the Siachen Glacier and the demarcation of the Sir Creek maritime border in the marshlands of the Rann of Kutch.[2] However, few expect such dialogue fundamentally to shift perceptions, especially in Pakistan, where opposition to India is still heavily laden with the significance of what it means to be Pakistani.

Indeed, much of the uncertainty over Pakistan's identity stems from the nagging question of whether its identity is fundamentally dependent on India and what its construction might entail outside of opposition to the latter. This has prompted the suggestion that Pakistan is a state burdened with a negative identity shaped by the circumstances of Partition. The League's rejection of 'Hindu domination', it is argued, has since fed Pakistan's national obsession with India. Unable to escape the India syndrome, it has failed to craft an independent identity beyond that which it moulded as a challenger to India.[3] The broad thrust of this argument is difficult to resist. With the creation of Bangladesh in 1971, the idea that Indian Muslims were a self-contained nation, whose attachment to Islam qualified them to seek separate statehood, became even harder to sustain. Yet, this vision rested on a further assumption that still exercises a powerful hold on the national imagination in Pakistan. It centres on the claim that the Muslims of India, distinguished by their political and historical importance as the dominant power in the region for over six centuries, had risen to a status of coequality, or parity, with their Hindu counterparts.[4] The creation of two separate states, India and Pakistan, appeared to the founders of Pakistan to validate this claim, even if it only did so in the Westphalian language of the *de jure* equality of states.

This argument has been vital to Pakistan and explains why its relations with India have been almost exclusively dictated by the need to defy the asymmetry of its position *vis-à-vis* its neighbour. While asymmetrical relations between states are by no means exceptional, Pakistan's experience has honed the belief that India still rejects the *rationale* of Pakistan's statehood, even if it has been forced to accept its reality. The roots of this perception also lie in diverging interpretations of Partition. For while Partition is widely represented in Pakistan as a triumph of Muslim nationalism and evidence of the irrefutable historical truth about Muslim nationhood, many in Pakistan live with the awareness that in India Partition is mourned as a tragedy—a painful reminder of the failure of India's secular project that could only be redeemed by undoing Pakistan. India's intervention in the civil war in Bangladesh in 1971, which led to the disintegration of Pakistan, still serves as proof for Pakistanis of India's intentions to cast doubt on the soundness of Partition, and by extension, the legitimacy of Pakistan.

This enduring rivalry[5] between India and Pakistan is grounded not only in rival interpretations of Partition, but also in two opposing national projects tied to distinct visions of nationhood: one (Indian) predicated on the principles of secularism, the other (Pakistani) founded somewhat problematically on the idea of a Muslim nation. At the same time, the designation of India and Pakistan as, respectively, secular and confessional states is far from straightforward. Indeed, the construction of these differences and their significance in the shaping of each state's identity are deeply contested in ways that have also influenced their relations with one another. Since its inception Pakistan has vigorously resisted any suggestion by India that it represents a theocratic or confessional Islamic state, while holding firm to its Muslim identity. However, the uncertainty attached to this identity has encouraged Pakistan to seek its most tangible expression in opposition to India's putative Hindu identity, which involves denying India's secularity. The instinct to shape Pakistan's Muslim identity in contradistinction to India's Hindu identity was epitomized by Jinnah, who set the tone by choosing to refer not to India, but to Hindustan.

But the affirmation of Pakistan's Muslim identity (against India's assumed Hindu identity) has been far from smooth. Since independence it has been vigorously contested by the protagonists of ethnic and regional groups on the periphery of the state, who oppose its right to appropriate the definition of Pakistan's Muslim identity. This has been especially marked with regard to military regimes which, by casting Pakistan's conflict with India as a civilizational[6] issue, have appeared to tighten the state's links with Islam and used them as a pretext to crush the articulation of ethnic differences. Another important consequence of projecting foreign policy issues in these terms has been to strengthen the impression that there exists a national consensus, especially on Kashmir.[7] This has been vital to military regimes in Pakistan, which more often than not have used the conflict with India over Kashmir as a pretext for retaining control over national politics. Tensions such as these have accentuated the uncertainty over Pakistan's national identity *vis-à-vis* India: for so long as Pakistan chose to subscribe to a Muslim identity shaped in response to the communal rhetoric of Partition, it seemed to acquire meaning only in relational opposition to India. However, by opting, as it did after 1971, to reorient itself more firmly in line with an Islamic identity attached to the Muslim world of the Middle East, it risked authenticating India's long-held portrayal of Pakistan as primarily a confessional state.

Thus, Pakistan's struggle against India is deeply embedded in a painful awareness of its own lack of a national history. The fact that India has had a historical identity (however ill-defined) that predated Pakistan's own has compounded the latter's need for external validation. Although the Independence Act of 1947 recognized India and Pakistan as two independent and equal Dominions,[8] in reality it had made no provision for two successor states—assuming that the Union of India would inherit the mantle of British India's unitary centre with Pakistan contracting out of the Union and then laying claim to its share of Union assets.[9] Though Jinnah successfully disputed these assumptions, most notably by rejecting proposals for a common governor-general for both Dominions and insisting on a separate governor-general for Pakistan—a post he chose to assume himself[10]—the implications of this debate had a deep impact on Pakistan. By choosing to declare its independence on 14 August 1947, a day before India, it hoped to neutralize any suggestion that it lacked an independent international persona. Yet, since its inception Pakistan has wrestled with the knowledge of India's historical precedence. This has served both as a reminder of Pakistan's historical status as a second-class successor to Britain's Indian empire as well as a disturbing indication that Pakistan was born, not out of a national struggle against a colonial power but merely as the legacy of secession by a minority in India.

The fact that many of Pakistan's legal boundaries are still in dispute (with Afghanistan in the tribal areas and with India in Kashmir) has also cast a shadow on the clarity of its sovereign identity. This has further eroded Pakistan's sense of national self, which remains tied to the affirmation of Pakistan's parity with India and which seeks assurance through military alignments with great powers (notably the United States) or the control of subordinate powers like Afghanistan that could be relied to enhance Pakistan's regional profile. While perceptions of the imminent threat posed by India to Pakistan's physical survival have been crucial in lending urgency to these policies, the country's approach to issues of war and peace with India has deeper roots grounded in questions regarding the identity and purpose of the state. While it is true that issues of identity have also played an important role in shaping Indian attitudes to Pakistan, especially in the wake of resurgent Hindi nationalism, the implications are quite different for India. As Nasr points out, 'India does not depend on identity for legitimacy, stability and survival in the manner that Pakistan does'; furthermore, he observes, 'Indian identity is not dependent on Pakistan'.[11] By contrast, the question of identity remains central in Pakistan, where the debate over the role of Islam continues to be played out externally and in relation to India—projecting a Muslim identity to counter India's notional Hindi identity or resisting India's interpretation of Pakistan's supposed 'Islamic' purpose.

Nowhere have these issues been more salient than in Pakistan's dispute with India over Kashmir. The conflict dates back to Partition, but few at the time (with the possible exception of Nehru) appreciated how symbolically charged it would be for the rival national projects espoused by the National Congress and the Muslim League. Jinnah himself had clearly underestimated the role that Kashmir would come to play in Pakistan's search for a coherent national identity. His only visit there, in 1944, was to lend support to Kashmiri Muslim groups, which under the aegis of the conservative Muslim Conference had decided to throw in their lot with the Muslim League. But his visit did little to rouse the League's senior leadership from its complacency over Kashmir or to spur their efforts to engage more vigorously with Kashmir's Muslim population.[12] By contrast, Congress leaders assiduously courted Kashmiri Muslims. In 1940 Nehru accepted an invitation from the Kashmiri nationalist and prominent Muslim leader, Sheikh Abdullah, who was said to have taken offence at Jinnah's decision to question the representative credentials of his organization, the National Conference.[13] Nehru visited Kashmir on two further occasions in 1945 and 1946. Senior Congress leaders, including Abul Kalam Azad and Ghaffar Khan, followed suit: both attended the annual gathering of Abdullah's National Conference in 1945, where their presence underscored this difference in approach to Kashmir in comparison with their counterparts from the League.[14]

Nevertheless, there was little to suggest that the casual attitude adopted by Jinnah and the League with regard to Kashmir would result in such heavy penalties for Pakistan. As a Muslim majority area that was contiguous to the country's western regions, Kashmir appeared to fulfil all the necessary criteria for inclusion in Pakistan. Few doubted that geography and demography would both favour Pakistan's right to Kashmir. How and why these claims came eventually to be thwarted are questions that have been mired in controversy and stand at the historical origins of the conflict. They centre broadly on the questionable decision in October 1947 by the Dogra ruler of Kashmir, Maharaja Hari Singh, to accede to India in response to an armed incursion by tribal militants from Pakistan. The precise terms under which this accession was secured have been contested. Suggestions from Pakistan that they were obtained under duress and possibly even *after* the deployment of Indian troops, have always been vigorously rebutted by India—although its claims to have acted legally have been questioned by independent scholars.[15] What is not in doubt is that the bitterness that followed the Maharaja's accession was instrumental in persuading Jinnah to send in his troops in an effort to regain control of territory that Pakistan has since believed should rightly have been hers. The short war that ensued escalated in May 1948, forcing the United Nations to take notice and impose a truce in early 1949, which led to the drawing of a ceasefire line (designated since 1972 as the Line of Control). It also left India with more than two-thirds of the disputed territory, including the coveted Vale of Kashmir. Pakistan controlled a narrow strip, consisting of western Jammu and Kashmir, renamed 'Azad', or 'Free', Kashmir, along with a clutch of remote mountainous regions further to the north-west collectively known as the 'Northern Territories'.[16]

Since then the status quo has twice been challenged by Pakistan. In 1965, it sought to instigate a mass uprising in Kashmir and seize the region by orchestrating a series of decisive military moves. Again, in 1971, it attempted to break through Indian positions along the LOC in retaliation for India's involvement on the side of the Bengalis in East

Pakistan, thus forcing it to redeploy its troops from Bengal.[17] But over time, Pakistan's position on the issue of Kashmir has also been altered by fundamental shifts in the nature of its national identity. At independence its approach to the problem of Kashmir was still dictated by an emphasis on Pakistan's communal identity shaped by the ideology of Muslim nationalism, which challenged Indian nationalist claims to represent Muslims and which insisted on the right to a Muslim homeland carved out of territories where Muslims were a majority. According to this logic, based on the idea that Muslims and Hindus were two nations separated by religion, Kashmir became central to Pakistan's territorial and communal identity. Therefore, so long as Kashmir was excluded the communal project that defined Pakistan remained incomplete. But this communal project was itself linked to 'the Muslim Question on the subcontinent',[18] which was overwhelmingly a question of where Muslims belonged rather than where Islam could be protected (though in practice there was much overlap between the two). Until 1971 Pakistan's relation to Kashmir was framed primarily in these terms insofar as Kashmiri Muslims were regarded as 'belonging' to the Pakistani homeland specially conceived for Muslims. Pakistan's support for a plebiscite in Kashmir did not, and indeed could not, on the basis of its 'national' logic, accommodate an independent Kashmir.

But Pakistan's relation to Kashmir as an expression of Pakistani identity changed after 1971. The loss of East Pakistan dealt a grievous blow to the communal project and with it Pakistan's communal identity. It forced Pakistan to re-imagine itself in terms that enhanced its Islamic identity and brought it more self-consciously in line with radical interpretations of a state based on Islam. With it came a shift in how Kashmir's relation to Pakistan's identity came to be represented. The focus no longer lay in projecting Pakistan as a Muslim homeland to which Kashmir as a Muslim majority province belonged by virtue of the established claims of the two-nation theory. Instead, Kashmir was recast as sacred territory awaiting liberation through jihad—thus authenticating Pakistan's identity as the protector of Islam. It is perhaps no coincidence, as some have noted, that in recent years Kashmir has emerged as much more of a territorial concern for Pakistan. Earlier generations had attached importance to it, primarily as a symbolic representation of the idea of Pakistan.[19]

Over time, the complex relation between Pakistan's identity and the issue of Kashmir has also been accentuated by the country's internal ethnic differences. It is now commonly acknowledged that the Kashmiri cause has always enjoyed much greater support in Punjab than in any other region of Pakistan.[20] Indications of uneven support for the campaign in Kashmir were already in evidence in the early years when official sponsorship met with a lukewarm response among the Bengalis in East Pakistan, who were far less troubled by the threat posed by Kashmir to the claims of Pakistani nationhood than by their ambiguous relation to West Bengal and their place in an overarching Bengali nation. Bengali impatience with the question of Kashmir finally bubbled over in 1965, when the bulk of Pakistani troops were deployed to protect Pakistan's western borders and positions along the Line of Control in Kashmir, leaving East Bengal defenceless.[21] These grievances over the conduct of the war have been regarded by some as crucially responsible for deepening Bengali political alienation and hastening the momentum towards the disintegration of the country in 1971.[22]

Since then doubts about the centrality of Kashmir to Pakistan's identity have surfaced in Sind and in Balochistan, where on the whole devotion to the Kashmiri cause has always been much less pronounced than in Punjab.[23] This is in part due to the relative marginalization of these provinces from the centres of power[24] and to the consequences of their poor representation in key state institutions, notably the armed forces. Indeed, the military has traditionally nourished a keen interest in the Kashmir dispute and, since it is dominated by ethnic Punjabis, this has made them the keenest supporters of the Kashmiri cause. It has also been suggested that the absence of any clear ethnic ties between Sindhis and Balochis on the one hand and Kashmiri Muslims on the other has accentuated their sense of distance from Kashmir and made them far less ready to regard it as central to Pakistan's national identity.[25]

This would also explain in part the strong commitment to Kashmir in Punjab, where many Punjabis take pride in tracing their roots to Kashmir—roots that have no doubt been strengthened by the proximity of the two regions and over time, by over-lapping patterns of migration and settlement. Since the 1980s these ties have intensified and acquired a distinctly Islamic hue that has in turn coloured the participation of Punjabi groups fighting on the side of Kashmiri militants.[26] The strengthening influence of *jihadi* activism in Kashmir has also roused the sympathies of the Pashtuns. Although they were not known to feel strongly about Kashmir, reserving their sympathies for

Afghanistan, they were now encouraged by the role of the disputed province in the re-definition of an Islamic identity for Pakistan. Their engagement had grown stronger under the influence of Deobandi *ulama*, who had gained ground among Pakistan's Pashtun population following their active participation in the Afghan war in the 1980s and who now sought to emulate their tribal forefathers' attempts to wrest Kashmir from the control of Indian 'infidels' in 1947.[27]

While the role of Kashmir in shaping Pakistan's identity *vis-a-vis* India cannot be over estimated, equally important has been Pakistan's desire to overcome its power handicap by aiming for military and diplomatic parity. In the 1950s Pakistan had hoped to counter this asymmetry through formal military alignments with the United States, aiming thereby to redress the imbalance in conventional military forces and strengthen the perception of Pakistan's equality with India. But the decision by the United States to arm India in the wake of the Sino-Indian war of 1962 left Pakistan with no choice but to turn to China to lessen the effects of its asymmetry. India, for its part, had burnt its bridges with the Soviet Union and the non-aligned world by actively seeking military assistance from the United States. However, China was no more willing than the United States to provide Pakistan with the formal security guarantees that it considered vital to counter the power differential with India and to help it erase the memory of its minority complex towards India.

The legacy of this 'minority discourse of power'[28] has been a determining factor in shaping Pakistan's self-avowed status as the challenger to India—a status it has single-mindedly pursued often at the cost of destructive regional policies. Though it was expected that independent statehood would ease the pressure of these claims on Pakistan, the crippling disadvantages with which Pakistan emerged at independence[29] meant that the equality guaranteed by formal statehood amounted to little when set against its rival's size, resources but especially its military strength. While Pakistan recognized that it could do little to redress the balance of the first two, the temptation to match India militarily proved to be irresistible. For almost three decades after independence, Pakistan was single-mindedly dedicated to overcoming its military inferiority by forging close security relations with the United States—before turning to China to help compensate for the shortfall brought on by the suspension of US aid after the Indo-Pakistan war of 1965 [see below]. It was however the military confrontation with India in 1971 and the humiliation of defeat at the hands of Indian military forces in Bangladesh, while the United States and China looked on, that finally convinced Pakistan it could no longer depend on unreliable allies to overcome the military imbalance with India.

The search for parity now shifted to the unexplored terrain of nuclear weapons as the ultimate means of tackling the issue of deterrence posed by India's overwhelming military superiority. There were other considerations that prompted Pakistan to sign up to the nuclear option. One important factor involved increasing pressure on India to make concessions on Kashmir by using the nuclear threat as an umbrella under which to stage low-intensity conflicts of the sort witnessed in Kargil in 1999.[30] Another centred on Pakistan's long standing desire to enhance Pakistan's status in the Muslim world as *primus inter pares*.[31] More recently, it has even been suggested that Pakistan hoped to use its nuclear status to act as the guarantor of a new strategic dispensation in Central and West Asia and match India by acquiring strategic depth.[32] Whether any of these objectives have been well served by Pakistan's nuclear status remains a moot point. What is not in doubt is that Pakistan's role in the proliferation of nuclear technology in recent years has so deeply compromised its status as a nuclear power that few believe that it can now fulfil the country's ambitions to share the space that has come to be reserved for India as a mature and full-fledged member of the international community.

America's sullen mistress

Nowhere has Pakistan's determination to counter its perceived asymmetry with India exacted a higher cost on the country than in its relations with the United States, which have been defined by mutual dependence rather than mutual respect. While Pakistan has needed the United States to validate its claim to be the equal of India, the United States has relied on Pakistan to act as its local proxy in pursuit of America's foreign policy aims.[33] And while the United States has consistently refused to grant Pakistan the privilege of the formal security guarantees that would have secured its diplomatic and military parity with India, Pakistan has proved no less wily in resisting the leverage sought by the United States in pursuit of its objectives. The costs of sustaining this unstable relationship have been immeasurably higher for Pakistan, whose need to ally with great powers has been fashioned as much by its search for national validation as by the imperatives of national security. Having insisted on the principle of parity as the basis of any territorial arrangement between 'Pakistan' and 'Hindustan', it became imperative after independence for Pakistan to strike alliances with external powers that could help it sustain its claim to be geopolitically the equal of India.

But the alliance with the United States, which made Pakistan the beneficiary of large scale economic and military assistance,[34] brought with it no special status of the kind Pakistan craved. Nor did it fulfill Pakistan's hopes of having its sovereignty validated by an agreement formally to guarantee its frontiers. Indeed, it is precisely Pakistan's unfulfilled quest for guarantees, which would have sealed its status on the international stage as the equal of India that has contributed to its deeply troubled relationship with the United States. It also explains why this relationship is so laden with emotional overtones unusual in international relations. Plagued by uncertainty about a partner whose support it has reason to doubt, and lacking the formal protection that first prompted it to seek an alliance with the United States it is no wonder that Pakistan has resorted to the language of recrimination to describe its closest ally as both duplicitous and disloyal.

Evidence of US indifference towards Pakistan had surfaced early. At independence it was India that had held the attention of the United States and which the United States coveted as the diplomatic prize to ensure a durable American presence in South Asia. By contrast, there was little or no enthusiasm for Jinnah's Pakistan, which ran against the United States' preference for a united India. At the same time, the immense challenges of post-war reconstruction in Europe and perceptions of a growing Soviet threat discouraged the United States from any immediate engagement in the Indian region. What this implied in practice was that the United States was more than willing to delegate responsibility for the defence of Western interests in South Asia to Britain, who, as the former colonial power in the region, was still regarded as best placed to secure those interests.[35]

Two factors undermined the smooth progression of US plans to entrust South Asian affairs to its war-time ally, Britain. The first was India's determination to loosen its links with the Western bloc and chart a non-aligned course in foreign policy, which the United States regarded as a potential danger to US global interests at a time when it was locked in combat with the Soviet Union. The second was Pakistan's search for international security guarantees against India in exchange for its co-operation in the service of great-power politics. Both forced a major reassessment of US policy towards the region. By the early 1950s Nehru's hostility to the United States as the new face of Western colonialism had come to be perceived by the Western alliance as synonymous with Indian tolerance for Soviet communism.[36]

These sentiments would become common and heighten US impatience with India. Yet there was little or no suggestion even at this time that this impatience would ever translate into a US policy to leave India vulnerable to the risk of a communist invasion. Pakistan understood this but was confident that, even if the idea of a separate Muslim state with dubious democratic credentials held little popular appeal in the United States, the geo-strategic importance of this new country had not been lost on US policy-makers. As early as 1948, a series of US policy recommendations suggested that, from the perspective of US national security objectives, the most important South Asian nation was not India but Pakistan. Heavily influenced by the priorities of the military and intelligence communities, they pointed to two main considerations: Pakistan's contiguous border with the Soviet Union, which could serve as the site of US bases, and Pakistan's proximity to the Persian Gulf, which could enhance its role in defending vital oil routes.[37]

Pakistan's first generation of leaders demonstrated no less understanding of their country's geostrategic position and how best to sell it to eager buyers in the West. In 1947 Jinnah played on Western fears of Soviet expansion by making a case for Pakistan that some claim rested on a Cold War version of the Great Game between imperial Russia and British India.[38] It was predicated on the idea that the security of the north west of India was a global concern 'and not merely an internal matter for Pakistan alone'; as such, the defence of one was inextricably tied to the other. The theme of a common defence had long been familiar to Jinnah and other Muslim separatist leaders, including Iqbal, who had sought to justify the demand for a separate Muslim state in the northwest of India on the ground that a strong state in this strategic corner was vital to the defence of the subcontinent.[39] But Jinnah had also cleverly anticipated the imperatives of the Cold War by drawing attention not only to Pakistan's position as a frontier state but also to its character as a *Muslim* state, where 'communism does not flourish in the soil of Islam'.[40]

It mattered little that Jinnah's observations would soon be put in doubt by Pakistan's alliance with communist China, in retaliation for the United States' decision to arm India following the Sino-Indian border war in 1962. What counted in these early years was to cultivate Pakistan's image as a Muslim state, ill at ease with communism and somewhat out of place in a region (South Asia) not commonly associated with the Muslim world. In time these impressions would be strengthened by America's dependence on Pakistan as a key component of its Cold War strategy in the Middle East[41]—a situation which also yielded rich dividends for Pakistan in the pursuit of its own regional interests against India. These benefits came at the cost of having to decide upon a clearer identity for Pakistan. The country's close association with a Middle Eastern agenda pre-empted any immediate resolution of the country's internal Muslim character (now taken for granted) or an understanding of its South Asian past (now judged to be superfluous).

Concerns such as these fuelled Pakistan's obsession with securing territorial guarantees to protect its borders—an obsession that was matched at the time only by the United States' fixation on the need to fight communism. Despite their developing relationship, Pakistan and the United States were driven by different objectives. While Pakistan's search for territorial guarantees was dictated primarily by its fear of India, the United States debated the merits of such guarantees with reference to securing Pakistan's compliance with US Cold War objectives in the Middle East.[42]

The illusion of a common purpose would henceforth set the tone of this fundamentally flawed bilateral relationship. Yet Pakistan's willingness to be primed by the United States as the local captain of a wider pro-Western Muslim alliance in the Middle East was not altogether at odds with its self-perception. Founded as it was on the idea of a Muslim nation, Pakistan had initially sought to balance its geopolitical weakness in relation to India by appealing to religion (Islam), and by extension, to a wider community of Muslims, whose support it expected would help it match India. Jinnah had helped reinforce this impression by assuring American diplomats in May 1947 that, as a Muslim state, Pakistan's foreign policy would be decisively oriented towards the Muslim countries of the Middle East.[43] His commitment was echoed in 1950 by Prime Minister Liaquat Ali Khan, who impressed upon his American interlocutors that Pakistan's Islamic identity and its regional continuity with the Muslim Middle East put it in a unique position.[44] By doing so he appeared to underscore the depth acquired by the western part of Pakistan in relation to India, augmenting its efforts to achieve symmetry with India.[45]

But these early self-perceptions also point to uncertainties in the definition of Pakistan's identity, which continued to waver between an 'ideational' and 'local' understanding of the nation. While the former emphasized Pakistan's relation to Islam and made it more prone to identify with the wider Islamic world centred on the Middle East, its local understanding situated the country more firmly within the South Asian region dominated by India. This tension was skillfully employed by Pakistan, which relied on its ideational character as a Muslim state to offset the limitations imposed by its local identity. By looking beyond South Asia to a wider Islamic world, it avoided local bilateral arrangements that would have established India's regional dominance.[46]

At the same time, managing this tension in the context of its relationship with the United States was fraught with risk for Pakistan. It found itself at odds in the 1950s with radical trends in the Arab world opposed to the United States and its claim to speak on behalf of the 'Muslim world' was widely resented. Pakistan's conduct was judged 'over-optimistic and amateurish', as were its references to 'being the largest Muslim state and the fifth largest country in the world'. 'Such talk', some observed, 'from a country whose rationale was little understood at the time, and whose capacity to survive was still a question mark, was not well received by other [Muslim] countries, proud of their own heritage.'[47] Whatever hopes Pakistan may have entertained to establish a pre-eminent status among its Muslim peers in the Middle East finally vanished with its decision in 1955 to participate in the Baghdad Pact (renamed the Central Treaty Organization—CENTO—in 1958). It led to widespread condemnation, especially by Egypt, which saw Pakistan as complicit in the attempt by Westerns powers to tighten their control over oil shipments through the Suez Canal.

Nor was Pakistan's membership of the US-led Western defence system trouble free. Signs of strain had surfaced as soon as Pakistan realized that its accession to Western sponsored collective security arrangements, including the Southeast Asia Treaty Organization in 1954 and the Baghdad Pact, afforded no protection against an attack from India. This brought to a head Pakistan's simmering resentment against the United States—resentment accentuated by the former's awareness of the domestic and international liabilities incurred by its relationship with the United States. These losses were most acutely felt on three fronts: the failure to obtain credible guarantees for Pakistan against a military attack from India; the failure to internationalize the issue of Kashmir, and the failure to contain Pakistan's isolation from the Muslim world. Together they served as the basis on which Pakistan would feel justified in accusing the United States of betraying an ally.

The question of US aid served as an early cause for Pakistan to air its grievances. In 1951 Pakistan complained that US aid to India had left it feeling like 'a prospective bride who observes her suitor spending very large sums on a mistress, i.e. India, while she herself can look forward to no more than a token maintenance in the event of marriage'.[48] These emotions re-surfaced in 1953, when Pakistan clamoured for more US aid in exchange for its public alliance with the United States, claiming that to do otherwise 'would be like taking a poor girl for a walk and then walking out on her, leaving her only with a bad name'.[49] Though Pakistan's marriage prospects were gradually to dim with its formal disengagement from US-sponsored security arrangements, this signalled the end not so much of a tumultuous relationship as a change in Pakistan's position from wronged wife to sullen mistress.

As mentioned above, America's decision to arm India in the wake of the 1962 Sino-Indian conflict precipitated in Pakistan a radical reassessment of its relationship with the United States. Most explanations have focused on Islamabad's anger over the moves to strengthen its deadliest foe by its closest ally. This is very largely true, but it also brought to the fore the governing assumptions that had shaped Pakistan's alliance with the United States. They rested squarely on the expectation of a special bilateral relationship that would formally validate its claim to strategic parity with India. After 1962 this search for validation was transferred to China though Pakistan's reasons for doing so were no less governed by its shrewd appreciation of American fears of Chinese communist expansion in South Asia, which it hoped would revive American interest in Pakistan as the equal of India.

Yet Pakistan's quest for validation and geo-political parity with India was to prove as disappointing in its relations with China as with the United States. While it is now widely accepted that Chinese military aid to Pakistan, and possibly even Chinese nuclear co-operation, have been indispensable in reducing Pakistan's power disadvantage *vis-à-vis* India, Pakistan's desire for the unambiguous endorsement of its founding rationale has met with no more than rhetorical support from China. This was cruelly exposed in 1965 when China failed to assist Pakistan during the Indo-Pakistan war, making a mockery of Prime Minister Zulfiqar Ali Bhutto's warning in 1963 that an attack on Pakistan would be challenged by 'the largest state in Asia'.[50] During the war with India in 1971 China's verbal support proved again to be the only tangible evidence of its defence of Pakistan, which had entertained expectations of some material rewards for its part in facilitating the Sino-US rapprochement that year.[51] At the same time, Pakistan's willingness to accommodate a less than satisfactory partnership with China that did not directly address its security needs *vis-à-vis* India suggests that more is at play in Pakistan's complex relations with great powers than merely seeking military protection from India. At issue is the recognition of Pakistan as a state that seeks international sanction to assume a role out of all proportion to its real power. Given the continuing uncertainty over its national identity and the lingering doubts over the prospects of its survival, Pakistan has come to rely on great-power endorsement as a vital measure of its historical purpose.

The disintegration of the country in 1971 accentuated these concerns by encouraging Pakistan to seek new forms of international validation that could regenerate its historical claim to parity with India. The pursuit of a nuclear weapons programme, which began in earnest in the mid 1970s, was seen to be the most effective route to achieve these objectives.[52] But while the United States may have been willing to partner Pakistan in its quest for parity with India by agreeing to furnish it with modern weapons and military training, it clearly intended to draw the line over nuclear weapons. Indeed, no issue has estranged Pakistan from the United States more than the determination to pursue a nuclear weapons programme. Yet shock at the decision by the United States to suspend military aid to Pakistan (and to India) in 1965 and alarm over India's testing of a nuclear device in 1974, persuaded Pakistan that it could no longer entrust its security to the United States or continue to rely on external powers to guarantee its security.[53] But the pursuit of nuclear weapons also afforded a fresh opportunity for Pakistan to make a determined bid for entry into an exclusive club that it expected would assure the country the recognition it craved as the equal of India.

However, stiff opposition from the United States and growing international surveillance forced Pakistan to acquire nuclear technology in a manner that was more suggestive of an international pariah than of an aspiring member seeking entry into a privileged nuclear club. By the mid 1970s Pakistan had embarked on a covert campaign to secure, mostly by illegal means, the wherewithal for a uranium enrichment programme that would help it reach the status of nuclear power in 1998. Just how much the United States was privy to this information and what options it intended to pursue to curb the development of Pakistan's nuclear programme may never be fully known. However, what is now reasonably well established is that, following the Soviet invasion of Afghanistan, the United States effectively turned a blind eye to Pakistan's nuclear weapons programme in exchange for Pakistan's co-operation in the war against Soviet forces. By so doing, the United States gained Pakistan's co-operation as a frontline state while signalling that it was prepared to live with a nuclear Pakistan on condition that Pakistan did not go public by testing a nuclear device.[54]

At the time, Pakistan was interested in a US-backed security treaty to protect Pakistan against an attack by India in exchange for its frontline responsibilities. The then military ruler General Zia ul Haq expressed this priority by demanding a formal security agreement upgrading the 1954 Mutual Defence Assistance Agreement but with no loopholes in the definition of a 'threat' and with clear and unambiguous guarantees ratified by Congress.[55] Given that Pakistan had formally withdrawn from CENTO in early 1979 on the grounds that it wanted membership of the Non-Aligned Movement (into which it was admitted that year), the demand was received with bemusement by the United States, which rejected it as inappropriate. Instead, it persuaded Pakistan to settle, as in the 1950s and 1960s, for an enlarged economic and military aid package.

These concerns were central to Pakistan's involvement in Afghanistan in the 1980s, which catapulted Pakistan to international prominence and helped sustain the impression that it now commanded the respect and attention of the great powers as a state set to rival India. Working in close and covert co-operation with United State to support Afghan resistance forces, it was confident that this new partnership would finally confirm Pakistan's arrival on the international stage. These expectations were fuelled in part by the assumption that Pakistan's relations with the United States had shifted from an alliance with divergent objectives to a partnership based on the perception of a common Soviet communist threat. This placed Pakistan for the first time in a real position to guarantee the security of the United States much as America ensured the protection of Pakistan's security.[56] These assumptions failed to stand the test of time. Tension over Pakistan's determination to pursue its nuclear weapons programme and its stubborn refusal to sign the Non-Proliferation Treaty (NPT) soon marred the sense of common purpose. The withdrawal of Soviet forces from Afghanistan in 1989 finally forced open these cracks leading to the imposition in 1990 of US sanctions against Pakistan and a threat to declare the country a 'terrorist state'.

The closing decade of the twentieth century found Pakistan effectively bereft of the support of its most powerful patron and facing international isolation amid allegations that it now served as a haven for drug traffickers and international terrorists. Far from emerging as a frontline state in partnership with the United States on the international stage, it found itself edging towards the unenviable status of a rogue state under scrutiny by America's terrorism watch-list.[57] By the mid 1990s Pakistan was set on a dangerous course, since its search for international recognition now rested on its grotesque decision to assume the patronage of the Taliban regime in Afghanistan. In 1998, its determination to proceed with nuclear tests in response to similar ones by India, in defiance of the international community, brought fresh sanctions. They were tightened in 1999 following General Musharraf's military coup, which threatened to complete Pakistan's international isolation and confirm its reputation as a pariah state.

These developments were dramatically thrown off-course on 11 September 2001 following the terrorist attacks on New York and Washington. Accounts of how the United States forced Pakistan to abandon its support for the Taliban and their chief financier, Osama bin Laden, who was held responsible for the terrorist attacks, have been widely documented. But what has also held the attention of many concerned with Pakistan were the remarkable parallels between the crisis faced by the country at the time of the Soviet invasion of Afghanistan in 1979 and that which confronted it on the eve of 9/11. The most obvious similarities pertained to the military regimes that were in control on both occasions. Although the regimes led by generals Zia and Musharraf were divided by their preferences, respectively, for orthodox and more moderate varieties of Islam, both upon taking power faced diplomatic isolation to much the same degree over their disregard for the international community. In the case of Zia, it was compounded by his unwillingness to compromise on the development of Pakistan's nuclear programme; in the case of Musharraf, by his reluctance to sever Pakistan's links with the Taliban. Both military regimes also confronted severe financial pressures—brought on by the costly readjustments of a less than satisfactory nationalization programme in the late 1970s and by the debilitating effects of punitive US sanctions in the 1990s. Above all both military regimes craved legitimacy, which they hoped to secure by co-operating with the United States.

Yet the dilemmas faced by Musharraf were far greater than those with which Zia had to grapple. Like the US, Pakistan under Zia had a clear interest in opposing the Soviet occupation of Afghanistan. By contrast, even if General Musharraf had little choice but to support the ouster of the Taliban regime, in doing so he was reversing a long-standing effort by Islamabad to install a friendly government in Kabul. Moreover whilst General Zia was able to improve his domestic political standing by pursuing a policy that enjoyed the support of Pakistan's Islamic radicals, General Musharraf was forced to confront them at a time when militant Islam was becoming an ever-stronger force. But Musharraf also faced another problem. In General Zia's day, India leaned towards the Soviet Union and had cool relations with the US. Under Musharraf Pakistan witnessed the emergence of India as a key US economic partner and possibly even a strategic ally bound by the terms of a nuclear agreement, whose currently civilian purpose could develop a military dimension. Whilst 9/11 forced America to court Pakistan and secure its compliance in the 'war on terror' in the face of immense popular opposition, Pakistan is deeply aware that, should there be any deterioration in its relationship with the United States, then India would be poised to emerge as America's major ally in South Asia—fatally undermining Pakistan's carefully constructed edifice of parity with India.[58] There are now for Pakistan also disturbing signals to suggest China's long-standing hostility to India, which largely dictated its support for Pakistan, is being transformed by the need to improve trading and wider bilateral relations.

These factors together could herald a change in Pakistan's relations with the great powers, especially the United States, upon which it has depended to sustain its historical claim to parity with India and validate its national identity. However, Pakistan's quest to match India has not been restricted merely to enhancing its status through alignments with major powers, but also by seeking to exercise control over subordinate countries, notably Afghanistan. Influence over that country has been regarded as vital not only to the management of Pakistan's regional geopolitics but also to the projection of Pakistan's identity as the regional equal of India.

Taking charge of Afghanistan

Therefore, Pakistan's Afghan policy is best understood as an extension of its historical claim to parity with India. Just as nuclear weapons have served Pakistan as 'equalizers' in its quest for military parity with India, so too has Pakistan's Afghan policy come to represent the ultimate test of Pakistan's aspirations to rival India as a regional hegemon. This has entailed the delicate management by Pakistan of two mutually contradictory identities—as a revisionist state on the issue on Kashmir and a defender of the status quo in relation to Afghanistan. The strains involved in balancing these opposing identities explain, in part, Pakistan's longstanding ambition to reshape its regional environment by securing Afghanistan as a 'junior partner' with a friendly government and thus enhance Pakistan's capacity to challenge India.[59]

However, Pakistan's Afghan policy was initially framed in response to the irredentist threat posed by Afghanistan, which in 1947 had questioned Pakistan's right to legitimate statehood on grounds that its western borders were drawn on territory seized from Afghanistan by British colonial forces without the consent of the local Pashtun population. The claim has always been vigorously contested by Pakistan, which has refused to countenance any suggestion of the 'illegality' of the Pakistani state or the proposals to review its border with Afghanistan—the Durand Line.[60] But this resistance on the part of Pakistan was deeply tied to its awareness that its claim to represent a coherent national identity capable of matching India's could not be sustained without a territorially secure state. This consciousness was heightened by Pakistan's emergence in 1947 as a truncated state. Challenged by these unique features, which appeared to mock Jinnah's vision of a consolidated Muslim homeland, Pakistan was determined not to allow an assault on the legality of its borders or its right to speak on behalf of all those within these borders—claims opposed by Afghanistan.

The most contentious of these issues was the legality of the Durand Line. It had been negotiated in 1893 as the frontier separating Afghanistan and the British Indian Empire. Running south-west of Kabul, its demarcation brought to an end almost half a century of conflict between Afghanistan and British India that culminated in the recognition by Britain of Afghanistan's sovereignty in 1921. This frontier also divided the Pashtun population of the region, which had been accustomed to living together, and cut through territory they claimed in common. Although successive Afghan rulers had been forced to accept the Durand Line in exchange for Afghanistan's sovereignty and to head off the threat of military attacks by British forces in India, they failed to pacify Pashtun tribes under their nominal authority. The opposition of these Pashtun tribesmen also pre-empted all attempts by Britain's government in India to establish effective military control in the regions east of the Durand Line. In this they were covertly supported by Afghan leaders, who since the late 1920s had agreed to guarantee the autonomy of tribesmen west of the Durand Line. In so doing, they helped prepare a campaign that would eventually call into question the contractual basis of the Durand Line as an invalid agreement concluded between two unequal parties obtained under duress by the stronger of the two, namely Britain.[61]

This question came to a head as Britain set out to dismantle the Indian empire and devolve power to its two successor states, India and Pakistan. At issue were rival interpretations of the international status of the Durand Line. While the British insisted that it had served as an international frontier between Afghanistan and British India and that it would, upon the devolution of power, also serve to demarcate the frontier between Afghanistan and Pakistan, Afghan leaders claimed that the Line stood merely as the demarcation of zones of influence rather than as an international boundary.[62] Afghan leaders also insisted that any agreement concluded between two such unequal parties as Britain and Afghanistan in 1893 could not serve as the basis for future arrangements between two equally sovereign states. Nor could it endure indefinitely;[63] indeed the treaty of 1893 had called for the renegotiation of its terms after a hundred years. These objections soon cast a shadow over the legality of Pakistan, both as a valid successor state to British India and as the authentic voice of the Pashtun population east of the Durand Line. They were thereafter to determine Pakistan's relations with Afghanistan.

Pakistan's position was formally summed up in 1947. It maintained that the 'Durand Line is a valid international boundary recognized and confirmed by Afghanistan on several occasions [in 1905 and 1919]; that the Durand Line terminated Afghan sovereignty over the territory or influence over the people east of [the] Durand Line; and finally that Pakistan, as a successor state [to British India] derived full sovereignty over this area and its people and had all the rights and obligations of a successor state.'[64] Finally, Pakistan also insisted that the question of self-determination for Pashtuns had been decided by a British-supervised plebiscite held in 1947 in the North West Frontier Province in which 99 percent of the votes cast were in favour of joining Pakistan. The fact that Pashtun nationalists boycotted the plebiscite, resulting in a mere 55% of the electorate actually participating in the vote, was not seen to have prejudiced Pakistani claims.[65]

Not surprisingly, these developments were regarded with alarm by Jinnah. He was determined to resist any attempt to jeopardize his plans for a consolidated Muslim presence in the northwest and east of India in preparation for a bid to secure their independence. Any suggestion that the North West Frontier Province and its adjacent tribal areas with their Muslim majorities could be detached from the body of British India or that the Pashtuns represented a 'nation' were therefore firmly resisted. Both went against the grain of Jinnah's vision and threatened to diminish the strength of his claims. His argument was that there were only two legitimate nations-Hindus and Muslims, and only two legitimate successors to the British in India—Congress and League. Maintaining this rigid logic of parity was vital to Jinnah, who understood that the consideration of a third centre of national and territorial allegiance could compromise his own scheme for a Muslim nation-state.

He succeeded in persuading the British government (along with the Congress) to agree to a plebiscite in the North West Frontier Province (on the basis of a limited electoral franchise) that gave its Pashtun population the choice of joining either India or Pakistan. The agreement to go ahead with a plebiscite was unusual when compared to other provinces, where the decision to opt for India or Pakistan had been left to elected assemblies. In the North West Frontier Province, the Congress-dominated provincial government could not be relied upon to deliver a verdict in favour of Pakistan. Although Pashtun nationalist parties boycotted the referendum, their protest did not derail the referendum, which was held on 20 July 1947 and resulted in a vote overwhelmingly in favour of Pakistan.

Afghanistan's opposition to the terms of the plebiscite, and by extension, the legalization of the Durand Line were clearly expressed when

Afghanistan became the only country to vote against Pakistan's admission to the United Nations in September 1947. At the time the Afghan representative to the United Nations, Abdul Hussain Khan Aziz, justified his stance by declaring that 'Afghanistan cannot recognise the NWFP [sic] as part of Pakistan so long as the people of the NWFP [sic] have not been given the opportunity, free from any kind of influence, to determine for themselves whether they wish to be independent or to become part of Pakistan'.[66] These objections were withdrawn in February 1948, when Afghanistan became one of the first countries to establish diplomatic relations with Pakistan.[67] This reversal of Afghanistan's position was suggestive of the lingering influence of a section of Afghanistan's deeply divided political establishment that, under King Nadir Shah (d. 1933), had distanced itself from Pashtun nationalism in favour of recognition of the Durand Line as a legal border between Afghanistan and British India.[68]

However, its influence was clearly on the wane for it was not long before relations between Afghanistan and newly independent Pakistan deteriorated. In 1949 a declaration of independence by Pashtun tribesmen on the Pakistani side of the Durand Line was immediately supported by Afghanistan, which hailed the birth of Pashtunistan. Mounting tension led to border clashes, and Pakistan cut fuel supplies to Afghanistan. Bitterness continued for much of the 1950s, egged on by the fierce Pashtun nationalist agenda espoused by the Afghan Prime Minister, Mohammad Daoud. Though his policies were designed primarily to strengthen the Afghan state by harnessing it to the Pashtun ethnic cause, their consequences for Pakistan's fragile national identity, already beset by ethnic conflicts, were far-reaching.

Pashtun nationalism, with its pronounced irredentist bent, posed an immediate threat to this identity. Although it was the fault-line between East and West Pakistan that was eventually to shatter Pakistan's national identity, it was the historical position of the Pashtuns of the North West Frontier Province that singled them out as the greatest danger to the new state. The Afghan factor sharpened this perception insofar as the involvement of Afghanistan was seen to compound Pakistan's difficulty in assimilating the Pathans. And while there were similar movements elsewhere, notably in Bengal, which also threatened Jinnah's vision of a Muslim nation, their momentum was cut short by Partition.[69] By contrast there were few signs that Afghanistan intended to relinquish its claim to Pakistan's tribal areas (including at times vast tracts of northern Balochistan, which hosted a sizeable Pashtun population) or to withdraw its influence over Pashtun affairs after Pakistan's independence. Indeed, Afghanistan registered a strong protest in 1955 over a controversial decision by Pakistan to amalgamate its four western provinces into 'One-Unit', triggering Afghan accusations that the Pashtuns and their territory were being forcibly integrated into Pakistan. In response Pakistan not only vigorously defended its right to exercise control over the territories claimed by Afghanistan as the nucleus of an autonomous Pashtun state, but also refused to subscribe to the theory that Pashtuns were a nation entitled to self-determination.

It was in the 1960s that signs first emerged of a shift in Pakistan's instinctively defensive position *vis-à-vis* Afghanistan. This marked the onset of a strategy that sought to manage Pakistan's conflict with Afghanistan by recasting the Pashtun question as a threat to Afghanistan while neutralizing its political saliency for Pakistan. It relied on a combination of state policies that co-opted Pashtuns into the country's key state institutions, especially the army, and on the language of Islamic solidarity, to blunt the appeal of Pashtun ethnicity. By so doing Pakistan hoped not only to reaffirm its identity as a national homeland for all Muslims in the region, but also to establish its claim as a regional power with the potential both to absorb lesser rivals like Afghanistan and to mount an effective challenge to bigger contenders such as India.

The earliest manifestations of this strategy appeared in a White Paper published in 1962. Coming hard on the heels of a provocative suggestion by Pakistan that Afghanistan should test the wishes of its Pashtun population by arranging for a referendum that would offer them the choice of living in Afghanistan or Pakistan,[70] it warned that 'if the Frontier [sic] of a country has to be predetermined on linguistic and ethnic bases as claimed by the Afghans, it will result in the disintegration of Afghanistan'.[71] The report drew attention to the vulnerability of Afghanistan's 3.5 million Pashto speakers (as compared to Pakistan's 8 million Pashtuns at the time) by emphasizing that they formed a mere fraction of the country's total population of some 15 million non-Pashtuns, and highlighted the dangers that faced the country's other ethnic groups (Tajiks, Uzbeks, Persian and Turkish speakers), who could also be encouraged to seek integration into neighbouring states.[72] This attempt by Pakistan to threaten Afghanistan with a fate it feared itself—that of national and territorial disintegration—marked the beginning of a change of posture that appeared to lend credence to the observation by the eminent anthropologist, Olaf Caroe, who had declared that in time it was more likely that 'Peshawar would absorb Kabul, not Kabul absorb Peshawar'.[73]

This shift in Pakistan's position also came against the background of wider changes in the 1960s that confirmed Afghanistan's failure to internationalize the issue of Pashtunistan by calling on external powers, including the Soviet Union. Their reluctance to be drawn into the conflict over Pashtunistan encouraged Pakistan, even while it expressed dismay over the unwillingness of the international community to mediate in its separate conflict with India over Kashmir. Nevertheless, Pakistan's growing military strength, resulting from its alliance with the United States, did much to fuel its determination to set its relation with Afghanistan on a new and more belligerent footing.

This was accompanied by more decisive moves to defuse the Pashtun question by launching a concerted campaign to co-opt larger numbers of Pashtuns into centres of national power—that is, the army and the senior civil services.[74] This policy was significantly expanded in the 1970s and 1980s by General Zia, who helped raise Pashtun representation in the army to their current levels of around 20 per cent.[75] In the civil services these levels stood at an estimated 10 per cent, roughly in line with the share of Pakistan's Pashtun population at the time.[76] Economically too the Pashtuns have fared better than most. Investment, especially in the settled areas of the North West Frontier Province, boosted economic development. Elsewhere, in provinces like Sind and Balochistan, where Pashtuns formed a migrant population, they enjoyed relative economic predominance, especially in the booming transport and construction sectors. The success of these policies over time has nowhere been more forcefully demonstrated than in the recent decision by Pashtun nationalist parties in Pakistan to abandon their demand for a separate 'Pakhtunistan' in favour of a province of 'Pakhtunkhwa' to replace the North West Frontier Province.[77]

It was the Soviet invasion of Afghanistan in 1979 that provided the real impetus for Pakistan finally to address the historical challenge posed by Afghanistan and to implement a policy that promised to fulfill the country's strategic and ideological objectives. The strategic objectives centred overwhelmingly on securing its western border so as effectively to neutralize the effects of a so-called pincer movement involving a simultaneous military threat from India and Afghanistan. Afghanistan's tacit alliance with India, which made no secret of its moral support for Pashtun autonomy, had long been a cause of concern to Pakistan. The Soviet invasion provided Pakistan with just the opportunity to direct the course of events in a manner that it believed would finally address these security concerns. Islamabad's patronage of the mujahedin resistance forced to operate from Pakistan and its control over facilities for millions of Afghan refugees opened for the first time the real prospect of ensuring a friendly government in Afghanistan. While the strategy was clearly risky insofar as it was predicated on the vulnerability of Soviet forces and their eventual withdrawal from Afghanistan, the benefits were deemed (at least, at the time) far to outweigh the costs of a possible blowback and the strains imposed on Pakistan's infrastructure.

Among the benefits of direct concern to Pakistan's dominant military establishment was the prospect of gaining strategic depth. Although regarded by some military strategists as irrelevant to the conditions of modern warfare, the idea has exercised the minds of several generations of Pakistani military leaders.[78] Keen to overcome the limitations of Pakistan's narrow geographical space in the event of a war with India, they assumed that control over Afghan territory would provide Pakistan's armed forces with enough of a hinterland to enhance their 'ability to fight a prolonged war with India'.[79] A hinterland such as this, it is now understood, was also considered vital as a useful base to train and arm Pakistan-backed Kashmiri militants while extending Pakistan's influence in Central Asia and boosting its ambitions to rival India.[80]

The ideological considerations were no less compelling. By galvanizing the mujahedin resistance and favouring hard-line Islamist groups committed to the establishment of an Islamic state in Afghanistan, Pakistan's leaders hoped not only to defuse the Paktunistan issue but also to ensure that questions of religious solidarity took precedence over ethnic loyalties. According to Olivier Roy, this reflected as much a desire to project the merits of Pakistan's own political trajectory in the service of Zia's Islamization programme, as to use the Islamic option to by-pass the ethnic one. The implementation of this policy was subtle in the extreme. It entailed the use of the ethnic and religious connections to reinforce links between Pakistan's Pashtun population (by now key players on the economic and political scene) and their

Afghan counterparts, who were favoured by Pakistan at the expense of other ethnic groups in Afghanistan.[81] By so doing, Pakistan not only furthered a vision that insisted upon the primacy of religion over ethnicity, but also successfully transformed the ethnic Pashtun question into an Islamist project tailored to enhance Pakistan's identity as the natural homeland for the Muslims of the region.

The consolidation of these gains was vital for the military in Pakistan, which despite the restoration of civilian government, from 1988 to 1999, still exercised a decisive veto over the direction of Pakistan's Afghan policy. The military's prerogative over this policy was predicated on the confidence that it could always count on a national consensus with regard to the non-negotiability of the Durand Line. In 1993 Pakistan firmly rejected Afghanistan's appeal to re-negotiate the Durand Line in line with the provisions of 1893 treaty calling for a review after a hundred years and reiterated its original position—namely, that the Line was a valid international boundary.

Pakistan's power to insist on the status quo with regard to the Durand Line was not matched by its tenuous grip over mujahedin groups battling for supremacy following the withdrawal of Soviet forces from Afghanistan. This gap threatened to undermine the consolidation of Pakistan's strategic and ideological gains. The ascendancy of the Tajik-dominated leadership in Kabul, which was determined to resist Pakistan's attempts to determine Afghan affairs through its control of Pashtun groups, was an additional source of concern for Pakistan. By the mid 1990s Pakistan could no longer rely on its Pashtun protégés inside Afghanistan to secure its regional interests or to defuse the challenge to the status quo posed by differences over the status of the Durand Line. These concerns were a major impetus behind Pakistan's decision to regain the initiative by backing Afghan groups closer to home. They included the so-called Taliban, who started as a band of fighters born in Afghan refugee camps inside Pakistan and educated in make-shift schools dispensing crude varieties of Islamic education. Predominantly Pashtuns belonging to lesser tribes habitually removed from centres of power in Afghanistan, they were seen as ideal material by Pakistan to reinvigorate its Afghan policy and secure the gains that had so far eluded her.[82]

This policy rested on expectations that, once in power, the Taliban would recognize the Durand Line, curb Pashtun nationalism and absorb the threat of Islamic radicalism that now threatened to blowback into Pakistan. The entire strategy rested on the assumption that Pakistan would remain the master of events—an assumption that was fatally flawed. Not only did Pakistan soon find itself the victim of policies pursued by the Taliban, notably the decision to host Al Qaida, but it also failed to achieve the objectives designed to enhance its security. 'In fact', as Ahmed Rashid argues persuasively, 'just the opposite occurred. The Taliban refused to recognize the Durand Line or drop Afghanistan's claims to part of the NWFP [sic]. The Taliban fostered Pashtun nationalism, albeit of an Islamic character and it began to affect Pakistani Pashtuns.'[83] In time, these developments would leave Pakistan vulnerable once again to forces from Afghanistan—forces it helped create, but failed to contain. They are now held responsible for the spread of the so-called 'Talibanization' of Pakistan, thereby underscoring the cruel irony of Pakistan now seeming to provide strategic depth to the Afghan Taliban.

Events since 9/11 have forced Pakistan (publicly at least) to withdraw its support for the Taliban and, more generally, to refrain from the kind of close involvement in Afghan affairs to which it had grown accustomed since the early 1980s. This has raised the prospect of a shift in Pakistan's Afghan policy in exchange for guarantees involving a mutually acceptable resolution of its dispute with Afghanistan over the status of the Durand line. So far Pakistan has refused to consider any change in the status quo that would involve re-drawing its border with Afghanistan. While some have argued that Pakistan may now have good strategic reasons to maintain a porous border with Afghanistan rather than to press for the recognition of the Durand Line as an international frontier (that would constrain Pakistan's scope for interference in Afghan affairs),[84] both are suggestive of Pakistan's insatiable need to shore up its fragile national identity.

Compensating for the limitations of this identity has driven Pakistan to pursue policies that, while admittedly informed by considerations of security, have been overwhelmingly concerned to validate the country's historical purpose—whether by pursuing its historical claim to parity, forging alliances with super-powers, or aspiring to adopt the mantle of a regional power. Together they have dictated Pakistan's foreign engagements and determined the country's unending search for meaning.

EPILOGUE

It would appear that history, politics and geostrategic compulsions have all conspired to hasten the decline of Pakistan and deepen its uncertainty as a nation. Yet as this study has sought to demonstrate, it is the country's problematic and contested relationship with Islam that has most decisively frustrated its quest for a coherent national identity and for stability as a nation-state capable of absorbing the challenges of its rich and diverse society.

The ambiguous but ample role afforded to Islam in the creation of Pakistan (especially in the years immediately leading up to the country's independence in 1947) ensured that Islam would not only play a part in moulding the constitutional complexion of the new state, but also set the priorities of its public policy. That it had damaging political, economic and social consequences had less to do with Islam as such than with a perennial uncertainty about its influence over Pakistan's identity as well as with the lack of consensus over the very terms of Islam. It is this contestation over the multiple meanings of Islam that accounts today for the doubts about the meaning of Pakistan and the significance of being Pakistani.

Seen from this angle, Pakistan was in trouble from the start. Nevertheless, it is by no means certain that the country has exhausted all the resources needed to develop a more robust identity grounded in rules of political negotiation rather than on the questionable assumptions of a ready made Islamic consensus. Indeed, in recent years, Pakistan has witnessed enormous changes—changes that signal the determination of its people, if not of its governing elite, to be more receptive to new ways of imagining their country's identity. This identity, while still for the most part predicated on opposition to India—an opposition that has particularly suited the interests of a politically dominant military, is now under fresh scrutiny. An emancipated media, a newly galvanized

209

legal fraternity, an astonishingly vibrant artistic community, a clutch of combative historians and human rights activists are all in the forefront of new trends. Although their voices are far from being dominant, they seek nothing less than to restore to Pakistan its identity as an integral, rather than an exclusive, part of the South Asian region.

Their endeavours have been responsible for what some have (perhaps too optimistically) described as a paradigm shift, which has encouraged ever larger numbers of Pakistanis to begin to conceive of their country's purpose and of its Muslim identity as rooted in the common history of South Asia. This re-engagement with the history of the region rather than with religion has also prompted a fresh understanding of local dynamics that are now judged to be as conducive to co-operation as to conflict. The spread of Islamist violence in recent years has reinforced these perceptions. Many Pakistanis now believe that the magnitude of the threat posed to their country by such violence is so immense that its future can no longer be guaranteed without the support and co-operation of its neighbours, including erstwhile foes, notably India.

But tilting the balance more firmly towards co-operation rather than conflict as the basis for a new understanding of Pakistan will be a demanding exercise. The most urgent (but also the most ambitious) objective will involve changes in the country's political dispensation. For too long it has favoured the preferences of a military leadership that has exploited the uncertainty over the country's national identity to pursue confrontation with Pakistan's regional neighbours and to consolidate its grip on power. While the military's success in securing its objectives owed much to its coercive capabilities, its gains have also been facilitated by support from Pakistan's political classes. Their own ambivalence and uncertainty about the relationship between Islam and the state has led them all too easily to seek the protection of successive military regimes. This chronic uncertainty has been no less to blame for their tendency (on the rare occasions when they held power in the guise of elected civilian governments) to fall back on authoritarian rule in order to establish a monopoly over political and religious expression.

Breaking this vicious cycle of authoritarian rule will not be easy. The military can be expected jealously to protect its privileges while the political classes will be loath to forfeit the benefits that have flowed from their partnership with the praetorians. Their symbiotic relationship, which has so damaged Pakistan's prospects of securing governments by consent, could now be poised to exact an even heavier price. Far from serving as the glue that held the country together in the absence of a consensus over Islam, the military and its allies among the political classes now preside (much as they did during the disintegration of the country in 1971) over the collapse of the state's authority across large parts of the country that are controlled by so-called 'non-state' actors. The mortal threat presented by these developments could serve as precisely the catalyst for a fresh alignment of forces—one driven as much by the desire for change as by the awareness that any further division of the country would be terminal.

Such speculation may of course prove to be futile. The troubles of a nuclear-armed Pakistan are now a matter of global concern and the danger of state failure is not an option that the international community is willing to countenance. What is certain is that the international community is determined to secure Pakistan against all risks—including those of political reform. It is this rather than any reluctance to pursue change inside Pakistan that is likely to act as a brake on the much-needed overhaul of the country's political system. Though many abroad recognize that an unreformed Pakistan could eventually pose a greater threat to world peace than one able to call on the genuine consent of all its citizens (whatever their ethnic, religious and sectarian persuasion), most Western governments still remain fearful of what such reform could entail in a pivotal state, whose fate is now widely believed to determine global security.

This is not to suggest that the international community is solely concerned to restrain the transformation in Pakistan. On the contrary: there is now strong pressure on Pakistan to re-orient itself away from its perennial stance of confrontation with India. The aim is not only to ease relations with New Delhi, but to distance Pakistan from the appeal of a type of militant Islam that is at odds with Islamic traditions indigenous to South Asia. Historically, these traditions, characterised by their strong syncretistic bias in favour of exploring common ground between Islam and India's indigenous religions, have been judged to be especially responsive to the region's culturally plural character. Many now also recognize that they may offer the best hope yet of ensuring that the affirmation of cultural difference does not become a source for discrimination.

Reviving these traditions, with their strong syncretistic foundations, could alleviate the pressures on Pakistan. By recasting its enduring quest for religious consensus in terms of a cultural heritage rooted in the discourse of Indian Islam, it may yet salvage a pluralist alternative consistent with democratic citizenship. Though any such endeavour will be forced to confront (and adapt to) the challenge of orthodoxy in Pakistan, it remains the only meaningful model for a country that seeks still to project an identity founded on reconciling Islam's universalist message with respect for the rich diversity of its peoples.

NOTES

INTRODUCTION

1. See Hamza Alavi, 'Class and state' in Hassan Gardezi and Jamil Rashid (eds), *Pakistan—the roots of dictatorship: the political economy of a praetorian state* (London: Zed Press, 1983), pp. 40–93 and his 'Ethnicity, Muslim society and the Pakistan ideology' in Anita Weiss (ed.), *Islamic re-assertion in Pakistan* (Lahore: Vanguard Books, 1987), pp. 21–47.
2. Alavi, 'Ethnicity, Muslim society and the Pakistan ideology' in Weiss (ed.), *Islamic re-assertion*, pp. 23–46.
3. See among others, Ayesha Jalal, *The sole spokesman: Jinnah, the Muslim League and the demand for Pakistan* (Cambridge: Cambridge University Press, 1985) and Yunus Samad, *A nation in turmoil: nationalism and ethnicity in Pakistan, 1937–58* (Delhi: Sage, 1995) and more recently, his 'Pakistan: from minority rights to majoritarianism' in Gyanendra Pandey and Yunus Samad, *Faultlines of nationhood* (Delhi: Roli Books, 2007), pp. 65–138.
4. See among others, David Page, *Prelude to Partition: the Indian Muslims and the imperial system of control, 1920–1932* (Oxford: Oxford University Press, 1982) and Francis Robinson, *Separatism among Indian Muslims: the politics of the United Provinces' Muslims, 1860–1923* (Cambridge: Cambridge University Press, 1974).
5. Farzana Shaikh, *Community and consensus in Islam: Muslim representation in colonial India, 1860–1947* (Cambridge University Press, 1989).
6. Yunus Samad, 'Reflections on Partition: Pakistan perspective', *International Journal of Punjab Studies*, Vol. 4, no. 1 (January-June 1997), pp. 43–63.
7. Ian Talbot, *Pakistan: a modern history* (London: Hurst, 2005).
8. Ibid., p. 5.
9. See Barbara Metcalf, 'The case of Pakistan', in Barbara Metcalf, *Islamic contestations: essays on Muslims in India and Pakistan* (Delhi: Oxford University Press, 2004), p. 219.
10. Ibid.

11. S.V.R. Nasr, 'National identities and the India-Pakistan conflict' in T.V. Paul (ed.), *The India-Pakistan conflict: an enduring rivalry* (Cambridge: Cambridge University Press, 2005), pp. 178–201.

12. See among others, Hasan Askari Rizvi, *The military and politics in Pakistan, 1947–77* (Lahore: Sang-i-Meel, 2000); Shahid Javed Burki, *Pakistan: fifty years of nationhood* (Boulder, CO: Praeger, 1999) and Lawrence Ziring, *The Ayub Khan era: politics in Pakistan, 1958–69* (Syracuse, NY: Syracuse University Pres, 1971).

13. Ayesha Siddiqa, *Military Inc: inside Pakistan's military economy* (London: Pluto Press, 2007).

14. It is instructive in this regard to compare the stability that flowed from the success of the Islamization programme in Malaysia with the sharp fissures it opened up in Pakistan during the 1980s. See S.V.R. Nasr, *Islamic Leviathan: Islam and the making of state power* (New York: Oxford University Press, 2001).

15. This relationship was first elaborated by Alavi in his seminal piece 'Class and state' in Gardezi and Rashid, (eds), *Pakistan: the roots of dictatorship*, pp. 54–56. Since then it has been extended by others, notably Ayesha Jalal, *The state of martial law: the origins of Pakistan's political economy of defence* (Cambridge: Cambridge University Press, 1990) and more recently (and rather more vigorously), by Tariq Ali, *The duel: Pakistan on the flight path of American power* (London: Simon & Schuster, 2008).

16. Stephen Cohen, *The idea of Pakistan* (Washington, DC: Brookings Institution Press, 2004).

1. WHY PAKISTAN?

1. Salman Rushdie, *Shame* (London: Jonathan Cape, 1983), p. 87.

2. Barbara Metcalf, 'The case of Pakistan' in Peter Merkl and Ninian Smart (eds), *Religion and politics in the modern world* (New York: New York University Press, 1982), p. 171.

3. For an extended discussion of the influence of an 'Islamically informed' discourse on the conduct of Indo-Muslim politics see Farzana Shaikh, *Community and consensus in Islam: Muslim representation in colonial India, 1860–1947* (Cambridge: Cambridge University Press, 1989).

4. Matiur Rahman, *From consultation to confrontation: a study of the Muslim League in British Indian politics, 1906–1912* (London: Luzac, 1970). See also Francis Robinson, *Separatism among Indian Muslims: the politics of the United Provinces' Muslims, 1860–1923* (Cambridge: Cambridge University Press, 1974).

5. T.N. Madan, *Modern myths, locked minds: secularism and fundamentalism in India* (fourth impression) (Delhi: Oxford University Press, 2003), p. 269.

6. See Gyanendra Pandey, *The construction of communalism in colonial North India* (Delhi: Oxford University Press, 1990).

7. Ayesha Jalal, 'Exploding communalism: the politics of Muslim identity in South Asia' in Sugata Bose and Ayesha Jalal (eds), *Nationalism, Democracy and Development: state and politics in India* (Delhi: Oxford University Press, 1996), pp. 76–103.

8. For an account of the uneven support for the idea of Pakistan among Indian Muslims across different regions in India see among others, Ian Talbot, *Pakistan: a modern history* (revised edition) (London: Hurst, 2005), pp. 66–94; Christophe Jaffrelot (ed.), *A history of Pakistan and its origins* (London: Anthem Press, 2002), pp. 12–20; Yunus Samad, *A nation in turmoil: nationalism and ethnicity in Pakistan, 1937–1958* (New Delhi: Sage, 1995) and Ayesha Jalal, *The sole spokesman: Jinnah the Muslim League and the demand for Pakistan* (Cambridge: Cambridge University Press, 1985).

9. Ayesha Jalal, *Self and sovereignty: individual and community in South Asian Islam since 1850* (London: Routledge, 2000), p. 41.

10. Ibid., p. 44.

11. Sunil Khilnani, *The idea of India* (revised edition) (Delhi: Penguin,1999), p.163.

12. According to Jinnah, 'They [the Hindus] fathered this word upon us. Give the dog a bad name and then hang him ... You know perfectly well that Pakistan is a word that is really foisted upon us and fathered upon us by some section of the Hindu press'. See his speech to the All India Muslim League in April 1943 in S.S Pirzada(ed.), *Foundations of Pakistan: All India Muslim League Documents, 1906–1947*, II (Karachi: National Publishing House, 1970), p. 425.

13. See Asim Roy, 'The high politics of India's Partition: the Revisionist Perspective', *Modern Asian Studies*, Vol. 24, no. 2 (May 1990), esp. pp. 400–408.

14. Jalal,'Exploding communalism', pp. 80–90.

15. Of these, clearly the most important was the eponymous movement in Deoband, near Delhi, founded in 1867. For the best single account of this movement and its precursors see Barbara D. Metcalf, *Islamic revival in British India: Deoband, 1860–1900* (Princeton: Princeton University Press, 1982).

16. See Ayesha Jalal, *Partisans of Allah: jihad in South Asia* (Cambridge, Mass.: Harvard University Press, 2008).

17. A phrase used by a critic against the prominent Indian Muslim leader, Abul Kalam Azad, who emerged in the 1940s as a senior spokesman for Congress. He was accused of boiling down all religions (including Islam) to a single faith-based essence consisting of a belief in God to justify his support for Congress and its brand of 'composite nationalism'. See Ian Henderson Douglas, *Abul Kalam Azad: an intellectual and religious biography*, edited by Gail Minault and Christian Troll (Delhi: Oxford University Press, 1988), p. 279.

18. Muzaffar Alam, 'Sharia and governance in the Indo-Islamic context', in David Gilmartin and Bruce B. Lawrence (eds), *Beyond Turk and Hindu: rethinking religious identities in Islamicate South Asia* (Delhi: Indian Research Press, 2002), p. 239.

19. T.N. Madan, *Modern myths. Locked minds* (fourth impression) (Delhi: Oxford University Press, 2003), p. 129.

20. Madan singles out 'the quest power for power' as a 'key variable' in the trajectory of Indo-Muslim thinking, noting how the challenges involved in maintaining scriptural authority (orthodoxy) and recovering the purity of the faith (revivalism) were held to be indistinguishable from the gaining or re-gaining of Muslim power—an objective he nevertheless most closely associates with 'fundamentalism'. Ibid., pp. 106–49.

21. Metcalf, *Islamic revival in British India*, pp. 150–51.

22. Madan, *Modern myths*, p. 137.

23. See Muhammad Qasim Zaman, *The ulama in contemporary Islam: custodians of change* (Princeton: Princeton University Press, 2002), p. 13.

24. Husain Ahmed Madani, *Muttahida qawwmiyat aur Islam* (originally published [1938?]) (Delhi: Qawmi ekta trust, 1972). See also Barbara Metcalf, 'Re-inventing Islamic politics in inter-war India: the clergy commitment to "composite nationalism"' in Mushirul Hasan and Asim Roy (eds), *Living together separately: cultural India in history and politics* (Delhi: Oxford University Press, 2005), pp. 389–403 and Ziya ul Hasan Faruqi, *The Deoband school and the demand for Pakistan* (Bombay: Asia Publishing House, 1963).

25. Barbara Metcalf, 'Deobandis' in John L. Esposito (ed.), *The Oxford Encyclopedia of the modern Islamic world,* I (New York: Oxford University Press, 2001), p. 363.

26. Zaman, *The ulama in contemporary Islam*, p.33.

27. See Kenneth Cragg, *The pen and the faith* (London: George Allen and Unwin, 1985), p. 28. See also Farzana Shaikh, 'Azad and Iqbal: the quest for the Islamic "Good"', in Mushirul Hasan(ed.), *Islam and Indian nationalism: reflections on Abul Kalam Azad* (Delhi: Manohar, 1992), pp. 59–76.

28. A view held especially by his critics in Pakistan. For a classic Pakistani exposition see I.H. Qureshi, *The Muslim community of the Indo-Pakistan subcontinent, 610–1947* (Gravenhage: Mouton and Co., 1962), pp. 258–60.

29. Aijaz Ahmad, 'Azad's careers: roads taken and not taken' in Mushirul Hasan (ed.), *Islam and Indian nationalism*, p. 139.

30. Peter Hardy, *Partners in Freedom and true Muslims: the political thought of some Muslim scholars in British India, 1912–1947* (Lund: Scandinavian Institute of Asian Studies, 1971), p. 34.

31. Madan, *Modern myths*, p.160.

32. Al Hilal, 1 (8): 2–3, quoted in Douglas, *Abul Kalam Azad*, p. 144.

33. On the 'salariat' see Hamza Alavi, 'Ethnicity, Muslim society and the Pakistan ideology' in Anita Weiss(ed.), *Islamic reassertion in Pakistan: the*

application of Islamic laws in a modern state (Lahore: Vanguard, 1987), pp. 24–27. See also Hamza Alavi, 'Class and state' in Hassan Gardezi and Jamil Rashid (eds), *Pakistan—the roots of dictatorship: the political economy of a praetorian state* (London: Zed Press, 1983), pp. 57–59.

34. For the most definitive study of Sir Sayyid Ahmed Khan and his reform movement see David Lelyveld, *Aligarh's First generation: Muslim solidarity in British India* (Princeton: Princeton University Press, 1978).

35. Shahid Javed Burki, *Pakistan: fifty years of nationhood* (Boulder, CO: Westview Press, 1999), p. 2.

36. See his speech in Meerut in A.M. Zaidi(ed.), *Evolution of Muslim political thought in India*, I (New Delhi: Michiko and Panjathan, n.d.), p. 51.

37. This legacy notwithstanding, the relationship between Islam and ethnicity was likely to be deeply problematic within the terms of Islam which, as Verkaaik shows in his brilliant study of *mohajir* (migrant) identity, has forced the ingenious option of 'ethnicizing' Islam. He observes: 'Islam claims universal relevance transcending ethnic and territorial attachments … For this reason [it] has been considered incompatible with ethnic solidarity from the first days of Pakistan's existence onwards … Yet the close and problematic linkage between the nation and Islam …. also meant that Islam largely set the limits of public debate. Although it is possible to support a wide range of positions on the interpretation of Islam … one can hardly speak out against Islam as such lest one be accused of both heresy and unpatriotic loyalties. Hence, regional groups resisting the authoritarian regime in Islamabad legitimized the regional basis of their protest by articulating an ethnicized Islam of their own'. Oskar Verkaaik, *Migrants and militants: fun and urban violence in Pakistan* (Princeton: Princeton University Press, 2004), pp. 20–21.

38. Lelyveld, *Aligarh's first generation*, p. 311.

39. Shaikh, *Community and consensus in Islam*, pp. 93–96; 114–18. See also Abbas Rashid, 'Pakistan: the ideological dimension' in Asghar Khan (ed.), *Islam, politics and the state: the Pakistan experience* (London: Zed Press, 1985), pp. 73–74.

40. Verkaaik, *Migrants and militants*, p. 25.

41. Jalal, *Self and sovereignty*, p. 167.

42. See Iqbal's presidential address to the All India Muslim League on 29 December 1930 in Sharifuddin Pirzada (ed.), *Foundations of Pakistan: Documents of the All India Muslim League, 1906–47*, II (Karachi: National Publishing House, 1970), p. 159.

43. Ibid.

44. Ibid.

45. See Farzana Shaikh, 'Azad and Iqbal' in Hasan, (ed.), *Islam and Indian nationalism*, pp. 59–76.

46. Quoted in Muhammad Daud Rahbar, 'Glimpses of the man' in Hafeez Malik (ed.), *Iqbal: Poet-Philosopher of Pakistan* (New York: Columbia University Press, 1971), p. 53.

47. Iqbal to R.A. Nicholson, 24 January 1921 in B.A. Dar (ed.), *Letters of Iqbal* (Lahore: Iqbal Academy, 1978), p. 144.
48. For a classic exposition see Pandey, *The construction of communalism in colonial North India.*
49. See Ian Talbot, *Pakistan: a modern history* (London: Hurst, revised edn, 2005), pp. 53–94. See also David Gilmartin, *Empire and Islam: Punjab and the making of Pakistan* (Berkeley, CA: University of California Press, 1988) and David Page, *Prelude to Partition: the Indian Muslims and the imperial system of control, 1920–1932* (New Delhi: Oxford University Press, 1982).
50. See Seyyed Vali Reza Nasr, *Islamic Leviathan: Islam and the making of state power* (New York: Oxford University Press, 2001), pp. 41–47.
51. See Mohammad Shah, 'The Bengal Muslims and the world of Islam: Pan-Islamic trends in colonial Bengal as reflected in the press' in Rafiuddin Ahmed (ed.), *Understanding the Bengal Muslims: Interpretative essays* (New Delhi: Oxford University Press, 2001).
52. Talbot, *Pakistan*, pp. 59–61.
53. See Sarah Ansari, *Sufi saints and state power: The pirs of Sind, 1843–1947* (Cambridge: Cambridge University Press, 1992).
54. See Gilmartin, *Empire and Islam.*
55. C.A. Bayly, *Origins of nationality in South Asia: patriotism and ethical government in the making of modern India* (New Delhi; Oxford: Oxford University Press, 1998), p. 106.
56. Ibid., p. 105 (italics added).
57. The standard interpretation remains Paul Brass, *Language, religion and politics in North India* (Cambridge: Cambridge University Press, 1974). See also his 'Elite groups, symbol manipulation and ethnic identity among the Muslims of South Asia' in David Taylor and Malcolm Yapp (eds), *Political identity in South Asia* (London: School of Oriental and African Studies, 1979). The argument has resurfaced more recently in Christophe Jaffrelot, 'Nationalism without a nation: Pakistan searching for its identity' in Christophe Jaffrelot (ed.), *Pakistan: nationalism without a nation?* (London: Zed Books, 2002), pp. 10–11.
58. Bayly, *Origins of nationality*, p. 105.
59. 'Now suppose that all the English were to leave India,' he mused, 'Then who would be the rulers of India? Is it possible that two *qaums*—the Muslim and Hindu—could sit on the same throne and remain equal in power? Most certainly not.' See his speech in Meerut on 16 March 1888 in Shan Muhammad (ed.), *Writings and speeches of Sir Sayyid Ahmad Khan* (Bombay: Nachiketa Publications, 1972), p. 184.
60. Referring to the creation of a common language—Urdu—that belonged to neither Hindus or Muslims, he observed in 1883: 'the blood of both have changed, the colour of both have become similar ... we mixed with each so much that we produced a new language—Urdu, which was neither our language nor theirs'. See his speech in Patna on 27 January 1883, ibid., p. 160.

61. 'Do not forget', he declared, 'that Hindu and Muslim are words of religious significance otherwise Hindus, Mussalmans and Christians who live in this country form one nation regardless of their faith.' See his speech in Gurdaspur, 27 January 1884, ibid., p. 266.

62. Lelyveld, *Aligarh's first generation*, p. 311.

63. See his speech in Ghazipur on 9 January 1864, in Shan Muhammad (ed.), *Writings and Speeches*, p. 114. See also G.F.I. Graham, *The life and work of Syed Ahmed Khan* (London: Hodder and Stoughton, 1909), pp. 56–57.

64. See Sir Sayyid's clarification of his speech delivered in Lucknow on 28 December 1887, in Shan Muhammad (ed.), *Writings and Speeches*, pp. 218–20. See also Christian Troll, *Sayyid Ahmed Khan: reinterpretation of Muslim theology* (Delhi: Vikas, 1978), p. 303.

65. Bayly, *Origins of nationality*, p. 113.

66. A term borrowed here from Olivier Roy, who uses it to explain the emergence of a Muslim 'ethnicity', especially in the West, that is shaped by religion 'as a set of cultural patterns that are inherited and not related to a person's spiritual life'. See Olivier Roy, *Globalised Islam: the search for a new ummah* (London: Hurst, 2004), p. 124.

67. See Farzana Shaikh, '"Millat" and "mazhab": rethinking Iqbal's political vision' in Mushirul Hasan and Asim Roy (eds), *Living together separately: cultural India in history and politics* (Delhi: Oxford University Press, 2005), pp. 366–88.

68. See his presidential address to the All India Muslim League, 29 December 1930 in Pirzada (ed.), *Foundations of Pakistan, II*, p. 159.

69. Iqbal to R.A. Nicolson, 24 January 1921 in Dar (ed.), *Letters of Iqbal*, p. 144.

70. See his presidential address to the All India Muslim League, 29 December 1930 in Pirzada (ed.), *Foundations of Pakistan, II*, p. 158.

71. See Iqbal's letter to Jinnah, 21 June, 1937 in Sharifuddin Pirzada (ed.), *Quaid-e-Azam Jinnah's correspondence* (Karachi: Guild Publishing House, 1966), p. 163.

72. See Iqbal's letter to Jinnah, 28 May, 1937 in ibid., p. 159.

73. S.V.R. Nasr, *Mawdudi and the making of Islamic revivalism* (Oxford: Oxford University Press, 1996), pp. 34–39.

74. Seyyed Vali Reza Nasr, *The Vanguard of the Islamic revolution: the Jamaat-i-Islami of Pakistan* (Berkeley, CA: University of California Press, 1994), p. 20.

75. Ibid., p. 109.

76. Ibid.

77. Ibid., p. 110.

78. Ibid., p. 110.

79. Lawrence Ziring, *Pakistan: at the cross-current of history* (Oxford: Oneworld, 2003), pp. 14–15.

80. Gyanendra Pandey, *Remembering Partition: violence, nationalism and history in India* (Cambridge: Cambridge University Press), p. 153

81. Pnina Werbner, *Imagined diàsporas among Manchester Muslims: the public performance of Pakistani transnational identity politics* (Oxford: James Currey, 2002), p. 83.

82. Talbot, *Pakistan*, p. 92.

83. Yunus Samad, 'Reflections on Partition: Pakistan Perspective', *International Journal of Punjab Studies*, Vol. 4, no. 1 (January-June 1997), pp. 43–63.

84. David Gilmartin, 'Religious leadership and the Pakistan movement in the Punjab', *Modern Asian Studies*, Vol. 13, no. 3 (July 1979), p. 498.

85. Jaffrelot, 'Nationalism without nation: Pakistan searching for its identity' in Jaffrelot (ed.), *Pakistan*, pp. 15–16.

86. See Hamza Alavi, 'Ethnicity, Muslim society and the Pakistan ideology' in Anita Weiss(ed.), *Islamic re-assertion in Pakistan: the application of Islamic laws in a modern state* (Lahore: Vanguard, 1987), pp. 21–47.

87. Quoted in Harun-ur-Rashid, *The foreshadowing of Bangladesh: Bengal Muslim League and Muslim League politics, 1936–47* (Dhaka: Asiatic Society of Bangladesh, 1987), p. 181.

88. Werbner, *Imagined diasporas*, p. 78.

89. Mohammad Waseem, *Politics and the state in Pakistan* (Islamabad: National Institute of Historical and Cultural Research, 1994), p. 80.

90. Werbner, *Imagined diasporas*, p. 78.

91. Ibid., p. 91.

92. S.V.R. Nasr, *Islamic Leviathan*, p. 47.

93. Benedict Anderson, *Imagined communities: reflections on the origin and spread of nationalism*, revised edition (London: Verso, 1991), p. 7.

94. Rafiuddin Ahmed, *Understanding the Bengal Muslims* (New Delhi: Oxford University Press, 2001), pp. 14–15.

95. Khilnani, *The idea of India*, p. 162.

2. WHO IS A PAKISTANI?

1. The violence of Partition has recently received close scholarly attention. For two of the best recent accounts see Gyanendra Pandey, *Remembering Partition: Violence, nationalism and history* (Cambridge: Cambridge University Press, 2002) and Yasmin Khan, *The great Partition: the making of India and Pakistan* (New Haven: Yale University Press, 2007). See also Mushirul Hasan, *India Partitioned: the other side of freedom* (Delhi: Roli Books, 1995).

2. See Theodore Wright, 'Indian Muslim refugees in the politics of Pakistan', *Journal of Commonwealth and Comparative Studies*, Vol. 12, no. 2 (1974), pp. 189–205. See also Talbot, *Pakistan: a modern history,* pp. 102–06.

3. Talbot, *Pakistan*, p. 102.

4. The creation of this community followed the Prophet Muhammad's emigration from the Arab city of Mecca to Yathrib (renamed Medina) in 622 AD.

5. For a thoughtful exploration of the ambivalent relationship between the 'Muslim' and the 'Pakistani', and its sinister legacy in the construction of modern India and Pakistan see Vazira-Fazila Yacoobali Zamindar, *The long Partition and the making of modern South Asia: refugees, boundaries, histories* (New York: Columbia University Press, 2007). The struggle to reconcile the Islamic with the national has also received the attention of others. Jalal spells out the 'contradiction attending the construction of the discourse on Pakistani nationhood' as 'the willingness to sever all ties with co-religionists in India whose geographical location denied them the rights of citizenship in the Muslim state even while they were theoretically constitutive elements of not only the *ummah*, but more importantly, the pre-1947 "Muslim nation"'. See, Ayesha Jalal, *Democracy and authoritarianism in South Asia: a comparative and historical perspective* (Cambridge: Cambridge University Press, 1995), pp. 235–36.

6. Talbot, *Pakistan*, pp. 68–70.

7. Ibid., p. 109.

8. Ibid., p.46.

9. Ibid., p. 47.

10. Ibid.

11. See Raunaq Jahan, *Pakistan: failure in national integration* (New York: Columbia University Press, 1972) and Hasan Zaheer, *The separation of East Pakistan: the rise and realization of Bengali Muslim Nationalism* (Karachi: Oxford University Press, 1995).

12. For an account of the background to these riots see Ziring, *Pakistan: at the cross-current of history*, pp. 56–58.

13. For the use of Urdu as a symbol in the consolidation of a separate Muslim identity in India see Robinson, *Separatism among Indian Muslims*, pp. 69–76 and Brass, *Language, religion and politics in North India*, pp. 127–38.

14. According to Tariq Rahman, it was the shift in the attitude of the *mohajirs* towards Urdu that led to its becoming a divisive issue. He argues that while in the early years Urdu-speaking *mohajirs* had agreed that Urdu would represent no more than a *lingua franca* for Pakistan, it was the claim in the 1970s that Urdu was also one of the languages of Sind that transformed the issue into a source of division by pitting Urdu-speaking migrants settled in large numbers in urban Sind against local Sindhis. See Tariq Rahman, *Language and politics in Pakistan* (Karachi: Oxford University Press, 1996), pp. 110–32.

15. Anwar Dil and Afia Dil, *Bengali language movement in Bangladesh* (Lahore: Ferozesons, 2000), p. 82.

16. For a fine discussion of syncretistic Islam in Bengal see Asim Roy, *The Islamic syncretistic tradition in Bengal* (Princeton: Princeton University Press, 1983).

17. Rafiuddin Ahmed, *The Bengal Muslims, 1871–1906: a quest for identity* (New Delhi: Oxford University Press, 1981), pp. 5–27.

18. Cohen, *The idea of Pakistan*, p. 169.
19. Burki, *Pakistan: fifty years of nationhood*, p. 216.
20. Ibid., pp. 217–18.
21. Yunus Samad, 'Pakistan or Punjabistan: Crisis of national identity', *International Journal of Punjab Studies*, Vol 2, no. 1 (1995), pp. 23–41.
22. Verkaaik, *Migrants and militants*, p. 40.
23. Ibid.
24. Ibid., p. 41.
25. Ibid., pp. 42–55. This was a key demand of the main *mohajir* organization, the Mohajir Qaumi Movement (Mohajir National Movement—MQM), founded in the mid 1980s and since renamed the Muttahida Qaumi Movement (United National Movement).
26. Their claims have been articulated by the Paktunkhwa Milli Party. See Jaffrelot (ed.), *A history of Pakistan and its origins*, p. 30.
27. See Frédéric Grare, *The resurgence of Baluch nationalism*, Carnegie Paper, no. 65, January 2006, http://www.carnegieendowment.org/files/CP65.Grare.FINAL.pdf
28. A.H. Dani (ed.), *Indus Valley: New Perspectives* (Islamabad: Quaid-i-Azam University, 1981).
29. Aitzaz Ahsan, *The Indus saga and the making of Pakistan* (Karachi: Oxford University Press, 1996).
30. Ibid., p. 9.
31. Ibid.
32. Shahnaz Rouse, 'The outsider(s) within: Sovereignty and citizenship in Pakistan' in Amrita Basu and Patricia Jeffrey (eds), *Appropriating gender: women's activism and policiticized religion in South Asia* (New York: Routledge, 1998), p. 59.
33. S.V.R. Nasr, 'International politics, domestic imperatives, and identity mobilization: sectarianism in Pakistan, 1979–1998', *Comparative politics*, Vol. 32, no. 2 (January 2000), pp. 171–190. See also Zaman, *The ulama in contemporary Islam*, pp. 135–43.
34. This is not say that there were no sectarian riots in these early years. One of the most ferocious took place during the Shia month of mourning (Muharram) in Khairpur district in Sind in 1963. Later, in 1970 there were reports of posters in some districts of Pakistan which called on Sunnis to take over the country with the slogan 'Jaag Sunni, jag, Pakistan tera hai' (Wake up Sunnis, Pakistan is yours). See Mariam Abou Zahab, 'The regional dimension of sectarian conflicts in Pakistan', in Christophe Jaffrelot (ed.), *Pakistan: nationalism without nation*, p. 125, fn. 2.
35. Mohammad Waseem, 'Origins and growth patters of Islamic organizations in Pakistan' in Satu P. Limaye, Mohan Malik and Robert Wirsing (eds), *Religious radicalism and security in South Asia* (Honolulu: University of Hawaii Press, 2004), p. 31.
36. S.V.R. Nasr, *The Shia revival: how conflicts within Islam will shape the future* (New York: W. W. Norton, 2006), pp. 63–80.

37. F. Daftary, *The Ismailis: their history and doctrine* (Cambridge: Cambridge University Press, 1990).
38. Mariam Abou-Zahab, 'Sectarianism as a substitute identity' in Soofia Mumtaz, Jean-Luc Racine and Imran Ali (eds), *Pakistan: the contours of state and society* (Karachi, Oxford University Press, 2002), p. 78; see also S.V.R. Nasr, 'The rise of Sunni militancy in Pakistan: the changing role of Islamism and the ulama in society and politics', *Modern Asian Studies*, Vol. 34, no. 1 (2002), pp. 139–80. On the Deobandi tradition see Metcalf's unrivalled *Islamic revival in British India*.
39. The Ahmedi controversy centres on the messianic status attached to its founder, Mirza Ghulam Ahmed (1830?-1908), which is regarded by orthodox Muslims as a rejection of Islamic dogma centring on the claim that Muhammad was the last prophet. See Yohanan Friedmann, 'Ahmadiya' in Esposito, *The Oxford Encyclopedia of the modern Islamic world* (New York: Oxford University Press, 2001), pp. 545–7. For a more extended discussion see, Yohanan Friedmann, *Prophecy continuous: aspects of Ahmedi religious thought and its medieval background* (Berkeley, CA: University of California Press, 1989).
40. L. Binder, *Religion and politics in Pakistan* (Berkeley, CA: University of California Press), pp. 258–96.
41. S.V.R. Nasr, *Islamic Leviathan: Islam and the making of state power* (New York: Oxford University Press, 2001), pp. 146–47.
42. For a comparable Indian perspective, but with rich insights into the case of Pakistan see Gyanendra Pandey, 'Can a Muslim be an Indian?', *Comparative Studies in Society and History*, Vol. 41, no. 4 (1999) and his 'Disciplining difference' in Gyanendra Pandey, *Remembering Partition: Violence, Nationalism and History* (Cambridge: Cambridge University Press, 2001), pp. 152–74.
43. See his presidential address to the Constituent Assembly of Pakistan in Karachi, 11 August, 1947, in *Speeches and Writings of Mr Jinnah*, edited by Jamil-ud-din Ahmad, Vol. II (Lahore: Shaikh Muhammad Ashrag, 1964), p. 403.
44. Ibid.
45. See Jinnah's speech to the Sind Bar Association in Karachi in *Dawn*, 24 January 1948.
46. Hamid Khan, *Constitutional and political history of Pakistan* (Karachi, Oxford University Press, 2005), p. 93.
47. For a background to Ahmedi thought and practice see Friedmann, *Prophecy continuous*.
48. *Report of the Court of Inquiry into the Punjab disturbances, 1954* (Munir Report) (Karachi: Government of Pakistan, 1954), p. 35.
49. Ibid.
50. A.S. Pirzada, *The politics of the Jamiat ul Ulema-i-Pakistan, 1971–77* (Karachi: Oxford University Press, 1996), p. 2.
51. *Dawn*, 1 July, 1974.

52. *National Assembly's verdict on finality of prophethood of Hazrat Muham-mad*, The National Assembly of Pakistan, *Debates*, 7 September 1974, (Islamabad: 1974).

53. Yohanan Friedmann, *Prophecy continuous*, pp. 42–43.

54. It is estimated that more than 4,000 people have died in sectarian violence in Pakistan since 1980. See Zaffar Abbas, 'Pakistan's schism spill into the present', http://news.bbc.co.uk/1/hi/world/south_asia/3724082.stm. These figures have since rise sharply in 2008 with the escalation of sectarian violence, especially in the tribal agency of Kurram, which has killed more than 400 people.

55. See S.V.R. Nasr, 'The rise of Sunni militancy in Pakistan', pp. 145–54.

56. Afak Haydar, 'The politicization of the Shias and the development of the Tehrik-e-Nifaz-e-Fiqhe-Jafaria in Pakistan' in Charles H. Kennedy (ed.), *Pakistan, 1992* (Boulder, CO: Westview Press, 1993), pp. 75–93.

57. See S.V.R. Nasr, 'International politics, domestic imperatives and identity mobilization', *Comparative Politics*, Vol. 32, no. 2 (January 2000), p. 176.

58. On the intricacies of Sunni politics in Pakistan see S.V.R. Nasr, 'The rise of Sunni militancy in Pakistan', pp. 143–85 and Muhammad Qasim Zaman, 'Sectarianism in Pakistan: the radicalization of Shia-Sunni identities', *Modern Asian Studies* , Vol. 32, no. 3, 1998, pp. 687–716.

59. Mariam Abou Zahab, 'The regional dimension of sectarian conflicts in Pakistan' in Jaffrelot, (ed.), *Pakistan*, pp. 115–128.

60. Ibid.

61. Zaman,'Sectarianism in Pakistan', p. 691.

62. Ian Talbot, *Pakistan: a modern history*, pp. 117–118 and Ahmad Hasan Dani, *History of the Northern Areas of Pakistan* (Islamabad: National Institute of Historical and Cultural research, 1989). See also International Crisis Group, *Discord in Pakistan's Northern Areas*, Asia Report 131, 2 April 2007, http://www.crisisgroup.org/library/documents/asia/south_asia/131_discord_in_pakistan_s_northern_areas.pdf

63. See Cohen, *The idea of Pakistan*, p. 163.

64. See Pandey, *Remembering Partition*, p. 152.

65. See Jinnah's presidential address to the Constituent Assembly of Pakistan, August 11, 1947 in *Speeches and writings of Mr Jinnah,* II, p. 402.

66. See R.J. Moore, 'Jinnah and the Pakistan demand', *Modern Asian Studies*, Vol. 17, no. 4 (1983), pp. 529–61.

67. Gyanendra Pandey, 'Can a Muslim be an Indian?' *Comparative Studies in Society and History*, Vol. 41, no. 4 (October 1999), pp. 608–629.

68. See Shaun Gregory, 'The Christian minority in Pakistan: issues and options', University of Bradford, Pakistan Security Research Unit, Briefing no. 37, 17 July 2008, p. 5, http://spaces.brad.ac.uk:8080/download/attachments/748/Brief+37.pdf

69. Kingsley Davis, 'India and Pakistan: the demography of Partition', *Pacific Affairs*, Vol. 22, no. 3 (September 1949), pp. 243–52.

70. Theodore Wright, 'Indian Muslim refugees in the politics of Pakistan', *Journal of Commonwealth and Comparative Studies*, Vol. 12 (1975), p. 194.

71. Quoted in Hassan Zaheer, *The separation of East Pakistan: the rise and realization of Bengali Muslim nationalism* (Karachi: Oxford University Press, 1994), p. 18.

72. Hamid Khan, *Constitutional and political history of Pakistan* (Karachi: Oxford University Press, 2005), p. 96. Italics added.

73. Ibid., p. 104.

74. The system of separate electorates was introduced by the British under the Government of India Act 1909. It was granted in response to demands by a group of aristocratic and high-ranking Indian Muslims—the so-called 'Simla Deputation'—which successfully lobbied the Viceroy, Lord Minto, in Simla in October 1906 to approve a separate electoral list for Muslims. Their case rested on the claim that the Muslim minority had separate 'communal' interests that could not be protected so long as it was left vulnerable to voters representing the Hindu or non-Muslim majority. Though vigorously challenged by Indian nationalists at the time, the institution of separate electorates was adopted as a key element of the manifesto of the Muslim League (founded in December 1906), which relied on it to reinforce the idea of a separate Muslim 'nation' driven by distinct concerns—an idea that was later to become an integral part of Pakistan's founding ideology. For a discussion of the historical background of the demand for separate electorates see Shaikh, *Community and consensus in Islam*, pp. 119–59.

75. Jalal, *Democracy and authoritarianism in South Asia*, p. 234.

76. Ziring, *Pakistan: at the cross-current of history*, p. 135.

77. Burki, *Pakistan*, pp. 219–20.

78. The referendum proposition asked voters: 'Whether the people of Pakistan endorse the process initiated by General Zia ul Haq, the President of Pakistan, to bring the laws of Pakistan in conformity with the injunctions of Islam as laid down in the Holy Quran and the Sunnah of the Holy Prophet (peace be upon Him) and for the preservation of the ideology of Pakistan, for the continuation and consolidation of that process for the smooth and orderly transfer of power to the elected representatives of the people'. For a further analysis of the referendum see William Richter, 'Pakistan in 1884: digging in', *Asian Survey*, Vol. 25, no. 2 (February 1985), pp. 145–54.

79. A.H. Nayyar & Ahmad Salim (eds), *The subtle subversion: the state of curricula and textbooks in Pakistan* (Islamabad: Sustainable Development Policy Institute, 2003) http://www.sdpi.org/whats_new/reporton/State%20 of%20Curr&TextBooks.pdf.

80. Ibid., p. 11.

81. Ibid., p. 9.

82. For a systematic treatment of the erosion of Pakistan's secular and plural legal system through the introduction in the late 1970s and 1980s of a parallel legal code claiming to rest on the *sharia*, see Shaheen Sardar Ali

and Javaid Rehman, *Indigenous peoples and ethnic minorities of Pakistan: Constitutional and legal perspectives* (London: Curzon, 2002). According to a recent report by the Christian non-government organization, Centre for Legal Aid and Settlement (CLAAS), its main features included the establishment of *sharia* benches as integral parts of Pakistan's superior judiciary to rule against laws judged to be 'repugnant to Islam'; the introduction in 1979 of Islamic punishments (Hudood Ordinance); the enforcement in 1984 of the Law of Evidence that reduced by half the value of court testimony given by a non-Muslim in comparison to that of a Muslim; the introduction of blasphemy laws, which after 1986 carried the death penalty for remarks deemed to be derogatory to the Prophet Muhammad; the Eighth Amendment of the constitution passed in 1985 re-introducing separate electorates that by relieving Muslim candidates from seeking the support of non-Muslims contributed to their disenfranchisement, and the 1988 and 1998 amendments extending the supremacy of the *sharia*. See Nasir Saeed, *Faith under Fire: a report on the second class citizenship and intimidation of Christians in Pakistan* (London: Centre for Legal Aid and Settlement, 2002), pp. 12–18.

83. Devirupa Mitra, 'Political voice of minorities still stifled in Pakistan', http://www.thaindian.com/newsportal/uncategorized/political-voice-of-minorities-still-stifled-in-pakistan_10019217.html. See also http://www.elections.com.pk/newsdetails.php?id=384.

84. Pandey, *Remembering Partition*, p. 160.

3. THE BURDEN OF ISLAM

1. Faisal Devji, *Landscapes of the Jihad: militancy, morality, modernity* (London: Hurst, 2005), p. 123.

2. See Barbara Metcalf, 'Nationalism, modernity, and Muslim identity in India before 1947' in Barbara Metcalf, *Islamic contestations: essays on Muslims in India and Pakistan* (Delhi: Oxford University Press, 2004), p. 183.

3. See Jinnah's presidential address to the All-India Muslim League in Lahore, March 1940 in *Speeches and writings of Mr Jinnah*, Vol. II, edited by Jamil-ul-din Ahmad (Lahore: Shaikh Muhammad Ashraf, 1960–6th edition), p. 159.

4. Ibid. p.160.

5. For insights into the destructive nexus of religion, politics and violence at Partition, see Ian Talbot (ed.), *The deadly embrace: religion, politics and violence in India and Pakistan 1947–2002* (Karachi: Oxford University Press, 2007), especially the contributions by Talbot (pp. 1–16) and Khan (pp. 36–60). See also the now classic study by Pandey, *Remembering Partition*.

6. See Jinnah's presidential address to the Constituent Assembly of Pakistan, August 11, 1947 in *Speeches and writings*, II, pp. 403, 404.

7. Leonard Binder, *Religion and politics in Pakistan* (Berkeley, CA: University of California Press, 1961), p. 6.

8. Jinnah reserved his opprobrium for those who might well have lined up behind him in support of his passionate defence in the Constituent Assembly of Pakistan as a secular state. 'I cannot understand,' he observed, 'why this feeling of nervousness that the future of constitution of Pakistan is going to be in conflict with Shariat Law. There is one section of the people who keep on impressing everybody that the future constitution of Pakistan should be based on the Shariah. The other section deliberately want [sic] to create mischief and agitate that the Sharia Law must be scrapped.' *Dawn*, 26 January 1948.

9. For a fine discussion of the inherent ambiguities that lay at the heart of the Resolution see Binder, *Religion and politics*, pp. 116–53.

10. S.M. Zafar, 'Constitutional development' in Hafeez Malik (ed.), *Pakistan: founders' aspirations and today's realities* (Karachi: Oxford University Press, 2001), p. 31.

11. Binder, *Religion and politics*, p. 22.

12. Nasr, *The vanguard of the Islamic revolution*, pp. 117–31.

13. For the full text of the Resolution see *The Constituent Assembly of Pakistan Debates, V* (Karachi: Government of Pakistan, 1964), p. 2.

14. See Liaquat's speech introducing the Resolution on 7 March 1949 in Hamid Khan, *Constitutional and political history of Pakistan* (Karachi: Oxford University Press, 2001), pp. 92–93.

15. *The Constituent Assembly of Pakistan Debates, V*, p. 2.

16. Khan, *Constitutional and political history*, p. 93.

17. Ibid.

18. Ibid., pp. 54, 55.

19. See speech by Abdur Rab Nishtar in the Constituent Assembly on 10 March 1949 in Khan, *Constitutional and political history*, p. 101.

20. Ibid., p. 102.

21. Usmani, who spoke at length in favour of the Resolution on 9 March 1949, drew attention to an address by Jinnah to Muslim students in July in 1943 in which he was quoted as saying 'in my opinion our system of government was determined by the Quran some 1350 years ago'. Usmani used this to dismiss claims by critics of the Resolution, who suggested that had Jinnah been alive, the Resolution would not have come up before the Constituent Assembly. Ibid., pp. 100–01.

22. See speech by Birat Chandra Mandal in the Constituent Assembly on 9 March 1949, ibid., p. 97.

23. See speech by Bhupendra Kumar Datta in the Constituent Assembly on 9 March 1949, ibid., p. 99.

24. See speech by Liaquat Ali Khan in the Constituent Assembly on 12 March 1949, ibid., p. 103.

25. Nasr, *Islamic Leviathan*, p. 61.

26. See Ayub's speech to a gathering of Deobandi *ulama* in May 1959 in Muhammad Ayub Khan, *Speeches and Statements*, Vol. 1 (Karachi: Government of Pakistan Press, 1961), pp. 110–11.

27. Lawrence Ziring, *Pakistan: at the crosscurrent of history* (Oxford: Oneworld, 2003), pp. 87–88.

28. Muhammad Ayub Khan, *Speeches and statements*, I (Karachi: Oxford University Press, 1961), p. 57.

29. Waseem, *Politics and the state in Pakistan*, p. 158.

30. The decision to secularize family law in Pakistan dated back to the 1950s though the weakness of the leadership at the time meant that it had to wait for support from Ayub's military-backed regime. The fierce controversy unleashed by its proposals also meant that it was never put to the vote in parliament and remains in the statute books as an executive ordinance. Among its key provisions were changes in the right of Muslim men under Islamic law to contract polygamous marriages, which were made subject to review by an Arbitration Council responsible for protecting the claims of existing wives and children likely to be affected by a polygamous marriage. Other provisions related to divorce, where the scope for abuse by Muslim men was limited by curbing their right under Islamic law to unilateral divorce by bringing it in line with morally approved practices that would secure the fair treatment for women. Islamic laws on inheritance were also modernized by extending the right to inherit property to orphaned grand children, hitherto excluded from any claim on their grand-parents' property. See Fazlur Rahman, 'The controversy over the Muslim Family Laws' in Donald E. Smith (ed.), *South Asian religion and politics* (Princeton: Princeton University Press, 1966), pp. 414–27. See also Christele Dedebant, *Le voile et la banniere: l'avante-garde feministe au Pakistan* (Paris : CNRS Editions, 2003), pp. 112–20.

31. Bruce Lawrence, *Shattering the myth: Islam beyond violence* (Princeton: Princeton University Press, 1998), p. 144.

32. Katherine Ewing, 'The politics of Sufism: redefining the saints of Pakistan', *Journal of Asian Studies*, Vol. 42, no. 2 (1983), pp. 257–60, 266.

33. Saifur Rahman Sherani, 'Ulema and pir in Pakistani politics' in Hastings Donnan and Pnina Werbner (eds), *Economy and culture in Pakistan: Migrants and cities in a Muslim society* (London: Macmillan, 1991), pp. 216–46.

34. David Gilmartin, *Empire and Islam: Punjab and the making of Pakistan* (Berkeley, CA: University of California Press, 1988), pp. 216–17.

35. See *The report of the Hamoodur Rehman Commission of Inquiry into the 1971 war [as declassified by the Government of Pakistan]* (Lahore: Vanguard, nd), p. 285.

36. Ibid., p. 289.

37. Zulfiqar Ali Bhutto, *Speeches* (Islamabad: Government of Pakistan, 1973), p. 13.

38. The phrase was first used by Libyan President Muammar Gaddafi during his address to the 1974 Summit in Lahore, where it received an enthusiastic public reception orchestrated by Bhutto's government. See Stanley Wolpert, *Zulfi Bhutto of Pakistan* (Oxford: Oxford University Press, 1993), p. 234.

39. Bhutto's close interest in promoting government patronage of local holy men and their shrines, especially in rural Sind, are explored in Sherani, 'Ulema and pir in Pakistani politics' in Donnan and Werbner (eds), *Economy and culture*, p. 235. See also Verkaaik, *Migrants and militants*, pp. 37–39.

40. See report on General Zia's address to the nation in *Dawn*, 8 July 1977.

41. The change followed amendments to the 1973 Constitution contained in a presidential order issued in March 1985. Under the newly introduced Article 2A, the 1949 Objectives Resolution was reproduced as an annex rather than a preamble, thereby making it an operative part of the Constitution. Its status has, since then, remained unchanged.

42. Nasr, *Islamic Leviathan*, p. 159.

43. See David Taylor, 'The politics of Islam and Islamization in Pakistan' in James Piscatori (ed.), *Islam in the Political Process* (Cambridge: Cambridge University Press, 1983), p. 195.

44. Ziring, *Pakistan at the cross-current of history*, p. 165.

45. For a classic study exploring the many facets of Zia's Islamization programme see Anita Weiss (ed.), *Islamic re-assertion in Pakistan: the application of Islamic laws in a modern state* (Lahore: Vanguard, 1987).

46. Quoted in Parvez Amirali Hoodbhoy and Abdul Hameed Nayyar, 'Rewriting the history of Pakistan' in Asghar Khan (ed.), *Islam, politics and the state: the Pakistan experience* (London: Zed Books, 1985), p. 165.

47. Ibid., pp. 167–68.

48. Ibid., p. 168.

49. Ibid., pp. 169–71.

50. See Hasan Askari-Rizvi, 'Is Pakistan an ideological state?', *Daily Times* (Lahore), 9 May 2005.

51. Taylor, 'The politics of Islam,' in Piscatori (ed.), *Islam in the political process*, p. 196.

52. Nasr, *Islamic Leviathan*, 137.

53. S.V.R. Nasr, 'International politics, domestic imperatives, and the rise of politics of identity: sectarianism in Pakistan, 1979–1997', *Comparative Politics*, Vol. 32, no. 2 (January 2000), p. 176.

54. For contrasting views of the impact of these reforms on women see Charles Kennedy, 'Islamization in Pakistan: implementation of the Hudood Ordinance', *Asian Survey*, Vol. 28, no. 3 (March 1988), pp. 307–16, and Anita Weiss, 'Implications of the Islamization programme for women' in A. Weiss (ed.), *Islamic re-assertion in Pakistan*, pp. 97–114. For a fine discussion of the clout of upper-class women in resisting these reforms see, Dedebant, *Le voile et la banniere*, pp. 133–47.

55. Kennedy, 'Islamization in Pakistan', pp. 312–13.

56. Barbara Metcalf, 'Islamic arguments in contemporary Pakistan' in Metcalf, *Islamic contestations*, pp. 258–59.

57. Ayesha Jalal, 'The convenience of subservience: women and the state in Pakistan' in Deniz Kandiyoti (ed.), *Women, Islam and the state* (London: Croom Helm, 1991), pp. 77–114.

58. Ibid., p. 79.
59. Christophe Jaffrelot, 'Islamic identity and ethnic tensions' in Christophe Jaffrelot (ed.), *A history of Pakistan and its origins*, pp. 29–30. See also S. Mahmud Ali, *The fearful state: power, people and internal war in South Asia* (London: Zed Books, 1993), p. 155.
60. Verkaaik's study of the ethnic-religious movement, the Mohajir Qaumi Movement (the MQM), representing Urdu-speaking migrants (*mohajirs*) in Pakistan skillfully traces this transformation. He shows how the MQM began by challenging the 'high' cultural Islamic modernist tradition associated with state ideology and appropriating the 'low' Islam of saints and shrines to carve out a *mohajir* ethnic space before reverting to 'high' Islamic traditions of martyrdom and sacrifice to sharpen its opposition to the state. See Oskar Verkaaik, *Migrants and militants*, op. cit.
61. I owe my use of the term 'shariatize', and later of the term 'shariatization', to Mumtaz Ahmad. His reference to 'shariatization' to describe the policies pursued by General Zia ul Haq in the late 1970s and 1980s helped capture the essence of a process that marked a radical break with earlier attempts at Islamization. See Mumtaz Ahmad, 'Pakistan', in Shireen Hunter (ed.), *The politics of Islamic revivalism: diversity and unity* (Bloomington, IN: Indiana University Press, 1988), pp. 236–239. My aim here is to amplify the meaning of that process by teasing out more rigorously its differences with Islamization and to identify the main agents driving that process with a view to elaborating how it transformed the debate on national identity in Pakistan. See also Saeed Shafqat, 'From official Islam to Islamism' in Jaffrelot (ed.), *Pakistan: nationalism without a nation?*, pp. 131–47.
62. Nasr, *Islamic Leviathan*, p. 134. See also Robert LaPorte, Jr, 'Urban groups and the Zia regime,' in Craig Baxter (ed.), *Zia's Pakistan: politics and stability in a frontline state* (Lahore: Vanguard, 1985), p. 14.
63. Mustapha Kamal Pasha, 'Savage Capitalism and Civil Society in Pakistan', in Anita Weiss and S. Zulfiqar Gilani (eds), *Power and civil society in Pakistan* (Karachi: Oxford University Press, 2001), p. 32.
64. Mustapha Kamal Pasha, 'The Hyper-Extended State: Civil Society and Democracy', in Rasul Bakhsh Rais (ed.), *State, Society and Democratic Change in Pakistan* (Karachi: Oxford University Press, 1997), p. 196.
65. Pasha, 'Savage Capitalism', p. 35.
66. Nasr, *The Vanguard of the Islamic Revolution*, p.193.
67. See Sarah Ansari, *Sufi Saints and State Power: The Pirs of Sind, 1843–1947* (Cambridge: Cambridge University Press, 1992); David Gilmartin, *Empire and Islam: Punjab and the Making of Pakistan* (Berkeley, CA: University of California Press, 1988); Usha Sanyal, *Devotional Islam and politics in British India: Ahmed Riza Khan and his movement, 1870–1920* (New Delhi: Oxford University Press, 1996); and Jamal Malik, *Colonialization of Islam: dissolution of traditional institutions in Pakistan* (New Delhi: Manohar, 1998).

68. Mariam Abou-Zahab and Olivier Roy, *Islamist networks: the Afghan-Pakistan connection* (London: Hurst, 2004), pp. 19–46.
69. Gilles Kepel, *Jihad: the trail of political Islam* (London and New York: I.B. Tauris, 2002), pp. 98–105.
70. Nasr, "The Rise of Sunni Militancy in Pakistan", p. 149.
71. For a classic exposition of the founding principles of the school at Deoband see Metcalf, *Islamic Revival in British India*.
72. For an excellent discussion of contemporary Islamic neo-fundamentalism and its basic tenets, see Olivier Roy, *Globalised Islam: the search for a new ummah* (London: Hurst, 2004). For an earlier discussion see also Olivier Roy, *The failure of political Islam* (London and New York: I.B. Tauris, 1999) pp. 75–88.
73. Mumtaz Ahmad, 'Revivalism, Islamization, Sectarianism and Violence in Pakistan', in Craig Baxter and Charles Kennedy (eds), *Pakistan, 1997* (Boulder, CO: Westview Press, 1998), pp. 101–21. For a discussion of the role of a similar class of preachers or 'peripheral ulama' on the margins of the clerical establishment in Egypt, see Malika Zeghal, 'Religion and Politics in Egypt: The Ulama of Al Azhar, Radical Islam, and the State (1952–94)', *International Journal of Middle East Studies*, Vol. 31, no. 3 (1999), pp. 401–27.
74. For an analysis of the ways in which this discourse shaped the conduct of Indo-Muslim politics in late nineteenth and twentieth centuries see, Shaikh, *Community and consensus in Islam*, pp. 200–07.
75. Aziz Ahmad, *Studies in Islamic culture in the Indian environment* (Oxford: Clarendon Press, 1964), pp. 210–212. For the best survey of this and other similar Islamic movements, see also Peter Hardy, *The Muslims of British India* (Cambridge: Cambridge University Press, 1972).
76. Gail Minault, *The Khilafat movement: religious symbolism and political mobilization in India* (New York: Columbia University Press, 1982).
77. Barbara D. Metcalf, 'Nationalism, modernity, and Muslim identity before 1947' in Barbara Metcalf, *Islamic Contestations: Essays on Muslims in India and Pakistan* (New Delhi: Oxford University Press, 2004), p.182. See also Khalid Masud (ed.), *Travellers in faith: studies of Tablighi Jamaat as a transnational islamic movement for faith renewal* (Leiden: E.J. Brill, 2000); Yoginder Sikand, *The origins and development of the Tablighi Jama'at* (New Delhi: Orient, Longman, 2002) and Mumtaz Ahmad, 'Islamic Fundamentalism in South Asia: the Jamaat-i-Islami and the Tablighi Jamaat' in Martin E. Marty and R. Scott Appleby (eds), *Fundamentalisms Observed* (Chicago and London: University of Chicago Press, 1991), pp. 510–523.
78. See Farzana Shaikh, 'Millat and Mazhab: re-thinking Iqbal's Political Vision' in Mushirul Hasan and Asim Roy (eds), *Living together separately: cultural India in history and politics* (New Delhi: Oxford University Press, 2005), pp. 366–88.
79. Nasr, *Vanguard of the Islamic revolution*, pp. 103–15.

80. For a detailed report into the legally anomalous position of the tribal areas, formally designated as the Federally Administered Tribal Areas (FATA), see International Crisis Group, *Pakistan's tribal areas: appeasing the militants,* Report no. 125, 11 December 2006, http://www.crisisgroup. org/library/documents/asia/south_asia/125_pakistans_tribal_areas___ appeasing_the_militants.pdf.

81. Lawrence Ziring, *Pakistan: at the cross-current of history* (Oxford: Oneworld, 2003), p. 130.

82. Nasr, 'The Rise of Sunni Militancy in Pakistan', pp. 145–154.

83. Ibid., p. 152.

84. Muhammad Qasim Zaman, *The Ulama in Contemporary Islam: custodians of Change* (Princeton: Princeton University Press, 2002), pp. 111–143.

85. Nasr, *Islamic Leviathan*, p. 143.

86. Muhammad Qasim Zaman, 'Religious Education and the Rhetoric of Reform: the Madrasah in British India and Pakistan', *Comparative Studies in Society and History*, Vol. 41, no. 2 (April 1999), pp. 294–323.

87. See International Crisis Group, *Pakistan: madrasahs, extremism and the military,* Asia Report no. 36, 29 July 2002, p. 2 http://www.crisisgroup. org/library/documents/report_archive/A400717_29072002.pdf.

88. Jamal Malik, 'Dynamics among traditional religious scholars and their institutions in contemporary South Asia', *The Muslim World*, Vol. 87, no. 3–4 (July-October 1997), pp. 216–17.

89. For a thorough exploration of this struggle in Pakistan and elsewhere in the Muslim world, see Robert Hefner and Muhammad Qasim Zaman (eds), *Schooling Islam: the culture and politics of modern Muslim education* (Princeton: Princeton University Press, 2007).

90. See Nasr, *The vanguard of the Islamic revolution*, p. 201.

91. See, among others, Ahmed Rashid, *Descent into chaos: how the war against Islamic extremism is being lost in Pakistan, Afghanistan and Central Asia* (London: Allen Lane, 2008) and his *Taliban: the story of the Afghan warlords* (London: Pan Books, 2001). See also Gilles Dorronsoro, *Revolution unending: Afghanistan—1979 to the present* (London: Hurst, 2005); William Maley (ed.), *Fundamentalism Reborn? Afghanistan and the Taliban* (London: Hurst, 1998); Olivier Roy, 'The Taliban: A Strategic Tool for Pakistan' in Christophe Jaffrelot (ed.), *Pakistan: nationalism without a nation?*, pp. 161–178; and Peter Marsden, *The Taliban: war, religion and the new order* (London: Zed Books, 1998).

92. Shaikh, 'Millat and mazhab', pp. 379–80.

93. Kepel, *Jihad*, p. 104.

4. THE DILEMMAS OF DEVELOPMENT

1. The term 'salariat' was famously employed by Hamza Alavi to describe the social group that served as the main driver of Muslim nationalism in colo-

nial India. He describes it as a class (falling somewhere between the middle class and the petit-bourgeoisie) of urban professionals 'who had received education that would qualify them for employment as scribes and functionaries in the expanding colonial state apparatus'. Hamza Alavi, 'Ethnicity, Muslim society, and the Pakistan ideology' in Anita Weiss (ed.) *Islamic Reassertion in Pakistan*, p. 24.

2. Rural and landless peasants Bengal were no strangers to the powerful appeal of Islam in the pursuit of economic objectives. The first half of the nineteenth century had witnessed the emergence of the revivalist Faraizi movement, which politicized Muslim rural communities in Bengal by organizing resistance against Hindu landlords and money-lenders. Rafiuddin Ahmed, *The Bengal Muslims, 1871–1906: a quest for identity* (New Delhi: Oxford University Press, 1981).

3. For one of the most comprehensive and insightful assessments of Pakistan's economic development since independence see S. Akbar Zaidi, *Issues in Pakistan's economy* (2nd edition) (Karachi: Oxford University Press, 2005).

4. Only eleven of the thirty-five members of the Simla Deputation (which in 1905 won the right for the separate representation of Indian Muslims in new legislative councils and in 1906 formed the nucleus of the All India Muslim League), were not titled. Members were required not only to demonstrate an ability to read and write 'with facility', but to be in command of an income of not less than Rs 500 a year. See Mohammad Waseem, *Politics and the state in Pakistan* (Islamabad: National Institute of Historical and Cultural Research, 1994), p. 62.

5. Mushirul Hasan, 'India and Pakistan: Why the difference?' in Mushirul Hasan and Nariaki Nakazato (eds), *The unfinished agenda: nation-building in South Asia* (New Delhi: Manohar, 2001), pp. 328–337.

6. Stanley Wolpert, *Jinnah of Pakistan* (Delhi: Oxford University Press, 2005 edn), pp. 144–45. This is confirmed by more recent reports. In what is described as 'a revealing portrait of his priorities' in the early months after the independence, Jinnah is said to have repeatedly pressed the US ambassador to Pakistan in March 1948 to buy Jinnah's residence 'Flagstaff' for use by US embassy personnel'. See Tariq Ali, *The duel: Pakistan in the flight path of American power* (London: Simon and Schuster, 2008), pp. 43–44.

7. Ian Talbot, *Pakistan: a modern history* (London: Hurst, rev edn, 2005), pp. 67–87.

8. Ibid., p. 88.

9. A.H. Beruni, *Makers of Pakistan and modern India* (Lahore: Shaikh Mohammad Ashraf, 1950), p. 209.

10. K.B. Sayeed, *Politics in Pakistan: the nature and direction of change* (New York: Praeger, 1980), p. 13.

11. For details see Ian Talbot, 'Planning for Pakistan: The Planning Committee of the All India Muslim League 1943–46', *Modern Asian Studies*, Vol. 28, no. 4 (October 1994), pp. 875–889.

12. Quoted in ibid., pp. 880–81.
13. Ibid.
14. Syed Sharifuddin Pirzada (ed.), *Quaid-e-Azam Jinnah's correspondence* (Karachi: Guild Publishing House, 1966), p. 159.
15. Ibid.
16. Ibid.
17. Ibid.
18. Ibid., p. 160.
19. In his famous presidential address to the League in 1940, Jinnah had declared that Islam and Hinduism were 'not religions in the strict sense of the word'. See *Speeches and writings of Mr Jinnah*, I, p. 160. Metcalf explains Jinnah's interpretation of Islam as possibly 'his own gesture stemming from the cosmopolitanism and isolation from mainstream religious practice he shared with Nehru, toward self-presentation as a "modern"'. See Metcalf, *Islamic contestations*, p. 183. Nehru though was unequivocally persuaded that religion (Hinduism) was outmoded and destined for a natural death with no prospect whatever of representing a modern nation-state. Jinnah's very different understanding of religion (Islam) would complicate the uncertainties that beset Pakistan in its own troubled passage to modernity.
20. Jamil Rashid and Hassan Gardezi, 'Independent Pakistan: Its political economy' in Hassan Gardezi and Jamil Rashid (eds), *Pakistan: the roots of dictatorship: the political economy of a praetorian state* (London: Zed Press, 1983), pp. 5–6.
21. Khalid bin Sayeed, *Politics in Pakistan: the nature and direction of change* (New York: Praeger, 1980), p. 59.
22. Bhashani was eventually to abandon the Muslim League and create the more radical Awami National Party (ANP) in 1957, which enjoyed strong support in rural districts of East Bengal.
23. Their views were reflected in the Report of the League's Agrarian Committee submitted in 1949. See Talbot, *Pakistan*, p. 123.
24. Hamza Alavi,'Class and state' in Gardezi and Rashid (eds), *Pakistan*, p. 58.
25. Omar Noman, *The political economy of Pakistan* (London: Routledge and Kegan Paul, 1988), p. 41.
26. See Akbar Zaidi, *Issues in Pakistan's economy* (Karachi: Oxford University Press, 2005, 2nd edn), pp. 97–103.
27. 'Functional inequality' was a central pillar of the economic doctrine favoured by Ayub's regime. It was predicated on the thesis that resources should be directed towards sectors with the propensity for the highest returns on the assumption that such returns would automatically 'trickle down' to less favoured sectors as development proceeded. Ibid., pp. 101–02.
28. Raunaq Jahan, *Pakistan: failure in national integration*, pp. 67–85.

29. Ibid., p.103.
30. Vaqar Ahmed and Rashid Amjad, *The management of Pakistan's economy, 1947–82* (Karachi: Oxford University Press, 1984), p. 90.
31. See Omar Noman, *Economic and social progress in Asia: why Pakistan did not become a tiger* (Karachi: Oxford University Press, 1997).
32. Talbot, 'Planning for Pakistan', p. 887.
33. Metcalf, *Islamic contestations*, p. 225.
34. Ibid., p. 223.
35. Gustav Papanek, a member of the so-called Harvard Advisory Group that exercised a powerful influence on economic policy under Ayub, described the doctrine as one based on the notion that 'great inequalities were necessary in order to create industry and industrialists' and that the pursuit of profit and high incomes were both acceptable 'because they are used chiefly for investment, rather than for conspicuous consumption'—an assumption that was to prove fatally flawed in the case of Pakistan. See Gustav Papanek, *Pakistan development: social goals and private incentives* (Cambridge, MA: Harvard University Press, 1967), pp 242–43.
36. Nevertheless, it has been widely noted that despite Zia's much heralded public advocacy of the private sector, which ensured the support of the business and entrepreneurial classes, he did not rush to denationalize industries brought under state control by Bhutto. This has strengthened the view that, as with the rest of his Islamizing agenda, Zia's economic policies were driven primarily by the need to shore up his regime and secure its bases of support. According to Zaidi, 'the Zia regime took a far more pragmatic and politically clever line by not denationalizing in haste. It encouraged the private sector by giving it greater incentives and removing controls ... Once the government realized that ownership and control of the public sector industries was an effective tool for granting political patronage and favour, there seemed little recourse to gift such a means away.' See Zaidi, *Issues in Pakistan's economy*, pp. 117.
37. Nasim Ahmed Jawed, *Islam's political culture: religion and politics in pre-divided Pakistan* (Austin, TX: University of Texas, 1999), p. 105.
38. Philip E. Jones, *The Pakistan People's Party: rise to Power* (Karachi: Oxford University Press, 2003), p. 101.
39. Jawed, *Islam's political culture*, pp. 108–09.
40. Metcalf, *Islamic contestations*, pp. 236–37.
41. Ibid., p. 260.
42. Nasr, *Islamic Leviathan*, p. 79.
43. Jones, *The Pakistan People's Party*, p. 223.
44. Jawed, *Islam's political culture*, p. 114.
45. Ibid., p. 116
46. A *fatwa* issued by leading *ulama* during the 1970 general elections warned voters against the 'evils' of capitalism, including indecent exposure and immodesty. Ibid., p.115.

47. For a fine exposition of Mawdudi's theory of Islamic economics see S.V.R. Nasr, *Mawdudi and the making of Islamic revivalism* (New York, Oxford: Oxford University Press, 1996), pp. 103–06.
48. Jawed, *Islam's political culture,* pp. 118–22.
49. Ibid., p. 123.
50. Nasr, *The vanguard of the Islamic revolution,* p. 164.
51. Shahid Javed Burki, *Pakistan under Bhutto, 1971–77* (London: Macmillan, 1980).
52. Ibid., p. 138.
53. Talbot, *Pakistan,* p. 244.
54. Zaidi, *Issues,* p. 117.
55. Shahid Javed Burki, *Pakistan: Fifty years of nationhood,* pp. 118–19.
56. Noman, *The political economy of Pakistan,* p. 157 and Jonathan Addleton, *Undermining the centre: the Gulf migration and Pakistan* (Karachi: Oxford University Press, 1992), pp. 127, 207.
57. Addleton, *Undermining the centre,* pp. 154, 158.
58. For a detailed exposition of the report and its implications for the creation of an Islamic economic system see Shahid Javed Burki, 'Economic management within an Islamic context' in Anita Weiss (ed.) *Islamic reassertion in Pakistan: the application of Islamic laws in a modern state* (Lahore: Vanguard Books, 1987), pp. 49–58.
59. Ibid., p. 53.
60. 'An Agenda for Islamic economic reforms: the report of the committee on Islamization appointed by the Finance Minister, 1980', quoted in ibid. p. 52.
61. Quoted in Burki, 'Economic management', p. 51. Italics added.
62. Shahid Javed Burki, 'Pakistan's Sixth Plan: helping the country climb out of poverty', *Asian Survey,* Vol. 24, no. 4 (April 1984), pp. 400–22.
63. Jamal Malik, *Colonialization of Islam: dissolution of traditional institutions in Pakistan* (New Delhi: Manohar, 1998), pp. 85–86.
64. S.V.R. Nasr also makes a convincing case to show that economic as much as political considerations may have influenced the regime's decision to introduce Islamic taxes. He argues that they helped reduce the budget deficit, and though accounting for only some 2% of government revenue, were 'important in a country where tax evasion is pervasive' and where 'some segments of the population such as the landed elite pay little or no taxes'. Nasr, *Islamic Leviathan,* pp. 144–45.
65. Zaidi, *Issues in Pakistan's economy,* p. 504. See also Burki, *Pakistan,* pp. 107–08 and Stephen Cohen, *The idea of Pakistan* (Washington, DC: The Brookings Institution Press, 2004), pp. 251–52.
66. The most widely used guide to corruption is the Corruption Perceptions Index (CPI) published annually by the Berlin-based organization Transparency International. In 2007 Pakistan's performance was still judged to rate poorly with a CPI score of 2.4 in a range of 10 (not corrupt) to 0 (highly corrupt) out of 179 countries surveyed. See http://www.transparency.org/policy_research/surveys_indices/cpi/2007.

67. Based on the slogan: *'pehley ehtesaab, baad intikhab'* ('accountability first, elections later'), it was popularised in a series of articles by one of the country's most widely read newspaper columnists, Ardeshir Cowasjee, *Dawn*, 1999.

68. Such movements are not of course exceptional to Pakistan. See J. P. Olivier de Sardan, 'A moral economy of corruption in Africa', *The Journal of Modern African Studies*, Vol. 37, no. 1 (1999), pp. 25–52.

69. One recent assessment concludes that, unlike its 'founding fathers' (Jinnah and Iqbal) Pakistan's new 'political leadership has enriched itself by plundering ("borrowing") the nationalized banks, and receiving kickbacks from foreign sellers of industrial and military hardware. This may sound like excessive generalization, but is not without truthful comment'. See Hafeez Malik, *Pakistan: founders' aspirations and today's realities* (Karach: Oxford University Press, 2001), p. 2.

70. Roedad Khan, *Pakistan: a dream gone sour* (Karachi: Oxford University Press, 1997), p. 207.

71. Burki, *Pakistan*, 179.

72. For a discussion of the Pakistani *ulama's* conception of the Islamic state see Zaman, *The Ulama in contemporary Islam*, pp. 93–99.

73. The Jamaat's leader, Maulana Mawdudi, traced the historical origins of corruption to the Ummayyad dynasty, which he accused of transforming the Caliphate into a tyrannical regime. See Nasr, *Mawdudi*, p. 92.

74. Ibid., p. 105.

75. According to Nasr 'Although the two had different aims, little separated Mawdudi's position from that of the Islamic modernists. He sought to appropriate modern scientific thought and Islamize it; they accepted modern scientific thought and attempted to interpret Islam according to it. The modernists wanted to modernize Islam whereas Mawdudi wanted also to Islamize modernity. The distinction was enough to permit Mawdudi to inveigh against his modernist rivals.' Ibid., p. 53.

76. Metcalf, 'The case of Pakistan' in Merkl and Smart (eds.) *Religion and Politics*, p. 178.

77. Burki, *Pakistan: Fifty years of nationhood*, p. 182.

78. Metcalf, 'The case of Pakistan' in Merkl and Smart (eds.) *Religion and politics*, pp. 180–181.

79. Ibid., p. 226.

80. Shahid Javed Burki, *Pakistan under Bhutto, 1971–77* (New York: St Martin's Press, 1980).

81. Oskar Verkaaik, *Migrants and militants*, p. 36.

82. Ibid., p. 36. See also Akbar S. Ahmed, *Discovering Islam: Making sense of Muslim history and society* (New York: Routledge and Kegan Paul, 1988), pp. 81–83.

83. The PNA was formed in January 1977 as an electoral alliance against Bhutto. Dominated by the Islamist opposition, it included nine parties headed by the Jamaat-i-Islami, the Jamiat-ul Ulama-i-Islam, the Jamiat-ul

Ulama-i-Pakistan and six other moderate and left-leaning factions belonging to the Tehrik-i-Istiqlal, the Pakistan Muslim League-Pagaro, the
National Democratic Party, the Pakistan Democratic Party, the Khaksar-
i-Tehrik, and the Azad Kashmir Muslim Conference.

84. Quoted in Nasr, *Mawdudi and the making of Islamic revivalism*, p. 132.
However, the Jamaat's political ambitions eventually led it towards a
qualified acceptance of Sufism resulting in the late 1980s in visits by
prominent Jamaat leaders to popular Sufi shrines. See Nasr, *Mawdudi and
the making of Islamic revivalism*, pp. 123–24.

85. Burki, *Pakistan*, p. 182.

86. Omar Noman, 'An uncivil society: the role of shadow privatization, con-
flict and ideology in the governance of Pakistan', in Anita Weiss and S.
Zulfiqar Gilani (eds), *Power and civil society in Pakistan* (Karachi: Oxford
University Press, 2001), p. 173.

87. Ibid., 178.

88. Barbara Metcalf, 'Traditionalist Islamic activism: Deoband, Tablighis,
and Talibs' in Metcalf, *Islamic contestations*, p. 274. See also Mumtaz
Ahmad, 'Tablighi Jamaat' in Esposito, *The Oxford Encyclopedia of the
modern Islamic world*, Vol. 4 (New York: Oxford University Press, 2001),
pp. 165–69.

89. Aftab Ahmad, 'Historical antecedents of corruption in Pakistan' in Arvind
K. Jain (ed.) *The political economy of corruption* (London and New York:
Routledge, 2001), p. 142.

90. Ayesha Siddiqa, *Military Inc: Inside Pakistan's military economy* (London
and Ann Arbor, MI: Pluto Press, 2007).

91. Ibid., p. 174.

92. Hamza Alavi, 'Class and state' in Gardezi and Rashid (eds), *Pakistan: the
roots of dictatorship*, pp. 66–67.

93. Imran Anwar Ali, 'Business and power in Pakistan' in Weiss and Gilani
(eds), *Power and civil society*, p. 110.

94. One of those implicated was General Fazle Haq, Zia's governor in the
North West Frontier Province from 1978–85. He was also briefly chief
minister of the province in 1988. See Tariq Ali, *The duel*, p. 123.

95. See Veena Kukreja, *Contemporary Pakistan: political processes, conflicts
and crises* (New Delhi and London: Sage Publications, 2003), pp. 201–02.

96. See also, Omar Noman, 'An uncivil society' in Weiss and Gilani (eds)
Power and civil society in Pakistan, p. 179.

97. Quoted in Muhammad Qasim Zaman, *The ulama in contemporary Islam*,
p. 87.

98. There is heated controversy over the share of madrassa education in Pakistan. While some estimates suggest that it comprises a very small proportion (possibly no more than 1 per cent) of the education market, others
claim that it could occupy as much as a third of the market though this
estimate has since been revised downwards. For these conflicting claims
see Tahir Andrabi, Jishnu Das, Asim Ijaz Khwaja and Tristan Zajonc,

'Religious School Enrollment in Pakistan: A Look at the Data' (Washington DC: World Bank, February 2005), http://papers.ssrn.com/sol3/papers.cfm?abstract_id=667843 and International Crisis Group, 'Pakistan: Madrasas, Extremism and the military', 29 July 2002, ICG Report 36, http://www.crisisgroup.org/library/documents/asia/south_asia/036___pakistan_madrasas__extremism_and_the_military_amended.pdf.

99. See Barbara Metcalf (ed.) *Moral conduct and authority: the place of adab in South Asia Islam* (Berkeley, CA: University of California Press, 1987).

100. Zaman, *The ulama in contemporary Islam*, p.74.

101. Barbara Metcalf, 'Madrasas in secular India' in Robert W. Hefner and Muhammad Qasim Zaman (eds), *Schooling Islam: The culture and politics of modern Muslim education* (Princeton: Princeton University Press, 2007), p. 99.

102. See Matthew Nelson, 'Religious education in non-religious schools: a comparative study of Bangladesh and Pakistan', *Journal of Comparative and Commonwealth Politics*, Vol. 46, no. 3 (July 2008), pp. 337–67. See also his 'Muslims, markets, and the meaning of a "good" education in Pakistan', *Asian Survey*, Vol. 46, no. 5 (2006), pp. 690–720, and 'Dealing with difference: religious education and the challenge of democracy in Pakistan', *Modern Asian Studies*, Vol. 43, no. 2 (March 2008), pp. 361–90.

103. *Report of the committee set up by the governor of West Pakistan for recommending improved syllabus for the various darul ulooms and Arabic madrasas in West Pakistan* (Lahore: Government Printing, 1962), p. 3. See also Jamal Malik, *Colonialization of Islam: dissolution of traditional institutions in Pakistan* (New Delhi: Manohar, 1998), pp. 125–28.

104. Ibid., p. 7.

105. Zaman, *The ulama in contemporary Islam*, p. 78.

106. Malik, *Colonialization of Islam*, pp. 125, 128.

107. Zaman, *The ulama in contemporary Islam*, p. 77.

108. Malik, *The colonialization of Islam*, pp. 136–39.

109. See, *Education in Pakistan: A White Paper (revised) document to revise and finalize the national education policy, February 2007* http://www.moe.gov.pk/nepr/WhitePaper.pdf, p. 56.

110. Ibid., pp. 56, 57.

111. Ibid., p. 57.

112. P.W. Singer, *Pakistan's madrassas: ensuring a system of education not jihad*, analysis paper #14; http://www.ciaonet.org/wps/sip02/sip02.pdf.

113. See, The Boston Group, *Higher education in Pakistan* http://web.mit.edu/bilal/www/education/education_report.pdf, p. 6.

114. Tariq Rahman, *Denizens of alien worlds: a study of education, inequality and polarization in Pakistan* (Karachi: Oxford University Press, 2004), p. 149.

115. There is currently great controversy over the number of *madrassas* in Pakistan, the number of students actually enrolled in *madrassas*, over what qualifies as a *madrassa*, and even over whether they serve as incubators of militant politics. For a critical review see Christine Fair, *The madrassah challange: militancy and religious education in Pakistan* (Washington, DC: United States Institute of Peace Press, 2008).

116. The term 'worldly' education is employed by some experts in deference to Pakistanis, who are said to prefer the term to 'secular' education with its overtones of the irreligious. See Fair, *The Madrassa challenge*, p. 119, fn. 1.

117. Tariq Rahman, 'Passports to privilege: the English medium schools in Pakistan' in *Peace and Democracy in South Asia* (online), Vol. 1, no. 1 (January 2005), http://www.thdl.org/texts/reprints/pdsa/pdsa_01_01_04. pdf, p. 36. See also Tariq Rahman, 'The Muslim response to English in South Asia: with special reference to inequality, intolerance and militancy in Pakistan', *Journal of Language, Identity and Education*, Vol. 4, no. 2 (January 2005), pp. 119–35.

118. Khaled Ahmed, 'Islamist school chains and the coming New Order', *The Friday Times*, 10–16 September 1999.

119. Fair, *The madrassah challenge*, p. 98.

120. Ibid.

5. BETWEEN CRESCENT AND SWORD

1. There are, by now, a number of fine studies on the military in Pakistan and its undisputed primacy as a political player. Stephen Cohen, *The Pakistan army*, first published in 1984, but since re-issued in a new edition (Karachi: Oxford University Press, 1998), remains a classic for its insights into the sociology of the army and the mind of its high command. Since then several Pakistani scholars have made outstanding contributions to the study of civil-military relations. Among the best are Hasan Askari Rizvi, *The military and politics in Pakistan*, first published in 1974, but since re-issued as a new edition (Lahore: Sang-i-Meel Publications, 2000), his *Military, state and society in Pakistan* (Lahore: Sang-i-Meel, 2003) and Ayesha Jalal, *The state of martial law: the origins of Pakistan's political economy of defence* (Cambridge: Cambridge University Press, 1990). These studies have more recently been matched (if not surpassed) by ground-breaking work based on painstaking research and unparalleled access to military sources. See, in particular, Ayesha Siddiqa, *Military Inc: Inside Pakistan's military economy* (London: Pluto Press, 2007) and Shuja Nawaz, *Crossed swords: Pakistan, its army, and the wars within* (Karachi: Oxford University Press, 2008).

2. Askari-Rizvi, *The military and politics*.

3. Jalal, *The state of martial law*.

4. Siddiqa, *Military Inc*.

5. Nawaz, *Crossed swords*, p. xxxi.

6. Askari-Rizvi, *Military, state and society*, pp. 245–247.
7. The tension between these two versions of 'Islam' in the construction of Pakistan's national identity has also been richly pursued by Barbara Metcalf and S.V.R. Nasr. See Barbara Metcalf, *Islamic contestations: essays on Muslims in India and Pakistan* (Oxford: Oxford University Press, 2004), pp. 217–35 and S.V.R. Nasr, 'National identities and the India-Pakistan conflict' in T.V. Paul (ed.), *The India-Pakistan conflict: an enduring rivalry* (Cambridge: Cambridge University Press, 2005), pp. 178–201.
8. Markus Daechsel, 'Military Islamisation in Pakistan and the spectre of colonial perceptions', *Contemporary South Asia*, Vol. 6, no. 2 (1997), p. 150.
9. Brian Cloughley, *A history of the Pakistan army: wars and insurrections* (Karachi: Oxford University Press, 1999), p. 29.
10. Nawaz, *Crossed swords*, pp. 83–84.
11. Ibid., p. 82. See also Jalal, *The state of martial rule*, pp. 119–123.
12. Pakistan's 1965 military operation in Kashmir was code-named Operation Gibraltar harking back to the Muslim conqueror of Spain, Tariq bin Ziad, who established a beach-head at the rock named after him—Jebel al Tariq, later Anglicized to Gibraltar. The trained guerrillas under Pakistani command, who were instructed to infiltrate into Indian-controlled Kashmir, were organized into five units, each named after an Islamic military hero: Tariq (bin Ziad), Mahmud (of Ghazni), Salahuddin (Saladin), Muhammad (bin Wasim), and Khalid (bin Waleed). See Nawaz, *Crossed swords*, p. 206.
13. Daechsel, 'Military Islamisation in Pakistan', pp. 150–51.
14. Mumtaz Ahmad, 'The crescent and the sword: Islam, the military, and political legitimacy in Pakistan, 1977–1985, *The Middle East Journal*, Vol. 50, no. 3 (Summer 1996), pp. 372–386.
15. Hamza Alavi, 'The state in post-colonial societies: Pakistan and Bangladesh' in Kathleen Gough and Hari Sharma (eds), *Imperialism and revolution in South Asia* (New York and London: Monthly Review Press, 1973), pp. 155–56.
16. Ibid., p. 156.
17. Hasan-Askari Rizvi, 'The military' in Weiss and Gilani (eds), *Power and civil society*, pp. 202, 207. In his exhaustive study of the army, Shuja Nawaz also notes the emergence of 'a different breed of officers'. Citing hitherto restricted recruitment data provided by official army sources he confirms 'that since the 1970s recruitment moved from the traditional districts to new cities. With increased urbanization and increased remittances from overseas workers [mainly from the Gulf States] to their families in the countryside, many newly rich rural people migrated to the fringes of smaller towns and cities. The expansion of cities, particularly in the Punjab, created a new base for recruitment to the volunteer army: the children of the lower middle class, akin to Zia's own background, who chose the military because of its economic and social advantages rather than military traditions.' See Nawaz, *Crossed swords*, p. 385.

18. Kukreja offers a typical assessment of this period. She observes that 'The definite appeal of Islamic slogans to General Headquarters could plausibly be interpreted in terms of the changing ethos of Pakistan's military leadership. A throwback to Islamic slogans appeared very attractive to the homespun officers—trained at Quetta and Karachi—who had suffered the humiliation of 1971 when Sandhurst-trained generals were in command.' See Veena Kukreja, *Contemporary Pakistan: political processes, conflicts and crises* (New Delhi and London: Sage Publications, 2003), p. 168.

19. For an outstanding recent study of the economic opportunities afforded to the military by its control of political power and its interest in continuing to hold on to this power to consolidate this 'economic empire', see Siddiqa, *Military Inc.*

20. Stephen Cohen, *The Pakistan army* (Karachi: Oxford University Press, 1998—first published 1984).

21. Ibid., pp. 55–63.

22. Ibid., pp. 63–70.

23. Ibid., p. 70.

24. Ibid., pp. 113–17.

25. Ibid., p. 54. See also Owen Bennett-Jones, *Pakistan: eye of the storm* (New Haven: Yale University Press, 2002), pp. 253–54.

26. Rizvi, *Military, state and society in Pakistan*, pp. 245–248.

27. Ibid., pp. 240–45.

28. On one such occasion junior officers are said to have hurled abuse at a senior general seeking to offer an explanation of Pakistan's military defeat in 1971 by accusing him of being a 'drunkard'. See Salmaan Taseer, *Bhutto: a political biography* (London: Ithaca Press, 1979), p. 130.

29. Cloughley, *A history of the Pakistan army*, p. 278.

30. For a controversial insider's view of this nexus between the military and militant groups see Husain Haqqani, *Pakistan: between mosque and military* (Washington: Carnegie Endowment for Peace, 2005). For another perspective 'from the inside' see Hassan Abbas, *Pakistan's drift into extremism: Allah, the army, and America's war on terror* (Armonk, NY: M.E. Sharpe, 2005).

31. Rashid, *Taliban*, pp. 181–95; Abou Zahab and Roy (eds), *Islamist networks*, pp. 19–46. See also William Maley, *Fundamentalism reborn? Afghanistan and the Taliban* (London: Hurst, 1998).

32. See Nasr, *The vanguard of the Islamic revolution*, p. 169.

33. Kepel, *Jihad*, pp. 101–05.

34. Olivier Roy, 'The Taliban: a strategic tool for Pakistan' in Jaffrelot (ed.), *Pakistan*, p. 151.

35. Masud (ed.), *Travellers in faith*, p. xvi.

36. Stephen Cohen, *The idea of Pakistan* (Washington, DC: Brookings Institution Press, 2004), p. 116.

37. Hasan-Askari Rizvi, 'The military' in Weiss and Gilani (eds), *Power and civil society*, p. 207.

38. Khalid Masud, 'Ideology and legitimacy' in Masud (ed.), *Travellers in faith*, p. 99.
39. Mumtaz Ahmad, 'Tablighi Jama'at' in John L. Esposito (ed.), *Oxford Encyclopedia of Islam*, p. 168.
40. Masud, 'Ideology and legitimacy', p. 105.
41. Yoginder Sikand, 'The Tablighi Jama'at and politics', International Institute for the Study of Islam in the Modern World (ISIM) *Review*, 13 (December 2003), p. 43.
42. Ahmed, 'Tablighi Jama'at' in Esposito, *The Oxford Encyclopedia of the Modern Islamic World*, p. 169.
43. Brig. S.K. Malik, *The Quranic concept of war* (Lahore, Wajidalis, 1979), p. viii.
44. Masud, 'Ideology and legitimacy', p. 99.
45. Bennett-Jones, *Pakistan*, p. 260.
46. Nasr, *Vanguard*, p. 194; Nasr, *Islamic Leviathan*, p. 136.
47. Daechsel, 'Military Islamisation', p. 150.
48. See speech by General Zia ul Haq in *Dawn*, 6 September 1977.
49. Nasr, *Islamic Leviathan*, pp. 61–65.
50. One recent assessment goes so far as to conclude that 'contrary to widespread perception Ayub Khan was not a secularist [but] ... Being a straightforward soldier, he did not have time for an elaborate theory of the Islamic state ... He simply wanted to do what he perceived was good for the state and declare it as Islamic'. Haqqani, *Pakistan: between mosque and military*, p. 41.
51. Nasr, *Islamic Leviathan*, p. 61.
52. Ziring, *Pakistan: at the cross-current of history*, p. 83.
53. According to Cohen, it was under Ayub that 'Pakistan began the process of official myth-creation in earnest'. See Cohen, *The idea of Pakistan*, pp. 67–68. One of the main engines tasked with the responsibility of furthering this process was the Bureau of National Research and Reconstruction, which was granted sweeping powers by Ayub to target any section of the news media that questioned the regime's national security policies predicated on rivalry with India. See Nawaz, *Crossed swords*, pp. 173–74.
54. Hamza Alavi, 'Ethnicity, Muslim society and the Pakistan ideology' in Weiss (ed.), *Islamic re-assertion in Pakistan*, pp. 21–48.
55. See Ayub Khan's address to the nation, *Dawn*, 7 September 1965.
56. Ayub Khan, *Friends not Masters* (Karachi and London: Oxford University Press, 1967), pp. 196–97.
57. Sumit Ganguly, *The crisis in Kashmir: portents of war, hopes of peace* (Woodrow Wilson Center and Cambridge: Cambridge University Press, 1997), pp. 55–57.
58. Quoted in Haqqani, *Pakistan: between mosque and military*, p. 46. For a discussion of the broader remit of the Bureau see Nawaz, *Crossed swords*, pp. 173–77.
59. Abbas, *Pakistan's drift into extremism*, p. 45.

243

60. See General A.A.K Niazi, *The betrayal of East Pakistan* (Karachi: Oxford University Press, 1998), p. 78. See also Nasr, *The vanguard of the Islamic revolution*, pp. 66–67, 169 and Haqqani, *Pakistan: between mosque and military*, pp. 79–80.

61. Talukder Maniruzzaman, *The Bangladesh revolution and its aftermath* (Dhaka: Bangladesh Books, 1980), pp. 102–06.

62. The Hamoodur Rehman Commission appointed by the government in January 1972 to conduct an inquiry into the 1971 civil war makes no mention of the army's use of counter-insurgency groups in East Pakistan tied to pro-Islamic parties. As for the claim of what it describes as the 'alleged killing of [Bengali] intellectuals in December 1971', it concluded that while there was 'some talk' of arresting persons on a 'list of names' of 'miscreants, heads of Mukti Bahini ... known leaders of the Awami League ... produced by the agencies concerned', it could not proceed 'unless the Bangladesh authorities can produce some convincing evidence'. Without it the Commission noted that 'it is not possible to record a finding that any intellectuals or professionals were indeed arrested and killed by the Pakistan Army during December 1971'. See, *The report of the Hamoodur Rehman Commission of Inquiry into the 1971 War—as declassified by the Government of Pakistan* (Lahore: Vanguard Books, nd), pp. 511–12.

63. Nasr, *The vanguard of the Islamic revolution*, p. 169.

64. Talbot, *Pakistan* (expanded and updated edition, 2005), p. 244.

65. Nasr, *Islamic Leviathan*, p. 97.

66. See Anwar Syed, 'Z.A. Bhutto's self-characterizations and Pakistani political culture', *Asian Survey*, Vol. 18, no. 12 (December 1978), p. 1260.

67. See Farzana Shaikh, 'Pakistan's nuclear bomb: beyond the non-proliferation regime', *International Affairs*, Vol. 78, no. 1 (January 2002), p. 39.

68. Dennis Kux, *The United States and Pakistan: disenchanted allies* (Washington and Baltimore: Woodrow Wilson Center and The Johns Hopkins University Press, 2001), p. 220.

69. Nasr, 'National identities', p. 187.

70. Abou-Zahab and Roy, *Islamist networks*, p. 26.

71. Talbot, *Pakistan*, p. 272.

72. For an extended discussion of the social basis of the Lashkar and its roots in Salafi Islam see Abou Zahab and Roy, *Islamist networks*, pp. 32–44.

73. Explaining the relation between the two, Hafiz Saeed, one of the founders of the *Dawat-ul-Irshad* and currently leader of the Lashkar-i-Tayyaba, declared: 'Islam propounds both Dawa and Jihad. Both are equally important and inseparable ... If beliefs and morals are not reformed, Dawa alone develops into mysticism and Jihad alone may lead to anarchy ... This is the only way to bring about change among individuals, society and the world.' Quoted in Saeed Shafqat, 'From official to Islamism: the rise of the Dawat-ul-Irshad and the Lashkar-e-Taiba' in Jaffrelot (ed.), *Pakistan: nationalism without a nation*, p. 143.

74. Abou Zahab and Roy, *Islamist networks*, p. 35.

75. See Jamal Malik, *Colonialization of Islam: dissolution of traditional institutions in Pakistan* (Delhi: Manohar, 1998), pp. 85–113.
76. See Ayesha Jalal, *Partisans of Allah: jihad in South Asia* (Cambridge, MA: Harvard University Press, 2008), pp. 291–92.
77. On the background to the Red Mosque crisis and the links between the mosque's leadership and Zia's military regime see Farzana Shaikh, 'Battered Musharraf playing with fire', *The Times* (London), 11 July 2007.
78. Quoted in Diego Cordovez and Selig Harrison, *Out of Afghanistan: the inside story of the Soviet withdrawal* (New York: Oxford University Press, 1995), p. 92.
79. See Muhammad Amir Rana, *A to Z of Jehadi organizations in Pakistan* (Lahore: Mashal Books, 2004), pp. 263–74.
80. Ibid., pp. 436–38.
81. Abbas, *Pakistan's drift into extremism*, p. 134.
82. See Zahid Hussain, *Frontline Pakistan: the struggle with militant Islam* (London: I.B. Tauris, 2007), p. 21.
83. Abbas, *Pakistan's drift into extremism*, p. 148.
84. See Rana, *A to Z of Jehadi organizations*, p. 272; ibid., pp. 152–53; Cloughly, *A history of the Pakistan army*, pp. 354–55 and Hussain, *Frontline Pakistan*, pp. 73–74.
85. Cohen, *The idea of Pakistan*, p. 172.
86. Nasr, 'National identities', p. 197.
87. Vernon Hewitt, *Towards the future? Jammu and Kashmir in the 21st Century* (Cambridge: Granta, 2001), p. 122.
88. Abbas, *Pakistan's drift into extremism*, p 148.
89. Amir Rana, *A-Z of jehadi organizations in Pakistan*, pp. 24–45; Hewitt, *Towards the future*, p. 165; Abou-Zahab and Roy, *Islamist networks*, p. 54.
90. See Khalid Hasan, 'Invisible Soldiers Inc (ISI)'s hallucination yielded terrorism', *Friday Times*, 7–13 January, 2005.
91. Olivier Roy, 'Islam and foreign policy: central Asia and the Arab Persian World' in Jaffrelot (ed.), *A history of Pakistan and its origins*, p. 145.
92. Ahmed Rashid, *Taliban: The story of the Afghan warlords* (London: Pan Books, 2001), p. 187.
93. See S.V.R. Nasr, *The Shia revival: how conflicts within Islam will shape the future* (New York and London: Norton, 2007), p. 161. See also, Mariam Abou Zahab, 'The regional dimension of sectarian conflicts in Pakistan' in Jaffrelot (ed.) *Pakistan: Nationalism without a nation?*, p. 118.
94. See S.V.R. Nasr, 'Islam, the state and the rise of sectarian militancy in Pakistan' in ibid., p. 94.
95. Abou Zahab and Roy, *Islamist networks*, p. 55. See also Rana, *A to Z of Jehadi organizations*, pp. 214–36.
96. Rashid, *Taliban*, p.186.
97. S.V.R. Nasr, 'Islam, the state and the rise of sectarian militancy' in Jaffrelot (ed.), *Pakistan: Nationalism without a nation?*, p. 96.

98. See Aoun Abbas Sahi, 'The Punjab connection', *Newsline*, October 2008, pp. 35–36.
99. See *The Friday Times*, 24–30 April, 1998.
100. Hewitt, *Towards the future?*, p. 198.
101. Abbas, *Pakistan's drift towards extremism*, p. 214.
102. Abou Zahab and Roy, *Islamist networks*, p. 30. Others support this view of a regional and sectarian nexus. According to Zahid Hussain: 'Most of the LeJ [Lashkar-i-Jhangvi] cadres were also involved in Pakistan's proxy war in Kashmir. The continuing state patronage of Islamic militancy in return produced an escalation in domestic sectarian conflict. The two were closely intertwined.' See Hussain, *Frontline Pakistan*, p. 96.
103. For a fine discussion of successive government initiatives to reform the *madrassas* in Pakistan and the role of religio-activism in thwarting these efforts, see Muhammad Qasim Zaman, 'Deobandi madrassas in South Asia' in Robert W. Hefner and Muhammad Qasim Zaman, *Schooling Islam*, pp. 59–86.
104. In May 2000 Musharraf formally reneged on his promise to reform the blasphemy laws, apparently on the advice on the Chief of General Staff, General Aziz Khan, known for his pro-Islamist sympathies, who warned that it would trigger Islamist unrest. See Rashid, *Descent into chaos*, p. 414 n. 24.
105. See Christophe Jaffrelot, 'Musharraf and the Islamists: from support to opposition after September 11' in Jaffrelot (ed.), *A history of Pakistan*, p. 260.
106. Two commanders who played a vital role in helping Musharraf to plan and execute the operation in Kargil were Lt. General Mahmud Ahmed, Commander of X Corps, and Lt General Mohammad Aziz Khan, Chief of General Staff. Ahmed, who made no secret of his sympathies for the Islamist cause, later joined the Tablighi Jamaat; Aziz, who was scrupulously religious, sported a flowing black beard in the late 1980s. See Nawaz, *Crossed swords*, p. 512.
107. See Rashid, *Descent into chaos*, p. 220.
108. For the full text of President Musharraf's speech see, *The Nation*, 13 January 2002. Among the groups banned were the LT and the Jaish-i-Muhammad, which represented the two largest militant organizations fighting in Kashmir. Other groups included the Sipah-i-Sahaba-i-Pakistan and its Shia counterpart, the Tehrik-i-Jafria.
109. See Frederic Grare, 'Pakistan: the myth of an Islamist peril', Policy Brief 46 (New York: Carnegie Endowment for Peace, February 2006), http://www.carnegieendowment.org/files/45.grare.final.pdf.

6. DEMONS FROM ABROAD

1. For a discussion of the background to changes in the formulation of the Kashmir policies of India and Pakistan, see P.R. Chari, 'Sources of New

Delhi's Kashmir policy' and Hasan-Askari Rizvi, 'Islamabad's new approach to Kashmir' in Waheguru Sidhu, Bushra Asif and Cyrus Samii (eds), *Kashmir: new voices, new approaches* (New York: International Peace Academy, 2006), pp. 117–37.

2. For a background to the Siachen dispute see Sumit Ganguly, *Conflict unending: India-Pakistan tensions since 1947* (New York: Columbia University Press, 2001), pp. 79–10. On the maritime border dispute see Ashutosh Mishra, 'The Sir Creek boundary dispute: a victim of India-Pakistan linkage politics', *IBRU Boundary and Security Bulletin*, Winter 2000–2001, http://www.dur.ac.uk/resources/ibru/publications/full/bsb8-4_misra.pdf. See also A.G. Noorani, 'Easing the Indo-Pakistan dialogue on Kashmir: confidence-building measures for the Siachen Glacier, Sir Creek, and the Wular Barrage disputes', Occasional Paper, no. 16 (Washington, DC: Henry L. Stimson Center, 1994).

3. Jean-Luc Racine, 'Pakistan and the "India Syndrome": between Kashmir and the nuclear predicament' in Jaffrelot (ed.), *Pakistan: Nationalism without a nation?*, pp. 113–16.

4. The idea that Indian Muslims were entitled to special representation that reflected their political importance was a key demand of Muslim separatists seeking to influence plans to introduce political reform in British India. By doing so, they hoped to compensate for the numerical weakness of India Muslims in relation to the Hindu majority. In time it served as a powerful argument to justify the claim that the special status of Indian Muslims qualified them for parity with the Hindu majority. See Farzana Shaikh, *Community and consensus in Islam*, pp. 141–54, 194–227. Pakistan's compulsive need to maintain parity with India after independence was driven largely by these perceptions of co-equality.

5. An 'enduring rivalry' is described by theorists as a conflict that lasts for more than two decades, is punctuated by militarized conflicts and 'characterized by a persistent, fundamental and long term incompatibility of goals between two states'. See T.V. Paul, 'Causes of the India-Pakistan enduring rivalry' in Paul, *The India-Pakistan conflict*, pp. 3–4.

6. See Mohammad Waseem, 'Dialectic between domestic politics and foreign policy' in Jaffrelot (ed.), *Pakistan: Nationalism with a nation?*, pp. 266–67.

7. Ibid., p. 267.

8. Hamid Khan, *Constitutional and political history of Pakistan*, pp. 67–68.

9. See Ayesha Jalal, 'Inheriting the Raj: Jinnah and the Governor-Generalship Issue', *Modern Asian Studies*, Vol. 19, no.1 (February 1985), pp. 29–31.

10. Jinnah's decision to assume the post of Pakistan's first Governor-General has been mired in controversy. Some claim that, by doing so, he perpetuated the vice-regal system and undermined the prospects of democracy in Pakistan. See Khalid bin Sayeed, *The formative phase, 1867–1948* (London: Oxford University Press, 1968), pp. 223–57; 279–300. Others

argue that Jinnah distorted the powers of the Governor-General by politicizing them and allowing him to ride roughshod over parliament. See Allen McGrath, *The destruction of Pakistan's democracy* (Karachi: Oxford University Press, 1996). Their position is lent some credence by Mountbatten's suggestion that Jinnah coveted the role of Governor-General because he had no intention of encouraging a Westminster-style parliamentary democracy in Pakistan. When reminded by Mountbatten that Jinnah should have been seeking the role of Prime Minister, Jinnah is said to have replied: 'Not in my Pakistan, there the Prime Minister will do what the Governor-General tells him', adding 'that's the way I am going to run Pakistan'. See John R. Wood, 'Dividing the Jewel: Mountbatten and the transfer of power to India', *Pacific Affairs*, Vol. 58, no. 4, (Winter 1985–86), p. 660. Jalal's position, which is that Jinnah was motivated by the need to establish Pakistan's equality with India and safeguard its sovereignty, is designed primarily to salvage Jinnah's reputation from charges that he suffered from vanity—charges detailed in Alan Campbell Johnson, *Mission with Mountbatten* (Westport, CT: Greenwood Press, 1972), p. 217.

11. Nasr, 'National identities' in Paul (ed.), *The India-Pakistan conflict*, p. 179.

12. This is recognized by some Pakistani scholars. According to Hasan Zaheer: 'The Muslim League leadership, overwhelmed by the issues arising from the creation of the new state, did not apply itself seriously to the Kashmir situation in the period preceding independence day, while India was systematically working at securing the accession of the state by any means.' See Hasan Zaheer, *The Rawalpindi conspiracy case 1951* (Karachi: Oxford University Press, 1998), p. 63.

13. Sumantra Bose, *Kashmir: roots of conflict, paths to peace*, pp. 21–22. Abdullah's National Conference was founded in 1932 as the All Jammu and Kashmir Muslim Conference. In 1939 it was renamed the National Conference after conservative Muslim factions re-grouped to form the Muslim Conference, claiming that Abdullah's pro-secular stance and radical social policies had tied the organization too closely to Congress. Ibid., pp. 20–21.

14. Bose, *Kashmir*, p. 22.

15. This impression is strongly conveyed in the account by the respected historian, Victoria Schofield, who quotes the senior Indian Foreign Ministry official, J.N. Dixit, in 1994 as acknowledging that 'everybody who has a sense of history knows that legality only has a relevance up to the threshold of transcending political realities. And especially in inter-state relations ... so to quibble about points of law and hope that by proving a legal point you can reverse the process of history is living in a somewhat contrived utopia. It won't work.' See Victoria Schofield, *Kashmir in the crossfire* (London: I.B. Tauris, 1996), p. 291. For an extended, if somewhat

controversial, discussion of the merits of rival interpretations of the legality of Kashmir's accession to India see Ganguly, *The crisis in Kashmir*, pp. 8–13.

16. For a discussion of the anomalous status of Azad Kashmir and its relations with Pakistan see Leo Rose, 'The politics of Azad Kashmir' in Raju Thomas (ed.), *Perspectives on Kashmir: the role of conflict in South Asia* (Boulder, CT: Westview Press, 1992), pp. 235–253. For a detailed and vigorous critique of the indeterminate status imposed on the Northern Territories by Pakistan see *Discord in Pakistan's Northern Areas*, International Crisis Group, Asia Report no. 131, 2 April 2007, http://www. crisisgroup.org/library/documents/asia/south_asia/131_discord_in_ pakistan_s_northern_areas.pdf. It suggests that Pakistan's decision to deny these Territories the right to a constitutional personality comparable to Azad Kashmir stems largely from the fear that it will empower the region's Shia majority. Others appear to be less persuaded by the sectarian argument claiming that Pakistan's interest in retaining direct control over the Northern Territories is designed to ensure that in any future plebiscite on Kashmir these Territories can be counted upon to vote in favour of Pakistan. See Bennett Jones, *Pakistan*, p. 70. Yet others have pointed to the strategic importance of districts such as Baltistan within the Northern Territories, which have served as vital staging posts for Pakistan-backed military incursions into Indian-held Kashmir. See Vernon Hewitt, *Towards the future*, p. 111.

17. For details of these military campaigns in Kashmir see Nawaz, *Crossed swords*, pp. 217–238; pp. 303–310.

18. Ashutosh Varshney, 'Three compromised nationalisms: why Kashmir has been a problem' in Thomas (ed.), *Perspectives on Kashmir*, p. 198.

19. Cohen, *The idea of Pakistan*, p. 52.

20. See Mehtab Ali Shah, *The foreign policy of Pakistan: ethnic impacts on diplomacy, 1971–1994* (London: I. B. Tauris, 1997). See also Iffat Malik, *Ethnic conflict, international dispute* (Karachi: Oxford University Press, 2001), p. 208.

21. The decision was predicated on military strategy at the time that rested on the theory that East Pakistan's defence lay in West Pakistan and that, as such, the army would remain heavily concentrated in the West. Though some senior military commanders questioned the wisdom of the strategy and also recognized the political costs incurred by fuelling Bengali 'apprehensions … about the inadequacy of their defence', the military leadership was reluctant to change course. See Nawaz, *Crossed swords*, pp. 240–41.

22. Raunaq Jahan, *Pakistan: the failure of national integration* (New York: Columbia University Press, 1972), p. 166. See also Talbot, *Pakistan*, p. 119.

23. Bhutto's ardent support for Kashmir was never widely espoused in Sind and must be seen as a reflection, above all, of his desire to consolidate his national standing and neutralize any suggestion that he represented Sindhi regionalism.

24. Waseem, 'Dialectic between domestic politics and foreign policy' in Jaffrelot (ed.), *Pakistan*, p. 267.
25. Mehtab Ali Shah, *The foreign policy of Pakistan: ethnic impacts on diplomacy, 1971–1994* (London: I. B. Tauris, 1997), pp. 83, 107.
26. Ibid., p. 145.
27. See Sana Haroon, *Frontiers of faith: Islam in the Indo-Afghan borderland* (London: Hurst, 2007), pp. 179–85, 197–215.
28. Nasr, 'National identities' in Paul (ed.), *The India-Pakistan conflict*, p. 180.
29. For a fine survey of the extent of Pakistan's liabilities at independence see Talbot, *Pakistan*, pp. 95–111. See also Jalal, *The state of martial law*, pp. 25–44.
30. According to Ahmed Rashid: 'Musharraf had calculated that India would never escalate the [Kargil] conflict for fear it could lead to an unsheathing of nuclear weapons. He expected the United States to step in and mediate a ceasefire, after which Pakistan could demand talks on Kashmir.' In the event, Rashid concludes, 'Pakistan lost on all counts. Rather than highlighting the Kashmir dispute. Musharraf's adventurism had ensured that Kashmir was further eclipsed and that India would win the propaganda war.' See Rashid, *Descent into chaos*, pp. 41–42. A more benign version of events is presented by Nawaz, who observes that while 'there are clearly many sides to the story of the [Kargil battle]', one of its aims (apparently endorsed by Prime Minister Sharif at the time), was 'the idea of raising the political temperature of political discussions on Kashmir with India'. Unlike Rashid, Nawaz is more than willing to accept the view that 'the Kargil infiltration plan was a resounding [military] success' [p. 515] and far less forthcoming about the irreparable damage caused by the military decision over Kargil to Pakistan's already fragile image as a responsible nuclear power. See Nawaz, *Crossed Swords*, pp. 508, 510, 515.
31. See Robert Wirsing, *Pakistan's security under Zia, 1977–88: the policy imperatives of a peripheral Asian state* (Basingstoke: Macmillan, 1991), p. 114. See also Shaikh, 'Pakistan's nuclear bomb', p. 47.
32. Cohen, *The idea of Pakistan,* p. 88.
33. This has recently been reiterated in a strong (and strongly worded) account by Tariq Ali, who observes that 'the new rulers of Pakistan developed an early communal awareness that to survive they had to rent their country' to the highest bidder, namely the United States. Since then, he argues, the United States has used its position as paymaster to ensure that Pakistan's foreign policy serves American rather than Pakistani interests. See Tariq Ali, *The duel: Pakistan on the flight path of American power* (London: Simon and Schuster, 2008), p. 195. While Ali makes a convincing case he tends to underestimate Pakistan's own skilful manipulation of its relations with the United States that has allowed Pakistan to borrow power to sustain its historical claim to a valid national identity and to advance its own strategic agenda against India.

34. According to US Congressional sources, 'a total of about US$16.5 billion in direct, overt US aid went to Pakistan from 1947 through to 2007, including some US$4.5 billion for military programmes. Since the 2001 renewal of large US assistance packages and reimbursement for militarized counterterrorism efforts, Pakistan will by the end of FY 2008 have received more than US$11 billion, the majority of this in the form of coalition support reimbursements , with another US$3.5 billion for economic purposes and nearly US$2.2 billion for security related programmes.' See Congressional Research Service Report for Congress, *Pakistan-US relations* by Alan Kronstadt, updated 25 August 2008, Library of Congress, http://www.fas.org/sgp/crs/row/RL33498.pdf p. 89.

35. See Dennis Kux, *The United States and Pakistan, 1947–2000: disenchanted allies* (Washington & Baltimore: Woodrow Wilson Centre & The Johns Hopkins University Press, 2001), p. 16.

36. See Robert J. Mcmahon, *The Cold War on the periphery: the United States, India, and Pakistan* (New York: Columbia University Press, 1994), pp. 106–08.

37. Ibid., p. 17.

38. Kux, *The United States and Pakistan*, p. 20.

39. See Sisir Gupta, *A study in India-Pakistan Relations* (New Delhi: Asia Publishing House, 1966), p. 440.

40. Jinnah quoted in Kux, *The United States and Pakistan*, p. 20.

41. McMahon, *The Cold War on the periphery*, pp. 143–53.

42. Pakistan of course understood this. In April 1950 Pakistan's Prime Minister Liaquat Ali Khan, during his first official visit to the United States, formally mooted the idea of a US-sponsored backed territorial guarantee for Pakistan, claiming it would free up Pakistani troops for use in Korea as well as, eventually, against a possible Soviet threat in the Middle East. But this tempting proposal received short-shrift owing to fierce opposition from Britain, which warned the United States against alienating India. See Jalal, *The state of martial rule*, p. 111.

43. Kux, *The United States and Pakistan*, p. 13.

44. See Liaquat Ali Khan, *Pakistan: the heart of Asia* (Cambridge, Mass: Harvard University Press, 1951), p. 83. See also, S.M. Burke and Lawrence Ziring, *Pakistan's foreign policy: an historical analysis* (New York: Oxford University Press, 1991), p. 123.

45. Thomas Perry Thornton, 'Pakistan: fifty years of insecurity' in Selig Harrison, Paul Kreisberg and Dennis Kux (eds), *India and Pakistan: the first fifty years* (Washington & Cambridge: Woodrow Wilson Press and Cambridge University Press, 1999), p. 171.

46. Thornton, 'Pakistan' in Harrison et al. (eds.), *India and Pakistan*, p. 173.

47. Burke and Ziring, *Pakistan's foreign policy*, p. 66.

48. Pakistan's Governor-General, Ghulam Mohammad, quoted in Jalal, *The state of martial rule*, p. 128.

49. Pakistan's Governor-General, Ghulam Mohammad, quoted in Kux, *The United States and Pakistan*, p. 60.

50. Kux, *The United States and Pakistan*, p. 143. Much was also made at the time by Pakistan of China's trumpeted but never realized ultimatum to India in 1965 to dismantle a string of border posts and return 800 sheep and 59 Chinese yaks that India was alleged to have kidnapped. See Bennett Jones, *Pakistan: eye of the storm*, p. 79.

51. For an insider's view of these unrealistic expectations see Sultan Moham-mad Khan, *Memories and reflections of a Pakistani diplomat* (London: London Centre for Pakistan studies, 1998), pp. 368–69, 343–48.

52. For discussion of these and other compulsions at the time see Adrian Levy and Catherine Scott-Clark, *Deception: Pakistan, the United States and the global nuclear weapons conspiracy* (London: Atlantic Books, 2007), pp. 11–137. See also Shaikh, 'Pakistan's nuclear bomb', pp. 42–48.

53. See Haidar Nizamani, *The roots of rhetoric: politics of nuclear weapons in India and Pakistan* (Westport, CT: Praeger, 2000), p. 72.

54. This relationship of mutual deception has been most comprehensively explored by Levy and Scott-Clark, who argue that the United States actively connived in concealing the truth about Pakistan's nuclear weap-ons capability on the dangerous assumption that it exercised enough influ-ence over Pakistan to control its consequences. See Levy and Scott-Clark, *Deception*. According to Kux, there was a 'tacit understanding' during the Reagan administration for much of the 1980s that the United Statas 'could live with Pakistan's nuclear programme as long as Islamabad does not explode a bomb'. Kux, *The United States and Pakistan*, p. 257.

55. A.Z. Hilali, *US-Pakistan relationship: Soviet invasion of Afghanistan* (London: Ashgate, 2005), pp. 69–70.

56. Ibid., p. 70.

57. See Craig Baxter, 'Pakistan becomes prominent in the international arena' in Shahid Javed Burki and Craig Baxter (eds), *Pakistan under the military: eleven years of Zia ul Haq* (Boulder, CO: Westview Press, 1991), pp. 137–153.

58. This was squarely recognized by Musharraf. Explaining his decision to withdraw Pakistan's support for the Taliban, he acknowledges that 'I also analyzed our national interest. First India had already tried to step in by offering its bases to the US. If we did not join the US, it would accept India's offer. What would happen then? India would gain a golden oppor-tunity with regard to Kashmir ... Second, the security of our strategic assets would be jeopardized. We did not want to lose or damage the mili-tary parity that we had achieved with India by becoming a nuclear weap-ons state.' See Parvez Musharraf, *In the line of fire: a memoir* (London: Simon and Schuster, 2006), p. 202.

59. Olivier Roy, 'The Taliban: a strategic tool for Pakistan' in Jaffrelot (ed.), *Pakistan: nationalism without nation?*, p. 151.

60. The Durand Line is named after the British plenipotentiary, Sir Mortimer Durand, who negotiated its demarcation in 1893.

61. For a detailed historical background see Mahnaz Ispahani, *Roads and rivals: the political uses of access in the borderlands of Asia* (Ithaca, NY:

Cornell University Press, 1989), pp. 83–144. See also Leon Poullada, 'Pushtunistan: Afghan domestic politics and relations with Pakistan' in Ainslee T. Embree (ed.), *Pakistan's western borderlands: the transformation of a political order* (Durham, NC: Academic Press, 1977), pp. 126–44 and David Loyn, *Butcher & bolt: Two hundred years of foreign engagement in Afghanistan* (London: Hutchinson, 2008), pp.125–42.

62. Poullada, 'Pashtunistan' in Embree (ed.), *Pakistan's western borderlands*, p. 137.

63. See, S.M.M. Qureshi, 'Pashtunistan: the frontier dispute between Afghanistan and Pakistan, *Pacific Affairs*, Vol. 39, no. 1/2 (Spring-Summer 1966), p. 102.

64. Poullada, 'Pashtunistan', p. 134.

65. Qureshi, 'Pakhtunistan', pp. 104–05. The most passionate advocate of Pashtun nationalism was the Pashtun leader, Abdul Ghaffar Khan or Badshah Khan, also known to his followers as the Frontier Gandhi for his heady mix of Islamic rhetoric with Gandhian principles of non-violence. Opposed to Jinnah's plans for Pakistan, his quasi-political movement, the *Khudai Khidmatgars* (Servants of God) rejected allegiance to both India and Pakistan and pressed instead for a third choice of forming a separate political entity, *Pakhtoonkhwa* (land of the Pakhtuns) to unite Pashtuns from both sides of the Durand Line. See Mukulika Banerjee, *The Pathan unarmed: opposition and memory in the north west frontier* (Oxford: James Currey, 2000), pp. 167–91. Closely watched by Afghanistan, Khan's defiant stance encouraged Afghan leaders to press for a fourth option: union with Afghanistan. Though couched in the language of self-determination, it clearly envisaged a Pashtun state on the territory of British India that would be friendly to Afghanistan. See Amin Saikal, *Modern Afghanistn: a history of struggle and survival* (London: I.B. Tauris, 2004), p. 113. The hope was that, 'before long it [Afghanistan] would be able to incorporate a state of this kind in its own territory'—thus serving as the mirror image of policies that would come later to be associated Pakistan's Afghan strategy. See L.F. Rushbrook Williams, *The state of Pakistan* (London: Faber and Faber, 1962), p. 66. More recently Barnett Rubin, a leading authority on Afghanistan, has also suggested that Afghanistan's argument in favour of an independent Pashtunistan rested on the assumption that 'it would have been integrated into Afghanistan'. See Barnett Rubin, *The fragmentation of Afghanistan: state formation and collapse in the international system* (New Haven: Yale University Press, 2nd edition, 2002), p. 62.

66. Quoted in Kalim Bahadur, 'Pakistan's policy towards Afghanistan' in K.P. Misra (ed.), *Afghanistan in crisis* (New York: Advent Books, 1981), pp. 92–93.

67. See Barnett Rubin and Abubakar Siddique, *Resolving the Pakistan-Afghanistan stalemate*, Special Report no. 176 (Washington: United States Institute of Peace, October 2006), p. 7.

68. Saikal, *Modern Afghanistan*, p. 102.
69. The frustrating course of the movement for a United Bengal and the hostility it aroused among sections of the Bengali political classes on both sides of the communal divide in the run up to Partition are discussed in Harun ur Rashid, *The foreshadowing of Bangladesh: Bengal Muslim League and Muslim politics, 1936–1947* (Dhaka: Asiatic Society of Bangladesh, 1987) and Joya Chatterji, *Bengali divided: Hindu communalism and Partition* (Cambridge: Cambridge University Press, 1994).
70. See statement by Pakistan Foreign Minister, Manzur Qadir, *The Times*, 9 March 1961.
71. See Government of Pakistan, *White Paper on the reality of Pakhtun issue* (Rawalpindi: Press and Publication, 1962), p. 18.
72. Ibid., pp. 18–19.
73. Olaf Caroe, *The Pathans* (London: Macmillan, 1958), p. 437.
74. Talbot, *Pakistan*, p. 252. According to others, the process of co-opting Pashtuns was already in train by the 1960s, when some Pashtuns along with Punjabis and *mohajirs* emerged as the main beneficiaries of the state's economic and social policies at the expense of the Bengali, the Sindhis and the Baloch. See Yunus Samad, 'Pakistan: from minority rights to majoritarianism' in Gyanendra Pandey and Yunus Samad, *Faultlines of nationhood*, p. 101.
75. See Siddiqa, *Military Inc.*, p. 59.
76. Tahir Amin, *Ethno-national movements of Pakistan* (Islamabad: Institute of Policy Studies, 1993), pp. 82, 175.
77. On 30 October 2008 the ruling Awami National Party (ANP) in the NWFP announced that it had ordered all official correspondence for the existing province of the North West Frontier Province to be conducted in the name of 'Pakhtunkhwa'. See *Daily Times* (Lahore), 31 October 2008. This fell short of the restructuring of the Pakistani state demanded by more radical Pashtun groups, which had pressed for all Pashtun regions, including the Federally Administered Tribal Areas (FATA), the North West Frontier Province and northern Balochistan to be amalgamated into a new province of' Pakhtunkhwa'. See Rubin and Siddique, 'Resolving the Pakistan-Afghanistan stalemate', p. 14.
78. Haqqani, *Pakistan: between mosque and military*, pp. 166–67.
79. Rashid, *Taliban*, p. 186.
80. See Rashid, *Descent into chaos*, pp. 110–15.
81. Olivier Roy, 'The Taliban: a strategic tool for Pakistan', in Jaffrelot (ed.), *Pakistan: nationalism without nation?*, p. 151.
82. See Gilles Dorronsoro, *Revolution unending: Afghanistan 1979 to the present* (London: Hurst, 2000), pp. 266–68; 272–78 and Rashid, *Taliban*, pp. 17–30; 82–94. See also William Maley (ed.), *Fundamentalism reborn? Afghanistan and the Taliban* (London: Hurst, 1998).
83. Rashid, *Taliban*, p. 187.
84. Among those who have called in to question the credibility of Pakistan's official position on the Durand Line is Ahmed Rashid. He maintains that

Pakistan's military, which controls Pakistan's Afghan policy, has never insisted on pressing for the recognition of the Durand Line by Afghanistan. This reluctance, he argues, is a legacy of the 1980s when General Zia promoted the vision of a Pakistani influenced region extending from Afghanistan into Central Asia that 'depended upon an undefined border with Afghanistan, so that the army could justify any future interference in that country and beyond'. See Rashid, *Descent into chaos*, pp. 267–68.

GLOSSARY

adab	code of right conduct
ahl-i-hadis	people of the *hadis*; movement closely allied to Saudi Wahhabi Islam
akhlaq	system of ethics
al adl wal ahsan	Islamic standards of justice and kindness
amr bil maruf wa nahiy anil munkar	Islamic injunction to enjoin good and forbid evil
ashraf (sing. *sharif*)	well-born or distinguished by high birth
bida	innovation in contravention of Islam
dar-ul-harb	abode of war; realm of the infidel
dar-ul-Islam	abode of Islam
dawa	(lit. 'call') proselytizing
dhikr	ritual Muslim practice devoted to the remembrance of God
hadis	sayings of the Prophet Muhammad
hajj	pilgrimage to Mecca and one of the five pillars of Islam. The others are the affirmation of God and his Prophet Muhammad; five daily prayers; observing the fast during the month of Ramazan, and payment of *zakat*
hawala	used interchangeably with *hundi* to refer to informal money transfers based on trust and sanctioned by Islamic law
hijrat	migration marking the Prophet Muhammad's journey from Mecca to Medina in 622 AD
hudood	Islamic penal code

hundi	see *hawala*
ijtihad	individual judgement
ijtima	congregation
ismaili	second most important branch of Shia Islam; also known as Seveners
ithna ashari	dominant branch of Shia Islam; also known as Twelvers
jagirdar	land-owner
jamaati-i-jahiliya	party of the ignorant or pagans
jihad	struggle; Islamic holy war
jihadi	individual or group dedicated to Islamic holy war (*jihad*)
jirga	tribal council
kafir	unbeliever or apostate
kathrat	plurality
madrassa	Quranic school or religious seminary
mazhab	religious doctrine or religious legal code
millat	faith-based organization or religious community that also applies to non-Muslim communities
mohajir	migrant
mujahedin	Muslim holy warriors
mujtahid	Muslim formally qualified to interpret Islamic law and exercise judgement (*ijtihad*)
mulk	country
musawat-i-Muhammadi	system of Muhammadan or Islamic egalitarianism
muttahida qaumiyyat	united political or national community
nizam-i-mustapha	order of the Prophet Muhammad
pir	Muslim holy man; spiritual mentor
qanoon-i-shahadat	Islamic law of evidence
qaum	nation
rais (pl. *ruasa*)	traditional political leader
raj	British sovereignty over India
razakars	armed volunteers
riwaj	custom or habit commonly associated with patronage

sajjida nashin	guardians of Sufi shrines; also successor to a *pir*
salafi	(lit. pious); trend favouring restoration of strict and 'original' Islam
sardar	tribal chief
sharia	Islamic law
shirk	polytheism
sulh-i-kul	social harmony
sunnah	normative conduct of the Prophet Muhammad
tablighi	one who proselytizes; also member of the Tablighi Jamaat
tamaddun	culture
tariqah	Sufi ritual practice
tasawwuf	Sufi mysticism
ulama (sing. *alim*)	body of formally trained Muslim theologians
umma wahidah	united spiritual community
umma	the global Islamic community
ushr	Islamic land tax
wahdat al-wajud	unity of being signifying the oneness of God
watan	territorial homeland
zakat	Islamic alms tax

ABBREVIATIONS

FATA	Federally Administered Tribal Agencies
HAM	*Harkat-ul Mujahedin* [Movement of the Mujahedin]
HM	*Hizb-ul Mujahedin* [Party of the Mujahedin]
HUA	*Harkat-ul Ansar* [Movement of the Helpers (of the Prophet Muhammad)], formerly the HAM
HUJI	*Harkat-ul Jihad al-Islami* [Movement for Islamic Jihad]
IJI	Islami Jumhoori Ittehad [Islamic Democratic Alliance]
IJT	*Islami Jamiat-i-Tulaba* [Islamic Students' Movement]
ISI	Inter-Services Intelligence
JI	*Jamaat-i-Islami* [Islamic Society]
JM	Jaish-i-Muhammad [Army of Muhammad]
JUI	*Jamiat-ul Ulama-i-Islam* [Association of the Ulama of Islam]
JUP	*Jamiat-ul Ulama-i-Pakistan* [Association of the Ulama of Pakistan]
LT	*Lashkar-i-Taiba* [Army of the Pure]
LJ	*Lashkar-i-Jhangvi* [Army of the People of Jhang]
MMA	*Muttahida Majlis-i-Amal* [United Council of Action]
PNA	Pakistan National Alliance
PPP	Pakistan People's Party
SSP	*Sipah-i-Sahaba-i-Pakistan* [Pakistani Force of the Companions (of the Prophet Muhammad)]
TNFJ	*Tehrik-i-Nifaz-i-Jafariya* [Movement for the Implementation of Jafari (Shia) Law]

SELECT BIBLIOGRAPHY

Abbas, Hassan, *Pakistan's drift into extremism: Allah, the army, and America's war on terror* (Armonk, NY: M.E. Sharpe, 2005).

Abou Zahab, Mariam and Olivier Roy, *Islamist networks: the Afghan-Pakistan connection* (London: Hurst, 2004).

Abou-Zahab, Mariam, 'Sectarianism as a substitute identity' in Soofia Mumtaz, Jean-Luc Racine and Imran Ali (eds), *Pakistan: the contours of state and society* (Karachi: Oxford University Press, 2002), pp. 77–95.

Ahmad, Aftab, 'Historical antecedents of corruption in Pakistan' in Arvind K. Jain (ed.), *The political economy of corruption* (London and New York: Routledge, 2001), pp. 142–154.

Ahmad, Aziz, *Studies in Islamic culture in the Indian environment* (Oxford: Clarendon Press, 1964).

Ahmad, Mumtaz, 'The crescent and the sword: Islam, the military, and political legitimacy in Pakistan, 1977–1985', *The Middle East Journal*, Vol. 50, no. 3 (Summer 1996), pp. 372–386.

Ahmed, Rafiuddin, *Understanding the Bengal Muslims* (New Delhi: Oxford University Press, 2001).

———, *The Bengal Muslims, 1871–1906: A quest for identity* (New Delhi: Oxford University Press, 1981).

Ahmed, Vaqar and Rashid Amjad, *The management of Pakistan's economy, 1947–82* (Karachi: Oxford University Press, 1984).

Ahsan, Aitzaz, *The Indus saga and the making of Pakistan* (Karachi: Oxford University Press, 1996).

Alavi, Hamza, 'Class and state' in Hassan Gardezi and Jamil Rashid (eds), *Pakistan—the roots of dictatorship: the political economy of a praetorian state* (London: Zed Press, 1983), pp. 40–85.

———, 'Ethnicity, Muslim society and the Pakistan ideology' in Anita Weiss (ed.), *Islamic reassertion in Pakistan: the application of Islamic laws in a modern state* (Lahore: Vanguard, 1987), pp. 21–47.

Ali, Shaheen Sardar and Javaid Rehman, *Indigenous peoples and ethnic minorities of Pakistan: Constitutional and legal perspectives* (London: Curzon, 2002).

Ali, Tariq, *The duel: Pakistan on the flight path of American power* (London: Simon and Schuster, 2008).

Ansari, Sarah, *Sufi saints and state power: the pirs of Sind, 1843–1947* (Cambridge: Cambridge University Press, 1992).

Banerjee, Mukulika, *The Pathan unarmed: opposition and memory in the north west frontier* (Oxford: James Currey, 2000).

Bayly, C.A., *Origins of nationality in South Asia: patriotism and ethical government in the making of modern India* (New Delhi: Oxford University Press, 1998).

Bennett Jones, Owen, *Pakistan: eye of the storm* (New Haven, CT: Yale University Press, 2002).

Bhutto, Zulfiqar Ali, *Speeches* (Islamabad: Government of Pakistan, 1973).

Binder, Leonard, *Religion and politics in Pakistan* (Berkeley, CA: University of California Press, 1961).

Bose, Sumantra, *Kashmir: roots of conflict, paths to peace* (Cambridge, Mass: Harvard University Press, 2003).

Brass, Paul, *Language, religion and politics in North India* (Cambridge: Cambridge University Press, 1974).

Burke, S.M. and Lawrence Ziring, *Pakistan's foreign policy: an historical analysis* (New York: Oxford University Press, 1991).

Burki, Shahid Javed. *Pakistan under Bhutto, 1971–77* (London: Macmillan, 1980).

Burki, Shahid Javed and Craig Baxter (eds), *Pakistan under the military: eleven years of Zia ul Haq* (Boulder, CO: Westview Press, 1991).

Burki, Shahid Javed, *Pakistan: fifty years of nationhood* (Boulder, CO: Westview Press, 1999).

Cohen, Stephen, *The idea of Pakistan* (Washington, DC: The Brookings Institution, 2004).

———, *The Pakistan army* (Karachi: Oxford University Press, 1998).

Cragg, Kenneth, *The pen and the faith: eight modern Muslim writers and the Quran* (London: George Allen & Unwin, 1985).

Daechsel, Markus, 'Military Islamisation in Pakistan and the spectre of colonial perceptions', *Contemporary South Asia*, Vol. 6, no. 2 (1997), pp. 141–160.

Dani, Ahmad Hasan, *History of the Northern Areas of Pakistan* (Islamabad: National Institute of Historical and Cultural Research, 1989).

Dar, B.A. (ed.), *Letters of Iqbal* (Lahore: Iqbal Academy, 1978).

Dedebant, Christele, *Le voile et la banniere: l'avante-garde feministe au Pakistan* (Paris : CNRS Edns, 2003).

Devji, Faisal, *Landscapes of the Jihad: militancy, morality, modernity* (London: Hurst, 2005).

Donnan, Hastings and Pnina Werbner (eds), *Economy and culture in Pakistan: migrants and cities in a Muslim society* (London: Macmillan, 1991).

Dorronsoro, Gilles, *Revolution unending: Afghanistan 1979 to the present* (London: Hurst, 2000).

Douglas, Ian Henderson, *Abul Kalam Azad: an intellectual and religious biography*, edited by Gail Minault and Christian Troll (Delhi: Oxford University Press, 1988).

Embree, Ainslee T. (ed.), *Pakistan's western borderlands: the transformation of a political order* (Durham, NC: Academic Press, 1977).

Fair, Christine, *The madrassah challange: militancy and religious education in Pakistan* (Washington, DC: United States Institute of Peace Press, 2008).

Friedmann, Yohanan, *Prophecy continuous: aspects of Ahmedi religious thought and its medieval background* (Berkeley, CA: University of California Press, 1989).

Ganguly, Sumit, *Conflict unending: India-Pakistan tensions since 1947* (New York, NY: Columbia University Press, 2001).

———, *The crisis in Kashmir: portents of war, hopes of peace* (Cambridge: Cambridge University Press and Woodrow Wilson Center Press, 1997).

Gilmartin, David, *Empire and Islam: Punjab and the making of Pakistan* (Berkeley, CA: University of California Press, 1988).

Haqqani, Husain, *Pakistan: between mosque and military* (Washington: Carnegie Endowment for Peace, 2005).

Hardy, Peter, *Partners in Freedom and true Muslims: the political thought of some Muslim scholars in British India, 1912–1947* (Lund: Scandinavian Institute of Asian Studies, 1971).

Harrison, Selig, Paul Kreisberg and Dennis Kux (eds), *India and Pakistan: the first fifty years* (Washington and Cambridge: Woodrow Wilson Press and Cambridge University Press, 1999).

Hasan, Arif, 'The roots of elite alienation', *Economic and Political Weekly* (special issue: Pakistan—socio-political dynamics), Vol. 37, nos. 44 and 45 (November 2–8/9–15, 2002), pp. 4550–4553.

Hasan, Mushirul, 'India and Pakistan: Why the difference?' in Mushirul Hasan and Nariaki Nakazato (eds), *The unfinished agenda: nation-building in South Asia* (New Delhi: Manohar, 2001), pp. 328–337.

———, (ed.), *India's Partition: Process, Strategy and Mobilization* (New Delhi: Oxford University Press, 1993).

Hassan Gardezi and Jamil Rashid (eds), *Pakistan—the roots of dictatorship: the political economy of a praetorian state* (London: Zed Press, 1983).

Hefner, Robert and Zaman, Muhammad Qasim (eds), *Schooling Islam: the culture and politics of modern Muslim education* (Princeton: Princeton University Press, 2007).

Madani, Husain Ahmed, *Muttahida qawwmiyat aur Islam* (originally published 1938?) (Delhi: Qawmi ekta trust, 1972).

Hussain, Zahid, *Frontline Pakistan: the struggle with militant Islam* (London: I.B. Tauris, 2007).

Iqbal, Muhammad, *Thoughts and reflections of Iqbal*, edited by S.A. Vahid (Lahore: Shaikh Muhammad Ashraf, 1964).

Ispahani, Mahnaz, *Roads and rivals: the political uses of access in the borderlands of Asia* (Ithaca, NY: Cornell University Press, 1989).

Jaffrelot, Christophe (ed.), *A history of Pakistan and its origins* (London: Anthem Press, 2002).

———, (ed.), *Pakistan: nationalism without a nation?* (London: Zed Books, 2002).

Jahan, Raunaq, *Pakistan: failure in national integration* (New York: Columbia University Press, 1972).

Jalal, Ayesha, *The sole spokesman: Jinnah the Muslim League and the demand for Pakistan* (Cambridge: Cambridge University Press, 1985).

——, *Self and sovereignty: individual and community in South Asian Islam since 1850* (London: Routledge, 2000).

Jawed, Nasim Ahmed, *Islam's political culture: religion and politics in pre-divided Pakistan* (Austin, TX: University of Texas, 1999).

Jinnah, Muhammad Ali, *Speeches and writings of Mr Jinnah*, Volumes I & II, edited by Jamil-ud-din Ahmad (Lahore: Shaikh Muhammad Ashraf, 1960, 1964).

——, *Speeches and Statements as Governor-General of Pakistan, 1947–48* (Islamabad: Ministy of Information and Broadcasting, Government of Pakistan, 1989).

Jones, Philip E., *The Pakistan People's Party: Rise to Power* (Karachi: Oxford University Press, 2003).

Kepel, Gilles, *Jihad: the trail of political Islam* (London and New York: I.B. Tauris, 2002).

Khan, Hamid, *Constitutional and political history of Pakistan* (Karachi: Oxford University Press, 2005).

Khan, Muhammad Ayub, *Speeches and Statements*, vol. 1 (Karachi: Government of Pakistan Press, 1961).

Khan, Yasmin, *The great Partition: the making of India and Pakistan* (New Haven: Yale University Press, 2007).

Khilnani, Sunil, *The idea of India* (revised edn) (Delhi: Penguin, 1999).

Kukreja, Veena, *Contemporary Pakistan: political processes, conflicts and crises* (New Delhi and London: Sage Publications, 2003).

Kux, Dennis, *The United States and Pakistan, 1947–2000: disenchanted allies* (Washington and Baltimore: Woodrow Wilson Centre and The Johns Hopkins University Press, 2001).

Lelyveld, David, *Aligarh's First generation: Muslim solidarity in British India* (Princeton: Princeton University Press, 1978).

Levy, Adrian and Catherine Scott-Clark, *Deception: Pakistan, the United States and the global nuclear weapons conspiracy* (London: Atlantic Books, 2007).

Madan, T.N., *Modern myths, locked minds: secularism and fundamentalism in India* (fourth impression) (Delhi: Oxford University Press, 2003).

Maley, William (ed.), *Fundamentalism reborn? Afghanistan and the Taliban* (London: Hurst, 1998).

Malik, Hafeez (ed.), *Iqbal: Poet-Philosopher of Pakistan* (New York: Columbia University Press, 1971).

Malik, Iftikhar, *Jihad, Hindutva and the Taliban: South Asia at the crossroads* (Karachi: Oxford University Press, 2005).

Malik, Jamal, *Colonialization of Islam: dissolution of traditional institutions in Pakistan* (New Delhi: Manohar, 1998).

Masud, Khalid (ed.), *Travellers in faith: studies of Tablighi Jamaat as a transnational Islamic movement for faith renewal* (Leiden: E.J. Brill, 2000).

McGrath, Allen, *The destruction of Pakistan's democracy* (Karachi: Oxford University Press, 1996).

Mcmahon, Robert J., *The Cold War on the periphery: the United States, India, and Pakistan* (New York: Columbia University Press, 1994).

Merkl, Peter and Ninian Smart (eds), *Religion and politics in the modern world* (New York, NY: New York University Press, 1982).

Metcalf, Barbara D., *Islamic revival in British India: Deoband, 1860–1900* (Princeton, NJ: Princeton University Press, 1982).

———, *Islamic contestations: essays on Muslims in India and Pakistan* (Delhi: Oxford University Press, 2004).

Muhammad, Shan (ed.), *Writings and speeches of Sir Sayyid Ahmad Khan* (Bombay: Nachiketa Publications, 1972).

Nasr, Seyyed Vali Reza, *Islamic Leviathan: Islam and the making of state power* (New York, NY: Oxford University Press, 2001).

———, *Mawdudi and the making of Islamic revivalism* (Oxford University Press, 1996).

———, *The Vanguard of the Islamic revolution: the Jamaat-i-Islami of Pakistan* (Berkeley and Los Angeles, CA: University of California Press, 1994).

———, 'National identities and the India-Pakistan conflict' in T.V. Paul (ed.), *The India-Pakistan conflict: an enduring rivalry* (Cambridge: Cambridge University Press, 2005), pp. 178–201.

Nawaz, Shuja, *Crossed swords: Pakistan, its army, and the wars within* (Karachi: Oxford University Press, 2008).

Nayyar, A.H. and Salim, Ahmad (eds), *The subtle subversion: the state of curricula and textbooks in Pakistan* (Islamabad: Sustainable Development Policy Institute, 2003).

Nelson, Matthew, 'Muslims, markets, and the meaning of a "good" education in Pakistan', *Asian Survey*, Vol. 46, no. 5 (2006), pp. 690–720.

———, 'Dealing with difference: religious education and the challenge of democracy in Pakistan', *Modern Asian Studies*, Vol. 43, no. 2 (March 2008), pp. 361–90.

———, 'Religious education in non-religious schools: a comparative study of Bangladesh and Pakistan', *Journal of Comparative and Commonwealth Politics*, Vol. 46, no. 3 (July 2008), pp. 337–67.

Nizamani, Haidar, *The roots of rhetoric: politics of nuclear weapons in India and Pakistan* (Westport, CT: Praeger, 2000).

Noman, Omar, *Economic and social progress in Asia: Why Pakistan did not become a tiger* (Karachi: Oxford University Press, 1997).

———, *The political economy of Pakistan* (London: Routledge and Kegan Paul, 1988).

Pandey, Gyanendra and Yunus Samad, *Faultlines of nationhood* (Delhi: Roli Books, 2007).

———, *Remembering Partition: Violence, nationalism and history* (Cambridge: Cambridge University Press, 2002).

————, *The construction of communalism in colonial North India* (Delhi: Oxford University Press, 1990).

Pirzada, Syed Sharifuddin (ed.), *Foundations of Pakistan: All India Muslim League Documents, 1906–1947*, Vols I & II (Karachi: National Publishing House, 1970).

————, *Quaid-e-Azam Jinnah's correspondence* (Karachi: Guild Publishing House, 1966).

Rahman, Tariq, *Denizens of alien worlds: a study of education, inequality and polarization in Pakistan*, (Karachi: Oxford University Press, 2004).

Rahman, Tariq, *Language and politics in Pakistan* (Karachi: Oxford University Press, 1996).

Rais, Rasul Bakhsh (ed.), *State, Society and Democratic Change in Pakistan* (Karachi: Oxford University Press, 1997).

Rana, Muhammad Amir, *A to Z of Jehadi organizations in Pakistan* (Lahore: Mashal Books, 2004).

Rashid, Ahmed, *Descent into chaos: how the war against Islamic extremism is being lost in Pakistan, Afghanistan and Central Asia* (London: Allen Lane, 2008).

Rashid, Ahmed, *Taliban: the story of the Afghan warlords* (London: Pan Books, 2001).

Report of the Hamoodur Rehman Commission of Inquiry into the 1971 war [as declassified by the Government of Pakistan] (Lahore: Vanguard, nd).

Rizvi, Hasan Askari, *Military, state and society in Pakistan* (Lahore: Sang-i-Meel, 2003).

————, *The military and politics in Pakistan* (new revised edn) (Lahore: Sang-i-Meel Publications, 2000).

Robinson, Francis, *Separatism among Indian Muslims: the politics of the United Provinces' Muslims, 1860–1923* (Cambridge: Cambridge University Press, 1974).

Rubin, Barnett *The fragmentation of Afghanistan: state formation and collapse in the international system* (2nd edn) (New Haven, CT: Yale University Press, 2002).

Saeed, Nasir, *Faith under Fire: a report on the second class citizenship and intimidation of Christians in Pakistan* (London: Centre for Legal Aid and Settlement, 2002).

Samad, Yunus, 'Pakistan or Punjabistan: Crisis of national identity', *International Journal of Punjab Studies*, Vol. 2, no. 1 (1995), pp. 23–41.

Sayeed, Khalid bin, *Politics in Pakistan: the nature and direction of change* (New York, NY: Praeger, 1980).

————, *The formative phase, 1867–1948* (London: Oxford University Press, 1968).

Schofield, Victoria, *Kashmir in the crossfire* (London: I.B. Tauris, 1996).

Shah, Mehtab Ali, *The foreign policy of Pakistan: ethnic impacts on diplomacy, 1971–1994* (London: I. B. Tauris, 1997).

Shaikh, Farzana, *Community and consensus in Islam: Muslim representation in colonial India, 1860–1947* (Cambridge: Cambridge University Press, 1989).

———, 'The language of representation: towards a Muslim political order in nineteenth century India' in Penelope Corfield, (ed.), *Language, History and Class* (Oxford: Basil Blackwell, 1991), pp. 204–226.

———, 'Azad and Iqbal: the quest for the Islamic "Good"', in Mushirul Hasan(ed.), *Islam and Indian nationalism: reflections on Abul Kalam Azad* (Delhi, Manohar, 1992), pp. 59–76.

———, 'Pakistan's nuclear bomb: beyond the non-proliferation regime', *International Affairs*, Vol. 78, no. 1(January 2002), pp. 29–48.

———, '"Millat" and "mazhab": rethinking Iqbal's political vision' in Mushirul Hasan and Asim Roy (eds), *Living together separately: cultural India in history and politics* (Delhi: Oxford University Press, 2005), pp. 366–88.

———, 'From Islamisation to Shariatisation: cultural transnationalism in Pakistan', *Third World Quarterly*, Vol. 29, no. 3, 2008, pp. 593–610.

Siddiqa, Ayesha, *Military Inc: Inside Pakistan's military economy* (London and Ann Arbor, MI: Pluto Press, 2007).

Sikand, Yoginder, *The origins and development of the Tablighi Jama'at* (New Delhi: Orient, Longman, 2002).

Talbot, Ian, *Pakistan: a modern history* (London: Hurst, revised edn, 2005).

Thomas, Raju (ed.), *Perspectives on Kashmir: the role of conflict in South Asia* (Boulder, CT: Westview Press, 1992).

Troll, Christian, *Sayyid Ahmed Khan: reinterpretation of Muslim theology* (Delhi: Vikas, 1978).

Verkaaik, Oskar, *Migrants and militants: fun and urban violence in Pakistan* (Princeton: Princeton University Press, 2004).

Waseem, Mohammad, *Politics and the state in Pakistan* (Islamabad: National Institute of Historical and Cultural Research, 1994).

Weiss, Anita and Gilani, S. Zulfiqar (eds), *Power and civil society in Pakistan* (Karachi: Oxford University Press, 2001).

Weiss, Anita, (ed.), *Islamic re-assertion in Pakistan: the application of Islamic laws in a modern state* (Lahore: Vanguard, 1987).

Wirsing, Robert, *Pakistan's security under Zia, 1977–88: the policy imperatives of a peripheral Asian state* (Basingstoke: Macmillan, 1991).

Wolpert, Stanley, *Jinnah of Pakistan* (Delhi: Oxford University Press, 2005 edn).

———, *Zulfi Bhutto of Pakistan* (Oxford: Oxford University Press, 1993).

Zaidi, S. Akbar, *Issues in Pakistan's economy* (2nd edn) (Karachi: Oxford University Press, 2005).

Zaman, Muhammad Qasim, *The ulama in contemporary Islam: custodians of change* (Princeton: Princeton University Press, 2002).

Zamindar, Vazira-Fazila Yacoobali, *The long Partition and the making of modern South Asia: refugees, boundaries, histories* (New York: Columbia University Press, 2007).

Ziring, Lawrence, *Pakistan: at the cross-current of history* (Oxford: Oneworld, 2003).

INDEX

Index

84, 85, 86, 95, 103; and non-
Muslims, 70, 73,88; lack of
consensus over, 2, 4, 5, 6, 7, 11,
47, 57, 85, 88, 117, 118, 123,
124; sectarian discourse of, 4, 47,
57, 59, 64; communal discourse
of, 11, 149, 159; Islamist
discourse of, 11, 149; 'Bengali',
6, 25, 46, 53, 76; 'Pakistani', 6,
90; and Islamic socialism,
126–127, 128; and Pakistani
military, 8, 148, 149, 150, 151,
153, 154, 157, 179, 198; and
militant Islamists, 8, 149, 150,
165,; and Indo-Muslim salariat,
8–10, 32; and role in Afghan civil
war, 106, 113, 114; and *mohajir*
ethnic identity, 106; as aspect of
shariatization, 107–115; and
debate on corruption, 133–140
Islami Jamiat-i-Tulaba, 93
Islami Jumhoori Ittehad (IJI), 169
Islamic socialism, 95, 117, 119,
123, 126–127, 129, 132
Islamic Summit Conference (1974),
96
Islamization, under Zia ul Haq,
101–106; comparison with
shariatization, 107–109
Ismaili Shia, 59, 66
Ispahani, M.A. H., 58
Israel, comparison with Pakistan, 3
Ithna ashari Shia, 59, 64

Jaish-i-Mohammad, 170, 172, 173,
175
Jalal, Ayesha, 73
Jamaat-i-Islami (Pakistan), 4, 6, 89,
93, 97, 101, 108,110, 114, 128,
130, 135, 136, 154, 165, 167;
campaign for Islamic state,
84–85, 87, opposition to Ayub
Khan, 91,134; relations with
Yahya Khan, 161, 162; under Zia

ul Haq, 99; on corruption, 134,
136; and *madrassas*, 142,
influence on military, 152
Jamaat-i-jahiliya, 35
Jamaat-ud Dawa, *see* Lashkar-i-
Taiba
Jamiat-ul Ulama-i-Islam (JUI), 106,
108, 109; 113, 113, 155, 165,
relations with Zia ul Haq,
108–109, 112; and shariatization,
108–115
Jamiat-ul Ulama-i-Pakistan (JUP),
97, 108, 162
Jamiat-ul Ulum al-Islamiya, 144
Javed, Nasim, 127
Jehangir, Mughal emperor, 20
Jinnah, Fatima, 93
Jinnah, Muhammad Ali, 2, 6, 9, 23,
25; 34; 36; 38, 39, 40, 43, 44,
48, 49, 50, 60, 68, 69, 80, 82,
83, 84, 85, 86, 91, 94, 96, 102,
123, 133, 177, 180, 183, 200;
correspondence with Iqbal,
35,122, and Muslim community
15, ambivalence towards Islam,
5; death of, 5; as sole spokesman,
6, 43; on Muslim homeland,
37–38; myths attached to, 41–42;
on constitutional safeguards for
Muslims, 38; on Muslims as a
minority, 39; on Muslim nationhood, 39–40; 41; and Islamic
universalism, 41, 43; and Bengali
Muslims, 42, 121; and Bengali
language issue, 52–53; Shia roots
of, 58; and non-Muslim minorities, 68–69; and capitalism,
118–119, 120, 122, and private
property, 120; and socialism,
126; and Kashmir, 185, 186;
attitude to Western powers, 192,
193; on Pashtun nationalism,
202–203

Kalashnikov culture, 173
Kargil, 75; use of mujahedin groups
in, 175, 176

270

Kashmir, 8, 160; militant Islamists in, 169–170; 175, 176; 177;and Jinnah, 185, Ayub Khan's policy on, 161; and Benazir Bhutto, 169; and Nawaz Sharif, 169–170; Musharraf's policy on, 176, 192; as expression of Pakistani identity, 187–89

Kepel, Gilles, 108

Khan, Ayub, 88, 89, 97, 100, 117, 134 and *pirs*, 6, 62, 91, 92, 93, 94, 114, 137, 148, and non-Muslims, 74; and secularization programme, 74–75; and Muslim modernism, 89, use of Islam, 90; 158–160; reform of Family Laws, 90–91; economic policies, 125; and Islamic modernism, 135

Khan, Ghaffar, 186

Khan, Liaquat Ali, 49, 61, 72, 133; position on Islamic constitution, 85, 88; relations with the United States, 193–94;

Khan, Sayyid Ahmad, 73, 82; and Muslim community, 23–25, and Caliphate, 28; and Muslim nation, 28, 31, 34; and Iqbal, 26; antipathy to Congress, 28; class bias of, 28, and Bengalis, 25, 31

Khan, Yahya, 94, 161, 162

Lahore Resolution (of 1940), 54

Lashkar-i-Jhangvi, 172, 174, 175

Lashkar-i-Taiba, 165, 166, 174, 175

Law of Evidence, 104

Line of Control (in Kashmir), 111

Madani, Husain Ahmed, on universalism, 3; on nation and community, 21–22

Madrassas, under Ayub Khan, 142; under Zia ul Haq, 110, 143; under Parvez Musharraf, 111, 143; and Afghan refugees, 114;

as microcosm of Islamic society, 140; in South Asia, 141

Mahmudabad, Raja of, 58

Majlis-i-Ahrar, 61, 66

Mansur, Abul, 42

Mawdudi, Abul Ala, on universalism, 4; 31, 33, 134, 138; on Muslim homeland, 35–36; opposition to nationalism, 35–36, 110; on two-nation theory, 36, hostility to Muslim League, 35; on Muslim 'right-of return', 36; association with Iqbal, 36; death of, 110, on Islamic economic system, 128–129

Metcalf, Barbara, 11, 82, 105, 126, 127, 135, 136

Milbus, 147

Military, and use of Islam, 8, 148, 149, 150; and Pakistani identity, 149, 158–159; and preference for jihad, 167–168; and corruption, 139–140; policy on Kashmir, 150, 153, 154, 166–167, 177; policy on Afghanistan, 153, 154, 166, 177; relations with militant Islamists, 154, 160, 161–162; 165–166; 175, 177; and use of militant groups in Kashmir, 170–175, 176; and Jamaat-i-Islami, 151, 152; changing patterns of recruitment into, 152; and impact of separation of East Pakistan, 153; and Tablighi Jamaat, 154, 155–156, 157

Millat, 22, 55

Mohajirs (Urdu-speaking), 48–50; 51–52; in Sind, 55, as Pakistan's fifth nationality, 55–56

Mohammedan Anglo-Oriental College, 24

Muhammad, Prophet, 42, 46, 97

Mulk, 29, 31, 71

Musharraf, Parvez, 79, 149, 198; and *madrassa* reform, 111, 143; coup against Sharif, 139, 175;

Islamic constitution, 5; 83–88, 91, 95–96; constitution of (of 1956), 72, 83, 84, 86, 88 (of 1962), 74, 83, 88, 91 (of 1973), 75, 83, 88, 95; and Islamization under Zia ul Haq, 99–106; and debate over Islamic economic system, 6, 123–128; and corruption, 6, 132–140; role and reform of *madrassas*, 141–146; historical roots of policy towards India, 9, 181–184; and disputed boundaries, 182; (1948) war with India, 186; (1965) war with India, 186, 189; (1971) war with India, 186; relations with the United States, 189, 190–199; relations with China, 189; 195–196; nuclear weapons programme, 1, 190, 196–197, 198; relations with Afghanistan, 197, 200–20; support for Taliban, 198
Pandey, Gyanendra, 37, 68, 69
Parsis, 67, 77
Pashtuns, 2, 10; nationalism 201–202; and Afghanistan, 203–204; integration under Zia ul Haq, 205, 206
Punjabi, 2, 10; salariat, 10, refugees, 50–51, settlers in Balochistan, 56

Qalandar, Lal Shabaz, 97
Qanoon-i-Shahadat, see Law of Evidence
Qawm, 21, 31, 55

Ramay, Hanif, 127
Rao, (Sir) Dinkar, 28
Rashid, Ahmed, 173, 208
Rawalpindi conspiracy case, 150
Red Mosque, assault on, 166
Roy, Olivier, 206

Sajjida nashin, 28
Salariat, 9, 10, 32

Saudi Arabia, 64
Sectarian conflict, and Islamization, 64; and ethnic conflict, 65; in Punjab, 66, in FATA, 66–67; in Northern Areas, 66–67; in Gilgit, 176; links to jihadist groups, 174
Separate electorates, 73, 74, 77, 79
Sevener (Shia) *see* Ismaili Shia
Sharia courts, 76
Sharia, 19, 20, 26, 28
Shariatization, 102, 106, 107, 108, 110, 113, 115; differences with Islamization, 107–109; military and, 154
Sharif, Mian Nawaz, 79, 168; economic policies of, 132; corruption under, 138–39, and Tablighi Jamaat, 139; military coup against, 139; on Kashmir, 169; links with jihadist groups, 168, 169, 170
Sheikh Abdullah, 185
Shia Muslims, 4, 57, 58, 59; 61, 64, 101, 107; percentage in Pakistan, 58; among Pashtuns, 66; opposition to *zakat*, 104
Siachen Glacier, 192
Siddiqa, Ayesha, 12
Sikhs, 71, 77
Simla Agreement (1972), 182
Sindhis, 2, ethnic nationalism, 54, conflict with Urdu-speaking migrants, 51, 55–56
Singh, Maharaja Hari, 186
Sipah-i-Sahaba-i-Pakistan (SSP), 64, 172, 175
Sir Creek (maritime border dispute), 182
South East Asia Treaty Organization (SEATO), 194
Suhrawardy, H.S., 71
Sulh-i-kul, 20
Sunni Muslims, 4, 57, 58, 59; 64, 65, 101, percentage of population in Pakistan, 58
Sunnification, 64

Tablighi Jamaat, history of, 110;
  influence on Nawaz Sharif, 139;
  influence on military, 154–55,
  157; and Zia ul Haq, 155;
  relations with JUI, 155
Talbot, Ian, 10, 11, 51
Taliban, 169, 171, 173, 177;
  'Punjabi', 172, 207, 208
Talpur, Rasul Bakhsh, 128
Tasawwuf, 26
Tehrik-i-Nifaz-i Fiqh-i Jafariyya
  (TNFJ), 64
Turi (tribe), 66
Turkish Caliphate, 28
Twelver (Shia), see ithna ashari Shia

Ulama, and Islamic constitution,
  84–88; opposition to Ayub Khan,
  91–92; hostility to Bhutto,
  96–97; co-operation with Zia ul
  Haq, 99, 108–110, 112–114; and
  private property, 128; attitude to
  corruption under Ayub, 134; and
  madrassa reform, 141–143
Umma, 23, 25, 26, 38, 43, 55, 73,
  109, 110, 156
Umma wahida, 22

United Front (in East Bengal), 71
Urdu, as national language (of
  Pakistan), 2; opposition to, 2;
  52–53; contested role of, 1, 49,
  52, 53; as aspect of mohajir
  identity, 50–51, 55
Usmani, Rafi, 141
Usmani, Shabbir Ahmed, 86
Usmani, Taqi,

Verkaaik, Oskar, 51, 55

Wahhabi (Islam), 113
Waliullah, Shah, 19, on Islamic
  universalism, 4; and sharia,
  19–20; and Muslim power, 20
Watan, 29, 71
Werbner, Pnina, 38
Women's Action Forum, opposition
  to Zia ul Haq, 104–105; class
  bias of, 105

Zakat, 64, 124, and ulama, 128;
  under Zia ul Haq, 131
Zaman, Muhammad Qasim, 141,
  142
Ziring, Lawrence, 76, 89

ABOUT THE AUTHOR

Farzana Shaikh is an Associate Fellow of the Asia Programme at the Royal Institute of International Affairs (Chatham House) in London, where she directs the Pakistan Study Group. After receiving a Ph.D in Political Science from Columbia University she was elected to a Research Fellowship in Politics at Clare Hall Cambridge. Since then she has lectured at universities in the United Kingdom, Europe and the United States, and has commented widely on Pakistan for the media in Britain and abroad. She is the author of *Community and Consensus in Islam: Muslim representation in colonial India, 1860–1947* (Cambridge University Press, 1989) and has written extensively on the history and politics of Muslim South Asia.